THE PORTUGUESE EMPIRE IN ASIA, 1500–1700

Summary of !'s 213-5

The Portuguese Empire in Asia, 1500–1700: A Political and Economic History

Sanjay Subrahmanyam

Longman
London and New York   1993

Longman Group UK Limited
Longman House, Burnt Mill,
Harlow, Essex CM20 2JE, England
and Associated Companies throughout the world.

*Published in the United States of America
by Longman Publishing, New York*

First published 1993

ISBN 0 582 05069 3 CSD
ISBN 0 582 05068 5 PPR

British Library Cataloguing-in-Publication Data

A catalogue record for this book is
available from the British Library

Library of Congress Cataloging in Publication Data

Subrahmanyam, Sanjay.
  The Portuguese empire in Asia. 1500–1700 : a political and
  economic history / Sanjay Subrahmanyam.
      p.   cm.
  Includes bibliographical references and index.
  ISBN 0-582-05069-3 (CSD). -- ISBN 0-582-05068-5 (PPR)
  1. Portuguese--Asia--History. 2. Asia--History. 3. Portugal--History--
  16th century. 4. Portugal--History--17th century.
  I. Title
  DS33.7.S83 1993   92–10236
  950'.04691--dc20   CIP

Set by 7 in 10 pt Bembo
Produced by Longman Singapore Publishers (Pte) Ltd.
Printed in Singapore

Contents

Contents

vii

List of Abbreviations

ACE	*Assentos do Conselho do Estado*, ed. P. S. S. Pissurlencar
AHU	Arquivo Histórico Ultramarino, Lisbon
ANTT	Arquivo Nacional da Torre do Tombo, Lisbon
APO	*Archivo Portuguez-Oriental,* ed. J. H. da Cunha Rivara
ARA	Algemeen Rijksarchief, The Hague
BFUP	*Boletim da Filmoteca Ultramarina Portuguesa*
BNL	Biblioteca Nacional de Lisboa, Lisbon
BNP	Bibliothèque Nationale de Paris
BPADE	Biblioteca Pública e Arquivo Distrital, Évora
CAA	*Cartas de Afonso de Albuquerque*, eds. R. A. de Bulhão Pato and H. Lopes de Mendonça
CC	Corpo Cronológico
CSL	Colecção de São Lourenço
DRI	Documentos Remetidos da Índia (published and unpublished)
HAG	Historical Archives, Panaji, Goa
IOLR	India Office Library and Records, London
VOC	Verenigde Oost-Indische Compagnie

List of Maps

List of Tables and Acknowledgements

Acknowledgements

The publishers would like to thank the following for permission to reproduce copyright material: Carolina Academic Press for table 5.1 from John TePaske's chapter in *Precious Metals in the Later Medieval and Early Modern Worlds*, ed. John F. Richards (1983); Studentlitteratur AB, Magistratsrägen for table 6.2 from *Carracks, Caravans and Companies. The Structural crisis in the European-Asian trade in the early seventeenth century*, Niels Steensgaard (1973); Macmillan Ltd. for tables 7.2 and 7.4 from *Economy and society in Baroque Portugal, 1668–1703*, Carl Hanson (1981).

Preface

Writing the preface of a book is often a greater pleasure than writing the book itself, since discharging debts is usually more pleasurable than incurring them. The germ of this book emerged in the summer of 1988, while I was giving seminars and teaching in Paris and Lisbon. It was stimulated by conversations with friends in both places, and particularly by the demands made on me by classes of the Mestrado in the History of Portuguese Expansion at the Universidade Nova de Lisboa. For the opportunity to teach in Lisbon, I thank Artur Teodoro de Matos and Lúis Filipe Thomaz. The stimulating ideas of the latter – surely the leading Portuguese historian today of the Estado da Índia – are directly reflected here, and breathed life into the project; I also thank him for his comments and suggestions on a first draft. The perspective of the foreign visitor to Portugal often tends to be excessively Lisbon-centred; a visit to Braga and the 'other' Portugal with Maria Augusta Lima Cruz and Arlindo Fagundes was of great utility in putting Portugal in perspective, besides being a pleasure in itself. I hope they will all forgive the presumptuous character of this book.

In the autumn of 1988, when the outline of this book was defined at Cambridge, Chris and Susan Bayly, who were there, and Kenneth McPherson, who was visiting London, played the role of sounding boards. Geoffrey Parker, generous as ever with his time as a correspondent, also helped give the idea shape, and a single, useful afternoon with John Elliott helped clarify matters Iberian. Seminar audiences in Cambridge and Leiden responded positively to an early draft outline (which has now appeared as a joint essay with L.F. Thomaz in James Tracy, ed., *The Political Economy of Merchant Empires*, Cambridge/New York, 1991), and helped sustain my confidence in the project.

As an economic historian based in India, I had tended to view the Portuguese materials in perhaps too limited and functional a fashion in my earlier work (e.g. Subrahmanyam 1990a). This book therefore represents a

shift in perspective, but it was not my intention to abandon Asian history
in the process. At the same time, this is a work of synthesis, more
concerned with the whole than the parts; it is not a book on the
nitty-gritty of the social, political and economic history of Goa, or Macau,
Timor, Mozambique, or of the other Portuguese possessions in Asia.
These are subjects deserving of far more detailed treatment than can be
afforded in a book of this size and nature. Thus, to the reader who finds
lacunae, an inadequate treatment of this or that aspect (be it Franciscan
ideology, household slavery or price history, to cite three random
examples), I can only offer my apologies and point to the bibliography
where possible.

The book itself was finished in far more trying circumstances than
those in which it began. Turmoil-ridden Delhi in 1990–91 has not been
the most congenial of academic or social atmospheres. But conversations
with friends, especially Muzaffar Alam and Sunil Kumar, have been a
consolation; both of them have partly read and made helpful comments
on the manuscript, as have G. Balachandran, Kenneth McPherson and
Gail Alterman. To all of them my thanks, and also especially to Jaivir
Singh, who has been a patient reader of half-finished drafts, delighting in
particular in the forays into Japanese history.

As an attempt at synthesis, this book naturally depends more than
monographs do on the work of colleagues. I should mention the following
persons in particular: Jean Aubin, Geneviève Bouchon, João Paulo Costa,
Teotonio R. De Souza, Anthony Disney, Maria Augusta Lima Cruz,
Jorge Manuel Flores, Pierre-Yves Manguin, Salih Ozbaran, Michael
Pearson, George B. Souza, Niels Steensgaard, Luís Filipe Thomaz, and
John Wills. One need hardly add that without the work of three pioneers
– Charles Boxer, Vitorino Magalhães Godinho and A. H. de Oliveira
Marques – a work like this would have been impossible. The work of the
Goan archivist and historian, the late P.S. S. Pissurlencar, has also been
extremely useful as a point of reference.

Finally, a word of appreciation for Longman for the confidence
reposed in an experiment in historical writing, and for patiently waiting
for a delayed manuscript. I also thank them for their wisdom in having
the manuscript read by Peter Marshall at the draft stage, even as I thank
him for his encouraging comments. I hope the end-product has been
made more 'user-friendly' by my response to them.

New Delhi
May 1992

Introduction: The Mythical Faces of Portuguese Asia

The dust has barely settled on Portuguese colonialism. It was less than two decades ago, in the aftermath of the 'Revolution of Flowers' – usually referred to by today's Portuguese simply as *vinte e cinco de abril* (or 25th April), with the year, 1974, being implicitly understood – that the Portuguese left their colonial possessions in Africa. In Southeast Asia, their last outpost, Timor, was wrested from them forcibly by the Indonesian Republic; only Macau remains today from an empire over which the sun once practically never set. And even today, Portuguese, Asians and Africans remain deeply divided over how to understand and interpret the imperial edifice that the Portuguese created in the sixteenth and seventeenth centuries: indeed, doubts even are raised on whether the Portuguese *truly* had an empire in any meaningful sense in that period. Since Portuguese expansion is intimately tied to Portuguese nationalism and collective identity – with the two most celebrated poets of the Lusitanian pantheon, the author of the *Lusíadas*, Luís Vaz de Camões (1524–80), and the 'modernist' author of *Mensagem*, Fernando Pessoa (1888–1935), both having held strong views on the subject – it is very difficult indeed to separate myth from history, and many do not even wish to try.

In writing this book, which is in the form of a long synthetic, interpretative essay in several chapters rather than an encyclopaedic survey, my desire is not to fight the colonial wars all over again. Nor is this book a foray into the myriad dimensions of the cultural interaction between the Portuguese and Asia. Instead, the book is a political and economic history, which will attempt to locate the Portuguese presence between the Cape of Good Hope and Japan in the sixteenth and seventeenth centuries on two intersecting planes. On the one hand, the Portuguese will be placed firmly in the Asian and East African contexts; at the same time, they will be located in the European (and more specifically Iberian) context. This exercise, which would be rather dull under the rules of Euclidean

1

geometry (where the intersection of the two planes would leave us with only a straight line!), hopefully has more potential in the rather more flexible discipline of history: historians of imperialism will doubtless recognise here echoes of the well-known debate on 'Eurocentric' and 'Ex-centric' explanations for nineteenth-century European imperial expansion (Bayly 1989). And indeed, the present work is conceived as a contribution to the larger debate on the nature of European empire-building in the early modern period. It will therefore attempt to grapple not merely with the issues mentioned above, but with the rather more thorny question of the extent of continuity and discontinuity between Portuguese, and later Dutch and English, expansion in Asia.

But how after all does one write such a history? On what sources can the historian who wishes to write a 'balanced account' rely? For the most part, we must fall back willy-nilly on the Portuguese sources themselves, but these are not the only materials available to us. It is also true that even the corpus of Portuguese documentation does not speak to us with a single voice. Differences exist depending on the nature of the source (whether it is a letter, an account-book or a chronicle), on the social status of the writer (for even chroniclers can afford us vastly different visions depending on the social group to which they pertained), and the time of the writing (for the early sixteenth century scarcely appeared so glorious to Portuguese of the 1540s as it did to those writing in the 1620s). In the case of writers belonging to the missionary orders, much depends on the nature of the order itself – for the Jesuit view of an event could be rather different from that of an Augustinian.

Besides the Portuguese sources, one also has other materials, in the form of travel-accounts by other Europeans like the Dutchman Jan Huyghen van Linschoten's famous late-sixteenth-century *Itinerario* (Tiele and Burnell 1885), later trading Company papers from the seventeenth century, and the memoirs and correspondence of Italian and German merchants who were resident in Portuguese Asia. Also, one has Asian and African materials, whether in written form (as chronicles, travelogues and letters), or preserved as oral traditions (Isaacman 1972). This last set of materials has very largely been disregarded by historians for several reasons. First, they are so scattered and diverse, and call for such extensive linguistic skills, that they remain only partially tapped. But second, and more importantly, there continues to be a widespread notion that these materials are unreliable, because they envelop the Portuguese in a cloud of myth, and fail basic tests, in particular of chronological accuracy. At best, it is therefore argued, they can be used to show that the Portuguese were unimportant in Asia (since many Asian sources largely ignore them) or that the Asians were too self-absorbed and too culturally involuted to need to bother with the newcomers.

But this last was not always true. Let us consider the example of an

Malacca

/ *near*

untitled Malay text from the late seventeenth or early eighteenth century,
describing the Portuguese arrival at the great Southeast Asian port-city of
Melaka, (at) the tip of the Malay peninsula, and encompassing their seizure
of it, how they fortified it and made it a centre of their own trade, and
how they were eventually expelled from it. It is, therefore, a complete
cycle of rise, prosperity and fall of which we read, self-contained and with
its own internal logic. It runs as follows.

> This is a history from long, long ago: The Franks arrive in the land of Melaka.
> Those who know the history tell us that there were, so it is said, ten
> Portuguese ships which came from Manila to trade in the country of Melaka.
> In that time, the king was the Sultan Ahmad Syah. In that epoch, the country
> of Melaka was very active in trade, and prosperous, and its government was in
> good order. But as time passed, the Portuguese ships arrive in the country of
> Melaka. Now in that time the fortifications of the city of Melaka were made
> of palm-tree trunks.
> Then the captain of the ship arrives to trade, with various other ships'
> captains, and they bring for the King Sultan Ahmad Syah a present of gold,
> reals, cloth, and chains from Manila; and the Sultan was most content with the
> Portuguese captain. And so, at the end of a little time, whatever the captains
> desired was done by the Sultan Ahmad Syah. Many times did the ministers
> (*bendahara* and *temenggong*) say respectfully:
>
> > Your Highness, My Lord, should not be too trusting with these white
> > people, because in the modest opinion of all your old servants, it is not
> > good that My Lord protects these recent arrivals.
> >
> > And then the Sultan Ahmad Syah spoke:
> > *Bendahara*, my uncle, and noble *temenggong*, I do not see how these white
> > people can cause the loss of our land!
> >
> > After this, the *bendahara* and *temenggong* still did not feel easy inside, and
> > observed respectfully to the King:
> > As for these white people, no good will come of them for Your Highness
> > and Lordship. ...
> >
> > However, the *bendahara* and *temenggong* could achieve nothing more. It was
> > then that the captains of the ships began to give out gold chains from Manila
> > to various notables in the country of Melaka. And all of the natives of Melaka
> > became most grateful to the captains of the Portuguese ships. Only the
> > *bendahara* and *temenggong* were not content.
> >
> > The Portuguese ships remained then in Melaka, trading for a space of forty
> > days, more or less. And the Portuguese came once again on land to offer reals
> > in boxes and boxes, and gold and many lovely cloths, which they offered to
> > His Highness Sultan Ahmad Syah. And the Sultan Ahmad Syah was content.
> > Once more then the Sultan Ahmad Syah spoke to the Portuguese captain:
> > What more is it that these friends of ours want of us, that they bring us
> > such a lovely gift?
> > Then all the captains of the ships said to him:
> > We want but one thing of our good friend; that is if our good friend
> > wishes to remain friendly with us, white people.
> > At which the Sultan Ahmad Syah replied to them:
> > Say it then for we permit it! If it is anything that we have, we will most
> > certainly satisfy the desire of our friends!
> > Then the captains of the ships said:

We would like to ask for a piece of land, the size of the dried skin of an animal.

And the King spoke:

Do not be sad, friends of ours: take the land that pleases you; and if it is of such size, keep the land.

Then the Portuguese captain was quite content. And at once the Portuguese come on land, bringing hoes to dig, bricks and lime. And they go to fetch that hide, made a cord from it, and with it measure out a square. And they make an extremely large building, fortified, and they at the same time make openings for cannon. And all the people of Melaka ask:

But what openings are these?

And the Portuguese responded:

These are the openings that white people use as windows. And the people of Melaka kept silent. Then, when the people were silent, on various occasions the *bendahara* and *temenggong* observed respectfully to the King:

My Lord! Do not permit these white people to make a great house!

And the King spoke:

In no way can these white people cause ruin to our land! I see very well that the white men are not many; and if their designs are evil, we will observe their behaviour; and if needed send in the amok.

After this the *bendahara* and *temenggong* were still not content in their hearts, because both were wise men. And the behaviour of the Portuguese was thus: at night, they unloaded cannon from their ships, and muskets hidden in boxes, saying that there was cloth inside them: such was the behaviour of the Portuguese to mislead the people of Melaka. And they did it so that the people of Melaka did not understand. Then, time having passed, the house of stone was complete and all their arms were ready. And more or less at midnight, when the people were all sleeping, then it was that the Franks bombarded the city of Melaka, and all the houses of the Melaka people were in ruins as was the fort of palm trees.

After this, under the bombardment of the Franks, at the midnight hour, thus it is that the King Ahmad Syah with all the people flees without knowing where, without having a chance to resist. And the Franks take Melaka. The Sultan Ahmad Syah flees to Muar; and from Muar, not long thereafter, shifts to Johor, to build a city; and from Johor moves again to Bintang. Such is the history of the Franks who snatched the city of Melaka from the hands of the Sultan Ahmad Syah once upon a time.

The history tells how the Franks remained in the city of Melaka for a duration of three months of time. Then the Franks sent a letter to their principal city, which is called Goa, saying that Melaka had been taken by the Franks. Then as soon as the great king of the Franks heard the news that Melaka was taken, he became very content. And when some time had passed, two months after the letter had reached his hands, their great king responded with a letter saying that they should erect a great fort of granite inside the city of Melaka; as for the form of this fortress, that it should be exactly like that of the great city that is called Goa. And thus the Portuguese made the fortress of Melaka equal to that of the country of Goa.

The history tells us then that when the letter of the King of Goa arrived in Melaka, the Portuguese who were there in the city sent the people of Melaka who remained to fetch granite. For the first time they went to fetch granite to make the fortress of Melaka, to Kuala Langai, and to Pulo Upeh, and to Bato Barus, and to Pulo Java, and to Tluk Emas, and to Pisau Peringgi, and to the island of Birds and to the backlands of Melaka. It was thus that the Melaka people went to fetch granite. As for its price: for a hundred pieces of granite, the Portuguese paid thirty patacas, for a hundred of the large, and twenty for a hundred small ones; at this time, hens were purchased by the Portuguese for one new coin each; and lime at this time was fifteen patacas the *koyang*. And the labourers dug on the hill at a rupia a day.

As for the fortification of the city of Melaka, it took, so they say, thirty-six years, three months and fourteen days. And the Portuguese remained in Melaka thereafter, so it is estimated, for another six years and a month. Such was the case of the Franks who remained in Melaka. And during the time that the Portuguese remained in Melaka, the city was most busy, and many were the merchants who came to trade in the port. So tells the history of long, long ago.

After this, it tells that a Dutch ship came to trade in Melaka. The name of the ship was *Aftar Lindir* and the name of its captain Inybir. It was this man who came to Melaka to trade; and he then saw Melaka in its beauty, with its fortress and its moat. And that Dutch ship traded in Melaka for fifteen days; and then set sail for its Europe.

Then, some time having passed, the Dutch ship arrived in its principal city; and the captain of the ship gave news to his great king concerning Melaka, which had active trade, of its fort and of its lovely moat. After which the great king of Europe says:

If such are the tidings, it will be good to have Melaka attacked.

And when time had passed, behold the great king of Europe sends twenty-five ships to go and attack Melaka. And the twenty-five ships make themselves ready, and are all equipped with soldiers. And behold those that sail in the direction of the city of Banten of Java. There was at the time in the city of Banten of Java a factory of the Dutch Company. Then those twenty-five ships arrived in Banten of Java, saying that they wished to go and attack Melaka. Now at this time in Banten there were also two Dutch ships and a galliot; and at once all of them filled their holds with all sorts of victuals; and without delay they set sail in the direction of Melaka.

So, once the ships had arrived at the bar of Melaka, the Dutch immediately sent the Portuguese a letter, saying they should prepare themselves, for next day at noon they would attack.

And the Portuguese replied:

As you wish! We are ready!

Then, on the next day, the Dutch attack, and they fight for about two months. But Melaka does not surrender at all. Then all the Dutch set sail in the direction of Banten. And after a few days all those ships arrive in the city of Banten and remain anchored there, with the intention of returning again to Europe.

All the Dutch feel ashamed, in front of the important people who had come in the ships. Then, once time had passed, the important people who had come in the ships sat down to discuss, deliberating with one another whether to attack anew.

Then, for the second time, the Dutch attack: Melaka does not yield.

The Dutch send letters to Johor, to ally themselves with the Sultan of Johor to attack the city of Melaka. And the King of Johor was content; and from then on, the Dutch and the King of Johor had an oath of alliance: Dutch and Malays became one only in order to go and attack Melaka. This was the agreement between the Dutch and the King of Johor: if they took Melaka, then the city and artillery would revert to Holland; and all the riches would be divided in two parts, one part for the Dutch, and the other part for the people from Johor. And this agreement was solemnized.

Then the people from Johor and the ships of the Dutch set sail in the direction of Melaka: and for some fifteen days they fight with the Franks. Many of the Franks died, but many of the Malays and Dutch died too.

After this the Malays thought to themselves:

Even if we fight white people of this sort for a whole year, they will not surrender!

On this account it was agreed amongst all the good Malays that the best thing would be to send fifty people into the place, who would go amok inside there.

The Malays fixed the time for the 21st of the month, at the beginning of the dawn oration. And the Malays entered the place, and made themselves amok. And the Franks were exterminated, some fleeing to the backlands of Melaka; they did not know where to go, those Portuguese!

And all the Malays found in Melaka an enormous prize. Then, as had been in the agreement between the Dutch and the people of Melaka, so it was, as promised, that all the riches obtained were exactly divided.

Those from Johor returned then to their land of Johor, and the Dutch established themselves, keeping for themselves the land of Melaka. Since then, the Dutch and the Malays of Johor have remained on good terms, until today.

This is what the history tells us of times long ago. As for this narration, it is composed by the Datu Bendahara of the King, His Majesty (Thomaz 1986b; Thomaz 1987).

What does one make of a text such as this? At the most mundane level, it is clear that it has many of the 'facts of the matter' wrong: the Portuguese did not arrive in Melaka from Manila, the 'great king' of the Portuguese resided not in Goa but in Portugal, the manner in which the city was taken in 1511 was not as is described here (if most other texts are to be believed), the Portuguese remained in Melaka for some one hundred and thirty years and not a mere forty-odd as is implied here, and so on. And so might one concur with the Portuguese Orientalist David Lopes, who wrote in 1899 that Asian sources in fact hold little of importance for the history of the Portuguese in Asia?[1]

Let us begin by noting that not all Asian texts fall within the same genre, and nor indeed do all Portuguese texts of the period. The reader of the famous *Peregrinação* of the Portuguese traveller Fernão Mendes Pinto will find himself in a Japan where the natives at times converse in Malay, and where other rather improbable events take place (Pinto 1983; 1989). This makes the *Peregrinação* a rather different sort of text from, say, the chronicler João de Barros's *Da Ásia* (Barros 1973); it does not render it valueless though. Similarly, Luís de Camões's epic poem, the *Lusíadas*, is scarcely to be treated as an historical source of the same type as the governor Afonso de Albuquerque's letters to his sovereign. In the case of sixteenth- and seventeenth-century Asian sources one must similarly make

---

1 See his introduction to Lopes (1899), pp. xc–xci

a distinction: the *Kitab-i Bahriye* of the Turkish admiral Piri Reis (1474–1554) cannot be equated to the Malay text glossed at length above, and nor can it be equated to a text like the Chinese *Yueh-chien pien* (1601) of Wang Lin-hsiang, which contains a quite elaborate discussion of Ming policy-making in respect of the European presence off Chinese shores (Reis 1988; Blussé 1988).

The utility of these sources can be approached from two perspectives. First, they often contain information of a sort wholly unavailable in contemporary Portuguese documentation: Leonard Blussé's analysis of the *Yueh-chien pien* shows, for example, that Chinese officialdom in the late sixteenth century included men who – contrary to conventional wisdom – had every desire to build contacts with foreigners, and that this influenced their policy decisions in respect of trade concessions. With the very best of will, the historian could never have arrived at this fact on the basis of Portuguese or Dutch sources, which very rarely discuss the issue of the Chinese 'official mind' at all (Blussé 1988). This is a relatively trivial instance, but many other examples can be brought out to show how Asian sources often give us useful 'facts' where the European materials are silent. But going beyond this, there is also the issue of the *perspective* embodied in different texts, whether 'true' or 'false' in terms of their facts. In a recent defence of Fernão Mendes Pinto's writings, scholars have pointed out that even though he often presents information that is patently erroneous, he also presents a unique moral critique of Portuguese actions in Asia: his account hence cannot be ignored, or relegated to the dustbin of historiography.

This is also the point with our anonymous Malay writer, the Datu Bendahara. First, we note how his account – written in all probability in the eighteenth century – carefully distinguishes the Dutch from the Portuguese; not all Europeans are seen as identical in relation to Asians. That stereotype was to come in a later age. Second, we note his use of the classical myth of the animal's hide as a device for territorial aggrandisement (common to much of Asia, the Mediterranean and North Africa, and which already appears in the *Aeneid*) to characterise the Portuguese conquest. The implication appears to be that contracts between strangers, and the ambiguities inherent in the letter thereof, are often apt to be exploited by one or the other party; this *was* indeed the case at times in Portuguese relations with Asian rulers. Third, we note how the Malays are still portrayed as ultimately holding the balance between Dutch and Portuguese; it is only when the amok are sent in that the struggle between the two European powers is resolved. It is almost as if, in a residual sense, the Malay writer wishes to assert that his community is still the most powerful.[2] Fourth, we note that the

---

2 Also see Andaya (1975) on this question

Portuguese are presented largely as an Asian power, with their headquarters in Goa, a superscription of what the Portuguese eventually had become by the late seventeenth century on their character in an earlier period. And finally, we note that in the latter part of the text, a creeping admiration emerges in describing the Portuguese: the apparent wonder at the trouble taken by them to construct the stone fort at Melaka is one aspect, as is the admission that they were hard to defeat even if one fought them 'for a whole year'.

Thus, whatever its inaccuracies and quirks, the text that we have cited above is not devoid of interest for the historian of the period. It lies admittedly in the area between fiction (or rather folk-tale) and history, but so too did the average Portuguese primary school text of the mid-twentieth century whose illustrations might well portray a black warrior wearing a loincloth and carrying a spear greeting Vasco da Gama at Calicut, or the blue-tile mural at Lisbon's Sociedade de Geografia, which shows a wholly fantastic meeting between Portuguese ambassadors and an Oriental potentate (probably the Samudri raja of Calicut). Separating myth from reality is of course a task that any historian must approach with trepidation, for while history is the stuff from which myth is made, myth-making too is part of the historical process. With this word of caution then, we may embark on our journey, to consider and interpret the history of the Portuguese Asian empire in the sixteenth and seventeenth centuries.

CHAPTER ONE

Early Modern Asia: Geopolitics and Economic Change

The world between the Cape of Good Hope and Japan, where the Portuguese strove to build a network of trade and power between 1500 and 1700, was not a static one. It was characterised by change, at times almost imperceptible, at other times more clearly visible, both at the institutional and at the functional level. To understand Portuguese actions in Asia, therefore, and to comprehend the accommodations they had to make as well as the avenues they used, one needs to do more than describe the 'Asian stage' on which they were actors. Rather, it is necessary to consider the problem of the dynamics of Asian history over these two hundred years.

The population of Asia in about 1650 was around 300 million, from a the world population of perhaps 500 million. A hundred years later, in 1750, the continent still accounted for roughly sixty per cent of the world's population, which had by then risen to around 700 million. Over the century and a half prior to 1650, when estimates are much harder to obtain, it is likely that there had already been a fair degree of expansion in numbers; after the mid-fifteenth century, all over Eurasia, the recovery from the Black Death takes decisive shape in the form of a demographic expansion. We would probably not be far wrong to place Asia's population in 1500 at between 200 and 225 million, which means that the Portuguese 'saw' over the first two hundred years of their presence in Asia something like a doubling of the continent's population.

This population was, needless to say, unevenly distributed. It appears clear that tropical and semi-tropical Asia accounted for a far larger share of the total population than regions farther north, but this was a difference that was not quite so marked at the end of our period as at its beginning. At the farthest limit of the space we are concerned with was Japan, whose modern historians are agreed that the period between 1500 and 1700 witnessed a far more rapid growth of population than either the fourteenth or the eighteenth century, which respectively preceded and

9

succeeded it. Indeed, if the estimates of scholars like Akira Hayami are acceptable, we may conclude that population growth rates in early modern Japan (which are said to have ranged between 0.8 and 1.3 per cent per annum) were amongst the highest anywhere in Asia (Hall et al. 1981). In sharp contrast is Southeast Asia, whose historians suggest very slow population growth over the period 1600 to 1800; while this period-isation does not permit us to speak directly of the sixteenth century, the impression is certainly left that rates of demographic change in that area (whose population may have been some 22 million in 1600) rarely exceeded 0.2 per cent a year over the entire period from 1500 to 1800 (Reid 1988: 11–18).

Sandwiched between Japan and Southeast Asia, the two outliers in early modern Asian demographic history, lie other regions, some closer to Japan in their experience, others better approximating the Southeast Asian case. In the former category is China, whose population grew from about 60 million in 1400 to 180 million by 1750, even if a significant accele-ration to this growth was given only after 1680 (at which point China's population has been estimated at a mere 120 million) (Banister 1987: 3–7). In the latter category, we must include much of South and West Asia, where one has to proceed on the basis of largely qualitative evidence, since population statistics are largely dubious until the eighteenth century. Taking one thing with another then, it is possible to assert that the balance of population in Asia gradually shifted from south and west to north and east over the period.

Not only did total population rise and its balance shift; the period also saw the consolidation of some great urban centres, and the decline of others. Cities like Delhi, Agra, Aceh, Kyoto, Isfahan and Istanbul (the last lying in a sense between Europe and Asia), were comparable in order of magnitude and complexity of social structure to any of the European cities of the sixteenth and seventeenth centuries. Nor was the change purely an urban phenomenon: partly under the pressure of population and partly for other reasons, land under cultivation expanded, as did manufacturing production, with India and China in the seventeenth century possibly accounting for over a half of the world's textile production. To reiterate our initial point, then, even the most obvious of indices do not support the idea of a static Asia that had to confront a dynamic and expanding Portugal.

FIFTEENTH- AND SIXTEENTH-CENTURY STATES

The changes that took place in Asia over these centuries are most obvious and visible, however, at the level of elite politics. In the sixteenth century, two very substantial and powerful states – of the Mughals and the Safavids – were formed in southern and western Asia, while still another state – the Ottoman one – grew considerably in strength. In southern India, the great political system centred around the metropolis of Vijayanagara first consolidated itself, and then, in the latter half of the century, entered into decline. Equally dramatic changes are to be observed in the careers of states of Southeast and East Asia: in the former case, Aceh, Arakan and to a lesser extent Makassar are three remarkable sixteenth-century success stories, while in the Far East, the turmoils of the sixteenth century eventually throw up a lasting institution in the *bakufu* – the 'curtain' government of the warlord house of the Tokugawas in Japan, who ruled behind the façade of imperial sovereignty until as late as 1868.

And yet, these changes can quite easily be dismissed as of no real consequence, as indeed they have often been by adherents of the 'Omar Khayyam approach', who insist – like the author of the *Rubaiyat* – that early modern Asian state-formation is well encapsulated in this verse:

> Think, in this batter'd Caravanserai
> Whose Portals are alternate Night and Day,
> How Sultan after Sultan with his Pomp,
> Abode his destined Hour, and went his way.   (Verse XVII)

That is to say that these changes represent no more than a replacement of one regime by another, all of which were much the same in essential character. This has, after all, for long been the central thrust of such theories as the 'Asiatic Mode of Production', or 'Oriental Despotism', which stressed the static and unchanging character of *both* Asian societies and the states that ruled over them. If it is indeed our contention that the states formed in Asia in this period (which we will call early modern) differed from those of an earlier epoch (extending from say the eighth to the fourteenth centuries, which we might term 'medieval'), how did they do so?

Before we enter into this question, however, it may be useful to differentiate *between* types of states in early modern Asia. It has been usual to distinguish Asian states of the period under two broad heads: *first*, the massive, agrarian-based imperial formations, such as the Ottomans, the Safavids, Vijayanagara and the Mughals, the Ming in China, and Mataram in Java; *in contrast*, the relatively small-scale (usually coastal) states like Kilwa, Hurmuz, Calicut, or Melaka, which are thought to have been essentially trade-based, thus drawing their resources not so much from the harnessing of force under prebendal systems as from the control of strategic 'choke-points' along key trade routes. Let us consider the Ottomans as an example of the first type. During the fifteenth and sixteenth centuries, their central fiscal institution is seen as the *timar*, a revenue-assignment given to *timariot* prebend-holders who rendered military and other services to the state. Despite the attempts to develop central institutions designed to reduce the dependence of the state on such

11

dispersed forces – attempts that are located by historians in particular during the reign of Sultan Suleyman 'the Magnificent' (r. 1520–66) – it is argued that the Ottomans could never throw off their character as a state whose fundamental institution was a combination of the classic Islamic *iqta* assignment, and a 'feudal' land-grant deriving from the Paleologues, the last dynasty to rule Byzantium. The *timar*, like its counterpart the *jagir* in Mughal territories, is thus often seen as holding the key to an understanding of how the Ottomans functioned, and also why they failed to modernise and compete with the West (Shaw 1976).

It is implicit in most characterisations of states like the Ottoman and Mughal empires that the bulk of their revenues must have come from the 'land', rather than from 'trade'. In practice, these categories prove rather difficult to disentangle in contemporary documents. Often, taxes on agricultural produce were collected through the control of trade in these goods; further, 'land' was a convenient category for purposes of assignment, since it concealed the fact that what was in fact being parcelled out was the right to use coercive force. Still, it is certainly true that if we were to examine the Ottoman budgets of the sixteenth century, the revenues of the greater part of the provinces under their control would show a preponderance of collections under categories other than 'customs-duties'. Thus, the provincial budget of the Yemen province in 1599–1600 shows that of total current revenues of 13,675,239 *para*, no more than 35 per cent came from port-duties, and this in an area with a relatively poor agricultural base. Again, the budget of Egypt in 1596–97 shows customs-duties accounting for a mere 8.2 per cent of total provincial revenues, and taxes on Cairo-based traders and artisans for another 6.6 per cent. Even for earlier years, such as the early 1560s, it has been suggested by Salih Ozbaran that the land-tax (*harac-i arazi*) dominates the Yemen budgets (Ozbaran 1986).

This is what is often thought to distinguish such states from, say, the Southeast Asian Sultanate of Melaka, or the East African Sultanate of Kilwa, ruled over from the late thirteenth century by a family of Yemeni *sharifs*, the Mahdali. In the case of Kilwa, or its northern neighbours and rivals Mombasa and Malindi (which emerged into prominence in the fourteenth century), we are not aware of any data on the fiscal foundations of the state, though links between the prosperity of these states and the Indian Ocean commercial triangle of Gujarat-Red Sea-East Africa are often asserted (as is the importance in the case of Kilwa of control of the gold trade) (Pouwels 1987). In the case of Melaka, we are rather better served, for early Portuguese observers resident in the town (after it fell into their hands in August 1511) meticulously described how the erstwhile Sultanate had functioned. In the early sixteenth century Melaka, which had been founded under somewhat obscure circumstances a century earlier, was the metropolis-capital of a state whose shadow reached to the other extremity of the Indonesian archipelago. The population of the city, variously estimated at between 100,000 and 200,000, was large by Asian standards of the time; in the late fifteenth century, Istanbul had a population of no more than 100,000, while only Kyoto of the Japanese cities of the early sixteenth century could boast of a population over 150,000.

While the greater part of the population of Melaka was made up of Malays of the labouring class (including a substantial slave sector – perhaps seven per cent of the total population), there were also sizeable resident foreign communities, amongst whom the most prominent were the Gujaratis and Kelings (Tamils), followed by the Javanese and the Fukien Chinese. There is little doubt that these merchants were accorded a high status in Melaka's society: in the *Hikayat Hang Tuah*, a Malay prose-epic, even the semi-divine progenitor of Melaka's Sultans (a certain Sang Perta Dewa) is constantly escorted in Heaven (the Malay *Keinderaan* or Kingdom of Indra) by a retinue of merchants! At a more mundane level, what we know of the Melaka Sultanate's revenue-base confirms that foreign trade was indeed the lifeblood of the kingdom. A complex system of taxes differentiated ships coming from the *negeri di-atas angin* – which is to say west of Melaka – from those coming from the *negeri di-bawah angin* (parts east of Melaka). In both cases, the rates of customs-duty are however much lower than those obtaining in contemporary Burma, Bengal and elsewhere (though not lower than in, say, Calicut). Despite this lower rate of duty, customs-collections and related surcharges accounted for something like ninety per cent of the Sultanate's revenues, swamping by far the tributes paid by the provincial governors and vassal kings of the Sultan. Besides this, Melaka's Sultans also participated directly in commerce, owning ships and plying routes between Melaka and the Indian coast of the Bay of Bengal. The presence of these ships, manned at times by the slaves of the Sultan, gives the state in Melaka a markedly mercantile character, thus strengthening the implicit divide between the character of large, agrarian states and small, trading ones (Thomaz 1986a).

We are aware that in about 1500, Melaka was one of the key nodes in Asian maritime trade, linked to China and eastern Indonesia, but also to India, the Persian Gulf and the Red Sea. In the last two areas, one equally finds political power seeking expression in the form of relatively small and compact trading states not dissimilar to Melaka, of which the two clearest examples are Yemen in the Red Sea, and Hurmuz in the Persian of Gulf, both of which also controlled key nodes in Indian Ocean trade – respectively the ports of Aden and Jarun.

Considering the case of Aden first, it emerges into importance as a centre in the late ninth or early tenth century, several centuries before the rise of Melaka. Together with the ports of Zafar and al-Shihr, Aden remained one of the centres where ships from India and Southeast Asia customarily made first landfall on the Arabian coast. Under the rule of the Ayyubid dynasty, the port duties (*ushur*) at Aden were first codified in the twelfth century, and these rulers also instituted a system of galleys, to patrol the coast and the mouth of the Red Sea in order to protect merchant shipping from pirates. The Ayyubid governor (*na'ib*) at Aden, Uthman b. Ali al-Zinjili (1175–83), is credited with rebuilding the port's harbour, and reorganising the markets in the town. The structure of trade and state in the area, somewhat obscure in the Ayyubid period, becomes somewhat clearer during the rule of the succeeding Rasulid dynasty. Of particular importance as evidence is a text of 1411–12, the *Mulakhkhas al-fitan*, which sets out at some detail the administration of the port, the nature of the communities resident there, the extent of revenues, and so on. From this work, it emerges that the Aden port-duties in 1411–12 amounted to as much as 1,470,000 *dinars*, and that they were the major source of revenue for the Rasulid Sultans resident at Ta'izz (Serjeant 1988).

It is natural enough then that from the early thirteenth century, the Rasulid Sultans should have taken great interest in developing the port, building a reputation of such dimensions that in 1374–75, the *qadi* of Calicut wrote to them, requesting that the Muslims of this Malabar port be permitted to read the *khutba* in the name of the Rasulids! The regulations of the port speak of a certain degree of bureaucratic order-liness; all vessels entering Aden were to carry a manifest, in the hands of the ship's scrivener (*karrani*), all goods were to be examined in detail, body-searches of passengers were to be conducted and so on.

But evidence also exists of conflict between the Rasulid Sultans and merchants, especially the substantial magnates (*a'yan al-tujjar*) of Aden, and in particular those of the Karimi community. These conflicts arose largely because the Sultans, like their counterparts at Melaka, were themselves engaged in commerce, and also because – as was to occur later in Aceh, and *unlike* what usually obtained in Melaka – they at times acted as monopsonists or monopolists. The royal trading establishment, called *al-Matjar al-Sultani*, was probably founded in the mid-fourteenth century by al-Mujahid, in imitation of the Fatimid practice at Cairo. The headship of the establishment, which was engaged in the trade in madder, pepper, aromatics and so on, appears to have been a hereditary post, that of the *ra'is tujjar al-Yaman*; the Sultan's traders were to be found at Mecca, Cairo and other centres in the late fourteenth and fifteenth centuries. It is likely that the Sultan also owned ships, though one has no evidence that they traded over long-distance routes. For the most part, the trade of the *matjar* seems to have been limited to the Arabian peninsula, the Red Sea littoral, and Egypt; this would also explain why the merchants who were most often in conflict with Sultan were the Karimis, rather than, say, the Indian *vanias*, whose quarter at Aden (the so-called *hafat al-baniyan*) is to be encountered already in the late fourteenth century (Serjeant 1988).

Prosperous and cosmopolitan, fifteenth-century Aden bears more than a passing resemblance to Melaka, although some differences – which we shall explore below – also existed between the two. It also resembles its nearer neighbour, Hurmuz (or rather Jarun) in the Persian Gulf, in more ways than one. Jarun, unlike either Aden or Melaka, was an island, with two port-sites on it, one for small vessels, the other for large ones. Founded in around 1300, the island-city was virtually impregnable from land, and succeeded quickly in superseding the centre of Qays that had earlier dominated Persian Gulf trade for two centuries. It became the centre of a kingdom, the kingdom of Hurmuz, ruled over by Sunni rulers of Arab extraction, but still closely linked by way of trade and political relations to the Iranian world. Hurmuz, like Melaka and Aden, was organised in quarters, where different communities resided: these included the Gujarati *vanias*, Iranian merchants, and also a substantial community of Jewish traders in the fifteenth century. More than the rulers of Melaka, the Shahs of Hurmuz appear to have run a semi-tributary, semi-trade-based state. They controlled a number of islands in the Persian Gulf, of which the most important – Qishm – was also the major supplier of agricultural products to feed Jarun. Other islands had a more clearly strategic function, such as Kharg which guarded the entrance to the Shatt-el-Arab waterway at the interior of the Gulf. Besides these islands, Hurmuz's rulers also collected revenues from their dominions on the mainland, both on the Iranian and the Arabian sides. The latter were more significant from the viewpoint of revenue yield, and included a number of settlements of which Qalhat and Maskat were the most significant. Frequently in revolt, the Arab part of Hurmuz's 'exterior districts' was however not so necessary for the day-to-day survival of the port-city as connections on the other side (Aubin 1973).

As a city located on a salinated, infertile island, with a population of over 50,000 in the late fifteenth century, Jarun was not merely deficient in food but also in drinking-water, for which huge storage tanks had been built by the rulers on the island, and which arrived from the Iranian side. On this side of the waterway, the rulers of Hurmuz claimed the allegiance of parts of Mughistan, as well as three other districts – Minab, Manujan, and Vashkird – which together yielded about a half in revenues of what was obtained from the Arabian dependent territories. It was also from this direction that the major overland caravans came and went, linking Hurmuz to the cities of the Iranian plateau and thence to the entrepots of the Levant. In view of the strategic and commercial importance of these routes, the Shahs of Hurmuz paid a fixed sum, called *muqarrariya*, to the dynasties that ruled fifteenth-century Iran – the Timurids, the Qara-Qoyunlu and then the Aq-Qoyunlu – to ensure that the caravan links remained unbroken (Aubin 1973: 141).

Over a half of the total revenues of the kingdom came from trade and

15

customs, in particular the trade to India. Fifteenth-century observers, as well as early Portuguese writers, suggest that as in Melaka, customs rates in Hurmuz were quite low: Nimdihi, writing in about 1500, suggests that all goods arriving in the kingdom by sea paid 10 per cent of their value, and that all goods from Khorassan paid 5 per cent. The Portuguese writers suggest a far more complex system, in which some Indian goods like raw cotton, rice and butter paid no more than 5 per cent, Indian textiles 10 per cent, and textiles exported to Hurmuz via Melaka as much as 16½ per cent. It is interesting to note that the bulk of customs duties were collected on imports rather than exports; neither of the major exports in the eastward direction, namely horses (exported at the rate of two thousand a year in the early sixteenth century), nor bullion – the major component in Hurmuz's trade to India – seem to have been taxed. This is not difficult to comprehend, for the bulk of Hurmuz's trade was a re-export trade, and to tax both imports and exports would have been tantamount to a double tax on the same commodity (Aubin 1973).

The total revenues of Hurmuz's rulers in the early sixteenth century are shown in Table 1.1.

Table 1.1 The Hurmuz Kingdom's Revenues, *c.* 1500

Head	Amount *(in* ashrafis)
Customs-duties	100,000
Other taxes at Jarun	41,300
Qays pearl-fishery	6,000
Revenue from Arabian lands	28,200
Revenue from Persian lands	16,700
Other	5,800
TOTAL	198,000

(*Source*: Aubin 1973: 233–37)

The meticulous researches of Jean Aubin, based on both Persian and Portuguese sources, permit us to have a close look at the internal functioning of the Hurmuz kingdom in the fifteenth century, and point to an internal political structure somewhat different from that which obtained in either Melaka or Aden. It turns out that Hurmuz's rulers owned no ships, and did not participate directly in trade; the sort of conflict that emerges between the Rasulids and the Karimi community at Aden is thus absent here. For the most part, Hurmuz's rulers led an insecure existence: of ten Shahs between 1400 and 1506, five were deposed, and four assassinated, with only one, Turan Shah II, (r. 1436–70/71) dying of natural causes, and that too because (in the words of a Persian chronicler) 'he ate only what he had fished with his own hands' (Aubin 1973: 129)!

On the other hand, a major role was played here by a series of powerful *vazir* families, the Baghdadi, the Iji, and the Fali. The Portuguese in their early dealings with Hurmuz had to contend with the figure of Khwaja Ata (Cojeatar), who had risen to power in about 1475, and who virtually ran the kingdom over the head of first Salghur Shah (r. 1475–1505) and then his successor.

Thus, despite the apparent similarities, Hurmuz provides us with a quite distinct case from Melaka and Aden at one level, being somewhat closer perhaps to the situation in the south-western Indian kingdom of Calicut, where the Samudri raja (or Zamorin) derived a great part of his revenues from taxing trade, but still did not run a fully-fledged mercantilist state. In Calicut, as in certain other small kingdoms with access to the seaboard like Kotte in western Sri Lanka, the rulers left trade in the hands of specific communities – be they indigenised Muslims, like the Mappilas of Malabar, or foreigners (*paradesis*) from as far as Baghdad and Shiraz (Bouchon 1973).

On the other hand, whatever the distinctions between them, Aden, Hurmuz and Melaka still appear to conform to a certain category of state – one that depended on trade – and thus appear to confirm the divide between such states, and other, agrarian-based, states that we described earlier. But if one is to take such a divide seriously, contrary evidence must be explained away. For instance, in the early fifteenth century, between 1405 and 1433, at roughly the same time that the Melaka state was founded, the Ming Chinese state mounted a series of maritime expeditions, as far as East Africa, the most celebrated of which were commanded by a Muslim eunuch-admiral, native of Yunnan, Cheng He. Involving several thousand crew, and a number of vessels, these expeditions have remained a source of embarrassment to those who argue that such large agrarian states as the Ming should by all rights have had no interest in the sea or maritime trade. Of course, explanations can be found in specific circumstances, the pressure of nomads from the north, for instance, which might have caused the Mings to seek an alternative to the caravan routes through Central Asia. But taking resort to such *ad hoc* explanations does tend to weaken the general characterisation. Nor is the sudden termination of these expeditions in the early 1430s susceptible of easy explanation, although one possible contributory factor may have been the humiliating defeat and withdrawal from Vietnam in much the same period. Examples of this type can very easily be multiplied: the Ottomans in the sixteenth century most certainly had an interest in maritime trade, as did some of the Mughal emperors like the builder of the Taj Mahal, Shahjahan, who had a whole fleet of substantial craft operating out of the western Indian port of Surat in the 1650s (Van Santen 1982: 71–78).

The issue of the extent of thalassophobia (or fear of the sea) of such states as the Chinese Ming, the Mughals, and the Safavids, therefore,

17

remains a vexed one. For the sixteenth century, John Wills has made a case for the continuing validity of the traditional view, based on an examination of the South China coast between the Yangtze delta and Hainan, including the Pescadores and Taiwan. Arguing that maritime China offered relatively meagre opportunities for the interaction of power and profit, with its trade to Vietnam, Luzon, Taiwan, the Ryukyus, and Japan either too fraught with risk or too little substance economically to interest the state, Wills points to how in the 1540s and 1550s, relatively small bands of pirates (*wo-k'ou*) played havoc in the countryside of Chiangnan and northern Chekiang, attacking Hangchow, Ningpo and even Nanking with impunity. A state more driven to trade and maritime preoccupations, it is suggested, would surely have been more watchful of the coastline. While major *wo-k'ou* leaders like Wang Chih were eventually defeated by state forces over the period 1557–61, the crisis of these decades on the coast seems to lend credence to the notion of Ming thalassophobia (Wills 1979). In the case of the Mughals, a similar argument has been put forward; whether in terms of the contribution to the exchequer or otherwise, trade – and especially maritime trade – could apparently never hold much attraction for this Central Asian warrior clan, who understood only the control of land as the currency of power (Pearson 1976).

Two intertwined strands in these arguments need to be separated here. There is first the issue of the lack of trading *opportunities*; states that occupied poorly monetised regions, or which had little control over either maritime or overland routes could never, even with the best of wills, really have been trade-oriented. The second question is that of ideological *barriers* to participation in trade, even in the presence of opportunities: thus, it is argued that certain political cultures were instinctively hostile to the very idea of trade, while others would embrace trade readily. Now, these two issues are naturally related, but we should not assume that one flows directly out of the other, or that ideology would necessarily accommodate itself to changing opportunities. Indeed, the coexistence of divergent ideological streams on the question of trade even within the same political culture can clearly be seen by juxtaposing two medieval Arabic texts, each of which is equally emphatic. The first, written 'in praise of merchants' by Al-Jahiz, assures us that 'Muslims know that Exalted God's elect, His most sincere worshipper, the one entrusted with His revelation, was a member of a merchant house'; the other, the *al-Sadaqah wa-'l-sadiq* of Al-Tawhidi, is equally firm in stating that 'Concerning merchants, the gaining of pence sets up an obstacle between them and manly virtue and interposes a barrier for them from all that is connected with chivalrous qualities' (Serjeant 1988).

It is no coincidence, of course, that those historians who are disposed to favour the idea that the large continental polities of Asia in the early

18

modern period subscribed to the views of Al-Tawhidi rather than
Al-Jahiz, tend to see these states' ideologies as largely formed *sui generis*,
rather than by a process of interaction with other states. The contrast is
thus often drawn between 'trading states' – mercantilist in spirit, outward
looking, and eclectic in ideology – and 'agrarian states' – anti-mercantile,
but also inward looking, and characterised by ideologies that stem from
their own, unique, internal experiences. While there is undoubtedly some
utility in these as ideal-types, locating most of the states of early modern
Asia in either one of these two 'boxes' proves difficult. The central
problem lies in the fact that from the latter half of the fifteenth century,
many states – even those that ruled over substantial and fertile agricultural
tracts – were increasingly formed through the mediation of migratory
elites, who circulated in two circuits: one embracing East Africa, West
Asia, South Asia and Southeast Asia, the other being formed by East Asia,
and Southeast Asia. Ideas and ideologies thus rarely retained a pristine
character, and can seldom be sited in a unique polity. Different states of
the period show striking and unexpected parallels in the development of
political institutions, and it is hard to dismiss these as mere coincidence.

Let us take the case of Japan. After the long drawn-out Onin War
(1467–77), the *bakufu*, or shadow government, of the Ashikaga Shoguns
began to break down. Those of the family who succeeded Ashikaga
Yoshimasa (r.1443–90) were themselves manipulated by warlords, even as
they manipulated the Emperor. The last decade of the fifteenth century
and the first two-thirds of the sixteenth century are thus often
characterised as the period of the *sengoku daimyo* – or Civil War Barons –
all of whom struggled to reconstitute their domains, and eventually to
throw up a *primus inter pares*. The extent of economic disruption and
generalised 'disorder' that resulted is the subject of some debate; but what
is certain is that it is not until the late 1560s that the glimmerings of a
characteristically early modern order are visible, with the rise to
dominance of the military leader Oda Nobunaga. Nobunaga's purported
role when he entered the capital city of Kyoto was, however, not as a *new*
centre of power; rather he claimed to be the restorer of one of the rival
Ashikaga claimants to the Shogunate, Ashikaga Yoshiaki. Killed in June
1582, Nobunaga thus failed to transform his *de facto* power into control of
the Shogunate for his family, and this was also the case with his successor
as *supremo*, Toyotomi Hideyoshi (d. 1598). It was only the third of the
'Great Unifiers', Tokugawa Ieyasu, who in the early seventeenth century
managed to create a new *bakufu*, that of the Tokugawas, which remained
in place for over two and a half centuries (Hall et al. 1981).

But was the order that emerged an unique experiment in governance?
Did the concept of the 'shadow government', accompanied by a tight
control over the external trade sector, find no echoes elsewhere?
Proponents of Japanese political insularity in the period (or, to put it more

diplomatically, of the uniqueness of Japanese political institutions) would argue in the affirmative. Certainly, the comparison with Ming China is not a fruitful one in terms of suggesting parallels. But we are aware, on the other hand, that in the sixteenth and early seventeenth centuries, Japan was a significant exporter of skilled military manpower, to mainland Southeast Asia as well as to Indo-China. Did these migrations, at the level of intermediate and elite segments of society, have any significance for the institutional structures of the recipient regions? At least one case would bear investigation, that of Dai-Viet or northern Vietnam, a region which maintained fairly close trading relations with the Japanese ports in the period. In this area, the expulsion of Ming forces after a brief occupation in the early fifteenth century had brought to the throne of Dai-Viet the Le dynasty, founded by Le Loi (r.1427–33), a warrior-leader from the mountainous western region, bordering Laos. Despite his origins, Le Loi sought to distance himself from the 'turbulent barons' of his realm, the so-called *cong than*; his successors, in particular Le Thanh-ton (r. 1460–97), were essentially concerned to build a stable and bureaucratised state structure, based on the reformulation and assimilation of Confucian political concepts rather than on the model of charismatic leadership that had characterised earlier periods. What ensued in the fifteenth and sixteenth centuries was a see-saw battle, with alternating phases of *cong than* dominance (such as 1442–59 and 1505–26), and of the dominance of court-based scholar-bureaucrats, who had a quite different vision of the state and philosophy of government (Ungar 1983).

What is significant for our purposes, however, is the resolution that emerges eventually in the sixteenth century. After sixty-five years of rule by the usurper Mac clan, the Le lineage was restored to the throne in 1592. However, their position was now quite different from what it had been in the fifteenth century; their rule was a mere façade, and the real power was held by a lineage of hereditary regents, the Trinh, who ruled for eight generations, into the eighteenth century. The emergence of this system, strikingly different from what we observe in the Malay world in the period, but at the same time remarkably close to the system established by Hideyoshi and Ieyasu in precisely the same period, deserves closer exploration.

THE CIRCULATION OF ELITES

The formation of conquest states in medieval Asia – be it the Sultanate of Delhi, or the Khanates formed by the disintegration of the Mongol empire – had always been accompanied by the migration of elites, at least at the level of courts and central bureaucracies (whatever the size of the latter might have been) (Wink 1988). However, these migrants of the medieval period were usually military specialists, religious leaders and men of letters and the arts; their role was thus either to shore up the coercive power of the thin layer of conquering migrants, or to console them in their exile from their erstwhile homelands. In contrast to the bulk of these medieval migrations, the period from the latter half of the fifteenth century, and especially after 1550, marks something of a departure from the pattern. Now one has the circulation of elites proceeding even in the *absence* of conquest, elites who – moreover – are noted for their ability to combine commercial activities with the more conventional skills noted above.

The example of the Mughal state is instructive in this respect. As descendants of Timur and Chengis Khan, the Mughals were scarcely a new ethnic element in northern Indian politics in the early sixteenth century. The initial takeover of Agra by Babur, the first Mughal to rule there, was facilitated more by political factionalism in the court of the Lodi Sultans ruling there than by true 'conquest'. Babur's son and successor Humayun first set about quelling the opposition of rivals in the Indo-Gangetic plain, particularly because they stood in the way of his eastward expansion (his ambition being to conquer the Husain Shahi Sultanate of Bengal). But the Bihar-based Afghan chieftain, Sher Khan Sur, defeated him in battle, forcing him into a long exile in Iran (which exceeded the period of his actual reign). Sher Shah, as the new ruler titled himself in 1539, appears to have been particularly interested in promoting trade along the Gangetic valley, and thence to the Iranian plateau and Central Asia (Qureshi 1970: 37–40). In effective terms, despite brief periods in which he dominated Bengal, his reign too is characterised by a failure to transform the landlocked Delhi state into one with direct maritime links. This was eventually achieved by Humayun's son, Akbar (r. 1556–1605), who had by 1580 conquered both Gujarat and Bengal and gained access to their sea-ports (Streusand 1989).

In the course of their expansion, the Mughals had to make use of a variety of skills from the tool-box of contemporary statecraft. There was, first and most importantly, the issue of the power-holders in the localities, the ubiquitous *zamindars*, who had armed retinues at their disposal, and who could as easily rebel as accept the service (*khidmat*) of the Mughal. This armed rural gentry had to be placated, by the offer of a share of the fiscal take, and various other perquisites, and suppressed by main force only if they proved truly recalcitrant. Of them, the Dutch traveller Francisco Pelsaert wrote in the 1620s (during the reign of the Mughal Jahangir):

> The whole country is enclosed and broken up by many mountains, and the people who live in, on, or beyond the mountains know nothing of any king, or of Jahangir; they recognize only their Rajas, who are very numerous, and

to whom the country is apportioned in many small fragments by old tradition. Jahangir, whose name implies that he grasps the whole world, must therefore be regarded as ruling no more than half the dominions which he claims, since there are nearly as many rebels as subjects.   (Wink 1986: 191)

From the ranks of these *zamindars*, a chosen few – Rajputs, Afghans and so on – were elevated to a place of importance in the court, and given high *mansabs* (numerically calibrated ranks, denoting direct links with the Mughal emperor). There is a similarity between the policies followed by the Mughals in this respect, and the treatment by the Safavid Shahs of Iran of the Turkoman *amirs*; they also bear a certain resemblance to the manner in which earlier Sultans at Delhi had managed to keep the balance of forces. But the management of resources was now a far more complex affair; the sheer size of the court had increased, and the economy of even the core of the Mughal state – the Indo-Gangetic plain – was far more productive, monetised and populous than what the Khaljis or Tughluqs had ruled over in the thirteenth and fourteenth centuries.

The second building-block of the Mughal state was therefore the incorporation of migrant intermediaries, who flocked to their court from Iran and Central Asia. The latter, often generically designated 'Turanis', had been present under earlier rulers as well; it is the Iranian migration that increases dramatically in Mughal times. Whether or not these Iranians constituted a faction in court politics is an open question; but it can scarcely be doubted that they, as a collectivity, had a substantial presence in the highest echelons of Mughal service (the *mansabdari*). The process had begun to accelerate in the closing years of the sixteenth century, and is remarked in particular during the reign of the Mughal Jahangir (r. 1605–27), when the fortune of the most prominent Iranian family of the high Mughal period (of I'timad-ud-daula, his son Asaf Khan, and his grandson Shayasta Khan) was made. Though their dominance was checked somewhat later in the seventeenth century, the position of Iranians remained conspicuous even under the reign of Jahangir's grandson Aurangzeb.

Table 1.2 Mansabdars under Aurangzeb, 1658–1707

Rank	1658–78			1679–1707		
	Iranis	Turanis	Total	Iranis	Turanis	Total
5,000 +	23	9	51	14	6	79
3,000–4,500	32	16	90	40	22	133
1,000–2,700	81	42	345	72	44	363
Total	136	67	486	126	72	575

(*Source*: Athar Ali 1966: 35)

Iranian elite migration had already been a significant feature of state formation in the Deccan (or south-central India) from as early as the fifteenth century; the Mughals were thus in a sense latecomers to the process. In the Bahmani Sultanate of the Deccan, men like Khwaja Mahmud Gawan Gilani (d. 1481) had held both the post of *malik ut-tujjar* ('chief of the merchants') and simultaneously controlled fiscal administration as *vazir* (Aubin 1973). Circulation and spatial mobility characterised these operators, as did a willingness to combine fiscal and commercial operations with military commands. A contemporary English trader's description of the Iranian Mir Muhammad Sayyid Ardistani (1591–1663), who was head of the fiscal administration of the Golconda Sultanate in the Deccan before becoming a high Mughal official, is worth citing at some length:

> The whole kingdom of Gulcundah is governed by him, of whome the people stand in feare and subjection unto as to the Kinge himselfe. The revenue that hee yearly brings the King in amounts to twentye hundred thousand pegodaes. ... The revenues that he hath taken from the Jentue in the aforesayd countrye is to the somme of fortie hundred thousand pegodaes per annum. Hee hath of his proper owne four thousand horse, three hundred elephants, foure or five hundred cammels, and tenn thousand oxen, which transporteth his goods up into severall countryes, as Gulcundah, Vizapore and into dyvers partes of the Great Maguls country. ... Concerning forran navigation, he hath trade to Pegue, Tenasaree, Acheen, Rackan, Persia, Bengalla, Moka, Peruk, Maldeevaes and Macassar. He hath ten vessels of his owne, and intends to augument them, makeing much preparatyon for building of more
> (Subrahmanyam 1990a: 326).

Thus, on the one hand, we have fiscal intermediation, on the other the command of war-animals and military labour; but this is only the tip of the iceberg, for it is in respect of overland and overseas trade that Muhammad Sayyid truly distinguished himself. Had detailed materials been available on other operators of the same period, like Mirza Abu Talib (Shayasta Khan), we would have probably found a similar profile of activities.

Iranian elite migration follows a complex three-centuries-long cycle, extending from the early fifteenth century to the middle of the eighteenth century. In the first phase, their dispersion is largely across the littoral of the western Indian Ocean, to the Red Sea and East Africa, to Gujarat, and to the Deccan. The second phase, which commences in the last quarter of the sixteenth century, sees them concentrating on South Asia. This is the period in which an Iranian poet wrote:

> Great is India, the Mecca
>   of all in need
> above all for those who seek safety.
> A journey to India is of essence
>   to any man
> made worthy by knowledge and skill.   (Savory 1980: 205)

23

The third phase, which commences in about 1650, sees a further widening of operations by the Iranis. A minor Iranian presence is remarked in western Indonesia and mainland Southeast Asia even in the early sixteenth century; the first Portuguese to arrive there, for example, usually spoke of the Thai kingdom's capital of Ayuthia using its Persian name Xarnauz (*shahr-i nav*, or New Town). But it is only after 1650 that the Iranian political presence comes to dominate, being a particularly marked feature of the reign at Ayuthia of Narai (1656–88). Similarly, the Arakan court in northern Burma witnesses an influx of Iranians of some dimensions in the seventeenth century (Aubin 1980).

If the Iranians formed one circuit, the Chinese from the south-east coastal provinces formed another. From the fifteenth century, in the aftermath of Cheng He's expeditions, there are clear indications of ethnic Chinese in positions of political power in Southeast Asian kingdoms (one conspicuous exception, however, being the Melaka Sultanate). The Sultanate of Banten, formed in the course of the sixteenth century, boasted a considerable Chinese population, as did most important port-towns of the Javanese north coast (*pasisir*) by 1600. When, in the early seventeenth century, the major Javanese state of the early modern period, Mataram, was under consolidation by Sultan Agung (r. 1613–45), it was with the aid of Chinese traders and revenue-farmers that this was accomplished. These Chinese, who were often assimilated, and took on Javanese or Malay names, continue to be conspicuous in Javanese politics, as local lords (*bupatis*) in the phase of Mataram's decline. Again, whether one looks at the Philippines, Indo-China, or even Dutch Batavia, the Chinese community is an important one, which plays the role of intermediary in diplomacy, recruits and manages labour, conducts overseas trade, and so on (Blussé 1986).

Our purpose in pointing to these instances of substantial elite migration is not to deny the existence of local dynamics, or the role of 'auto-chthonous' groups in determining the shape of early modern Asian state formation. But at the same time, it is necessary to note that the political spheres of different Asian states inter-penetrated by this period to a far greater extent than is often assumed. In comparison with the period from the ninth to the fourteenth centuries, the later period – which dovetails fairly well with what Anthony Reid has recently termed an 'age of commerce' in Southeast Asia – represents a phase of far greater elite political mobility *without conquest* (Reid 1988). This flexibility, and ability to accept new elements into the elite as well as to make use of their services, were important factors in determining the nature of Portuguese interaction with early modern Asian kingdoms.

TOWARDS A TAXONOMY

The shapes and strategies of Asian states of the early modern period, we have seen, were at least partly determined by relations *between* these states and by the common conjuncture in which they at times found themselves. But differences also existed, and it would be misleading to see no essential distinctions between Tokugawa Japan, Aceh, and the Ottoman Empire – to take three examples that encompass the entire region we wish to survey. One such model of differentiation – which clearly distinguishes agrarian-based, trade-averse states, from trade-oriented ones, we have already examined with some scepticism. It is evident that, contrary to what such a model might lead us to believe, so-called agrarian empires grew increasingly attracted to trade, and to the management of their resources not through cash-less, prebendal systems, but by utilising the cash nexus. Three examples will suffice here.

In west Asia, the fiscal system of the Ottoman empire, founded in the late thirteenth century, had, we have already noted, for long been dominated by the *timar* – a prebendal assignment, which was appropriate to a relatively poorly monetised economy. Revenues tended to be collected in kind rather than cash, and were used to support a somewhat decentralised military system. In the sixteenth and seventeenth century, however, a new feature is evident: this is the system of the so-called *salyaneli eyaletler* ('provinces with salaries'), described by a contemporary, Ali Çavus, as follows in his *Risale* (1653):

> The [Sultan's] well-protected territories (*memalik-i mahrusa*) consist of thirty-four provinces; twenty-five of them are of *has*, nine of *salyane*. These are the *salyane* provinces: the Province of Egypt, Province of Yemen, Province of Habesh, Province of Basra, Province of Lahsa, Province of Baghdad, Province of Trablusgarb, Province of Tunus, Province of Jazair-i Garb. ... There are no prebends (*zeamet ve timar*) in the *salyane* provinces, but there exist janissary groups. All the revenues are held by the *Padis3ah*, the Protector. From these revenues the salaries of the governors, and wages of the janissary groups are given. The remaining sum is sent to the treasury in the capital.
>
> (Ozbaran 1986: 42)

Two remarks are in order here. First, we note that these provinces are for the most part areas captured by the Ottomans in the sixteenth century. Secondly, it is worth remarking that almost all of these are provinces where trade had a more important role to play than in the Ottoman heartland of Anatolia and Rumelia. The sixteenth century is also a period when the Ottoman state's direct interest in trade reaches its height. Not only are there substantial maritime interventions in the Indian Ocean and the Mediterranean, the Ottomans are seen as a potential source of support by distant Southeast Asian kingdoms like Aceh. The purportedly agrarian character of the state had thus been considerably modified; the prebendal assignment system was now giving way to a relatively centralised (and money-based) system controlled by the Treasury.

Our second example concerns Safavid Iran. Here, the Shi'i dynasty founded by Shah Ismail in the early sixteenth century ruled over what is often portrayed as the fourth largest agrarian despotism in early modern Asia (after China, the Mughals and Ottomans), although the balance between nomadic tribes and settled cultivators and townsmen was rather more favourable to the former here than in the other empires. Safavid rulers spent much of the sixteenth century in a delicate balancing act between the Turkoman tribesmen (or *qizilbash*) who had initially supported them politically, and the so-called Tajiks of the towns and settled countryside. However, by the last quarter of the century, a new situation emerged. In the reign of Shah Abbas I (r.1588–1629), the Safavid state turns its attention to trade – both overseas and overland – as a major source of state revenue. Embassies are sent out to places as distant as Muscovy and Spain; the Shah decides to monopolise the trade in the premier export commodity – silk; links are built up with a trading community, which emerges as the Shah's favoured client-group, the Armenians. A new coin, the *abbasi*, enters circulation in the Persian Gulf, and then the Indian Ocean, and it is in this coin that the Shah's *ghulam* corps of Georgian and Circassian mercenary and slave soldiers is paid. Thus, once again, we have the spectacle of an agrarian state taking recourse to trade and the cash-nexus (Savory 1980; Jackson and Lockhart 1986).

Our third and final example takes us far afield. This is the case of Japan under Toyotomi Hideyoshi and the early Tokugawas, that is to say in the 1580s and thereafter. We have already noted earlier that this period sees the re-emergence in Japan of a single central authority, after the period of *sengoku* beginning in the late fifteenth century. This period – namely the late sixteenth and early seventeenth centuries – is often associated with the rise in Japan of a sort of xenophobia, leading to the celebrated 'closure' (*sakoku*) of the country to Europeans. But, as has been argued by Ronald Toby, such an argument fails to take into account the restructuring of Japan's relations with her *Asian* neighbours – Korea, China, and the Southeast Asian states – that was taking place. The restructuring – partly mediated by military struggle – was part of an attempt to create a Japan-centred world-order; it is also significant that of all early modern states Japan is perhaps the most reluctant to permit the sort of elite migration into her domains that we have discussed earlier (Toby 1984).

We should equally note however that the restructuring of foreign relations was part of a far larger package. Hideyoshi and his Tokugawa successors implemented a wide-ranging set of social and economic policies, which set them apart from both the Ashikagas and the *sengoku daimyo*. Most celebrated of course is the cadastral survey (*taiko kenchi*) conducted on Hideyoshi's orders in the late 1590s, which entailed plot-by-plot measurement of agricultural land, assessment of its tax-potential, and identification of the assessee. This measure also had a clear political dimension: it facilitated the large-scale redistribution of *ryogoku* (or *daimyo* domains) by Tokugawa Ieyasu in 1602, in which process he undercut the power of some houses, while shoring up others. The net beneficiaries from all this were, of course, the Tokugawas themselves, in the sense that they emerged as the ultimate source of even land-based power. Table 1.3 sums up the impact of the early Tokugawa reform on the leading *daimyo* of the epoch.

Table 1.3: Japanese fiscal reorganisation, 1598–1602

(a) The largest *daimyo*, 1598–1602 (in *koku*)		
Name	Holdings in 1598	Holdings in 1602
Tokugawa Ieyasu	2,557,000	–
Mori Terumoto	1,205,000	369,000
Uyesugi Kagekatsu	1,200,000	300,000
Maeda Toshiiye	835,000	1,195,000
Yuki Hideyasu	101,000	751,000

(b) *Ryogoku* reorganisation by Ieyasu, 1602		
Domains	Number	Yield (in *koku*)
Total in 1598	204	18,723,200
Confiscations	90	4,307,000
Reductions	4	2,215,900

(*Source:* Sansom 1961: 414–16)

Furthermore, the period witnesses a growing *direct* control by the state of commerce, an attack on the guild system leading to the breakdown of guild monopolies, as well as a new system of registration of merchants and artisans with the state. The growing urbanisation that accompanies these changes – with Kyoto and Osaka attaining populations of 410,000 and 405,000 respectively in 1634 – suggests a shift in the structure not merely of state but of civil society. Once more, at the centre of things is the issue of the cash-nexus, and the growth in a sort of state interventionism (Hall et al. 1981: 327–72).

An alternative way of posing these phenomena might be to argue that if the two categories with which we began, namely agrarian-based, prebendally organised states, and trade-oriented ones, can be treated as two ends of a spectrum or distribution, what the period witnesses is a growing attraction towards the centre, as opposed to a polarisation. In part, this change is mediated through the growth of a sort of absolutism – and it is of some interest that both Hideyoshi and Shah Abbas have been characterised as absolutist in their own historiographies. To elaborate, the circulation of elites, the circulation of money-media, as well as certain other unifying phenomena, caused the direction taken by different Asian states in the period to appear similar. However, we may still speak in terms of differing *degrees* of interest and involvement in trade, of monetisation, of measurement and enumeration of resources and the tax-base; from a choice between two bald categories, we emerge with a spectrum of possibilities, within which we can place Aceh, Arakan, Iran, Japan, and the Ottoman empire.

One of the keys to where we locate particular states would appear to be the degree of autonomy and political power wielded by a land-oriented aristocracy, as opposed to an urban trading class. The central state itself tended to operate on two principles: first, it abhorred a vacuum, and strove to expand its activities to fill any space left by the opposite tugs of these groups; but beyond this somewhat mechanistic role was also an actor and initiator, partly because it was open to external winds, and partly on account of a semi-autonomous dynamic provided by its own evolving ideology. Thus, in different periods, the shifting balance between *orang kaya* (or urban mercantile aristocracy), and *hulubalang* (or landed chieftains) moulded and remoulded the character of the Acehnese state, even as the tussle between Tajik *tujjar* (merchant) and Turkoman *amir* shaped but did not *determine* the destiny of Safavid Iran (Reid 1979; Haneda 1987).

LONG-TERM TRENDS

This chapter has attempted to highlight certain features of the changing relationship between the state, economy and society in Asia in the centuries preceding the Portuguese arrival there, as well as in the two centuries after 1500. There appears to be little doubt from a survey of available materials that the Portuguese did not arrive in an Asia that was in stasis, nor did they act on a *tabula rasa*. Rather, it was in a world of forces in constantly shifting geo-political, social and economic balance that the Portuguese found themselves resident in the sixteenth and seventeenth centuries.

Besides the specific questions that we have raised above, which pertain largely to the domain of state–society relations, it may be worthwhile to point to certain rather broad changes that took place in Asia over the years 1300 to 1700. The first set of these was in the commercial sphere. Whereas during the age of the Cholas and Srivijaya (that is the late centuries of the first millenium, and the early centuries of the second millenium), the main direction of commercial flows in Asia appears to have been in the east-west direction (both on the caravan routes, and on sea), the years after 1300 saw the rise of commerce largely in the north-south direction. Indian trade with Southeast Asia and south-eastern Africa grew, as did Chinese trade with the lands of the *nanyang*, as they termed insular Southeast Asia. This growing trade was largely based on the exchange of tropical products, such a spices and woods, and minerals, against manufactures – Chinese porcelains and silks and Indian cotton textiles. At the same time, the rise of the port-centred states that we have described, such as Aden, Hurmuz and Melaka, led to the growth of a substantial trade in foodgrains and other items of bulk consumption. This trade, in relatively low-value and high-volume goods, may have existed earlier as well, but it would seem that the late fourteenth and fifteenth centuries witnessed a substantial expansion in its extent.

It has at times been assumed that the commercial expansion of these centuries was part of a phase of 'Arab dominance' of Indian Ocean trade. But this is surely too simplistic, for other Asian merchant groups participated in this trade on a large scale as well. These included Gujarati *vanias* and Bohras, Tamil and Telugu Chettis (known in Southeast Asia as *Kelings*), Mappila and Maraikkayar Muslims from southern India, Chinese from Fukien and other provinces of the southeast in the Celestial Empire, and the Iranian *tujjar* whom we have discussed above. However, even if we question the extent of Arab dominance, it remains true that the fourteenth and fifteenth centuries saw the expansion of Islam on the shores of the Indian Ocean, and the growing presence of Muslim mercantile communities, whether in East Africa, India, or Southeast Asia. The centuries immediately preceding the arrival of the Portuguese in Asia therefore saw a redefinition of the religious map of the continent, and the expansion of Islam, and to a lesser extent Theravada Buddhism, religions that laid greater stress on the individual and individual salvation. The Christianity that the Portuguese brought to Asia therefore competed with other religions freshly on the ascendant, which were being spread not merely by conquest but by acculturation and trading contacts. This second aspect of long-term change in maritime Asia must also be borne in mind if we are to view Portuguese actions in perspective.

29

CHAPTER TWO
Portuguese State and Society, 1200–1500

CROWN AND NOBILITY

Perched at one extremity of the Eurasian landmass, a *finisterra* looking out on to Africa and the still unknown Atlantic, Portugal in about 1450 was uniquely placed to create a model for a seaborne empire that would be imitated time and again in later centuries. In the eighth century, the south of what was later to become Portugal had fallen under the control of Musa bin Nusayr, who had just overrun Morocco, and who advanced as far as Galicia; his son Abd al-Aziz took the towns of Beja and Evora in AD 712. At one time or another, all parts of Portugal have been under Arab rule. The northern town of Braga, the heartland of Portugal in some eyes, was re-taken only in the tenth century, and the central Portuguese city of Coimbra in the next century. The conflict against Islamic (Arab and Berber) domination shaped to a great extent the mentalities of medieval Portuguese (Miranda 1970). Designated *mouros* or Moors, in view of their association with Mauritania (the Roman name for the Maghreb), these antagonists became the 'straw men' for Portuguese nationalist ideologues for many centuries. For, in a sense, the *mouros* were the midwives attendant on the birth of the nation of Portugal, and once in adolescence the nation still felt the need to define its identity in contradistinction to them.

Muslim rule over the future Portugal was quite uneven in extent and duration. In some areas, like those to the north of the river Douro, the Arabs had an intermittent career, being expelled already by the latter half of the eighth century, and returning only in the tenth century for a brief period. This area, comprising southern Galicia, Trás-os-Montes and Minho, became the cradle of the infant Portuguese nation: the name Portugal itself deriving from the city of Portucale, near modern-day Oporto, seat of the Count (*conde*) of Portucale in the time of Afonso III of Leon in the mid-ninth century. Further south, the region between the

Tagus

rivers Douro and Tejo – which is to say much of the area of Beira and Estremadura – remained contested between various forces, including the crowns of Leon and Castile on the one hand, and the Caliphs of Cordoba on the other. In the late tenth century, the *de facto* Cordoba ruler Muhammad bin Abi Amir (or al-Mansur 'the Victorious') carried out a series of devastating expeditions to Santiago, Coimbra, and other urban centres of this region. But a bare half-century later, the power of Cordoba had collapsed; Coimbra was re-taken in 1064, and from the early twelfth century, a new order emerged.

This order is usually associated with the founder-king of Portugal Dom Afonso Henriques (1106–85), whose father had acquired the *condados* (counties) of first Coimbra and then Portucale in the late eleventh century, and whose initial seat of power was the town of Guimarães. As recent detailed studies by José Mattoso and others show, by the late eleventh century a well-defined nobility had emerged in northern and central Portugal, in place of the earlier *condal* nobility, which had to a large extent been dependent on the support and legitimation of Leon (Mattoso 1985; 1988). The wars of the late tenth and early eleventh centuries broke the back of *condal* power; the line of the Counts of Coimbra, for instance, was extinguished by Muslim invasions, while the Counts of Portucale had to flee their territories for Galicia. When the Caliphate of Cordoba fell in 1031, and was replaced by the system of relatively small Muslim *taifa* states (or 'Party Kingdoms'), based at centres like Saragossa, Seville, Toledo and Badajoz, those who were able to gain from the ensuing confusion were therefore not the *condal* nobility but new men of a middle nobility, the so-called *infanções*.

The coalescence around Afonso Henriques, which effectively gained momentum after his defeat of the forces of his mother Teresa and her Leon-based allies in July 1128, thus consisted of a complex of processes. First, there was the demographic groundswell of the twelfth century, which shifted the balance of economic resources within Portugal itself in favour of the interior northern regions from which he operated. Second, Afonso Henriques had to mobilise and tie himself to the newly redefined nobility, while at the same time allowing it to retain certain military and juridical prerogatives. This nobility had to be mobilised in terms of a new 'nationalist' ideology; thus, on the one hand the crusading venture had to be prosecuted to the south against the *al-murabitin* (Almoravid) warriors who now controlled Coimbra and other southern centres, while at the same time Afonso Henriques had to distance himself from his troublesome relationship with Leon, ruled over by his cousin Alfonso VII. The former task had been achieved in large measure by 1147, with the conquest of Santarém, Lisbon and Sintra; the latter too was accomplished when in 1139–40 Afonso Henriques began styling himself *rex*, in place of *dux*.

Echoes of the two defining relationships of Portugal at birth, first the

31

opposition to the *mouros*, and second the need to distinguish Portugal from her eastern neighbours in the Iberian Peninsula, are to be heard much later in the country's history as well. By 1250, the Arabs and Berbers had effectively been expelled from Portuguese territories with the taking of the Algarve, thereby setting the seal on the processes of the half-century after Afonso Henriques's death (1185), when much of the Alentejo came to fall into the hands of his heirs. In 1250 then, the *reino* – the homeland of the Portuguese – had been more or less defined in its entirety. But what sort of kingdom was it which was ruled over by Afonso III (r. 1246–79), the monarch of the period?

If on the one hand Portugal was a compact and relatively well-defined territory, Portuguese society was also deeply divided. Three regions can be distinguished within the territories ruled over by D. Afonso. To the north of the river Douro, and especially in the region of Entre Douro e Minho, the social stucture was dominated by a traditional, locally-rooted nobility, in a typically seignorial structure. Further south, between the Douro and Tejo, the power of the nobility was far less, partly because the area had long been contested by Muslims and Christians, with neither side being able to put a firmly rooted structure of dominance in place. As a consequence, here the *concelhos*, which were communal structures of medium and large peasant proprietors, effectively controlled affairs, electing their own magistrates (with Arabised titles such as *alcaides* and *almotacés*). Still further south, the high degree of militarisation accompanying the *reconquista* (or reconquest) had given a disproportionate amount of power, on the one hand, to the nobility, and on the other hand to the so-called *ordens militares* (or Military Orders).

Of the latter, the first to establish itself on a long-term basis in Portugal was the Order of Christ (created by D. Dinis, the successor of Afonso III, from the properties that had belonged to the Knights Templar), which was largely based in the north of the Estremadura region, along the valley of the Tejo and its tributaries the Zezere and Nabão, with its centre at Tomar. This Order held control by the fifteenth century of some twenty-one towns and settlements, largely in the region defined above. Further south, around Évora, were territories associated with the Order of Avis, initially the Portuguese branch of the Spanish Order of Calatrava, but which broke off from its parent body in 1377. As for Lisbon, it came to be defended by the Order of Santiago, from its headquarters at Palmela. This last Order became lord over vast dominions in the extreme south, controlling something like a third of the region south of the Tejo (Livermore 1973: 54, 72–74).

The nobility for its part, while also deriving power and legitimacy through membership in the Military Orders, tended to guard its independent privileges as well. At the highest level of the nobility in the fourteenth century were the so-called *ricos-homens* (rich men), and at the lowest the *cavaleiros* (or knights); the middle ground was held by the *infanções*. The great noble families tended to come from Entre Douro e Minho, the region of origin of D. Afonso Henriques, and still today probably the core of the most deeply-rooted Portuguese nationalism. But their privileges were increasingly under threat from the time the *reconquista* had been completed; the fact that Afonso III in 1253 called together a gathering of the three estates (*cortes*), where for the first time 'commoners' were represented, is in itself suggestive. The assembly, held in 1253 in Leiria, was held again in 1285 by Dom Dinis, this time in Lisbon.

Between 1300 and 1500 then, Portugal witnessed a complex struggle between centralising tendencies inherent in the monarchy, and the resistance of other privileged groups: the Church, the Military Orders, and the nobility. As for the first of these, Crown and Church had already been engaged in a bitter struggle in the thirteenth century. There had already been fierce differences between Church and State in the reign of Afonso II, and Sancho II (r. 1223–46) was deposed by the Papacy, ostensibly on account of his incapacity and weakness. His brother and successor Afonso III also entered into conflict with the archbishops and various other high clergy, and this continued into the reign of Dom Dinis. But the moral power of church and clergy over city-dwellers and rural folk alike was considerable; and even if they held considerable lands, these economic bases of their power could not be attacked frontally. The real thrust of the monarchy's drive for centralisation was hence not directed at the Church but at the territorial nobility. In part, the Crown attempted to stabilise, limit and *define* this group: a law of D. Dinis claimed for the ruler the right, for example, of admitting new members into the nobility by making them knights (*cavaleiros*).

It was only after a long struggle that in the fifteenth century a well-defined hierarchy of titles was set out. In part this seems to have occurred in imitation of what obtained in England, and was probably the result of the influence of a Queen of English origin, D. Filipa de Lancastre, of the House of Lancaster. In descending order, the 'great nobility' (*grande nobreza*) were classified into *duque*, *marquês*, *conde*, *visconde*, and *barão*. These men, entitled to use the title *dom* (from the Latin *dominus*), comprised perhaps a tenth of the total nobility. They were the successors of the erstwhile *ricos-homens*, even if not always their lineal descendants – for some *arrivistes* too existed among the group in the fourteenth and fifteenth centuries. At the same time, under the rule of D. Afonso V, a second hierarchy of nobles, who held positions that were not necessarily heritable, was established. The purpose of this was evidently to strengthen the hand of the Crown, for the latter group was almost axiomatically far more dependent on the Crown than the former.

A roughly parallel division also came about in the course of the fifteenth century between the territorial nobility, based on the land, and the so-called court-nobility or *nobreza de serviço*. The term *fidalgo*, corresponding to the Castilian *hidalgo* and in vogue from the late thirteenth century, was initially used to describe a far larger class of persons, often no more than an upwardly mobile rural gentry, but in the fifteenth century was used in combination with other titles: thus, *cavaleiros-fidalgos*, *escudeiros-fidalgos* and so on. It is from the *nobreza de serviço*, comprising either nobles who actually attended the court, or who were the King's representatives in the provinces, that we later find much of the cutting edge of Portuguese expansion in Asia.

Where the Military Orders were concerned, the Crown followed a far more complex set of tactics. The schism in the Papacy, wherein Portugal followed the Pope in Rome, and Castile the Pope at Avignon, permitted the Portuguese branches of the Orders to cut loose from their initial, Castilian, moorings. In the case of the Order of Christ, which was exclusively Portuguese anyway, this did not have any significance. However, the Orders of Santiago and Avis became more 'nationalised' in the process; members of the royal family were given the Masterships of these Orders, as a means of holding them to the Crown. This tactic was primarily favoured in the reign of the House of Avis, which ruled from 1385 to 1580. The founder of the dynasty, Dom João I, came to the throne as Master of Avis; his son, the Infante Dom Henrique, was master of the Order of Christ, Dom João his brother was master of Avis, and his younger brother Dom Fernando of Santiago. Still later, the ruler Dom Manuel managed to have the Pope nominate him to the mastership of all three orders, a practice that continued under his son Dom João III.

Besides the clergy (*clero*) and the nobility (*nobreza*), the mass of the Portuguese in the fourteenth and fifteenth centuries were defined simply under the head of the *povo* ('people'). The best-off amongst them, the *cidadãos* or *homens-bons*, were often also termed *cavaleiros vilãos*, although this did not make them of the nobility. These were members of the service-classes, master-craftsmen and merchants, men who for the most part supported Dom João I in his bid for the throne in 1383–85. Lower in status, but far more numerous, were the *assoldados* and *jornaleiros* (journeymen), who worked for the master-craftsmen, or were domestic servants, cattle-tenders and agricultural labourers. These members of the *gente miuda* or *gente baixa* – the 'little people' – were permitted only limited mobility. Their status was thus considerably poorer than that of the *homens-bons*, or of the *doutores* (whether in law, medicine or religion), or indeed of the owner-cultivator peasant, the *lavradores* (Marques 1987).

The struggles of the period 1300 to 1500, which we have addressed briefly in earlier paragraphs, do not appear to have been *primarily* between the lower and the upper classes. Rather, they were struggles *between* elements in the upper classes: on the one hand, between clergy, nobility and Crown, and on the other clan and factional strife, of a type that finds

34

expression in Portuguese activity in Asia as well. In the course of such struggles, at certain moments, the subaltern groups like the journeymen-artisans could gain specific advantages, and at times decisively affect the outcome of such a struggle. Such was the case in 1383–85, when a bitter struggle occcurred between the adherents of Queen Leonor (the so-called 'Castilian party', which wished to proclaim Juan I of Castile King of Portugal), and João, bastard son of Pedro I (r. 1357–67), and Master of the Order of Avis. This struggle, often seen as the prototype for the later takeover of Portugal by Philip II of Spain in 1580–81, divided Portugal into two parties: an urban-based one, supportive of João of Avis, and the nobility and clergy who apparently believed that a Castilian succession would relieve them of the centralising pressures that we have already discussed. The divisions manifested themselves in two other ways. First, the tendency in the frontier territories was the inverse of what obtained on the Atlantic littoral; at the same time, there was a division between the south (which supported Avis) and the north. Amongst the towns themselves, it is of some interest that almost all the northern ones, except Oporto – traditional bastions of the aristocracy and conservative groups – like Bragança, Vila Real and Viana do Castelo supported the Castilians; but once south of the Tejo, almost all major towns and their garrisons were for Avis (Ribeiro et al. 1987: 695).

To understand this struggle, its context and its outcome, which was to have an important influence on early modern Portuguese history, we should recall that the late fourteenth and early fifteenth centuries had seen Portugal plunged into a serious economic and social crisis. In 1347, the population of Portugal was some 1.5 million; some two hundred years later, the population may still have been only 1.4 million. This was the result of the demographic collapse of the second half of the fourteenth century, with successive visitations of the Black Death in 1356, 1361–63, 1374, 1383–85, 1389, 1400 and so on. The mortality was particularly marked from the epidemic of 1384 onwards; in the early fifteenth century, life expectancy was so low that a man was reckoned to enter the 'autumn' of his life at thirty-five! One of the consequences of this high mortality was a fillip to horizontal mobility; inter-provincial migration increased, as did the attraction of Lisbon (which had replaced Coimbra as the capital in the mid-thirteenth century).

A. H. de Oliveira Marques has reckoned that at the close of the thirteenth century, the most densely populated area of Portugal was the northern province of Entre Douro e Minho, followed by Beira; both the Alentejo and the Algarve were extremely thinly populated in this period. Moreover, he finds that the population was dense not along the coast but along the upper river valleys, on the fertile interior plains, and along the main routes of overland trade linking Portugal to Galicia and Castile (Marques 1980: 51–73). All this was to change gradually in the fourteenth century, in a process that has been termed *meridionalização* (an untranslatable term meaning a southward shift), and which is certainly apparent by 1416, when we have the first geographical description of Portugal written by a Portuguese (Ribeiro et al. 1987: 691–93). Already in the 1380s, the domination of north and interior had been substituted by the growing importance of the south (not so much the extreme south as Lisbon and the Estremadura), and the coast. The maritime vocation of Portugal had begun to assert itself in a distinctive and definitive way.

Had the 'Castilian party', supported by the upper nobility from its base in Trás-os-Montes and Entre Douro e Minho, succeeded in 1383–85, it is certain that the history of Portugal would have been quite different. But it did not, and this failure must be seen as strengthening the hands of the city-dwellers, the 'cobblers and tailors' who were contemptuously described by Dom João I's denigrators as his prime supporters, and as a further blow to the entrenched upper nobility. In its aftermath, the immediate consequence was a more conspicuous role for the *cortes*, which in this period at times even met once a year (Thomaz 1989b). But ironically enough, it also possibly paved the way for the House of Avis to exercise a form of absolutism in the fifteenth century.

One may hence see Portuguese history in the period in terms of a series of oppositions: interior versus coast, north versus south, city-dwellers versus rural-based nobility, the court-nobility versus the territorial nobility, and so on. If 1385 marks an important shift in these balances, we would be naive to suppose that the reversal was total and complete. To be sure, Dom João I acted to curtail the power of both nobility and clergy; he also took the opportunity to seize hold of the key positions in the Military Orders. Some noblemen's estates were seized, and 'new men' like Nuno Álvares Pereira, who had masterminded João I's military success against the Castilians at Aljubarrota, were made high nobles. The guild-system was strengthened in the towns, and this suggests that the ruler's allies in the towns were *not* the journeymen and petty artisans (many of whose privileges were actually encroached upon after 1385), but rather the master-craftsmen, *homens-bons* et cetera, who were given explicit recognition in the corporate life of Portuguese towns through the strengthening of institutions like the Municipal Chamber (*Câmara Municipal*), and from the late fifteenth century the *Santa Casa de Misericórdia* (Holy House of Mercy). The specific place given in the *cortes* of 1385 to *letrados* (or clerks) is also significant in this context.

Still, the opposition of other elements to the centralising ambitions of the Crown had scarcely ended. It recurs time and again in the fifteenth century, as Portuguese expansion in the Atlantic and then the Indian Ocean takes place, at times expressing itself in terms of the opposition between city-based bourgeois and nobility, and at other times as the struggle to deny the Crown its preponderant share in the spoils of overseas expansion. It is revealed in Philip II's negotiations to take over Portugal in the late 1570s, and is a significant thread running across the apparently unbroken warp of nationalism often seen as 'unifying' Portuguese history. It helps explain why Dom João II (r. 1481–95), intent on pursuing his mercantile ambitions overseas, equally faced the opposition of the nobility, which he dealt with in a suitably sanguine fashion by executing the Duke of Bragança in June 1484, killing some of the latter's allies and forcing others into exile. It may also serve to explain why not *all* Portuguese were enthused by their compatriots' maritime exploits. One recalls here the oft-cited sixteenth-century verse of Brás da Costa:

> Why pass so many storms,
> and life and times so sore,
> forever at death's door?
> I'd give up pepper without qualms.

> Por passar tanta tormenta,
> Tempo e vida tão forte,
> E tão perto da morte,
> Antes não quero pimenta.   (Dias 1988: 20)

IN SEARCH OF A BOURGEOISIE

In 1497, the year that the first Portuguese fleet to the Indian Ocean left *Tagus* the estuary of the Tejo, the prevailing mood was rather different from that of 1385. On the throne was Dom Manuel I, who had succeeded Dom João II in 1495 in a most curious fashion, after the death of many better-placed candidates. The rivalry with Castile now appeared somewhat muted in comparison to 1385, though it was scarcely forgotten. A war was fought in 1475–76, and it was evidently no coincidence that the Genoese Christopher Columbus, who had once been a participant in the Portuguese overseas enterprise of the Atlantic, had gone over to Castile and Aragon on being spurned by the Portuguese court. Columbus discovered a westward-lying land a mere five years before, in 1492, and the possibility that disputes might arise between the Spaniards and the Portuguese over maritime possessions was still present. But the prevailing mood surely stressed not the rivalry with eastern neighbours, but with another old rival: Islam and the 'Moors'.

It is a significant fact that between 1249, when Faro in the Algarve was taken from its Muslim rulers, and 1415, when Dom João I took Ceuta in North Africa, some one hundred and sixty-six years passed. Yet historians often tell us that the spirit of *reconquista* survived of its own accord over this interregnum, and provided a reason for the Portuguese to discover new lands. Why did this spirit remain vigorous? One explanation, not particularly plausible, is that the failed Marinid expedition of 1340 (defeated by a Castilian-Portuguese combine at Salado) and the continuing presence at Granada of the enfeebled Nasrid dynasty were sufficient to keep alive the crusading fervour not merely of Castilians but of Portuguese. In the course of the fourteenth century, the rulers of Portugal sought Papal Bulls of Crusade on at least five occasions, in pursuit of plans to conquer Morocco and Granada. But nothing came of these plans, and the only form of conflict with Islam in these years was naval, in terms of the *guerra do corso*, or incessant corsair activity, in the Mediterranean. We should also consider the idea that the anti-Islamic spirit was deliberately kept alive as an ideological prop, in order to prosecute an expansionary venture whose real reasons were two: first, to check Castilian ambitions by placing Portugal at the cutting edge of the *Respublica Christiana*, and thereby gaining support from the Papacy and other European kingdoms; second, to defuse the internal situation in Portugal, since military expansion would give the territorial nobility something at which to direct their attention (as well as the possibility of rewards), while commercial expansion would strengthen the position of the *Fazenda Real* (Royal Treasury) and city-based mercantile elements (Thomaz 1989b; 1989c).

There is little doubt that the state's strategy at the time of Dom João I was two-pronged: if the North African expansion was more military than commercial, the Atlantic expeditions – which were conducted almost simultaneously, but largely through private entrepreneurs – were primarily commercial not military. To be sure, in both cases, the two spheres could never be kept *wholly* separate; if the outposts in North Africa assumed a commercial aspect with the settlement there of commercially-minded townsmen, maritime expansion had its predatory side, in the tradition of the *guerra do corso*. Further, executing this two-pronged strategy was no simple matter, for while the military wherewithal undoubtedly existed, the commercial expertise was not as easily forthcoming.

By 1418, when the Madeira Islands were first officially settled, by Tristão Vaz Teixeira and João Gonçalves Zarco, it was clear that the focal point of the commercial expansion would have to be Lisbon itself. The town itself was of great antiquity: even in pre-Roman times, it appears as Olisippo, and later under the Romans as the *municipium* of Olisipona. Under Muslim rule (which endured here from AD 714 to 1147, with interregna in 953–54, and again over the period 1093–95, when it was briefly held by Christians), Lisbon had been designated al-Ushbuna, capital of a local administrative unit (*kura*) but hardly a centre of great importance. However, its significance grew over the period 1150 to 1240 as a frontier garrison town; then, in the mid-thirteenth century, the ruler Afonso III shifted the normal residence of his court there from Coimbra, suggesting that it had attained fair dimensions by then. Thereafter, the town expanded fast, and though the growth in population was checked by

the plague of 1348, it continued until in the 1530s Lisbon had a
population of some 65,000 inhabitants (and over 100,000 in the early
seventeenth century).

Table 2.1 The growth of Lisbon, 1147–1500

Year	Population	Year	No. of parishes
1147	5,000	1300	10
1250	14,000	1400	23
1400	35,000	1500	30
1525	65,000		
1620	100,000–165,000		

(*Source:* Marques 1988 : 84–91)

Historians have been hard put to classify Lisbon, which was
undoubtedly one of the larger European cities of the sixteenth century.
Clearly it did not have the predominantly commercial character of, say,
Antwerp or Bruges, but at the same time it cannot be seen as a city where
the administrative apparatus dominated life. Rather, it was a hybrid town,
part-administrative and court-centred, part-mercantile – with a metro-
politan character deriving from its numerous and diverse resident
communities – and also partly a port-town, with mariners and fishermen
jostling for a place on the waterfront. In the mid-fifteenth century, the
chronicler Fernão Lopes provides us a vivid portrayal of Lisbon, still only
a town of 50,000 or less inhabitants: resident foreign merchants included
Italians (Genoese and Florentines in particular), Flemings, English and
French, while a number of prosperous Portuguese textile-traders and other
merchants lived there too (Marques 1988). This foreign mercantile class
was partly attracted by the prospects that Lisbon with its newly-created
Atlantic network held out for them, but their presence was also partly the
reason why Portugal had been able to build up its overseas network in the
first place. We are aware that in the first instance Genoese merchants had
been attracted to Lisbon as a midway point in their maritime trade to
Flanders, to which the taking of the Algarve in about 1250 had given a
fillip. To evaluate the relative importance of these two factors – cause and
effect – we must turn to the central question of the period: what indeed
was the strength of the Portuguese bourgeoisie in relation to resident
foreign merchants, as well as in relation to the Crown?

There exists abundant documentation concerning some of the
prominent Lisbon-based Italians of the fifteenth century; the activities of
the Florentine Bartolomeo di Jacopo di ser Vanni are to be traced, for
example, over a period extending from 1424 to 1470, during which he
acted as commercial agent, independent merchant, and banker, lending

39

money to the nobility and even to the Infante Dom Henrique (the misnamed 'Prince Henry the Navigator') (Rau 1971). Once the Atlantic islands of Madeira were settled, many prominent Italians took part in its sugar export and trade, including the families of Spinola and Lomellini. Again the Perestrelo family, later to play a prominent role in early Portuguese activities in the Indian Ocean, was settled at Porto Santo in Madeira, and traded from there to Portugal. Equally, from the early fourteenth century, Italians had played a prominent part as navigators and master-mariners in Portuguese maritime ventures, with Dom Dinis actually inviting a Genoese, Manuel Pessagna, to come to Portugal and command his corsair-galleys; thus, trade, prize-taking and maritime skills came together in a package. However, it is all too easy to focus on the activities of the Marchionnis, Perestrelos, Cà da Mostos and other Italians – for their careers are so well-documented at both the Portuguese and the Italian ends. A far more difficult question to answer is the place of Portuguese merchants themselves in the prosperity of, first, Lisbon itself, and second, of the Atlantic network built up from about 1420.

To begin with, to what social groups did they belong? Lisbon undoubtedly contained a core of Muslim residents in its *mouraria* (Moorish quarter) until the late fifteenth century; after the Christian conquest of the city in 1170, this community had received a letter-patent (*carta de foral*), specifying its rights and dues in respect of the majority – Christian – community, and the Crown. However, both this *foral*, and a later text of around 1400, make it clear that the Muslims were not considered citizens in the full sense, and that they were to be subject to a number of capitation fees (*libras de cabeça*), professional taxes (*dízimas do trabalho*), and so on. Despite this, they were allowed quite extensive freedoms: within their *arrabalde* (or main area of residence in Lisbon), they had mosques and an *imam*, a school (*madrasa*), public baths (*hammam*) and even a separate graveyard, until at least the mid-fifteenth century (Marques 1988: 97–102).

While some of these privileges were encroached on in the latter half of the fifteenth century, others – like the mosque – seemed to have remained intact to 1496. For our purposes, it is significant though to note that Lisbon's Muslim settlers were for the most part not merchants but artisans. A good number of them seem to have been potters, others were blacksmiths, glass-makers, carpenters, and so on. Their position in Lisbon is clearly summed up by the German traveller Popplau, writing in about 1484:

> This city and capital also has infidels in its surroundings, and they even occupy a part of the city itself; after the city was conquered by the Christians, they still remained in the castle for seven years, but soon there was an agreement between the victors and the vanquished, so that the latter were left with a quarter, in which they could live and build their houses without anyone molesting them, and where they are to the present day.   (Marques 1988: 104)

Malacca

This is a model that we shall see adopted later in such centres as Goa and Melaka. Still, whoever the substantial bourgeois may have been in the fifteenth century, they were evidently not the Muslims of Lisbon.

Policy re the Jews

The same cannot be said of the other minority community – the Jews. Although most Jews were, like the Muslims, artisans, there were also among them men-of-letters, physicians and surgeons, and merchants of substance. Their numbers had been swelled in the late fourteenth century, when persecutions in Seville and other Spanish cities (1391) brought them to the more tolerant climes of Portugal. Important fifteenth-century families like the Negros (or Ibn Yahia) controlled vineyards and other agricultural lands, besides trading in the city of Lisbon, and acting as revenue-farmers (*rendeiros*) under Dom Afonso V and his successors. Other Jewish traders participated in the overseas trade to the Atlantic islands and to North Africa, including in the *terras de mouros* (the parts of the Maghreb controlled by the Muslim opponents of the Portuguese, the Marinids and later the Wattasids). One finds them not only to the south of Iberia, but equally in the other great centres of the Portuguese intra-European network: in Bruges, members of the great Portuguese-Jewish banker families like the Abravanel, Latam and Palaçano acted as intemediaries between the Portuguese king and other private parties.

Now this trade was not conducted without opposition: if the Jewish merchant-bankers resented their Italian rivals and at times refused to enter into partnerships with them, others in Portugal – both artisanal groups from whom the Jews collected taxes as revenue-farmers, and Christian Portuguese merchants – sought by a variety of means to place checks on Jewish prosperity. In the *cortes* of 1472, for example, some representatives demanded that the overseas trade of the Jews be stopped, since it encouraged the corsair activity of rivals – for Castilian-licensed corsairs apparently regarded the goods of Jews of any nation as fair game. Since Jewish traders required royal permission (in the form of a *carta régia*) to participate in such trade, it was well within the Crown's powers to intervene decisively; but instead Dom João II took precisely the opposite line from his Christian subjects, demanding from Ferdinand and Isabel in 1481 that they protect all Portuguese Jews who were engaged in maritime trade. Equally, as late as the 1490s, we are aware that the family of José Alfaquim (including his son-in-law Benjamin Najarim) played a major role in trade to Ceuta, al-Qasr al-Saghir (Alcacér Ceguer), and other North African cities, all under the protection of Portuguese royal letters (Tavares 1982: 286–87).

Thus, there can be little doubt that the economic position of Portuguese Jews in the fifteenth century was far sounder than that of the small Muslim colonies, but it is equally certain that popular resentment existed against them in the urban areas – both as traders, and as artisans. Exaggerated views of their riches undoubtedly fed on this resentment, as

41

this verse from the *Cancioneiro Geral*, naming some of the principal families of Portuguese Jewish merchants, demonstrates:

> These men always hold the reins,
> and deny them you would in vain,
> the eight greatest lords.
> The first would be Latam,
> and the second Samuel,
> the third one Salamam,
> the fourth would be Fayam,
> the fifth Abravanel.
> Beloved is Palaçano
> Gualyte, and also Jacee,
> for every year it is always they. ...   (Tavares 1982: 328)

And it is undoubtedly this exaggerated view of their wealth which contributed to the acceptance in 1496 by Dom Manuel of the Castilian rulers' demand that he too expel the Jews from his kingdom, as they had done in 1492. The demand was made during the marriage negotiations, by which Dom Manuel was to marry the daughter of Ferdinand and Isabel, an alliance that was intended in turn to strengthen his hand both nationally and internationally.

But the supposed wealth of the Jewish community was not the only reason for what transpired. First of all, we should note that not only the Jews but *all* religious minorities, including the Muslims of Lisbon's *mouraria*, were mentioned in Dom Manuel's edict of December 1496. Thus, what was asserted was not merely anti-Jewish sentiment, but a feeling against all non-Christian peoples, something that scarcely augured well for a nation that was about to make direct contact with Asia and its tiny Christian population. Second, we should note that the expulsion order of 1496 and the ruler's other actions in 1496–97 contain curiously contradictory elements. On the one hand, Dom Manuel had begun his reign by freeing the Castilian Jews who had been incarcerated when they fled to Portugal in 1492, apparently because he valued their skills and commercial expertise. To follow this up the same year with the expulsion order speaks of an official mind that was – to put it mildly – somewhat confused.

The confusion possibly resulted from the fact that not all those in the King's Council were agreed that the Jews should indeed be expelled, some for reasons of religious tolerance, others for more pragmatic considerations. An example of the latter type, quite frankly stated, was that the Jews 'have subtle and delicate spirits, so that they can give advice to the Moors on what is necessary for them against us, and above all they will teach them their mechanical offices, in which they are very dexterous, principally in the making of arms ...' (Tavares 1982: 484); thus, it was thought to be necessary to ensure that the human and financial capital of the Jews remained in Dom Manuel's kingdom. As against this, there was the pressure from Castile (as part of the marriage negotiations between the two royal houses), as well as the internal pressure in Portugal from elements in the City Councils, and Dom Manuel's own peculiar brand of Messianism, of which we shall encounter more details below.

What finally emerged therefore was a compromise. The *conselhos* and the *letrados* in Portugal had argued that the continued existence of a Jewish community in Portugal would provoke reprisals (at the level not of open war but of corsair activity) by other European states against Portugal; their solution was hence expulsion. The ruler and many in his council for their part saw expulsion as fraught with too many problems; the extent of their dependence on Jewish skills cannot be underestimated, for we know that Dom João II, when planning the first (and as it happens, aborted) voyage around the Cape of Good Hope, turned not to the Italians but to Abraão Zacuto, Jewish astronomer, for advice. Thus, having promulgated the expulsion order in early December 1496, Dom Manuel sought by the end of the same month to find means forcibly to prevent Jews from leaving, instead demanding that they convert to Christianity. In the process, the Crown seized the ornaments and possessions of all synagogues and mosques, which according to one estimate came to over 1,250,000 reals in money, and over 500 marks of silver bullion. The premises of the religious establishments too were taken over, or reallocated; the great synagogue of Lisbon, for instance, became the church of Our Lady of Conception.

Thus, as a result of the processes of 1496–97, the Portuguese Jews became the so-called New Christians (*cristãos novos*), with the exception of a small minority – such as Guedelha Benefaçam of Évora – who managed to flee the country. Those who remained often managed to return to their original residences at the end of a year or two; some panic sale of property did take place, however, at inevitably depressed prices. In the sixteenth and seventeenth centuries, no study of the Portuguese bourgeoisie can afford to neglect the *cristãos novos*, whose networks extended from Lisbon and Evora to Medina del Campo and Madrid, Antwerp and Amsterdam, and eventually to Brazil, Peru and Goa.

In the forcible conversion of 1496–97, besides the destabilisation caused by the influx of a substantial number of Castilian Jews and the rivalry between Christian and Jewish artisan groups, a role was also played by the Christian Portuguese bourgeoisie – a social group that has thus far eluded our grasp. In the fifteenth century, some names do stand out: thus, Martim Leme, initially a Portuguese merchant at Bruges, and holder of a monopoly contract on the cork trade, later is to be found in Lisbon, and engaged in financial dealings with the Crown in the 1460s. Again, the famous Fernão Gomes, a native of Lisbon, may be termed a prominent example of the Portuguese *alta burguesia* (high bourgeoisie) of the 1460s and 1470s, who was neither Jewish nor resident Italian. The fact that other such men existed at the turn of the sixteenth century can be demonstrated by their participation in the commercial activities surrounding early Portuguese voyages to Asia. Between August 1509 and January 1511, sales of pepper, spices and 'drugs' at the *Casa da Índia* in Lisbon, in auction, were as shown in Table 2.2.

Table 2.2 Sales at the Casa da Índia, 1509–11

Buyer's ethnic origin	Amount (in reals)
Portuguese	35,752,069
German	10,727,720
Spanish	7,951,635
Italian	1,029,600
Other	11,473,873
TOTAL	66,934,897

(*Source*: Godinho 1981–83 (iii) : 195)

Prominent Portuguese merchants who figure in these transactions include Álvaro Pimentel, Duarte Tristão and Jorge Lopes Bixorda; Bixorda also sent ships on his own account on fleets to Asia in 1509, and again in 1523, controlled the trade in Brazil-wood together with two partners, and is known to have been a bullion trader on some scale. These activities, taken together with his substantial involvement in the sugar trade from Madeira, place Bixorda at the forefront of the big Portuguese bourgeois of the early sixteenth century, a position he shares with Pimentel, Fernão de Noronha, and a few others. The culmination of their careers is, significantly, usually an entry into the nobility; Martim Leme in the 1460s was made *escudeiro del-Rei*, Jorge Lopes Bixorda becomes a *cavaleiro da Casa Real*, and among the other purchasers of pepper and spices at the *Casa da Índia* in these years we find Francisco Fernandes, a *cavaleiro* (Godinho 1981–83, iii: 193–98). This is a pattern we shall see repeated, albeit with modifications, by the *cristão novo* magnates of the late sixteenth century.

Suffice it to say then, that the bourgeoisie of Portugal on the eve of Vasco da Gama's voyage to Asia in 1497 was complex. Elements of different origins found themselves performing much the same function, and Florentines, Genoese, native Lisboetas and erstwhile Castilian Jews (now New Christians) were all participants in the venture of overseas trade to a greater or lesser degree. Furthermore, solidarity was not always along the lines of ethnicity: when in the mid-sixteenth century, rivalries between consortia surfaced for the control of lucrative trading contracts, Germans from Augsburg allied with Genoese, and Florentines with New Christians, as well as vice-versa. To place such rivalries in context though, it is necessary to turn to the last of the significant players in the commercial circuit centred at Lisbon, the Portuguese Crown itself.

MERCANTILISM AND MESSIANISM

Modern historians tend to shy away from the term 'mercantilism', claiming that it simplifies far too complex a set of state policies. Yet, as we have seen in our earlier discussion of Asian states in the early modern period, certain policies can indeed be seen to transform states into quasi-commercial enterprises, and rivals of those of their subjects who were engaged in such activities – and this can help us distinguish between states across both space and time. In the case of Portugal, Manuel Nunes Dias has in a well-known work spoken of 'monarchical capitalism' (*o capitalismo monárquico português*), and it is this phenomenon that we shall seek to pose here within the framework of mercantilism (Nunes Dias 1963–64). When, in the late sixteenth century, a London-based venture attempted to enter Euro-Asian trade, it was a Company, a quasi-private entity with state sanction and some diplomatic privileges, that did so – and not the state itself. Similarly, Dutch trade to Asia – although sanctioned by the States-General – was conducted after 1602 by an ostensibly autonomous body, the Verenigde Oost-Indische Compagnie. In contrast, from the earliest Portuguese voyages to Asia, the state's involvement was considerable, even if it did recede towards the close of the sixteenth century, and then again in the late 1620s. But we are running ahead of our story, and should return to the fifteenth century, and the creation of Portuguese mercantilism.

We have already observed that the Portuguese monarchy was a crucial instrument, a fulcrum that from the fourteenth century held the balance between opposing elements not in the sense of a class struggle pure and simple, but a struggle between regions, between interior and coast, between a nobility attracted to Castile and an urban bourgeoisie and artisan class that saw trade as the obvious key to prosperity, given Portugal's – and especially Lisbon's – position at the cusp of the Mediterranean and the Atlantic. What made this struggle particularly complex was the fact that the nobility itself was divided on some crucial questions, which in turn was further exacerbated by the entry of some merchants into the lower nobility – as we have noted above.

The basic strategy of the Portuguese monarchs, whose sphere of influence was naturally enlarged as a consequence of the vacuum created by opposing groups pulling in different directions, does not seem all that different at times from the policies followed by Ferdinand and Isabel in Castile-Aragon. There, an alliance of the cities (the so-called *hermandad*) was built up in the 1470s to combat the power of the rural-based aristocracy; there too, the Crown sought to gain control of the Military Orders (though rather later than in Portugal, one should note); and not least of all, as in Portugal, the *cortes* – of Madrigal in 1476, and of Toledo in 1480 – were used to sanction what was in effect a growing tendency towards absolutism. But the crucial *difference* lay in the attitude towards trade itself. However hard the Spanish rulers may have tried at times to imitate the Portuguese model – setting up their own *Casa de Contratación* in January 1503 for example as an explicit mirror-image of the *Casa da Índia*, the former looking west where the latter looked east – the two remained very different in spirit until the mid-sixteenth century.

Perhaps the simplest way of comprehending this distinction is in terms of a crucial institution in the late fifteenth century Portuguese system – the *feitoria* or *factory*. Medieval cities in both Europe and Asia, which had numerous colonies of resident foreigners, tended to develop systems of internal regulation for these foreign communities, which at times gave them considerable social and juridical autonomy. In cities like fifteenth-century Melaka, for instance, this took the form of the system of multiple *syahbandars* – with the Gujaratis, Tamils, and other groups each having a 'representative' leader. In the Mediterranean, and also in the Low Countries, the system of consuls of different 'nations' had a similar aspect and function: thus, in medieval Bruges for example, the Venetians and Genoese each had their own consul, as did the Hanseatic merchants and the south Germans. But this post of consul must be distinguished, both in theory and in practice, from the factor (*feitor*), who derived his legitimacy (and also his remuneration) not from the merchant community in which he was resident but from some external authority. It is thus possible to see the post of *feitor* as close to the Italian concept of *fondaco* – a distant representative of a merchant company or banking house, who received a fixed salary, and carried out instructions sent to him by his principals. The major difference was that the *fondachi* more often than not acted within the private sphere; the *feitor* on the other hand was usually dependent on the public treasury for his remuneration and was a state employee. The problem, however, was that the distinction between the financial and economic activities of the royal household (the *Casa Real*) and those of the state was not wholly clear.

The earliest Portuguese *feitoria* whose history we can trace in detail is that located in the city of Bruges. The first mention of the *feitor de Flandres* occurs, interestingly enough, in 1386, when a new monarch, Dom João I, had just wrested the Portuguese throne from rivals. This factory remained in Bruges until the late fifteenth century, eventually shifting to Antwerp in 1498 after a decade of unstable existence due to local political turmoil. During these hundred-odd years, we are aware of the identities of some eight *feitores*, some of whom held the post for as many as seven or eight years, others for shorter periods. We are equally aware that from the 1430s, the posts of *feitor* and *consul* (earlier sometimes combined in the same person) were kept distinct: the former was appointed by a royal letter, the latter elected by the small Portuguese merchant community of Bruges (which numbered around twenty-five in the decades 1451–70, and about twenty in the decade 1481–90). The *feitor* drew a salary and maintenance allowance from the royal treasury (*Fazenda Real*), and sold Portuguese goods in Bruges – in the early fifteenth century figs and raisins, some wine, cork, and after the colonisation of Madeira also sugar – but more importantly acted as a purchaser (*comprador*) for the royal household, which he kept supplied with the textiles of Flanders, arms and ammunition, copper, and some other goods of less importance (Marques 1980: 159–93).

The *feitor*'s activities were also related to an increasingly important aspect of the royal household's interests in the fifteenth century: the trade conducted on royal ships (*naus del-Rei*). From at least as early as 1373, there is sporadic evidence of the Crown's direct interest in trade. The ruler Dom Fernando is stated to have involved several of his own vessels in a commercial company in that year, according to the testimony of Fernão Lopes in his *Crónica de Dom Fernando*. Later, in 1417, we have evidence of royal ships trading from Portugal to Flanders and Middelburgh, and then to Genoa and even Norway. In the middle years of the century, the Infante Dom Henrique both owned merchant ships, and even financed corsair ventures; the ruler Dom João II, while still heir-apparent, had vessels trading to Middelburgh. These royal merchant-capitalists, albeit still operating on a relatively small scale, traded in slaves and sugar, sold the grain, wine and fruit produced in their *reguengos* (estates), and were imitated by a number of other nobles – the Duke of Bragança, the Conde de Vila Real, and even the Duke of Beja (the future Dom Manuel I) who in the 1480s already had his own factor in Flanders. Thus, the epithet used by the French King François to describe Dom Manuel in the early sixteenth century – the 'grocer king' (*le roi épicier*) – had roots going back into the early fifteenth century, and can perhaps even be traced as far back as Dom Fernando (r. 1367–83), who – some evidence suggests – operated a mercantile fleet of around a dozen vessels (Thomaz 1989b).

The phenomenon of Portuguese royal mercantilism reached its apogee in the period from the 1480s to the 1520s, under Dom João II and his successor Dom Manuel I. Before this, the direct reign of Dom João II's father Dom Afonso V (r. 1448–81) had been characterised by a preoccupation with military adventurism in North Africa, rather than the direct control of maritime trade. Initially, it was the king's uncle the Infante Dom Henrique who concerned himself with the business of overseas expansion, and after his death, Dom Afonso in 1469 gave over to

47

Fernão Gomes, a prosperous Lisbon-based merchant, what was potentially the most significant of his mercantile avenues, namely the right to trade on the Guinea coast, for a period of six years. Gomes's contract also stipulated that he push the exploration of the African coast along, and as an unforeseen result, in 1471, the Portuguese were able to attain what was later called São Jorge da Mina, a major centre of gold trade and export. Little could be made of this discovery until the 1480s, although its significance was undoubtedly appreciated quickly. By the mid-1470s, the Castilians had staked *their* claim to Mina, as reprisal for Dom Afonso's indiscreet interference in the internal politics of Castile and Aragon. Only a peace signed in the early 1480s did away with this threat.

The policies of Dom João II are in direct contrast to those of his father. Resolutely turning his back on Castile and executing the Duke of Bragança were two early signs of his impatience with the territorial nobility and its predilections (Thomaz 1989a). Again, when it came to southward expansion, he did not opt for the costly route of North African adventures – pleasing though they may have been to the nobility, who could send their second sons and bastard offspring there – but rather the Atlantic route. In 1481, an armada of eleven vessels was sent out under the command of Diogo de Azambuja, who built a fortress at São Jorge da Mina in early 1482. With this base secured, and together with the chain of *feitorias* at Arguim, Uadam, Cantor, Sierra Leone and Axem, the Crown was in a few years able to reap returns sufficient to double its revenues. To monitor the functioning of this network, the Crown set up the *Casa de Guiné* and the *Casa da Mina*, each with its own Lisbon-based *feitor*, who supervised the transfer of the gold brought back from West Africa to the *Casa da Moeda* (mint) under strict guard. In the early sixteenth century, around a dozen caravels made the trip between Lisbon and the gold-trading factories each year, bringing back – in the words of the Venetian Cà Masser – 'from the Mine of Gold of Guinea 120 thousand ducats a year, for every month a caravel comes from there with 10 thousand ducats' (Godinho 1981–83, i: 171).

It is this preoccupation with commerce rather than military conquest that made Dom João a logical choice as patron for men like Ferdinand van Olmen or Columbus, who in 1486 presented the King with a proposal to seek a westerly route to India, basing himself on the calculations of the Florentine cosmographer Paolo dal Pozzo (or Toscanelli). As is well-known, Dom João rejected Columbus's proposal, even though he accepted van Olmen's equally speculative one, which eventually ended in disaster. But the rejection of Columbus was not because of a return to North African preoccupations. Instead, Dom João had his own plans; he had sent out emissaries overland to East Africa and India via the Mediterranean, and then in 1487–88 was able to savour the triumph of having his subject Bartolomeu Dias round the Cape of Good

Hope. The all-sea route to India was now open, though internal opposition in Portugal seems to have prevented its actual use for a decade (Thomaz 1991).

The building-blocks that we have stressed so far are two in number: first, capital and expertise, and second, an institutional structure founded largely on the *feitoria*, and its head the *feitor*. Since the exploration of the Atlantic was largely centred around the discovery and settlement of desert islands, force was of little importance there – save in the *guerra do corso*, the corsair activity equally practised by Portuguese, Spanish and French. Force – the preoccupation of one section of Portuguese society – was given full expression elsewhere, in the sanguinary campaigns of North Africa, such as in the capture (1418) and defence of al-Qasr al-Saghir (1463), Arzila (1471) or Tangier (1471). Taken to its logical extreme, it might seem that we are arguing that the Portuguese expansion enterprise of the fifteenth century was conceived in compartments: in one resided rational calculation and commerce, and in another the atavistic passions of anti-Muslim feeling were to be found. But this was not really the case, and in fact royal mercantilism itself cannot be seen in Dom Manuel's reign without its strange bedfellow – Messianism.

That Portuguese expansion in general had a religious side to it is a commonplace in writings on the subject, which speak of the 'Crusading spirit' of the Lusitanians, the residual momentum left by the *reconquista* and so on. Support for this view can be found in the writings of the greatest contemporary ideologue of Portuguese expansion, the chronicler João de Barros. Barros, charged by his sovereign to write 'of the deeds that the Portuguese did in the discovery and conquest of the seas and lands of the Orient', nevertheless began his *Da Ásia* in the following manner:

> There having risen in the land of Arabia that great anti-Christ Muhammad, more or less in the year 593 of our Redemption, he so worked the fury of his steel, and the fire of his infernal sect by means of his captains and caliphs, that in the space of a hundred years, they conquered all of Arabia, part of Syria, and Persia, in Asia, and in Africa all of Egypt beyond and before the Nile.
>
> (Barros 1973, i/1: 1–2)

It is thus the rise of Islam that, in Barros's view, provides the logical starting-point for an understanding of how the Portuguese came to be in Asia; he looks at the Muslim conquest of Iberia, the reconquest, the Atlantic explorations and the charting of the west coast of Africa, only arriving at Vasco da Gama's expedition to the Indian Ocean in the fourth book of his *Década Primeira da Ásia*.

However, the careful reader of Barros and of other contemporary writings and documents soon discovers that those who were so religiously motivated could often be equally the persons in whose breasts the mostly fervently mercantilist spirit resided. An example is the Infante Dom Henrique, Master of the Order of Christ and creator of the Portuguese

Crown patronage of missions (the *padroado da Ordem de Cristo*, later to become the *padroado real* under Dom Manuel) by virtue of Papal Bulls, but equally a trader in sugar and slaves, and a patron of corsair ventures. Still, religious though Dom Henrique was, he was no Messianist.

Portuguese Messianism is often associated quasi-exclusively with Dom Manuel's great-grandson, Dom Sebastião, the focal point of a Messianic cult after his death in North Africa in 1578. But, more recently, the Portuguese historian Luís Filipe Thomaz has pointed to the existence of a Messianism of a somewhat different sort in the court of Dom Manuel. Revealed in the writings of some of his courtiers like Duarte Galvão and Duarte Pacheco Pereira, the proximate psychological reason for this Messianism was the monarch's rather improbable accession to the throne, after the (for him) fortuitous deaths of six persons closer to the throne than he; also a possible factor was his quite unusual physical appearance, with eyes that were 'between green and white', and 'arms so long that the fingers of his hands reached below his knees' (the description is that of the chronicler Damião de Góis). Furthermore, in his early life, Dom Manuel's educators seem to have imbued him with religious ideas derived from Joachim of Fiore (1130/35–1201/2), a Cistercian monk born in Calabria, who holds a somewhat ambiguous reputation in Christian theology, being regarded by some as a saint and others as a heretic. Joachimite philosophising centred around some key ideas: the literalist belief that one had to wrestle with the letter of the scriptures to get at the spirit, a trinitarian approach to history, and an apocalyptic vision (in evidence in his writings such as *Expositio in Apocalypsim*) which held that a new age would dawn, when two new orders of men would emerge as guides (Thomaz 1990).

Fostered by some of those in his council after his accession to the throne, these Messianic beliefs enabled Dom Manuel at times to act in a highly autocratic fashion, since he believed that he was directly inspired by the Holy Spirit. But the Joachimite influence on the ruler also brought with it another effect: a preoccupation with the recapture of Jerusalem, which under Dom Manuel came to be seen as the logical culmination of overseas expansion, and the crowning achievement that would enable him to claim the title of Emperor of the East or perhaps even Universal Emperor. The Jerusalem enterprise was one that lived and died with Dom Manuel, for neither his predecessors nor his successors seem to have been particularly enamoured of the idea. We should stress though that even in tactical terms there was no necessary contradiction between royal mercantilism and Messianism, since the former could be accommodated to the former. Dom Manuel's plan was to mount a two-pronged attack on the Mamluk Kingdom of Egypt (or the 'Sultanate of Babylonia', as his Messianist supporters termed it), with one force attacking via North Africa, and the other via the Red Sea. It is true that this policy required reactivating the North African front, after a lull under Dom João II, and hence a diversion of resources from mercantile activity. But the Red Sea strategy was truly one of killing two birds with one stone: a blockade of the entry to the Red Sea would not only give the Portuguese a decisive advantage in the European market for pepper and spices over their Venetian rivals (who were supplied through Cairo and Alexandria), but also cut into the revenue-base of the Mamluks (Thomaz 1991).

In order to do this, however, the support of other Asian powers was deemed necessary, and here Dom Manuel and his supporters were badly misinformed; they believed the number of Christian kingdoms to be far larger than was in fact the case. Eventually, this meant a strategy centred around an alliance with Ethiopia, the state ruled over by the fabled Prester John (or Preste João). It was this alliance that was deeply opposed by other parties, both in Portugal and in Portuguese Asia. Thus, royal mercantilism was in part a necessary condition for the putting into effect of Messianist plans: making war required resources, especially a war that was unlikely to enthuse the nobility (as the Jerusalem campaign is unlikely to have done, had it ever been prosecuted). The idea of maintaining a larger standing army, that became popular in the reign of Dom Manuel, was a natural outcome of this logic: it was also the next step in the development of royal absolutism, albeit a step that was never wholly put into effect. The problem with the two guiding principles of Dom Manuel's overseas policy was hence not their mutually contradictory nature, but rather the hostility they evoked in certain quarters, and on account of which they remained circumscribed in reality.

SUMMING UP

In tracing the medieval background of Portugal's early modern presence in Asia and the waters of the Indian Ocean, this chapter has suggested that just as Asia was no *tabula rasa* on which the Portuguese inscribed what they chose, so too the Portuguese were more than mere bandits, who acted in a conceptual and historical vacuum. Tiny by the standards of Asia in the period, whether in terms of physical size or population, Portugal was nevertheless a complex and stratified society, comprising groups with vastly different levels of cohesiveness and with vastly different outlooks and interests. We have chosen here to focus on two aspects of stratification: social stratification, in terms of the nobility (itself divided into two broad strata), the clergy, the urban-based bourgeoisie (both Portuguese and foreign), and the relatively unknown sea of the *gente miuda*; and geographical stratification, in terms of coast versus littoral, north versus south, as indeed Lisbon versus the rest of the country. These two schemes of stratification run across each other, creating sub-categories and groups. Taking the example of the nobility, those who were most actively involved in the Indian Ocean enterprise in its first three decades were not so much the territorial nobility of the north and interior, but the court-nobility made up of upwardly mobile bourgeois, migrants from Castile, France and Galicia and so on, and holders of such titles as *estribeiro-mór*, *caçador-mór* and *alcaide-mór*. To understand the mentality of the first group, we should recall that the so-called *lei mental* of Dom Duarte (r. 1433–38) had created for this nobility a system of *morgadíos*, or entailed estates, which meant that all grants made to them by the Crown were inalienable, indivisible, and heritable by the oldest son. The younger sons were thus a 'surplus' to be exported, usually to North Africa, later – and somewhat reluctantly – to Asia. By training and inclination, this group had little direct mercantile interest – and even when they traded (as they did in the late sixteenth and early seventeenth centuries) it was through the use of skilled intermediaries. The *morgados* for their part wished to entrench themselves, and assert their autonomy from the Crown and its schemes, whether mercantilist or not; as one of them is supposed to have declared in the 1530s: 'He possessed nothing that belonged to the Crown, and if he did have something, they could as well take it away from him' (Cruz 1989: 323). Opposed to royal centralisation, supportive of overseas expansion only to the extent that it gave them an opportunity to put into practice their military training, the priorities of this group emerge clearly from their demands to the rulers Dom João I and Dom Duarte that the latter petition Castile to permit them (the nobility) to take Granada in the early fifteenth century. For while the Portuguese kings looked west and south towards the sea, they still looked east within the Iberian peninsula.

In contrast, urban bourgeois elements like Fernão Gomes were keen on overseas expansion, but their preferred field was the Atlantic islands and West Africa, rather than North Africa or – somewhat later – Asia. It was they who had supported the Crown in the course of the fifteenth century, but cracks had begun to appear in the alliance by the reign of Dom Manuel. For if the result of expansion was to be that the Crown got to keep the profits as well as the commerce, such a process was not exactly in their interest either.

Thus, residually, the Crown was left with the support of the service-nobility, of certain elements among Lisbon's Florentines and Genoese (who became the bankers and financiers to the royal household, and were allowed at times to share in various Crown monopolies), and finally of the urban labouring classes – the target of a veritable ideological bombardment in the sixteenth century. They too had to be incorporated, willy-nilly, into the Asian enterprise in a situation that was ambiguous, for if on the one hand Portugal was a net importer of food (and thus appeared over-populated), its population was by no means large in absolute terms. In the early sixteenth century (as in more recent times), the most densely populated areas were the Douro littoral, and southern Estremadura (25–40 persons per sq. km); they were followed by Trás-os-Montes, Alto Douro and the littoral south of Oporto (12–25 persons), then by the upper Alentejo and littoral Beira (8–12 persons), and finally by the lower Alentejo, the Algarve and lower Beira (less than 8 persons/sq. km). Thus, broadly speaking, the north was far more densely populated than the south in the sixteenth century, and would provide the bulk of the 'cannon-fodder' who went overseas (Ribeiro et al. 1987: 735, 786).

Table 2.3 The population of Portugal in 1527

Region	Number of Households	%
Trás-os-Montes	35,616	12.7
Entre Douro e Minho	55,099	19.6
Beira	66,800	23.9
Estremadura	52,402	18.7
Entre Tejo e Guardiana	48,804	17.4
Algarve	8,797	3.1
Lisbon	13,010	4.6
TOTAL	280,528	100.0

(*Source*: Ribeiro et al. 1987 : 735)

We may conclude this chapter then by reminding the reader that the orientation of the area that was defined in 1250 as the Kingdom of Portugal was not always maritime. To the modern Argentine poet Jorge Luis Borges, himself partly of Portuguese descent:

> Before our human dream (or terror) wove
> Mythologies, cosmogonies and love,
> before time coined its substance into days
> The sea, the always sea existed : was.　　　　　(Borges 1972: 234–35)

But the sea meant different things in different periods. In medieval Portugal, a maritime orientation had to be invented and sustained between the thirteenth and the fifteenth centuries, during the course of which the Portuguese learnt much from the Italians, even as later some Italians (like Columbus) were to learn from the Portuguese. In retrospect, the turning to the sea of Portugal may appear logical, in view of its strategic location, and its relatively limited agrarian resources. It also involved both conscious choices and a measure of serendipity, and was cast in terms of a nationalism determined in a matrix: on the one hand, the opposition Christian versus Moor, on the other hand Portuguese versus Castilian.

'Moorish' influence on a great part of Portuguese culture – from loan-words in the language, to the structure and instrumentation of popular music – are of course evident, and equally Castile was a pole that at one and the same time attracted and repelled. These contradictions and oppositions were to remain no less strong in the period 1500 to 1700 than they had been in medieval Portugal.

Two Patterns and Their Logic: Creating an Empire, 1498–1540

The Portuguese arrival in Asia in 1498 did not pass unnoticed in Asian historical writings of the period. One of the most detailed works devoted to their actions is the Arabic chronicle, *Tuhfat al-Mujahidin* (or 'Gift to the Holy Warriors'), written in the late 1570s by a certain Zain al-Din Ma'bari, who wished to glorify the deeds of the Muslim opponents of the Portuguese in Asia. But Zain al-Din also wished to make a theoretical argument, justifying the war against the Portuguese, and showing how the latter had transgressed acceptable modes of behaviour. Early in his text, he therefore wrote:

> It is to be known that the infidels can be divided into two categories. The first are those who live in their own countries; in this case, the holy war (*jihad*) is a precept of delegation, that is, it is enough that those believers who live with them make it, with other Muslims not being obliged to do so, unless they are sinning.
>
> The second is of those who invade the territories of the Muslims, as is the case here [in India]; and then the war cannot be delegated to another, but is the imperative of every Muslim, whether slave, woman, townsman or peasant, even without the authorisation of the lord, husband, creditor or landowner; both for those who are near, and those who are far away.   (Lopes 1899: 8–9)

Zain al-Din wrote almost three-quarters of a century after the arrival of the Portuguese on the coast of Malabar in the far south-west of the Indian peninsula. Since he wrote with the benefit of hindsight, his view cannot be thought to represent the spontaneous reaction of local Islamic elites to the newcomers. In fact it is his suggestion that the Muslims of the Malabar area (the so-called Mappilas) had 'sinned and disobeyed God. Then He sent them a Frankish people as their masters, the Portuguese – may God abandon them! – to oppress, vex and trouble them with all sorts of oppressions and travails' (Lopes 1899: 4–5).

As a vision of things, Zain al-Din's is disturbingly close to some of the early Portuguese texts concerning their 'deeds' (*feitos*) in Asia; the concept of the *guerra santa* (holy war) is as present in the latter, as in the former's 'Gift to the Holy Warriors' (*tuhfat al-mujahidin*). Zain al-Din's work is also remarkably accurate in tracing the chronology and geography of early Portuguese activity in the area, and the first two voyages commanded respectively by Vasco da Gama and Pedro Álvares Cabral, as well as their outcome, find extensive mention in the *Tuhfat*.

It is well-known that by the end of the second Portuguese voyage, the 'Holy War' of which Zain al-Din speaks had in a sense been inaugurated. Hostilities between the newcomers and the 'Moors' were however not indiscriminate; the Portuguese now carefully distinguished between the *mouros da terra* ('native Moors'), and the *mouros de Meca* ('Moors from Mecca' – which is to say the Middle East); they saw the latter rather than the former as their principal adversaries (Bouchon 1973). Such distinctions were, however, the result of hard-won experience. Despite the quite extensive contacts that medieval Europe had maintained with the Indian Ocean, the first Portuguese expedition of Vasco da Gama was conducted in considerable ignorance of the religious, political and economic geography of Asia and East Africa. Álvaro Velho, who maintained a log-book on board the *São Rafael*, one of the ships of the expedition, thus declares quite emphatically: 'This city of Calecut is of Christians, who are brown men; and some of whom go about with great beards and long hair on their heads, and others have shaven heads, and still others cropped hair' (Velho 1987: 55). Nor is he disabused of such views in the appendix of his *Roteiro*: here one finds listed, among the Christian kingdoms of Asia, Cranganore, Kollam, Kayal (which apparently has a Moorish king but Christian subjects), Coromandel, Ceylon, Sumatra, Siam (*shahr-i nav*), Tenasserim, Melaka and Pegu; only Bengal, which has 'many Moors and few Christians, and the King is a Moor', and Calicut, are excluded from the list. Significantly, the term *gentio* (later used to denote Hindus and Buddhists), finds no mention in the text at all.

THE EARLY EXPEDITIONS

But we have already advanced too far perhaps, without detailing the context in which our naive observer found himself in Calicut, on the Malabar coast. He was part of an expedition initially comprising four vessels, *São Gabriel* (captained by Vasco da Gama, head of the fleet), *São Rafael* (captained by Paulo da Gama, his brother), *Berrio* (commanded by Nicolau Coelho), and a fourth supply-vessel which did not go to India. Now the expedition has been termed a 'mystery' by some for a variety of reasons. There is, first of all, the issue of why nine years passed between the return of Bartolomeu Dias's expedition from the Cape of Good Hope and Da Gama's voyage. A second problem lies in the somewhat obscure past of the Captain-Major before he was appointed to this task; why was a relative unknown appointed for such an important purpose?

The answers to both questions, rather than lying – as sometimes has been suggested – in some mysterious, intermediate expeditions, whose documents have conveniently disappeared, appear to be as follows. First, we have already noted how woefully ignorant the Portuguese were of many of the basic facts concerning even the Indian west coast. This was surely a reason for some hesitation, and tentativeness. Secondly, it has been observed that a strong set of groups existed in Portugal which was opposed to the idea of direct trade to Asia, either because it would strengthen the hand of the Crown as trader and thus deprive *them* of commercial possibilities, or because they were more interested in North Africa than Asia. It is possible that such pockets of opposition gave pause to D. João II in the last years of his reign. And third, the confusion caused by the 'success' of Columbus in 1492 may well have worse confounded the situation. Thus, the small size of the expedition, as well as the choice of the obscure Da Gama as its leader, may have been precisely because D. Manuel did not as yet wish to sink a great deal of his prestige on the venture. Or, alternatively, it may well have been the case that Da Gama was not Dom Manuel's own choice, but rather imposed in him by the opposition, for we later see a certain reluctance on the Crown's part to reward him.

Da Gama's fleet eventually left the estuary of the Tejo on 8th July 1497, and arrived at the Cape of Good Hope on 19th November, but it finally arrived in Calicut, its true destination, only on 20th/21st May 1498. The reason for this long delay, which meant a total Lisbon-Calicut voyaging time of three hundred and sixteen days, was a four-month stay on the African east coast. Modern historians have somewhat neglected this part of the voyage, focusing instead on the Calicut visit; in fact, at least some of what occurred in Calicut can only be understood by examining the East African experience of Da Gama. The fleet's first major encounter with the East African trading network took place in early March, on Moçambique Island. In early April, Da Gama moved on to Mombasa, then to Malindi, whence he eventually set sail on 24th April for Calicut. In this period, several important incidents took place. Let us note, to begin with, that the fleet had on board several 'specialists' of one or the other sort: some men had spent time earlier in Manicongo (on the African west coast), and were hence regarded as expert in dealing with the *negros*; one other, Fernão Martins, had been a captive in North Africa and could speak Arabic. The account of Álvaro Velho comprises a compendium of their views. Here is how they saw Mozambique, in their first real encounter with the Indian Ocean trading network:

> The men of this land are dark and well-built, and of the sect of Mafamede and speak like Moors; and their clothes are made of cotton and linen, very fine

and multi-coloured, and striped, and they are rich and embroidered. And all of them have caps on their head, with silk tassels (*vivos*) embroidered with gold thread. And they are merchants, and trade with white Moors (*mouros brancos*), of whose ships there were four in this place, which brought gold, silver and cloth, and cloves, and pepper and ginger. ...   (Velho 1987: 36)

Two statements stand out: the rapid identification of the settlement as Muslim, but at the same time the desire to distinguish the 'native' Muslims from those of the Middle East. In fact, when relations with the local ruler soured, as they rapidly did, there is once again a clear attempt to point to the culpability of the *mouros brancos* in the matter.

The origins of the conflict are not wholly clear. Velho has it that the Portuguese were at first mistaken for Turks, and that when their identity as *Christians* became clear, the ruler secretly ordered them killed. This is possible but by no means certain; after all, the fact that Christian Italians traded with Muslims in the Levant could not have been unknown to the Arabs trading in Kilwa and Mozambique. At any rate, by 24th March, the situation had reached a state in which a three-hour engagement was fought between the Portuguese and those on the strand; the Portuguese also forced a ship belonging to a local *sharif* to run aground, and then departed for Kilwa and Mombasa. On failing to reach the former port due to contrary winds, they arrived at Mombasa on 7th April, but once again there were hostilities: the Portuguese by now had some Muslims captive on board, who confessed under torture to a conspiracy against them by the Mombasa ruler. The fleet now proceeded down the coast, took another vessel belonging to an 'honoured Moor', and arrived in Malindi on 16th April.

The language of Velho's journal has coarsened by this time – he now refers to those on the coast as 'dogs' (*perros*) – and much suspicion is evident in the Portuguese fleet's dealings at Malindi. But in fact, during the nine days they spent in this port, they were well-received, and succeeded in encountering four ships from the Malabar port of Cranganore, with St. Thomas Christians on board. They also took on board a Gujarati pilot (often incorrectly identified as the celebrated Arab navigator Ahmad ibn-Majid), sent them by the local ruler in exchange for his ambassador, whom the Portuguese had taken hostage. Da Gama refused, however, to set foot on land, feeling that he might be ambushed – and Velho for his part is clear that the Captain-Major was right in distrusting such men 'who did not speak from their hearts, nor of their will'.

This East African sojourn is surely crucial in defining Portuguese conduct in Malabar. We note extreme suspicion in Da Gama's attitude in Calicut; he waits for boats from the land to approach his ships, rather than making contact himself, and then sends on land an expendable member of his fleet – a convict-exile called João Nunes – rather than someone of authority. Nunes, on encountering two Tunisian traders in the port, is the real protagonist of the following celebrated scene:

> And he was taken to a place where there were two Moors from Tunis, who knew how to speak Castilian and Genoese. And the first greeting that they gave him was the following:
> What the Devil! What brought you here?
> And they asked him what he had come to seek from so far; and he replied:
> We came to seek Christians and spices.
> And they said to him:
> Why do the King of Castile and the King of France and the Seignory of Venice not send men here?
> And he replied that the King of Portugal did not permit them to do so. And they said that he did well.   (Velho 1987: 54–55)

What Nunes sought to establish then was the *power* of the Portuguese King in Europe. As for the Muslim traders, their response – as can be seen above – was far from negative. Indeed, one of them is reported by Velho to have told the Portuguese: 'You should give many thanks to God for having brought you to a land where there are such riches'! Contrary to what has been stated by some writers therefore, Islam and Christianity did not confront each other directly at the moment of Da Gama's arrival in Calicut. Such a total confrontation, despite the rhetoric of both Zain al-Din and some contemporary Portuguese writers, never actually took place in Calicut. It was however necessary for Zain al-Din, writing in the 1570s – when the conflict between Ottomans and Hapsburgs in the Mediterranean, on the one hand, and Bijapur, Calicut and Aceh, and the Portuguese, on the other hand, had reached fever pitch – to pose matters in this light.

What took place during the three months of Da Gama's stay (he left Calicut on 29th August) was far more complex: information was certainly gained, but the Portuguese – with their rather paltry gift of cloth, hats, coral and agricultural products – failed to create a favourable impression. Moreover, there was a fair deal of hostility in some of the dealings; the mutual distrust is evident in the fact that hostages and counter-hostages were taken. Velho's own account thus concludes:

> One Wednesday, which was the twenty-ninth of the said month of August, seeing that we had found and discovered what we had come to seek out, both spices and precious stones, and that we could not manage to leave the land in peace and as friends of the people, the Captain-Major decided, on consulting the other captains, to leave ...   (Velho 1987: 75)

The admission is frank: the Portuguese did not leave Calicut with pleasant thoughts in 1498. But by other standards, the expedition could be deemed a success, and it certainly strengthened the hand of D. Manuel. The next fleet, sent under Pedro Álvares Cabral, was a full-fledged affair, far larger than Da Gama's rather paltry trio of vessels; it comprised thirteen ships and carried over a thousand men on board.

skips Cabral.

The Portuguese Empire in Asia, 1500–1700

It would be tedious to detail the vicissitudes of each of these expeditions. Instead let us consider the broad features of the first phase, lasting until 1505, when D. Francisco de Almeida was named the first viceroy of Portuguese Asia, or rather 'viceroy of the Indies' (*visorey das Índias*) as he titles himself. This was a phase when the enterprise was characterised by great ambiguities in hierarchy; authority was exercised by persons holding the title of Captain-Major (*capitão-mór*), but there might be several of these in Asia at one and the same time. It is also a phase dominated by Cochin, the small port-town to the south of Calicut, to which Cabral had shifted in December 1500, after the Portuguese factory in the latter centre was razed and open hostilities between Calicut and the Portuguese broke out. Cochin has recently been termed 'the school of apprenticeship of the Portuguese in India'; and it certainly was the only serious contender for administrative centre before Albuquerque chose Goa in 1510.

The Cochin factory was set up by Vasco da Gama on his second voyage to Asia in 1502; its first factor was Diogo Fernandes Correia, earlier factor at Flanders. The early years were difficult ones, and not on account of difficulties faced with the Calicut ruler alone. The factional and intra-clan strife, that is later to characterise Portuguese Asia, already reared its head at an early stage: in 1503–04, the two Captains-Major in Asia, Francisco de Albuquerque, and his cousin Afonso de Albuquerque, quarrelled incessantly at Cochin. These quarrels had a more profound significance than that of a mere intra-family feud: Francisco de Albuquerque was a *fidalgo*, supported by a coterie at the court, and suspicious of the Crown's encroachment into mercantile and other spaces, while Afonso – an illegitimate son, who could not use the title *Dom* – was a creature of D. Manuel, a representative, already in 1503–04, of the spirit of Manueline imperialism. This is made clear from a quarrel that broke out between the two after a wooden fortress was constructed at Cochin in late 1503; Francisco wished to name it 'Castelo Albuquerque', while Afonso wished to call it 'Castelo Manuel' (Aubin 1987)!

The intense activity of these years shows up in terms of the most obvious index: the extent of shipping on the Cape route. It is equally in this period that the difference between Portuguese shipping arrivals in, and departures from Asia reaches its peak; thus, from 1497 to 1510, of some 40,300 tonnes of shipping that arrived, a mere 26,300 went back. There were two reasons for this: first, losses in Asian waters, and second (and more important), the need to build up a permanent Portuguese naval presence in Asia, already initiated by Da Gama on his second voyage in 1502–03.

What was the broad Portuguese strategy of these years? To put the matter baldly, for the Crown, it was to trade where possible, to make war where necessary. Trade initially meant developing the Lisbon–Malabar

60

axis, but this soon turned into a triangle, with East Africa playing the role of apex. The logic was simple: when Da Gama offered his paltry gifts at Calicut, he had been told that 'it was nothing to give a King, and that the poorest merchant who came from Mecca ... would give him more than that' (Velho 1987: 63). Instead, he was asked for gold, and it was precisely this that the East African ports provided, drawing on the trade of the inland caravans that arrived there from the Munhumutapa kingdom. But, once again, the problem was of what to sell in East Africa to 'ransom' (*resgatar*) the gold. Malabar pepper and Southeast Asian spices had a small demand there, and the only solution was to take recourse to textiles from Gujarat, buying them at the markets of Cochin and Cannanore, where the Portuguese had factories.

Table 3.1 Portuguese shipping tonnage on the Cape route, 1497–1520

| Years | Europe–Asia | | Asia–Europe | |
	Departures	Arrivals	Departures	Arrivals
1497–1500	2,665 (17)	1,640 (10)	290 (3)	170 (2)
1501–1510	42,775 (151)	38,695 (135)	26,085 (88)	21,115 (73)
1511–1520	38,690 (96)	35,830 (87)	26,060 (60)	25,760 (59)

(*Note*: Figures in brackets represent number of ships)
(*Source*: Duncan 1986: 22)

If this was the essence of the Crown's strategy, it was not the whole of Portuguese strategy. We may consider, by way of illustration, the Instruction (*Regimento*) given to D. Francisco de Almeida on his departure for India in 1505 by the King: after detailing the manner in which the voyage through the Atlantic is to be organised, there are then several sections on Sofala and Kilwa (on the African east coast), on Cochin and the Malabar coast, on a proposed expedition to the Red Sea, and on the return cargoes for Europe (CAA (ii): 272–334). But, interspersed through all this, a great part of the *regimento* is taken up by another subject, laconically designated '*presas*'. This refers to a part of Portuguese activity of lesser interest to the Crown, and more to the taste of *fidalgos*: corsair activity and the taking of prizes. We have already noted in an earlier chapter that such activity had been quite characteristic in the fourteenth and fifteenth century, off the African north coast and later in the Atlantic. Besides the Portuguese, many Italians, Spaniards and Frenchmen practised it, and the tradition was carried over into the Indian Ocean. The Crown, often not having the resources to give rewards of adequate dimensions to the nobility for their part in early voyages, acquiesced in this – albeit with a certain unwillingness. As we will see below, this aspect of Portuguese dealings in the Indian Ocean was to bring the Portuguese some disrepute even by

61

1520. But faced with a recalcitrant nobility, this was the Crown's sop, and it was felt that at least some check could be kept on it by making it 'official'. The division of spoils as it appears in Almeida's *regimento* is shown in Table 3.2.

Table 3.2 Division of prizes according to the 1505 *Regimento*

Claimant	Share (%)	Remarks
(a) Deductions		
Viceroy	?	Jewels worth below 500 *cruzados* etc.
King	20	One-fifth (*quinto*)
Treasury	53.3	Two-thirds of what remains
(b) Division of what remains (26.6)		
Viceroy	25	
Captains of Naus	10	— %
Caravel captains	6	—
Masters-cum-Pilots	4	
Masters only	3	
Pilots only	3	
Armed mariners (each)	1.5	—
Men at arms (each)	1.5	= total of remains?
Others	46	

(*Source*: CAA (ii): 325–26)

The King's fifth share (or *quinto*) was based on an interesting precedent: the Islamic tradition of the *khums*, the fifth share of plunder (Ar. *ghanima*) that was to be made over to the overlord, or to the Caliphate. This rule was meant to apply not only to corsair ventures carried out on royal ships (with which the 1505 *regimento* is primarily concerned); even private corsair ventures (which engaged in the activity described by contemporary chroniclers as *andar às presas*) were subject to the *quinto*. Those corsairs who did not do so were termed *alevantados*, a term that might be loosely translated as 'mavericks' or 'freelancers' rather than in the somewhat more literal sense of 'rebels'. The term was later to be used to categorise a whole sub-culture within Portuguese Asia, that of the north-eastern Bay of Bengal.

FROM ALMEIDA TO ALBUQUERQUE: DEFINING THE FIRST PATTERN

It is well-known that the profitability of Portuguese trade on the Cape route in the early years of the sixteenth century was based on the return cargoes from Asia to Europe: largely pepper and spices. The pepper came for the most part from Malabar in India, and to a lesser extent from Malaysia and Indonesia; of the spices, cloves and nutmeg came from the Moluccas, and cinnamon from Sri Lanka. Let us consider a return cargo of these early years, that of 1505, in the fleet commanded by Lopo Soares de Albergaria. The fleet was larger than usual; as Table 3.1 shows, the average annual departures from Asia in the decade 1501–10 was about nine vessels, and Lopo Soares's fleet had thirteen, of which one was lost en route. The return cargo, according to the cargo inventory, was as shown in Table 3.3 (for purposes of comparison we present the 1518 cargo as well).

Table 3.3 The return cargoes of 1505 and 1518 (in kgs.) *in kilograms*

Commodity	1505	1518
Pepper	1,074,003	2,128,962
Ginger	28,476	–
Cinnamon	8,789	1,342
Cloves	7,145	5,584
Indigo	1,336	–
Mace	–	986
Myrrh	514	678
Lac	411	66,443
Red sandalwood	–	27,978
Cassia	–	2,432
Incense	–	2,589
Silk	–	2,660
Brazil-wood	–	969
Cornelian	–	851
Spikenard	–	431
Tamarind	308	–
Cardamom	206	–
Others	771	207
TOTAL	1,121,959	2,242,112

(Handwritten annotations: 96% and 95% above the columns; "spice (aromatic) of nutmeg shell" by Mace; "shellac for lacquer" by Lac; "a bark or herb" by Cassia; "dried (resin) from insects" by Lac/Red sandalwood; "i.e. brazier (= red coals)" and "used as a red dye" by Incense/Silk; "Cornelian = carnelian (a translucent precious stone – quartz – of reddish color)" by Cornelian/Spikenard; "ginger-like spice" by Cardamom)

(*Sources*: Bouchon 1976a (1505 cargo), Bouchon 1977 (1518 cargo))

Now before the Cape route was opened up, these commodities – of which the most important by far was pepper, followed by spices – had reached Europe by a complex land and sea route. The Indian and Southeast Asian ports – especially Melaka and Calicut, but also others – exported these goods in the late fifteenth century to Hurmuz and Aden, whence they were taken on caravans to the ports of the eastern Mediterranean. Merchants from west Asia and North Africa, like the Tunisian 'Moors' whom João Nunes met at Calicut, had a significant interest in this trade. Once in the Mediterranean, however, the carrying trade was largely in another set of hands, that of merchants from the

(Handwritten margin note top: Moluccas; bottom right: "not (partly by sea?)")

Catalonia

Italian city-states, together with some Catalans, and a few other nationalities essentially of the *northern* littoral of the Mediterranean.

In the fourteenth century, merchants from Genoa had played a role of great importance in this trade with Alexandria, Beirut, and other ports. By the early fifteenth century, however, the Genoese participation seems to have declined and the growing dominance of the Venetians in this Mediterranean pepper and spice carrying-trade asserted itself. The size of the trade and its significance for the overall economy of Venice is not susceptible of precise quantification, save in a few years, but the combined *1,100 per annum* pepper and spice imports into Europe in the early 1400s are unlikely to have exceeded 1,100 tonnes, of which about 60 per cent was accounted for by Venice. By the late fifteenth century, the Venetian share in pepper imports had declined slightly, but to compensate, her trade in other spices (a faster growing branch, one should add) expanded at the cost of Genoese and Catalan rivals (Wake 1979; 1986).

Moreover, from a situation in the early fifteenth century when the bulk of Venetian pepper had come from Egypt (Alexandria), and the bulk of the other spices from Syria (Beirut), by the 1490s, Venetian dependence on Alexandria in both branches of trade was substantial. The overall picture is shown in Table 3.4.

Table 3.4 Venetian Pepper and Spice Sources, *c.* 1400 and 1500

Source	Pepper	Other spices
(a) *c.* 1400:		
— Egypt	80%	30%
Syria	20%	70%
(b) *c.* 1500:		
—Egypt	75%	80%
Syria	25%	20%

(*Source*: Wake 1986: 631–35)

It was this trade that the Portuguese Cape route trade, managed at the European end through the *Casa da Índia* in Lisbon, frontally challenged. There was great consternation in Venice at the Portuguese success, testified to in the diaries of merchant houses like the Sanudo and Priuli; and as the markets in the eastern Mediterranean collapsed, the Venetians saw an obvious coming together of their interests with those of the Mamluk Sultans of Egypt (whose customs-collections were similarly affected), and with other political entities in the Indian Ocean to whom the Portuguese presence was a blow – such as Kilwa and Calicut. Reasons of state, and the overwhelming logic of trading competition, thus saw Catholic republic allied with Islamic Sultanate against another Catholic power: juridically, this can be understood in terms of Zain al-Din's matrix, wherein it was of greater significance to fight the infidel who had 'invaded the territories of Muslims', than those who 'live in their own countries'. *I.e. Venetians let live; Portuguese destroy*

The alliance, already in the making in about 1500, was brought to *quick!* fruition in the early years of the first viceroyalty, that of D. Francisco de Almeida (1505–09). The alliance was not wholly anticipated by the Portuguese, for D. Francisco, when he came to Asia, had quite another battle–plan: he intended to construct a fortress at Socotora near the Straits of Bab-el-Mandeb, at the mouth of the Red Sea, which – when taken together with *other* forts that he hoped to build in Sofala, the Anjedive *Kanara* Islands (off the Kanara coast) and Kollam in Malabar – would preclude the *Coast* possibility of precisely such alliances. The logic of the Red Sea fort appears clearly in the *regimento* given to him:

> And since it seems to us [D. Manuel] that nothing could be more important for our service than to have a fortress at the mouth of the Red Sea or near it, either inside or outside as seems most convenient, for if that is sealed then no *Still looking to* more spices can pass through to the lands of the [Mamluk] Sultan (*Soldam*), *an* and everyone in India would give up the fantasy of being able to trade with *African* anyone save us, and also because it is close to the lands of Prester John, from *Christian* which it seems to us that there could follow great profits for us, firstly in terms *alliance* of the Christians there, and then a great increase in our treasury, and then in *of* war whenever we want to make it. ... (CAA (ii): 311) *puissance*

There is an implicit reference to the Jerusalem enterprise, and the will to monopolise by the use of force. Either the Portuguese King was not confident that the economic advantages of the Cape route were such that the *Casa da Índia* could sell spices and pepper cheaper than the Venetians or Genoese, or alternatively he believed that the blockade of the Red Sea would damage the economic interests of Egypt by cutting off supplies even to the north African market.

To understand the motives behind the Mamluk response, we should recall that the idea of seapower was by no means alien to these rulers of *Egypt* Egypt. This was because their kingdom was vulnerable to attack both from the Mediterranean and the Red Sea; in the thirteenth century, the Il-Khan Arghun had invited Genoese shipwrights to Baghdad, in order to help construct galleys to blockade Aden and the Red Sea, thus threatening trade flows into Egypt. Later, during the period of the Circassian Mamluks *Mamlukes* (1382–1517), maritime power was required at various points, to defend the kingdom's trading interests. The Mamluk Sultan Barsbay (r. 1422–38) built coastal defences as well as a fleet in the 1420s, to defend his kingdom's northern shores from the depredations of Christian pirates and privateers based at Cyprus, and in 1427 even launched a major maritime attack on Cyprus, reducing the island's ruler to dependent status. It is in the reign of this Sultan that Mamluk policies towards the Red Sea trade witnessed significant changes (Lewis 1970). A conscious policy was adopted of developing the trade of Jiddah, to the detriment of Aden, since the former port was far more closely linked to Cairo fiscally than the latter. In Barsbay's period, contemporary sources report that Jiddah alone yielded an average revenue of 200,000 *dinars* to the treasury each year.

The commercial policy of earlier Sultans, articulated for example by the contemporary writer al-Qalqashandi (who speaks of the need to receive merchants kindly 'and treat them justly, for the profits accruing from them ... are very great'), was reversed to an extent in Barsbay's time (Lewis 1970: 224). A series of commodity monopolies was created, first on local products like sugar, and later even on imported goods such as pepper. In the 1430s, the Sultan forbade the sale of pepper to Europeans by anyone save his own official apparatus, and this policy was periodically revived by later rulers like Khushqadam (r. 1461–67) and Qa'it Bay (r. 1468–95).

By the time of Cabral's return to Europe, the ruling Sultan was Qansawh al-Ghawri (r. 1500–16). He first initiated a series of diplomatic moves, by means of his Venetian connections, to have the Papacy restrain the Portuguese from the use of force in the Indian Ocean and particularly in the vicinity of the Red Sea. When this failed, the Sultan invoked the spirit of Barsbay, and – with the encouragement of the Venetians – had a fleet assembled at Suez, and sent into the Indian Ocean. To understand the extent of his anxiety, we may consider the economic consequences of the first few Portuguese Asian expeditions for the Venice-Levant trade.

Table 3.5 Collapse of the Venice-Levant trade, 1496–1506 (annual averages, figures in tonnes)

Route Commodity	Alexandria 1496–98	1501–06	Beirut 1496–98	1501–06
Pepper	480–630	135	90–240	10
Other spices	580–730	200	150–180	35
TOTAL	1060–1200	335	270–420	45

(*Source*: Wake 1986: 633)

As Table 3.5 clearly demonstrates, Venetian exports from Alexandria collapsed to less than a third what they had been, and to less than a sixth in the case of Beirut. The decline is far more steep in the case of pepper than in 'other spices'; a glance at Table 3.3 demonstrates why this was so. Up to 1511, the Portuguese had only limited access to spices other than ginger and cinnamon; it was only later that cloves, nutmeg and mace enter their return cargoes in a substantial fashion.

Mamluk

The fleet sent out from Suez eventually left only in 1507, and arrived off the Indian west coast late that year, after a brief punitive mission at Jiddah against the local Shaikh, who was withholding fiscal payments from Cairo. Led by a Kurdish admiral, Emir Hussain, the fleet comprised twelve ships and carried over 1500 men-at-arms; its first major engagement was against a Portuguese fleet at Chaul, and was a signal success. But a later naval battle, fought off the Gujarat port of Diu, was a total reversal; the fleet was largely destroyed, and the Indian adherents to the Mamluk party – such as Malik Ayaz, governor of Diu – had to negotiate a retreat (Pearson 1976: 70–71). This defeat of the Mamluk fleet is usually portrayed in Portuguese chronicles as the major event of D. Francisco de Almeida's viceroyalty, and was certainly a great loss of face for the declining Egyptian monarchy. Increasingly embroiled in difficulties with the Ottomans, and with their revenues in decline, the Mamluk Sultanate collapsed a mere seven years later, in 1516–17. But this was still an unforeseen outcome in 1509. It is very probable that the victory at Diu was, if anything, interpreted by D. Manuel and others of his coterie as a divine signal, demonstrating approval of *his* plans in respect of Jerusalem.

In November 1509, Almeida's viceroyalty ended. The man designated to succeed him – albeit with the lesser title of governor – was Afonso de Albuquerque, whom we have already encountered in the context of early sixteenth-century Cochin. Albuquerque represents a quite different type of figure from Almeida, for the latter was a typical *fidalgo*, anxious to create at best a system of tribute-collection, and one in which the nobility could demonstrate its prowess at arms. Albuquerque on the other hand was a creature of curious contradictions: a great believer in centralisation, but also a man who himself went far beyond what royal instructions in fact required. We see this already in 1507, when he was on a mission to Hurmuz, to force its ruler to pay tribute (*páreas* – a key term in the period) to D. Manuel; instead, he attempted to take over the fortress there, and only withdrew when other captains in his fleet refused to go along with his plans.

At the court in Portugal, Albuquerque enjoyed the support of a few influential persons, such as D. Martinho de Castelo Branco and Duarte Galvão, but the greater part of the *fidalguia* had little use for him, nor indeed did his predecessor Almeida. In fact, Dom Manuel had to nominate him secretly as Almeida's successor, for fear of opposition, and also gave him the title of governor (rather than viceroy) in order not to exasperate his denigrators further. Albuquerque hence had to take recourse to the support of a small coterie surrounding him, often his own near relatives, who were appointed by him into key positions in the six years of his governorship. Equally, he rested a great deal of trust in some of his Italian advisers, particularly in one Francesco Corbinelli, a Florentine, whom he made factor of Goa. Increasingly, as his governorship wore on, we also see Albuquerque influenced by the advice of a number of Asian merchants, especially while entering what were relatively unknown waters. This is the case with Timmayya on the Indian west coast, and Nina Chatu in Melaka.

The opposition to Albuquerque was far more than a question of personality differences. The main opponents of his policy, as Albuquerque himself saw it, were on the one hand the established nobility, which was opposed in principle to state centralisation, and on the other the men we may term the 'Cochin coterie': Lourenço Moreno, Duarte Barbosa, Diogo Pereira (nicknamed 'the Malabar'), António Real and Gaspar Pereira (Guerreiro and Rodrigues 1989). Some of these men later attained considerable success, with Gaspar Pereira for example being appointed treasurer at the *Casa da Índia* in 1519.

How did they sustain their opposition to Albuquerque, and on what was it based? Let us begin by noting that the Cochin coterie, almost to a man, belonged to the middle nobility, and were hence not averse to trade in principle. Rather, the issue for them was the manner in which trade was organised, and the extent to which it was state controlled. Initially, in the differences between Almeida and Albuquerque, they had supported the latter – seeing in him perhaps a man of their social stratum, rather than the higher one to which men like Almeida belonged. But when Albuquerque began to show his hand, in 1510, their disquiet increased. For Albuquerque seemed intent on acquiring a large number of fortified points, influenced in all probability by his earlier experience in North Africa. In 1510, on the advice of the corsair-trader Timmayya, he decided to acquire Goa – a port at the time in the control of the Bijapur ruler, Yusuf Adil Shah, and a key centre of horse-import into the Deccan. In 1513, he turned to Aden, which he failed to take, but in 1514, he recaptured Hurmuz after a gap of seven years. Taken together with Sofala, Cochin, Socotora, and Melaka (to which we shall turn later in this chapter), it seemed that Albuquerque had created a militarised chain – all largely answerable to himself.

The Cochin coterie and those allied to them had a quite different vision of things. For a variety of reasons, they were in a position to correspond directly with the court (and even with D. Manuel himself); the system of *feitores* ensured moreover that they did not fall strictly under the authority of the governor, but were instead answerable directly to Lisbon. Their view, and the view of *some* of the Italian merchants interested in the India trade, was that Albuquerque was in the process of creating a system both too militarised and too centralised. As António Real wrote to D. Manuel, in a celebrated letter of December 1512:

> Believe me, My Lord, if you expect to sustain Goa, then you will receive neither cargoes nor profits from India, because it lacks everything, and as for Mallaca, I do not know what will come of it. ... Thus, My Lord, everything is

wind, save Cochym. Make your feet firm here forever, because all the other fortresses, both made and to be made, will do you no good, and will only expend what there is there, and what there is here.   (CAA (iii): 337)

Elsewhere in the same letter, Real speaks disparagingly even of Albuquerque's pretensions as a warrior, declaring that his policy is of making 'little battles against unarmed, nude little negros (*negrinhos nuus*), and in constructing fortresses in places where there is little profit and much expenditure'.

The opposition took two concrete forms. First, it was suggested to Lisbon that Albuquerque harboured immense personal ambitions, wishing to become Duke of Goa, and to turn the Asian enterprise into his own demesne. Such rumours were seized upon by persons in the court, such as the Baron of Alvito, who were fervently opposed to both royal mercantilism and excessive centralisation. But besides acting through Lisbon, actions against Albuquerque were taken even in Asia. Two examples were the conspiracy to capture and sell as a slave Simão Rangel, Albuquerque's ambassador to Calicut, and the imprisonment on false grounds of Matthew, the ambassador sent from Ethiopia to India, with the intention of developing an anti-Islamic alliance between that state and Portugal (Aubin 1976: 23–25). From a series of tactical actions to frustrate Albuquerque, the opposition thus came little by little to acquire a quite distinct vision of how things should operate in Portuguese Asia; in this vision, neither the Jerusalem enterprise of D. Manuel, nor the state-trading and military adventurism of Albuquerque had any place. Rather, the anti-Albuquerque alliance wished to see an Asia in which corsair activity and the taking of prizes would be a significant form of activity, and where private initiative – in the hands of the middle nobility and their allies – would have greater expression.

Even the Florentines saw some point in this. The most powerful Florentine families like that of Sernigi, which had actually been permitted to send ships to Asia, were themselves at loggerheads with Albuquerque in 1510. The Sernigis and some others had obtained from D. Manuel permission to explore the Melaka trade, and arrived on the Indian west coast en route to Southeast Asia. But Albuquerque had his own ideas: he first commandeered their fleet for use in his attack on Goa (in late 1510), and then insisted that they desist from going to Melaka until he had his own expeditionary force ready. Frustrated and humiliated, Girolamo Sernigi returned to Lisbon, and added his voice to numerous others that were raised against Albuquerque's policies. Eventually, they were heard – and the Baron of Alvito succeeded in having his own nephew Lopo Soares de Albergaria replace Albuquerque as governor (Thomaz 1991).

THE SECOND PATTERN: EAST OF CAPE COMORIN

The action of the period surveyed thus far has largely taken place in the western Indian Ocean, between Sri Lanka and East Africa. As we have seen, from as early as 1505, the intention was always to build a string of fortresses, and Albuquerque only extended this conception to its logical end: by the close of his governorship, there were major fortresses in Kilwa, Hurmuz, Goa and Cannanore in Portuguese hands. Undoubtedly some gaps remained. One was Aden, which Albuquerque was unable to take, and the long and busy coastline of Gujarat and the Konkan too was as yet not host to any Portuguese settlement. In fact, the death of Albuquerque served to remind the Portuguese of the importance of Gujarat and the Gujaratis in Asian trade, for these merchants fomented a series of anti-Portuguese actions in ports as diverse as Bhatkal, Calicut and Martaban in this period. But for the moment, official attention was turned elsewhere.

The one major venture prosecuted by Albuquerque outside the western Indian Ocean was the capture of Melaka, which he took in August 1511. This act had profound and unforeseen consequences for the Portuguese enterprise, leading to the creation of a second pattern of activity, to the east of Cape Comorin. In the course of their protracted actions leading up to the taking of Melaka, the Portuguese had acquired allies from within the town's mercantile community. These were mostly Tamils, or Kelings, merchants of considerable standing in the trade within the Bay of Bengal and east of Melaka. The other major community in Melaka, the Gujaratis, concentrated for the most part on trade to Malabar, Gujarat, the Red Sea and Persian Gulf – and fled Melaka en masse on the Portuguese capture. It was through the Kelings that Albuquerque, and his representative in Melaka, the first captain Rui de Brito Patalim, sought to make contact with other parts of the Bay of Bengal littoral, insular Southeast Asia, and the Far East. Between 1511, and Albuquerque's death in 1515, a series of maritime ventures was organised on a cooperative basis between the Portuguese Crown and several Keling merchants (but especially a certain Nina Chatu): ships went to Martaban in Burma, to Pulicat in south-eastern India, to the Moluccas and so on. Such ventures continued until about 1518: thereafter, they were replaced by Portuguese Crown shipping with a captain, factor and scrivener on board, all of whom were Portuguese (Thomaz 1976). In the initial phase, one of apprenticeship and exploration, things were somewhat different: the Crown was no more than a partner in the venture, and the other (Keling) partner also sent *his* representatives on board the vessel.

From these ventures there emerged gradually the system of *carreiras* (or Crown trade routes), between designated ports in Asia such as Pulicat and Melaka, or Melaka and Chittagong (in Bengal). The system was not peculiar to the areas east of Cape Comorin: in the western Indian Ocean,

70

there was similarly a set of *carreiras* linking Hurmuz to several ports on the Indian west coast. We have details of one such voyage, between Goa and Hurmuz, in 1520–21: the ship was called *Santa Maria do Monte*, and it carried 140 persons on its outward voyage. The cargo loaded at Goa largely comprised rice and iron, and on the return seventy-one horses were shipped to Goa from Hurmuz. Although in this instance we do not have details concerning the cargo carried on behalf of private parties and the captain-cum-factor (who was Parigi Corbinelli, son of the erstwhile factor of Goa), it becomes clear from the 1520s that the *carreira* system represented a compromise between Crown and private interests. The Captain and other officials were allowed the free use of a certain proportion of the cargo-hold (their *quintalada*), in addition to being given a salary (Aubin 1988). It was not uncommon by the early 1520s for noblemen embarking from Portugal for Asia already to have letters of authorisation from the King, appointing them to the captaincy of this or that *carreira*. The Crown supplied the vessel, and its trading interests were secured in part by its control over the greater part of the cargo space.

Now, east of Cape Comorin, the first *carreiras* to emerge were those from the Indian west coast to the Banda Islands in the Moluccas via Melaka, to Coromandel (that is, Pulicat), and to Pegu in lower Burma. There then followed others, to Bengal, and to a whole host of ports on the Malay peninsula. The captains of these were at times asked to play the role of diplomats and ambassadors, and to establish relations between Goa and the rulers of the ports to which the *carreiras* were destined. This is the case with António Correia, sent to Martaban in 1519, and with António de Brito and his brother-in-law Diogo Pereira in Bengal in 1521. The Brito-Pereira embassy is a particularly significant one, for it also points clearly to the manner in which the second pattern of which we have spoken emerged.

To understand the vicissitudes of the Bengal embassy though, we should recall that the governorship of Lopo Soares had in its own way been as startling in its impact as that of Albuquerque. Lopo Soares was an avowed 'free trader': he is supposed to have proclaimed that Portuguese in Asia were free to go anywhere to seek profit, and thus set in motion what has been termed the 'great freedom' (*grande soltura*), the diametric opposite of Albuquerque's *dirigisme*. By 1520, this had had dramatic effects. Private Portuguese settlements sprang up in most major ports of the Bay of Bengal littoral, and in such places as Patani, and Pahang on the Malay Peninsula. The numbers of Portuguese involved were by no means negligible: in Pulicat, on the Coromandel coast of south-eastern India, it is reported that there were two or three hundred Portuguese by 1520, and smaller nuclei could be found in Martaban, Tenasserim and other centres on the facing littoral of the Bay of Bengal. The presence of the private Portuguese was undoubtedly an embarrassment for the captains of the *carreiras* which visited these ports, the more so since some of these Portuguese were not above turning pirate on occasion. Or worse still, from the official Portuguese viewpoint, they could turn renegade, convert to Islam, and seek entry into an Islamic polity such as that of Bengal.

The embassy of 1521 was sent after Lopo Soares's governorship, during the government of Diogo Lopes de Sequeira. Sequeira tried to strike a median path between the Albuquerque and Albergaria lines, as did his successor D. Duarte de Meneses. Their policies were oriented towards pulling back at least some of the Portuguese who had escaped during the *soltura* from the fold of the Portuguese state. By the early 1520s, the official settlements in the western Indian Ocean (which numbered perhaps a dozen in all) had been organised more or less in the fashion of the North African *praças*.[1] They had a garrison, a certain number of officials – a captain, a factor, a scrivener and so on – but also a group of private merchants, now termed *casados*. These *casados*, whose status was analogous to that of the *fronteiros* in North Africa, and juridically related in turn to the category of *homens-bons* in Portuguese urban society, represented the acceptable face of private mercantile activity.

In 1519, Diogo Lopes attempted to bring the private traders of Coromandel too under a similar regime, but his representative João Moreno was much too busy in private trade from Coromandel to Burma to make much headway. D. Duarte de Meneses did somewhat better, creating in 1521 the post of Captain and factor of Coromandel, but in the absence of a settlement over which the Portuguese had any juridical rights, the category of *casado* could not be applied yet.

Diogo Lopes's policy in respect of Bengal was, similarly, a poorly defined one. Bengal was an exporter of rice on a considerable scale, and hence useful for feeding Melaka; its textiles were also a profitable item of trade. But the choice of envoys – in particular Diogo Pereira – strikes one as curious. Pereira was, we have seen, one of the Cochin coterie, and a man who by 1518 is reported to have 'crammed all of India full of his trade in all the forbidden goods, and there is no factory in which he does not have his own agent' (Guerreiro and Rodrigues 1989). In Melaka, his brother-in-law Lopo Vaz conducted affairs for him, and he is said to have 'sent jongs and ships with his goods to many parts'. In their embassy to Bengal, at the time under the control of the Afghan Husain Shahi dynasty, which ruled from the interior city of Gaur, the intention of men like Brito and Pereira was obviously to secure better trading opportunities not merely for the Crown but for others like themselves.

---

1 The extant forts in 1521 were the following, with their construction dates being indicated in brackets: from west to east Sofala (1505), Mozambique (1508), Hurmuz (1515), Chaul (1521), Goa (1510), Cannanore (1505), Calicut (1513), Cochin (1503), Kollam (1519), Colombo (1518), Pasai (1521), and Melaka (1511). Forts earlier constructed and abandoned included Kilwa (1505–12), Socotra (1507–11) and Anjedive (1505–07).

But the embassy turned out to be a case of 'the biter bit'. On arriving in the port of Chittagong in October 1521, the Brito embassy found that a rival Portuguese embassy had already been sent to the court at Gaur by one Rafael Perestrelo, who had been instructed to go to China via Southeast Asia, but had 'missed the monsoon' and hence decided of his own initiative to go to Bengal. Perestrelo's envoy to Gaur was a resourceful man, a certain Cristôvão Jusarte. It was his feeling that the best way to proceed would be to make contact with the Portuguese *already* in Bengal, who were in fact renegades and converts to Islam. Thus we have the spectacle of Martim de Lucena, apparently a Portuguese renegade, aiding Cristôvão Jusarte (himself 'dressed as a Moor') to argue his case before the Bengal Sultan, and of the two Portuguese embassies making claims and counter-claims, much to the amusement of the Gaur court. The sort of factional struggle that runs like a thread through the early days of the Portuguese in Asia, from the time of the quarrel of the two Albuquerques at Cochin, thus surfaces here in dramatic form; it serves to remind us that the notion of a united European presence, practising 'divide and rule' on factionally divided Asians, Africans and American Indians bears little relationship to reality.

Here is Cristôvão Jusarte before the Sultan, in the words of the interpreter of the Brito-Pereira embassy:

> [He said] that he did not wish to reside with the Christians, because he was the son of the regent of Portugal, and we were no more than poor peasants who were unfit to serve him, and that the embassy we brought was a fraud, and especially that he was a Moor and did not wish to deal with us and so he went about dressed according to local usage, with his head and beard shaved just like them, and that he had come to bring prosperity to the land and we to diminish it, and other things that are ugly to relate.
>
> (Bouchon and Thomaz 1988: 240–41)

Even though Jusarte did not succeed in the final analysis in having his embassy accredited, the confrontation is significant. Here was one party, operating through the mediation of private Portuguese who were already entrenched in the land, and another party which, albeit still distant from Albuquerque's spirit, still represented 'officialdom'.

From this dialectic emerged the pattern of Portuguese dealings in the Bay of Bengal and in much of Southeast Asia. Here, fortresses were few and far between, for besides Melaka, the only other one was in the Moluccas – and this to combat Castilian ambitions on the Spice Islands more than for any other reason. In Coromandel, Bengal, Arakan, Pegu, the Malay Peninsula, Thailand, and a host of other places, the official Portuguese presence remained limited in the period up to 1570 to the *carreira* voyages and their captains, and – in some instances – to a locally resident captain with very limited powers. Some contemporaries believed that even the latter had no real function in places like Coromandel – for

73

they were often more interested in private trade than in controlling the uncontrollable. To the official mind in Goa, these areas in the 1530s remained a problem: inhabited by men who were at best undisciplined (which is to say, reluctant to respond to Goa's urgings), at worst a blot on the Portuguese reputation on account of their 'scandalous' lives.

THE LOGIC AT WORK: PORTUGUESE ASIA, 1525–40

The two patterns that we have described above have sometimes been compared to two earlier patterns in Portuguese expansion, that of the western Indian Ocean to North Africa, and that of the Bay of Bengal and Southeast Asia to the west coast of Africa. In the former case, the military dominated the commercial, and the upper nobility were a relatively strong presence, while in the latter case the mercantile impulse dominated the military one, with the middle and lower nobility and the marginal elements in Portuguese society being more in evidence. The processes of the period 1525–40 served for the most part to entrench rather than disturb this distinction; there were however a few processes that limit the extent of our generalisation.

Let us begin by taking stock of numbers. In 1516, it is stated that there were something like four thousand Portuguese in Asia; by 1540, D. João de Castro stated that the number was up to between six and seven thousand. Of these, something like four hundred were in Cochin alone, Melaka had some two hundred and fifty, and Hurmuz less than a hundred and fifty. But a large number were also outside the Portuguese state's control: in Ethiopia there may have been as many as two hundred by 1550, and something like three to four times that number in all the ports of Coromandel – Nagapattinam, Kunjimedu, São Tomé de Meliapor, Pulicat, Armagon and Masulipatnam – taken together. But equally important were centres acquired on the Indian west coast after Albuquerque: Bassein, Daman, Chaul and Diu. Two of these, Diu and Bassein, were ceded to the Portuguese by Sultan Bahadur of Gujarat in 1534, and the latter seems to have been acquired for two reasons: first to secure the supply lines of Goa, which suffered from a deficit of food, and second to provide a means to pamper the residual seignorial pretensions of the *fidalgos*, who were given estates (called *prazos*) in this area, which came to be known as the northern province (*província do norte*). Chaul, where a fortress was built as early as 1521, was meant to act together with Diu to serve as a check on Gujarati mercantile activity between the Indian west coast and the ports that were identified as 'enemies' of the Portuguese state (Pearson 1976: 71). We may see these as supplementing, but not fundamentally altering, the western Indian Ocean network of 1515. The

74

fact that they yielded a not inconsiderable revenue was a further reason for acquiring them.

Similarly, the changes in the Portuguese presence in East Africa in the 1530s were by way of consolidation rather than fundamental restructuring. Already in Albuquerque's time, the Portuguese had abandoned their fort at Kilwa, and in the 1530s, they began to penetrate up the Zambezi, in an attempt to come to grips with the inland supply-lines of the coastal ports. Small settlements were set up at Sena and Tete, and then, in 1544, in Quelimane.

The western Indian Ocean was also where the major part of the Portuguese state's maritime resources continued to be concentrated. The *Lembrança das Cousas da Índia* (Memorandum on India Affairs), anonymously authored in 1525, gives us data on the shipping available to the Portuguese governor at the time (see Table 3.6). The disposition of these vessels is of some significance. Three of the largest, totalling something like 1500 *toneis*, were in Hurmuz; several others were being deployed at Calicut. One galleon and a round-ship were at Melaka, another galleon was to go to Melaka. In the Bay of Bengal there was a single vessel, the round-ship *Pamtoso*, in which Ambrósio do Rego, captain of Coromandel, had left for Pulicat. This is in itself a demonstration of the relative weight given to different areas by Portuguese officialdom in the period.

Table 3.6 Shipping resources in Portuguese Asia,1525

Type of ship	Number	Remarks
Naus	6	3 in Hurmuz
Galleons	11	5 under repair, 2 in Calicut
Galleys	5	2 made in Chaul
Galliots	4	3 in Calicut
Brigantines	4	1 in Malindi
Round and Latin ships	9	2 at Cape Guardafui
Private ships	11	–
Small vessels and boats	34	–

(*Source*: Felner 1868, iv: 21–25)

Did these relatively weak shipping resources mean that the main Portuguese objective – securing the Asia-Europe pepper and spice trade – could not be attained? The curious fact remains that despite the relatively poor Portuguese position, trade to the Red Sea from India and Southeast Asia was rather limited in this period. The *Tarikh al-Shihri*, a chronicle of events in the late 1520s and 1530s from the vantage-point of the south Arabian port of al-Shihr, suggests that the only vessels conspicuous enough for the Portuguese to chase and capture in these years were some pepper-bearing ships from Bhatkal, south of Goa (Serjeant 1963). It is possible that there *were* others, from such ports as Kollam, Calicut and

Cannanore, to which the Portuguese routinely turned a blind eye, but that remains in the realm of speculation.

It is more or less clear, however, that the pepper and spice trade from South Asia and Southeast Asia to west Asia continued in the 1530s and 1540s. From the 1540s, we have the following discussion in the *Livro que Trata das Coisas da Índia e do Japão* (Book of India and Japan Affairs):

> The spices and drugs from India that arrive in Trypoly of Sorya first arrive in Ormuz and from Ormuz are taken by sea to Baçora, and from Baçora there are two routes to Trypoly of Sorya, that is, one by the desert of Arabia Deserta, which ends at the city of Damascus, and the other by Old Babylonya, which today is called Bagodade, and by land from Mesopotamya or Baçora to Damascus is a journey of eighteen days ... The route through the desert of Arabia which ends at Damascus is shorter, but even so, on account of the many robbers (*ladrões*) and highwaymen who inhabit the desert, the Turk has ordered that the caravans (*cafyllas*) and spice merchants should not go through there, and ordered that all of them should go through Babylonya and Mesopotamya, both because they will be safe from the thieves, and in order to enrich and ennoble his lands; from Babylonya the cafillas arrive in the city of Alepo, and from Alepo they take all the spices to Trypoly of Sorya, which takes four days' journey.   (Calado 1960: 74)

Thus, despite the fact that Hurmuz was controlled by the Portuguese, spices continued to pass through there; the key question is however the market for which these were destined. There appears to be a good case to be made for the fact that the spices that passed through here were intended in good measure *not* for the European market but to meet Iranian, Turkish and North African consumption. A marginal postscript to the anonymous account cited above makes mention of Tabriz in this context, and the account itself concludes by stating:

> The drugs and spices that are sold in Persia cannot pass to the seas of the Levant because of the great duties and expenses on the way and because the journey is so long that the expenses will be more than what the goods are worth.   (Calado 1960: 74)

The implication is clear: it was recognised that there was a Middle Eastern demand quite aside from that of Venice and Genoa, and since it was highly unlikely that this former demand would be fed by the spice distribution network centred at Lisbon (that is, the sales of the *Casa da Índia*) it made perfect sense for the Portuguese themselves to trade in these goods at Hurmuz.

Thus, in the case of the western Indian Ocean, the logic of the early years worked itself out, so that a species of compromise was attained. Once the *basic* network of fortresses was in place, and once the European distribution of pepper and spices was more or less in Portuguese hands, the true nature of Asian demand too could be gauged. As Table 3.3 shows, by 1518, the return cargoes to Europe spanned a great diversity of products, unlike the rather pepper-centred cargo that we have seen in

1505 (Bouchon 1976a; 1977). Pepper, lac, cloves, cinnamon, mace, sandalwood were among the goods taken back, all in all a cargo of 2,242 tonnes. The Crown's basic trade revenues were thus assured, and continued to be substantial through the 1520s and early 1530s. There remained the intra-Asian trade, run on the system of *carreiras*, and here the situation was rather more complex. From the late 1520s, a tendency becomes manifest to limit the number of *carreiras*: some, such as the Bhatkal-Hurmuz route, cease to function in about this period. Again, from 1521 to 1535, the clove trade from the Moluccas operated as a Crown monopoly, but from the latter date, private merchants were also permitted to participate, provided they paid the Crown a sum called the *choquel*, and also gave over one-third of the cloves they brought back to the Crown at a fixed price (lower than the market rate) (Thomaz 1975).

But what of claims of generalised monopoly over Asian trade, sometimes inferred from the title taken by the Portuguese monarch D. Manuel after Vasco da Gama's return from Asia: 'Lord of the Conquest, Navigation and Commerce of Ethiopia, Arabia, Persia and India'? It has been pointed out by scholars who have analysed the content of these epithets in the light of juridical usage in medieval Portugal, that the generalised doctrine of closed seas (or *mare clausum*) was not adhered to by all in the Portuguese court, and could only be justified if one adopted a radical position – one that had, incidentally, been refuted by theologians like St. Thomas Aquinas – to the effect that non-Christian peoples and powers were by definition illegitimate. To the extent that the Portuguese ruler had sanction for his rights, it came from the Papal Bull of Nicholas V in 1455, which was careful however to note that the monopoly was of navigation *to* India (that is, *usque ad indos*) and not in the Indian Ocean. Thus, what was being discussed was the right over the Atlantic, and in particular in relation to other Christian powers like Spain or France. Those Portuguese who extended this to navigation within Asia were in fact taking a rather wide interpretation of the Papal grant (Thomaz 1985).

The only manner in which the larger claim could be justified was thus as follows: first, the Portuguese ruler, as a ruler, had the right to assert a monopoly in relation to his *own* subjects, and could thus forbid them from trading in certain goods; second, the state of war could be used as a justification for the denial to certain ships of the right to navigate. From the latter stems the so-called *cartaz* system, a system of safe-conducts issued to Asian ships by the Portuguese, initially on the Malabar coast, and later on Coromandel, in Gujarat, and elsewhere. According to the chronicler Gaspar Correia, in 1502, *cartazes* were first issued to ships from the Malabar ports of Kollam, Cochin and Cannanore, in order to certify to the fact that they pertained to areas that were not at war with the Portuguese (Correia 1975, i: 298).

The *limited* claims that the Portuguese monarchs in fact made in this

77

period can also be seen from their preoccupation with *páreas, or tribute*. We have already noted that there is some suspicion that D. Manuel wished to declare himself Emperor in the years before he died, and was waiting for the Jerusalem enterprise to be brought to a successful conclusion before doing so. His proto-imperial pretensions rested, however, not on the exercise of sovereignty over large territories (for the colonisation of Brazil was still a thing of the future); instead, he wished to have himself declared suzerain over as many rulers as possible in Asia. Thus, in 1521, when the fortress at Chaul was constructed by Diogo Lopes de Sequeira, it was with the provision that the Nizam Shahs of Ahmadnagar (to whom the port belonged) would pay *páreas* worth 2,000 gold *pagodas* (or *hun*); this 'tribute' was raised to 7,000 *pagodas* after 1539 (Godinho 1982: 50–51). In Ternate, in eastern Indonesia, the *páreas* were in terms of palm-leaves and sago; in Kilwa, the Sultans were required in the early sixteenth century to pay *páreas* in gold.

The sums of money (or quantities of goods) involved are often so trivial as to seem risible, but the point was much more the *fact* of tribute than its amount. Harking back to the concept of *taifa*, in vogue in Iberia in the later Islamic period, the Portuguese monarch intended to assert a widespread rather than deep influence, as we see from other evidence as well. The most crucial evidence in this respect is the fact that the Portuguese did very little to interfere with local administrative systems in the first years of their rule. In Melaka, at first they tried to persuade the Sultan to return as their vassal; failing this, they strengthened the hand of the *bendahara*, and eventually made the office a hereditary one in the hands of a Tamil Keling family, that of Nina Chatu. In Hurmuz, they established not sovereign rights but a protectorate, permitting the Shah to remain in place, even though they gradually encroached on his revenue-base. Again in Goa, the crucial post of *tanadar-mór* was held for over two and a half decades by a certain Krishna Rao, who in the years 1520-23 visited Portugal, and managed to secure for himself the posts of *shahbandar, corretor dos cavalos*, and captain of the 'native infantry'. The charter of 1526 in Goa, put together by Afonso Mexia, was more an attempt to record existing rights than to redefine them; the same holds for the *província do norte*, where the *iqtadars* (prebend–holders) of the Gujarat Sultanate were not displaced in the initial phase after the Portuguese takeover. Much of this began to change however in the next phase, and particularly from the late 1540s.

TOWARDS THE 'CRISIS'

Unlike the earlier decades, the 1530s is a difficult period to characterise in the history of Portuguese Asia. This is partly because it is a period in which the logic defined in an earlier period seeks to work itself out: consolidation, rather than departure from the earlier trend, seems to be the rule. But it is also a period in which much is occurring at the fringes of the consciousness of Portuguese in Asia, processes that eventually impinged on their Asian enterprise in a major way. We can broadly sum these up under three heads.

First, the 1530s mark the creation in Brazil of the donatory-captaincy – /. system, due to which the colonisation of the Brazilian interior truly gets under way; the man initially given charge of this, Martim Afonso de Sousa, was later to be governor of Portuguese Asia in the 1540s. Brazil as a competitor of Asia for resources, both human and financial, was thus on the verge of coming to life.

Second, the Ottoman ruler Suleyman (r. 1520–66), whose expansionary 2 focus had mainly been to the west in the 1520s – with the revolt in Egypt of Arnavut Ahmet Pasha (1523–25), and the Hungarian campaigns (1526–29) – turned his attention in the 1530s and 1540s to the southern 'underbelly' of his domain. The first major Ottoman fleet, constructed at Suez, had been ready from the early 1530s, but it was only after the Ottoman conquest of Basra that the fleet was sent out, under the command of Hadim Suleyman Pasha. The expedition had mixed results, helping to consolidate Ottoman control over the Red Sea littoral, but being unsuccessful in its attack on the Portuguese stronghold of Diu *Diu* (fortified in 1535). But this expedition was only a portent of things to come in the next phase.

Third, the 1530s saw the gradual emergence in the Bay of Bengal of a 3. new complex of trade and political power. As the Husain Shahi Sultanate in Bengal – to which the Brito-Pereira embassy had been sent in 1521 – declined in the early 1530s, two processes became visible. On the one hand, the 1530s witnessed the emergence of two aggressively mercantilist states, Arakan in northern Burma, under Minbin (r. 1531–53), with his capital at the city of Mrauk-u, and the Taung-ngu (or Toungoo) empire in lower Burma under Tabin-shwei-hti (r. 1531–50) (Collis and Bu 1925; Lieberman 1984). Trade on the Burmese coast, which had earlier proceeded in fits and starts, became relatively stable, and the ports of Cosmin (in the western Irrawaddy delta) and Martaban (at the mouth of the Salween river) vie with Mrauk-u in the trade to Coromandel. At the same time, Bengal and Burma become the favoured hunting-ground of larger and larger numbers of Portuguese, perhaps several hundred by 1540. Engaged in petty coastal trade, and mercenary activities, these men carried the spirit of Martim de Lucena and Rafael Perestrelo to its logical conclusion.

CHAPTER FOUR
The Mid-Sixteenth-Century 'Crisis'

where?

By the late 1530s, and especially at the end of the prolonged governorship of Nuno da Cunha (1529–38) at Goa, the Portuguese Asian enterprise appears to have exhausted the energy provided by the dialectical interaction between what we have called, as a shorthand, the Albuquerque and Albergaria tendencies. João de Barros himself seems implicitly to have recognised this: in closing his *Década Quarta*, he writes at some length of Nuno da Cunha, and after describing him as something of a ladies' man (*inclinado a mulheres*), also notes:

> He had many rivals here in Portugal, more from envy for they believed him to be very rich than because he had done deeds in order to become so, and who did him much damage in the King's eyes, on account of the high esteem in which they [the rivals] were held by him [the King].

And, significantly, he went on:

> And [God] permitted that after his lifetime, the affairs of India should fall into such a state, that the ten years that he governed were always remembered, and even the enemies he had when alive had to praise his person, and works, after his death. (Barros 1973, iv/2: 750–51)

The implication is clear: the end of Cunha's governorship, and the phase inaugurated by D. Garcia de Noronha, mark the beginning even in Barros's eyes of a sort of crisis, which the chronicler in the manner typical of his age relates to God's vengeance on envious humans. From our perspective, we may appreciate Barros's view of the poor state of the 'affairs of India' without necessarily subscribing to his conception of historical causation, particularly because the former is echoed by any number of otherwise quite divergent contemporary observers, and testified to by abundant materials on the Portuguese Asian economy. The letters of the *vedor da fazenda* (financial superintendent) Simão Botelho to the King, dating from the period 1547 to 1552, as well as his *Tombo do Estado da Índia* finished in October 1554, are informed by this sense of financial

80

crisis, and equally urgently by the need for reform. However, we must note that the writings of this period differ substantially from a later genre of literature, that on 'decline' (or *decadência*), adumbrated by men like Diogo do Couto (1543–1616) at some length. The latter, which we shall discuss in later chapters, is informed by a sense of 'paradise lost', the former by an accumulation of problems of an *immediate* nature, which are weighing down on Portuguese Asia. To understand the nature of the 'crisis' that men like Barros and Botelho saw, let us begin with the situation in Portugal, and then move on to consider, step by step, the anatomy of the Asian situation.

THE DILEMMAS OF JOANINE POLICY

The long reign of D. João III (r. 1521–57) is surely one of the most complex in early modern Portuguese history, marked by twists and turns that defy simple characterisation. J. S. da Silva Dias, who has written extensively on the cultural history of this reign, appears to argue that the first half of the Joanine period – that is up to the late 1530s – was marked by one set of tendencies, and the latter half by another, which were further accentuated during the 1560s, when D. João III's Spanish wife was regent during the minority of her grandson, D. Sebastião (Dias 1969).

The characteristics of the first half of the reign are seen to be the desire to 'Europeanise' Portugal, and to promote a form of Renaissance humanism in intellectual life. In keeping with these intentions, D. João had his courtier Damião de Góis invite men like Erasmus to Portugal; other noted Portuguese literary humanists like Luís Teixeira and Aires Barbosa also flourished in the court in the first half of the reign. Furthermore, social change was promoted with the rapid growth of literacy, which meant however that D. João in the phase up to 1540 had to face the opposition of a substantial part of the nobility, who opposed the spread of access to written materials. In fact, Vasco da Pina actually wrote the King a letter in 1532, addressing the question, in which he declared: 'I have heard it said that the Bishop of Guarda has been saying that the worst thing a man of evil inclinations could be was well-read, and that letters combined with evil zeal were a plague on the people'. Contrariwise, the poet Francisco de Sá de Miranda wrote at much the same time:

They say of our dear forbears,
that they unlettered spent their days.
They were good, and never felt fear,
but ignorance I cannot praise,
though others may hold it dear.

81

> I fondly praise their customs,
> and regret their loss today.
> But from letters or from perfumes,
> whence comes the damage, pray?[1]

Eventually, in the second half of D. João's reign, conservative opinion on this question did come to dominate. This was reflected at various levels of social policy, and can in part be attributed to growing Spanish influence on the ruler. Liberal historians of the nineteenth century like Alexandre Herculano, who were torn between the desire to portray D. João III as a monster and the belief that he was actually an imbecile, argued that he was at best weak and indecisive, and increasingly manipulated in the latter half of his reign by his secretaries, all of whom belonged to the Carneiro family. But this interpretation, in which much blame is laid in particular at the door of Pero de Alcáçova Carneiro, has been modified in more recent times.

The picture that emerges is a more nuanced one: D. João was, it appears, overshadowed in the early part of his reign by the policies of his father, the momentum of many of which determined the Portuguese state's attitudes to overseas and internal problems until at least ten years into D. João's reign. However, the political relationship between father and son was also partly a hostile one; the latter did not share the Messianic zeal of the former, and as a consequence many of those at the Portuguese court who were opposed to D. Manuel's plans in respect of Jerusalem had formed a faction in the late 1510s around the heir-apparent. In this context, D. Manuel's decision in 1518 to marry Dona Leonor of Austria, sister of Charles V, who had been unofficially affianced to the heir-apparent, can only be interpreted as a profoundly aggressive political act within the family. D. João was humiliated, and many of the *fidalgos* who were his partisans are reported by Damião de Góis to have 'taken the affair badly' (Serrão 1980). The transition of 1521 was thus a sour one.

Still, at most levels, the real changes came only several years into the reign. True, the Jerusalem enterprise was immediately abandoned, but other policy shifts – whether in Brazil, Asia or even Portugal – can be traced at the very earliest to the 1530s. And even here, the development was not linear. Consider what is arguably the most important change in social policy inside Portugal – namely the institution of the Portuguese Inquisition. It is this act, more than anything else, that caused men like Herculano to see D. João as a disaster in the history of Portugal. But even here, we see a minor paradox, for the Inquisition is instituted in Portugal after a period that most historians see as one of humanistic cosmo-

---

1. Cited in Dias (1969), ii: Ch. 9. The original verse runs: Dizem dos nossos passados/ que os mais não sabião ler;/ eram bons, eram ousados./ Eu não louvo o não saber,/ como alguns as graças dados;/ louvo muito os seus costumes,/ doi-me hoje não são tais;/ mas, de letras ou perfumes,/ donde vem o dano mais.

politanism, namely the 1530s. While the Portuguese Inquisition was officially set up as early as 1531 by a Papal Bull, it remained a dead letter; a later Bull, *Cum ad nil magis* of 1536 was also rejected by the Portuguese state, leading to protracted diplomatic wranglings. The contrast with the flourishing condition of the Holy Office in neighbouring Spain could not have been more marked than in this period.

But by the end of the 1530s, the mood shifted. Censorship began in the early 1540s, and by 1547 – when the third Papal Bull *Meditatio cordis* was issued – as many as one hundred and eighty texts had already been banned in Portugal. In the years 1537–48, six tribunals of the Inquisition operated – at Tomar, Oporto, Lamego, Lisbon, Coimbra and Évora; after 1548, though the number was reduced to two (Lisbon and Évora), the intensity of scrutiny increased apace (Amiel 1986). In 1560, the Inquisition was exported to the overseas territories, with Goa acquiring a tribunal in that year. The Renaissance humanism of the first half of the reign thus gave way to the spirit of Counter-Reformation in an astonishingly rapid reversal.

Now the adoption of the Inquisition itself signals the growing subordination of the Portuguese court to currents from Habsburg Spain. Spain had instituted its own *Santo Oficio* as early as 1478, and the three-tiered organisational structure in use there was adopted by the Portuguese as well. In some respects, the pupils proved more adept than the masters; by 1551, the list of banned books in Portugal included four hundred and eighty-seven titles, and in 1559, the Spaniards and the Romans actually used the Portuguese list as a model for their own! But in many other respects, the actual measures taken by the Portuguese Inquisition were weaker than those followed in Spain; of 31,000 persons who appeared in over 760 *autos-da-fé* between 1536 and 1794, only six per cent were actually sentenced to death, and a mere four per cent (or five per year on average) executed (Amiel 1986). Thus, what is remarkable about the Portuguese Inquisition (like the earlier measures against minority communities in 1496) is not so much the *low level of* severity in comparison with Spain, but the reversal in direction that was implied in the Portuguese case.

Spanish influence can also be discerned in another important institution 'exported' to Portugal in D. João III's reign as part of the growing spirit of Counter-Reformation – namely the Society of Jesus. Founded by Ignatius Loyola (1491–1556), a Basque of the lower nobility, educated at Alacala and Paris, the Society was officially inaugurated by the Papal Bull *Regimini Militantis Ecclesiae* in September 1540; and possibly owing to its founder's early training as a soldier, it was organised in a quasi-military fashion, with Loyola himself being styled the first General of the Order. Its purposes were three in number: (a) to battle against the Protestant Reformation in Europe, (b) to promote the Catholic education of the aristocracy in its colleges, and (c) to recover in Asia, Brazil and Africa the ground that Catholicism had lost in Europe. The Society and its brand of militant Christianity soon had a substantial influence on both Portugal and her overseas empire; in the 1540s, Francis Xavier, a Navarrene, played a particularly prominent role in spreading the Jesuit message across maritime Asia. In Portugal itself, D. João III's brother, the influential Infante D. Luís, became a strong supporter of the Society, and correspondent of one of its Generals, Francisco de Borja. In 1551, the Infante openly declared himself to be an opponent of the Portuguese Renaissance and all that it stood for. Thus, the Jesuit influence also had a significant role to play in the reversals of social policy in the Joanine reign (Dias 1969, ii: Ch. 9).

Despite popular identification of the Jesuits with the Inquisition, we must note that the two institutions often represented radically different positions – albeit within the broad stream of the Counter-Reformation. Late eighteenth-century claims that every perversion of the Holy Office that had taken place was due to the Jesuits are surely vastly exaggerated, for the Inquisition seems to have been influenced and managed not by the Jesuits but by their rivals, the Dominicans. In particular, the Jesuits of the sixteenth century were far more tolerant of Jewish converts to Christianity than was the Inquisition itself. The Spanish cult of *limpieza de sangre* (purity of blood) was actively repudiated by Loyola himself, as well as by his successors, one of whom called it 'el humor o error nacional' ('the national humour or error') (Kamen 1985: 124–26). Only for a brief period from 1593 to 1608 did the Jesuits agree to deny converts from Judaism access to their Order, and that too under intense external pressure. But after 1608, there was effectively a return to the line espoused by Loyola and his immediate successors on the question.

The Jesuits and the Inquisition are two of the most conspicuous symbols of change in social policy in the middle decades of the sixteenth century. But there were also problems other than ones caused by religious heterodoxy or the Reformation, or even the suspicion that the New Christians were in danger of lapsing into their erstwhile practices. Thus, from the court's point of view, where did the central problems indeed lie? V.M. Godinho, whose work has been crucial in identifying the fluctuations in the economy of the Portuguese overseas empire, has suggested that crises were a cyclical feature of the economic system. He goes on to identify minor crises in 1521–24 and 1531–35, as well as 1545–52, but – significantly from our point of view – concludes, 'The crisis of 1545–52 attained a different dimension of perturbation, and its area too is incomparably greater to that of the earlier crises.' He terms it a 'structural break' (*viragem estrutural*), which is marked by three features: first, the recovery of the Levant route and the pepper and spice trade of Venice; second, the beginnings of stagnation in the Portuguese Asian economy; and third, the period when monarchic capitalism (and its allies

– the middle bourgeoisie) give way to a new set-up, dominated by powerful trans-national banker-merchants, allied to the Portuguese nobility (Godinho 1968: 177–205).

What are the symptoms of this crisis? First, let us consider the trade to Flanders, which is to say Antwerp. The annual average of Portuguese ships there falls from 22.5 in the years 1536–44 to 14 (or even less) in the period 1545–50. Moreover, in 1548, the Portuguese monarch decided to close down the Antwerp factory, and give the trade there over to private parties, a decision that was implemented in July 1549. Still, ships from Portugal continued to trade in the port, albeit in smaller numbers than before.

Table 4.1 Ships from Portugal at Antwerp, 1536–50

Year	Number	Year	Number
1536	24	1544	29
1537	32	1545	10
1538	14	1546	10
1539	22	1547	16
1540	20	1548	21
1541	14	1549	10
1542	23	1550	13
1543	28		

(*Source*: Godinho 1968: 190–91)

The contraction of these middle years is also visible at another level, namely the decline in the shipping on the Cape route in the 1540s, 1550s and even the 1560s, especially in terms of departures from Lisbon but also in return tonnage from Asia. A gradual recovery begins in the 1570s, but by that time the economic situation too had changed. D. João III himself expressed some concern over the state of affairs on the *Carreira da Índia* in letters written by him to his close associate, the *vedor da fazenda*, D. António de Ataíde, Count of Castanheira. The bind was a double one: if too little pepper and spices were to come in from Asia, the Crown's revenues would suffer, but – contrariwise – if too much were to come in, not enough buyers would be forthcoming. With the cloth trade between London and Lisbon, as well as the trade to Antwerp, in decline in these years, the trading community at Lisbon, whether Portuguese or foreign, was strapped for liquidity; the logical consequence was a cutback in the tonnage of ships sent out to Asia, by ten to fifteen per cent in the decades under consideration.

The other dimension of the crisis lay elsewhere, in North Africa. In D. Manuel's reign, as part of expansion in this direction, new fortified settlements had been created at Agadir (1504), Safi (1508), and Azemmour

(1513), the purposes of which seem to have been manifold. One of these was to deny the rulers of Morocco access to the seaboard and the sugar export trade of Agadir and Azemmour. But equally, North Africa was seen by D. Manuel as one of the prongs of his proposed attack on Jerusalem, in pursuit of which he tried and failed to take Mers el-Kebir in 1501. And finally, it was also the intention to use the wheat production of the region to supply the Portuguese settlements on the Guinea coast.

Table 4.2 Shipping tonnage on the Carreira da Índia, 1531–80

| Years | Lisbon-Asia | | Asia-Lisbon | |
	Departures	Arrivals	Departures	Arrivals
1531–40	44,660 (80)	42,610 (76)	39,110 (61)	36,410 (57)
1541–50	40,800 (68)	34,100 (56)	34,550 (58)	30,550 (52)
1551–60	39,600 (58)	32,500 (46)	33,650 (47)	25,750 (35)
1561–70	37,030 (50)	35,580 (46)	36,250 (45)	32,150 (40)
1571–80	42,900 (50)	40,800 (48)	38,250 (42)	35,150 (39)

(Figures in brackets are numbers of ships)

(*Source*: Duncan 1986: 22)

Now, at this time, the principal opponents of the Portuguese in the area were the Wattasids, whose region of control lay largely in and around Fez. Faced with this pressure from the north, the Wattasid ruler Muhammad al-Burtughali (r. 1505–24) was unable to consolidate his control over the south, from which a new challenge arose to his dynasty. The challenge, centering around the popular mysticism of the *murabitin* (or marabouts), was fired by the spirit of Holy War (*jihad*), and found the climate in southern Morocco particularly salubrious for its growth. The Banu Sa'd clan, claiming descent from the Prophet Muhammad, managed to weld together an alliance of the southern tribes, and aided by the revenues of the trans-Saharan gold trade from Sudan, first exerted control over the Sus region, and then the whole of the southern fringe of the High Atlas. In 1536, the Sa'dis fought a successful campaign against the Wattasid ruler Abu'l Abbas Ahmad (r. 1524–49), and took much of central Morocco; by the late 1530s, they posed a serious threat to Portuguese possessions like Agadir, Arzila, Azemmour, Safi and al-Qasr al-Saghir (Mantran 1970).

The strategy adopted by the first Sa'di ruler, Muhammad al-Mahdi, was a complex one. Notionally, he faced four opponents: the Ottoman Turks at Tlemcen, the Spaniards established in their north African outposts in Algeria such as Oran and Mers el-Kebir, the Wattasids, and the Portuguese. Not wishing to take all of these opponents on, he sought to neutralise the Spaniards through diplomatic relations, and focused his attention on first the Wattasids, then the Portuguese and finally the Ottomans. Here then was the dilemma that the court of D. João III faced in the late 1530s and early 1540s. Three possible fields of activity existed, over which human and financial resources had to be distributed. The first was North Africa, under imminent threat, and prestigious on account both of its proximity and the fact that it was here that overseas expansion had begun in 1415. The second was Asia, an enormous expanse whose returns were essentially commercial, but in which the Portuguese network was nevertheless quite militarised (especially in the western Indian Ocean). And third was the Atlantic network, on the west the great *terra incognita* of Brazil, whose agricultural potentialities were just beginning to be recognised, and on the east the African coast of Angola and Congo, which would supply the slave labour for Brazil. The debate that raged in the court was – quite literally – of which one of these three should be abandoned in order to shore up the other two.

The debate is an interesting and important one, prefiguring later debates of the 1620s and 1640s, in which the choice was rather more simple: Atlantic versus Indian Ocean. In the 1540s, the positions that were articulated in respect of Asia – our primary concern here – are quite startling. One group at the court argued that most of the Portuguese possessions in the western Indian Ocean were both unnecessary and illegitimate, unnecessary because they did not help trade, and illegitimate because they had been acquired by Afonso de Albuquerque without prior royal sanction (Fontoura 1966). One can almost hear the echo of António Real's voice, arguing that besides Cochin 'all else is wind', in these papers. Effectively, these 'free traders' wished to secure the Crown's withdrawal (or at least partial withdrawal) from Asia, in order to leave the trade of that region open to private parties, possibly with royal licence. Certainly, dear military resources were not to be expended on maintaining places such as Goa, Hurmuz, Diu or Melaka; they were far better spent in North Africa, and in the rather more cost-effective operations against Amerindians in Brazil.

But this was not the voice that prevailed. While expansion in Brazil certainly went on apace, North Africa was given step-motherly treatment: the Sa'dis took Agadir in 1541, Safi and Azemmour were hence abandoned hurriedly in 1542, and al-Qasr al-Saghir and Arzila in 1549. Fired by these successes, Muhammad al-Mahdi went on to drive the Wattasid ruler Ba Hassun from Fez in 1549, and entered thereafter into headlong conflict with the Ottomans. It was only in the 1570s that the Portuguese briefly returned to a more activist policy in respect of North Africa, during the reign of D. Sebastião (Serrão 1980: 70–79).

Why did the Portuguese state not have adequate resources to act on all these fronts at the same time? Why did the question of the choice between fronts arise? There are two answers to this question, one obvious and the other less so. At the most obvious level, there was the problem of human resources; Portugal simply did not have the manpower to do so. In the late 1540s, Brazil had some two thousand Portuguese, and Asia something like four times that number. It has been estimated that while in the 1530s, some 21,000 people embarked for Asia from Portugal, only half that number returned. Of the Atlantic islands, the Madeira archipelago had some 17,000 settlers by 1550, and São Tomé around half that number at the close of the sixteenth century. In this context, to sustain the level of manning of the North African *presídios* (or garrisons) at their late fifteenth century level of 25,000 was a hard task. The following letter, written by D. João III to the Count of Castanheira in 1537, suggests clearly that those who wished to leave Portugal for Asia in the period exceeded the number which could be accommodated on board the vessels of the Crown:

> Conde, amiguo. I, the King, send you hearty geeetings as one whom I love. I am informed that there are many people ready to go this year to India; and that some of them have my license to take their women along; and that there are also unmarried women who have my permission to go. ... And as for the women, the first to go should be the married ones, who are going with their husbands, brothers, or relatives who are taking them along. And of the unmarried ones only those who have a good reason and just cause should be allowed to go. (Ford 1931: 314)

The second factor, far less easy to demonstrate, is the financial stringency that the Portuguese Crown, and the monarchic capitalism of which it partook, was in all probability undergoing. Without this the withdrawal of the Flanders factory, the reduction in Crown participation in intra-Asian *carreiras*, and the reduction in shipping tonnage on the Cape route, all are difficult to comprehend. To be sure, we must also bear in mind that little by little, under the influence of the Spanish court of Charles V, the Portuguese monarch's inner circle had become nervous of the excessively commercial profile of the House of Avis, and there are the first rumblings in this period of the idea that trade was somehow 'beneath the dignity of the royal estate'. The chronicler and man-of-letters Damião de Góis, for example, wrote to the ruler D. João III congratulating him on withdrawing Crown participation from the trade to Flanders, seeing it as in the fitness of things. But it would be difficult to attribute the gamut of changes that one witnesses in the period – in Flanders, North Africa, Brazil and Asia – to an ideological shift alone. For the shift was slow, and uneven, and had not been completed even in the 1570s. It took direct Spanish rule in Portugal, in the period after 1580, to bring about a decisive shift in the attitude towards royal trade.

SÁS, SOUSAS AND CASTROS: PORTUGUESE ASIAN OFFICIALDOM IN THE CRISIS

The period immediately after Nuno da Cunha, the quinquennium 1538–42, saw two governments in Goa, first the viceroyalty of D. Garcia de Noronha, and then the governorship of D. Estêvão da Gama, the latter one of several members of the tribe of Vasco da Gama to play a prominent role in sixteenth-century Portuguese Asian affairs. The period marks a lull, after the dramatics of the siege of Diu, but it does contain one notable feature. D. Garcia, tired of the recalcitrance of the Portuguese of Coromandel, decided in 1539 to do away with their major settlement there, namely the town of São Tomé or Mylapur. From this we may infer that the governor was one of those who had little patience with private Portuguese enterprise, and the proximate reason for this decision is not far to seek. When asked to assist the anti-Ottoman operations at Diu with their private vessels, the Portuguese of Coromandel and Bengal sent a mere handful of representatives, causing D. João de Castro to conclude that less than a half of the Portuguese in Asia saw such official military operations as any concern of theirs. The reason why Mylapur was chosen as a particular target was that it was the only settlement in the Bay of Bengal which had any legitimacy beyond mercantile self-interest; the legitimacy derived, of course, from the fact that the Apostle St. Thomas's tomb was located there, and the Portuguese settlement built in its vicinity. D. Garcia's representative, Manuel da Gama, was hence instructed to go there with an armada, to dismantle the settlement, and perhaps to bring away the relics of the Apostle (Subrahmanyam 1990b: 52).

It would appear that the governor, like his successor in the early 1560s D. Constantino de Bragança, miscalculated in respect of Coromandel. By the late 1530s, the Coromandel settlements of the Portuguese – Nagapattinam to the south, São Tomé and Pulicat to the north – had men of influence and prestige resident in them, and not merely 'thieves, homicides and deserters', as more than one official at Goa put it at the time. Some of these entrepreneurs, like Miguel Ferreira (1466–1548), were celebrated figures in their own lifetimes, and capable of holding their own in correspondence with Portugal. With friends in the court, and among the powerful and entrenched *casados* of Cochin and Goa, dislodging Ferreira was no easy matter. Thus, Da Gama's expedition failed miserably, and trade between Sri Lanka, Coromandel and Bengal, and Burma and the Malay peninsula ports continued to provide a reasonable return to the Portuguese of the area.

Realism in respect of these trade networks already characterises the governorship of D. Estêvão da Gama, himself a considerable private trader in his own right during the period that he was captain of Melaka. It is taken a step further however during the most controversial of the 1540s governments, that of Martim Afonso de Sousa (1542–45). Martim Afonso's is one of the celebrated families in sixteenth-century Portuguese overseas history, showing how a small set of noble families were able to gain control of a vast set of networks. His brother Pero Lopes de Sousa was later donatory of Itamaraca in Brazil; one of his cousins, Manuel de Sousa, had been first captain of Diu, while still another – Tomé de Sousa – was made the first governor of Brazil in 1549. Martim Afonso himself was a characteristic representative of the northern Portuguese middle nobility; his father Lopo de Sousa was *alcaide-mór* of Bragança in the far north-west of Portugal, and Martim Afonso's early career was spent as page to the heir- apparent, the future D. João III. It emerges from the latter part of his career that Sousa was identified with the Spanish party in the Portuguese court, and especially with the Queen D. Catarina, and this enabled him after his return to Portugal to play a leading role in decision-making in the 1560s. The fact that he was married to a Castilian woman, and his rather mysterious exile to Salamanca in the late 1510s, may explain some of this, for – as we have noted on earlier occasions – while an orientation towards Castile was a not unnatural trait among the *upper* nobility, Martim Afonso can be thought to belong more properly to the service nobility (Couto 1973–74, v: 456–58).

It is a remarkable fact that, with the sole exception of the chronicler Diogo do Couto, all sources speak disparagingly of Martim Afonso de Sousa's Indian sojourn. The most trenchant of these criticisms is in an anonymous report sent to the Portuguese monarch in 1544, called 'True information on Indian affairs' (Gavetas, iii: 199–234). The anonymous critic leaves no stone unturned in attacking the governor (then still in office), and at least some of the details he provides are also to be found in other sources – such as the chronicle of Gaspar Correia. The fundamental criticism appears to be that the governor took factional and familial favouritism to a new height, filling the major posts with 'Sás and Sousas', his own clan and its relatives.

It is claimed that he, together with his nephew, Garcia de Sá (later also governor at Goa), traded extensively in spices, lac and pepper, very probably within the Bay of Bengal and Southeast Asia. Of sixteen *carreira* voyages granted by him, using his discretionary powers, four were to Bengal (probably Chittagong), six to China and one to Pegu, besides one to the Moluccas. The grantees too are often men with names like Francisco de Sá, António de Sá, and Belchior de Sousa; great powers were also given to another of the governor's relatives, Aleixos de Sousa Chichorro.

We thus have an inversion of the policy under D. Garcia de Noronha and D. Estêvão da Gama (the latter being the commander of a celebrated expedition into the Red Sea in 1541, which carried out a raid on Suez); in Martim Afonso's time, we see the governor and his clansmen turning away from the traditional focus of government – namely the western Indian Ocean – and instead looking eastward. This concern with Southeast Asia is most clearly expressed in two ways. First, Crown vessels were deployed in great measure in these areas, unlike what we have seen, say, for 1525. Second, it is in this period that an elaborate, and eventually unsuccessful, expedition was sent out under Jerónimo de Figueiredo to discover the 'Island of Gold' (*Ilha do Ouro*), rumoured to exist near Sumatra. This expedition followed earlier ones to this island (termed *Pulo Mas* by the Malays) in 1519 and 1521, but was certainly far more elaborate than either of its precursors.

Given the new orientation in this period, it is not surprising perhaps that the structure of alliances in India too changes. We have seen that in the earlier period, the primary contradiction on Malabar had been between the Portuguese state and the Middle Eastern Muslim traders (the *mouros de Meca* or *mouros da Arábia*, to the Portuguese). On the other hand, relations with the Mappilas – the local Muslim converts of the Malabar coast – remained peaceful in the first phase, and early Portuguese cargoes of Southeast Asian spices were in fact obtained through the big Mappila traders of Cochin. There were two foci of Mappila settlement in Malabar, one to the north – near Cannanore – the other farther south in ports like Ponnani, closer to Calicut (Bouchon 1973).

The first rupture between the Portuguese and the Mappilas occurred in respect of the Cannanore group, whose influence extended far afield, into the Maldives and Laccadives. Its reasons are not far to seek, for the Maldives in particular were an important intermediate point between Southeast Asia and the Red Sea; a fair proportion of the prizes taken by the Portuguese in the first decade and a half of their presence in the Indian Ocean was hence in this region. But the conflicts between the Portuguese state and Mammali, the leader of the Cannanore Mappilas, were far tamer than the hostilities that erupted later (Bouchon 1988). These difficulties have a good deal to do with the formation in Cochin of a nucleus of substantial Portuguese *casado* traders, who became interested in the coastal trade to Sri Lanka and to Coromandel (via the Gulf of Mannar), both largely in the hands of the Mappilas and their allies, the Tamil-speaking Maraikkayar Muslims of the Pearl Fishery Coast, lying between Cape Comorin and Rameswaram.

In the 1520s, and especially after 1524, a bloody and disruptive series of conflicts broke out between the Portuguese state (here acting as a front for *casado* interests) and the Mappilas, ranging across ports like Vedalai, Kayalpattinam, Kayamkulam, and Calicut, and extending down the west coast of Sri Lanka. At stake was, on the one hand, the trade in Sri Lankan cinnamon, and on the other hand, the low-value, high-volume trade in foodstuffs that passed through the Gulf of Mannar. The Portuguese won the battle in the 1530s (Flores 1990). This was done by three means, military, diplomatic and ecclesiastical. A series of naval engagements, culminating in the defeat in 1538 of the Mappila leaders, Ibrahim and Pate Marikkar, at Vedalai, and the killing in Sri Lanka of a third notable, was thus one factor that forced the Mappila representative Chinna Kutti Ali to sue for peace with Goa in 1540. The diplomatic negotiations between the Portuguese and the Samudri raja of Calicut, which had the effect of driving a wedge between the ruler and the Mappilas, also had their role to play.

But the third factor, equally crucial, was the mass conversion in 1532 of a low status community of the Pearl Fishery Coast, the Paravas. Negotiated between the head of this community, the *jati talaivan* who adopted the name D. João da Cruz, and Miguel Vaz, the Bishop of Cochin, the Parava conversion was the first major success that the Portuguese ecclesiastical mission enjoyed in Asia. But little credit for it can be given to the Church, which was effectively handed the opportunity on a platter. The logic of conversion was blatantly political: the maritime wars of the 1520s and early 1530s had made both pearl-fishing and even sea-fishing a hazardous occupation, and the Parava leaders were seeking a solution to this by allying themselves to the principal perpetrators of violence – the Portuguese. Implicitly, this constitutes a recognition by the Paravas that their interests could not be protected by the Maraikkayar-Mappila alliance, and also possibly stems from a pre-existent economic rivalry between the Maraikkayars (who, from the twelfth century, had controlled the lucrative pearl-fishery, as well as local tax-farms) and the notables of the Parava community (the so-called *pattankattis*) (Flores 1990).

But conflict resumed again in the 1540s, in the governorship of Martim Afonso de Sousa, in a manner that suggests that the governor was spoiling for a fight. Arriving in India in May 1542, he unceremoniously got rid of his predecessor D. Estêvão da Gama (in one version 'ejecting him from his bed, without even allowing him time to put on his shirt'), and immediately launched an expedition against the Kanara port of Bhatkal, south of Goa, apparently as an anti-Mappila measure. This raid, described at some length in the chronicles of Correia and Couto, was followed by a rather more mysterious expedition the next year (1543), involving some three thousand men, in which Martim Afonso apparently intended to launch a pillaging raid (rather in the style of the early Spanish *conquistadores* in the New World) against one of the major temple-complexes of south-eastern India. Warned off from this venture by Miguel Ferreira and others, he contented himself by a raid on the Tevelakkara temple in southern Kerala, taking – in the words of the author of the 'True Information' – 'much money and some jewels' therefrom.

About this time, the governor also entered into a complex set of negotiations with one of the leading Middle Eastern traders resident on the Indian south-west coast, the Iranian Khwaja Shams-ud-din Gilani of Cannanore (Albuquerque and Guerreiro 1985). These involved the grant to the Persian of a set of licences for trade to the Red Sea and elsewhere, in return for cooperation in Martim Afonso's private trade. Shams-ud-din thus emerged as a privileged trader to Jiddah, in an inversion of previous policy. Indeed, it is claimed that in Martim Afonso's regime, a great deal of trade on this route was permitted from the Malabar ports; the author of the 'True Information' lists thirteen ships departing Kanara and Malabar for the Red Sea in one year alone, including one each from Bhatkal and Mangalore. The reversal was thus two-fold: on the one hand, the trade of Middle Eastern Muslims was permitted, but on the other, the governor and his associates came down hard on the Mappilas. A crucial incident is the assassination of the *qadi* of Cannanore Abu Bakr Ali by Belchior de Sousa Chichorro, a half-brother of the *vedor da fazenda* Aleixos de Sousa, and a distant relative of the governor himself. Taken together with the heightened competition in this period between the Mappilas and the Portuguese *casado* traders of Cochin for the trade to Bengal – and especially Chittagong – this act had the effect of negating the peace that had been made with Chinna Kutti Ali. The initiative was now taken by the head of the Mappilas of Cannanore, who designated themselves the Ali Rajas; they forced the Samudri of Calicut to turn against the Portuguese once again.

These acts on the part of Martim Afonso, Belchior de Sousa, and others cannot be seen merely as a set of unrelated incidents. They suggest that two sets of factors were at work. First, by this period, the influence of the so-called *casados*, in the settlements of Goa and Cochin, was a major factor to which each governor had to accommodate himself, and policy had to be fashioned accordingly. Second, there is a very real suggestion in the desperation of Martim Afonso's period of a resource crunch; why else undertake such an improbable venture as a three-thousand-man expedition to raid a distant temple treasury? We note too that it is in this period that the Portuguese state takes the significant measure of assuming total control of the Hurmuz customs-house, even at the risk of alienating that ruler. Earlier, Hurmuz had functioned under the *páreas* system, paying 15,000 and later 25,000 *xerafins* a year to the Portuguese. In 1523, after quelling a revolt, the Portuguese governor raised the amount to 60,000 *xerafins*, and then in 1529 to 100,000 (Godinho 1982: 44–47). This last amount was an absurd demand, one that the ruler could not possibly meet, and so his debts to the Portuguese Crown steadily mounted, exceeding 500,000 *xerafins* in 1542. In fact, the revenues of Hurmuz by the 1540s, taking the information of Simão Botelho together with that of Bastião Lopes Lobato, who had served as factor there, were as shown in Table 4.3

Table 4.3 Customs-revenues of Hurmuz in the 1540s

(a) 'Normal' revenues:	
Source	Amount (in gold xerafins = 300 reis)
Trade from Gujarat	35,000 – 45,000
Trade from Persia	35,000 – 40,000
Trade to and from Basra	9,000 – 10,000
Trade from Sind	8,000 – 9,000
Duties paid by Portuguese	10,000 – 13,000
TOTAL	97,000 – 117,000

(b) Actual revenues:			
Year	Amount	Year	Amount
1540	93,512	1545	70,280
1541	111,779	1546	79,881
1542	87,882	1547	62,269
1543	108,930	1548	61,646
1544	93,603	1549	90,782
		1550	135,000

(Sources: Godinho 1982: 47–48; Calado 1960: 128–30)

Two things stand out from these figures. First, Portuguese private traders now accounted for over a tenth of trade at this important port, suggesting that they had become a significant force. Second, the years 1545–49 represent a low-water mark in Hurmuz's trade, a downturn possibly related to Godinho's hypothesis of a general contraction in global trade in this period (Godinho 1968). Some factors which influenced this contraction in the Hurmuz case were undoubtedly local – such as the Ottoman expedition against Gujarat in 1546. But other factors, such as the general prevalence of famine conditions in the early 1540s over a rather large territory extending from the Red Sea littoral to the Deccan and southern India did not pass unremarked by contemporary observers, and may have had a belated effect on trade flows. According to the chronicler Gaspar Correia, in these years 'there was so much hunger on Choromandel that almost the entire land was depopulated on account of the mortality of people. ... In the same year, there was such a lack of food in the ports of the Straits [Bab-el-Mandeb] that in Aden one bale of rice was worth forty xerafins' (Correia 1975, iv: 131–32).

The financial crisis that Martim Afonso faced was thus embedded in a larger economic downturn, reflected not only in Hurmuz customs-revenues but those of Melaka (Table 4.4).

If the period from the early 1550s witnessed a growth in customs-revenues in Melaka, which continued into the early 1570s, the middle and late 1540s represent a downturn, not dissimilar to that which we have observed in the case of Hurmuz.

Table 4.4 Melaka customs-collections in the 1540s

Year	Amount (in cruzados = 360 reis)
1542	27,530
1543	26,250
1544	23,600
1545–54 (ave.)	13,500
1550	12,000
1555	50,000
1568	60,000

(*Sources:* Godinho 1982: 115; Thomaz 1979)

This downturn, which had begun in the government of Martim Afonso de Sousa, continued into the best documented of the mid-sixteenth Portuguese Asian governments, that of D. João de Castro (extending from September 1545 to June 1548). The transition from Martim Afonso to Castro is a dramatic one, reminiscent in certain ways of that between Albuquerque and Albergaria, save that it was in the reverse direction. While Martim Afonso, we have seen, was an entrepreneur and oriented towards the Bay of Bengal, Southeast Asia and China, the focus in D. João de Castro's three-year government returns squarely to the western Indian Ocean. As the successful defender of Diu against the forces of Khwaja Safar-us-Salmani, an Italian renegade who controlled the port of Surat under the Gujarat Sultans, Castro occupies a prominent place amongst the pantheon of heroes of Portuguese nationalist historiography; when added to his talents as a navigator, astronomer and amateur scientific observer, they make him a veritable 'Renaissance man' to many Portuguese historians – perhaps the last gasp of the aborted Renaissance.

At a more mundane level, his government represents a vain attempt to return to a more centralised conception of empire, in the face of forces that were headed in quite another direction. To take a conspicuous example, Castro revived the idea first put forward under Albuquerque of having a standing army organised in the 'Swiss style' (*à suiça*), and which later viceroys like D. Luís de Ataíde had occasion to bring up once more in the following decades. Characteristically, Castro in the 1540s failed in his attempt at military reform, and this suggests that in order to function, therefore, the viceroy could not make a true break away from the policies of Martim Afonso de Sousa. Indeed, on many crucial matters, he wound up compromising. The compromise is most obvious in his choice of *vedor da fazenda* to succeed Brás de Araújo, who died in early 1547. To this post he appointed Rui Gonçalves de Caminha, native of Oporto, perhaps the most celebrated *casado* operator of his generation on the west coast of India, and a man of whom Castro himself wrote (in a letter to the King around this time):

> As soon as I knew of the death of Brás de Araújo, I spent many days wondering whom I could place in his post, and after running them all through my mind, I decided to give it to Rui Gonçalves de Caminha. The qualities that Rui Gonçalves has are these, to wit: he is very rich, extremely independent, and a great businessman (*homem de negócio*), commands great credit in the whole land, is zealous in fleecing *vedores* and *almoxarifes*, a great collector on behalf of Your Highness's treasury, and most tight-fisted in spending. (Felner 1868: xviii–xix)

He went on to confess though that his true motive was different; since Caminha was a great 'friend and counsellor' of Khwaja Shams-ud-din Gilani, he wished him to intervene in order to lay his hands on a large sum of money left with the Iranian by a Deccani noble, Asad Khan (possibly to be remitted to his heirs in the Middle East). Castro wished to use these funds to tide over the public treasury, once more a sure sign of financial crisis. The alliance with Caminha was thus a marriage of convenience stemming from reasons of state, but it is nevertheless significant. According to Simão Botelho, on account of Castro's protection, Caminha could get away with substantial frauds and misdemeanours; his familial connections in Portugal with at least one treasurer of the *fazenda real* may also have helped (Felner 1868, ii: 2).

Thus, in dealing with men like Caminha or Miguel Ferreira (the Coromandel-based military entrepreneur mentioned above), D. João de Castro had to turn a blind eye to the potentially destabilising effects of their private trade and personal power. Ferreira was used by Castro to bring together men and resources from Coromandel as part of the Diu campaign of 1546; the fact that he himself only followed Goa's orders to a limited extent was ignored. The reasons for such alliances are not far to seek, for Castro's main purpose was to break the hold of the 'Sás and Sousas', who opposed his policies quite consistently. In September 1545, Castro ordered a week-long public enquiry into Martim Afonso de Sousa's government, and followed it up with an investigation of his fiscal practices, and those of his *vedor da fazenda*, Aleixos de Sousa Chichorro. Thereafter, one who particularly bore the brunt of his wrath was Aleixos's half-brother, Henrique de Sousa Chichorro, captain of Cochin, whom he eventually removed from his post in November 1547 under charges of insubordination and illegal private trade in pepper to Bengal. In 1550, Chichorro was reinstated by Jorge Cabral, then governor at Goa, to serve out the last year of his captaincy (Goertz 1986).

It appears simplistic to see this conflict in terms of the Sousas' wrongdoing and Castro's uprightness, as is often the case in the historiography. Rather, we would be better off noting that D. João de

Castro represented a different interest and ideology than that of his
predecessor: at the personal level, he was less a trading *fidalgo* than Martim
Afonso (despite his close personal relations in Portugal with Luca Giraldi,
the celebrated Italian banker-merchant), and in terms of policy, saw the
primary concern of the state as the Red Sea, the Persian Gulf, Gujarat and
the Indian west coast. Faced with the hard fact that numerous Portuguese
were trading in the Bay of Bengal and Southeast Asia, he was forced to
adapt his ideology pragmatically, seeking to utilise both the *casado* interest
and the Coromandel Portuguese to the greatest extent possible.

THE MID-CENTURY DEBATE

It is of some significance, in view of the tensions delineated above, to
note that the crisis years of the 1540s and 1550s witness a major debate
among the administrators in Portuguese Asia, on the manner in which
commercial affairs and general administration are to be conducted. Those
who participated in the debate included such men as Julião Fernandes,
Jorge Cabral, and, somewhat later, Simão Botelho. What was at issue was,
above all, the question of whether the Crown should continue its
participation in intra-Asian trade, and if so in what form this should be.
Now, in the light of the dispute between the Cochin coterie and men like
Albuquerque in the 1510s, it may seem that not much was new about this
debate. To recapitulate briefly, the contention of the Cochin group was
that the elaborate system of fortresses and state trade that Albuquerque had
instituted was uncalled-for, and that trade within Asia should be made
over to private parties – and above all to the relatively few privileged
families from the service-nobility who had the ear of the Crown. In part,
their advice had been heeded in the Albergaria years, by demarcating a
space east of Cape Comorin that was relatively free of state interference,
though even here the *carreira*-system did find a place.

The *carreira* system had one major drawback: it committed the Crown
to providing merchant shipping within Asia, and given the number of
carreiras that existed by 1540, the number of substantial vessels that were
needed was at least a dozen, perhaps as many as twenty (and this in
addition to the ships of the Cape route and warships). In view of the great
shortage of vessels, several *carreiras* (such as the Bhatkal-Hurmuz route)
were given up in the 1530s, and on other occasions, when ships that had
just returned from one long voyage were immediately sent off on another,
disaster resulted. On the *carreira de Choromandel*, the Goa-Pulicat-
Melaka-Goa route, we are aware of one such case in the 1540s, the
Taforeia commanded by D. Pedro de Meneses, in 1546; another *nau
del-Rei* (royal vessel), commanded by Gonçalo Pacheco de Sousa and

probably en route to Pegu, was lost the same year off Sri Lanka (Subrahmanyam 1990b: 33–34). It is true that such losses could have been treated as part of the vagaries of a normal mercantile venture, but such was not the mood in the mid-1540s. For in this period, the Crown in Portugal, for reasons not wholly unrelated to the debate pitting Asia and Brazil against North Africa, had begun to question its own role. Was it in fact a *commercial* enterprise, a centre of royal mercantilism as envisioned by the ideologues around D. João II and D. Manuel? Or was it a military machine, designed to conquer new lands of the 'Moors', the atavistic enemies inherited from the Middle Ages? Or was it an absolutist monarchy like that of Spain, rooted in revenue-collection whether from the land or from commerce, but above the petty business of trade?

The voices in the debate are many and divergent, and address two major questions. The first concerns the future of the *carreira* voyages in Asia, and the second the issue of commodity monopolies (and more particularly the trade in pepper). Among those consulted were the *fidalgos* of long service in India, many of whom were asked to submit their opinions (*pareceres*) to the viceroy. Let us consider one of these, the 'Opinion of Jorge Cabral concerning the pepper trade and concerning the renting out of the voyages of Coromandel, Pegu etc.' The document, addressed to D. João de Castro, was written in November 1545; the author was himself later governor of Portuguese Asia in 1549–50. In it, Cabral argues against both propositions that were put to him, namely that pepper-trade within Asia be freed of some constraints, and that the *carreira* routes be rented out to the highest bidder. His logic is compelling in parts, dubious at others. He states:

> My Lord. Concerning what Your Lordship asks me, on the subject of what His Highness orders in his instructions (*regimento*) that he be informed of whether it would be to his service to rent out the voyages to Banda, and Melaka and Pegu, in fact it would be more to his service to rent all of them [the voyages] out had there not been many and great inconveniences which compel us not to do so; the first is that His Highness has many *fidalgos*, and servants and men-at-arms in this land to whom he has a great obligation, and who live and serve him solely in the hope that His Highness, or Your Lordship in his name, will grant them some of these voyages; because it is thus that they derive the wherewithal to sustain themselves in order better to be able to serve His Highness, and if the said voyages are rented out, these men will lose all their hope [and] this necessity will make them seek some other mode of living, which could well cause a greater loss to His Highness.
>
> (ANTT, CC, I/77/26)[2]

Cabral's argument here centres on the concept of the state as the giver of benefices, whose ties to its subjects are crucially dependent on being able to make such grants. It is a powerful argument, particularly in a

---

2 The document is titled 'Parecer de Jorge Cabral sobre o comércio da pimenta, e sobre o arrendamento das viagens de Coromandel, Pegu etc.', and is dated 22nd November 1545.

situation when the governor Castro himself conceded that over a half of the Portuguese in Asia refused to obey his mobilisation orders for the Diu campaign; the implicit threat is of seeking 'some other mode of living' as mercenaries, renegades or freelance private traders (*chatins* in the terminology then current).

The second leg to Cabral's argument is equally significant. How would the rentiers (*rendeiros*) behave, he asks, and concludes that 'they would leave no place for anyone else to go to the said places', seeking monopoly rights of a sort that *carreira* trade had not implied. He goes on that

> it does not seem to me to be to His Highness's service to rent them out, because on renting them out His Highness will lose a great deal in his customs-houses both in Melaka and in Goa, because the rentiers cannot load on board all the goods from the land, and for their own profit will have to ban other merchants from trading there. *Needs explaining*

On the pepper trade question, though, Cabral is less convincing. He argues that sending pepper from Malabar to China, Melaka and Bengal causes a significant rise in the price of pepper to be sent to Portugal, where this commodity finds its 'just value'. This is unconvincing for one obvious reason: with Portuguese pepper cargoes to Europe seldom exceeding 30,000 *quintais* in the mid-sixteenth century, it is difficult to believe that more than one-eighth or one-tenth of total Asian production (in Malabar, Kanara and Southeast Asia) made its way there. The real issue was therefore not one of whether pepper should be exported to China and Bengal, but of who should export it. This point is well made by the author of one of the other *pareceres*, Julião Fernandes, who points out that if the Portuguese do not supply Bengal, pepper will arrive there anyway from the Sunda region of western Java (ANTT, CC, I/76/8).

Simão Botelho, writing seven years later in 1552, takes a rather different tack from Cabral. His argument is that the *carreira* voyages have become completely unprofitable because of the system of *forros*, or grants of cargo-space as benefices. He writes: *carreira cargo space granted to private hands*

> Last year, there arrived two ships from Maluku of His Highness, and one brought ten *bares* of cloves for him, and the other none, for it was wholly occupied by *bares* of *forros* ... and it is a great shame to see the ships laden for private parties and nothing for him, and this is no less true of that which goes by way of Pulicat to Melaka, and this makes even less profit and has greater expenses; and if His Highness does not wish to lose the things that allow him to make grants to *fidalgos* and people of service, it would be much better to allow them to make this voyage of Pulicat, and that they should buy the ship, and take freight-goods, and pay duties in Melaka, and both they and His Highness would wind up gaining more, and the same could be done with the voyages of Bengal, that is no ships of His Highness should go there. ...
>
> (Felner 1868, ii: 28)

The positions in the debate are therefore clear. On pepper, Botelho did not differ greatly from Cabral, seeing private trade within Asia as a great problem (although the contradiction between this position and his position on intra-Asian voyages apparently did not strike him). On the *carreira* system, their views are opposed, though – significantly enough – neither favoured the idea of renting out the voyages to the highest bidder. The pressure from the *fidalgos* and 'men of service' was far too great, and territorial expansion and the distribution of benefices on land (as had been done in Bassein and its vicinity in the late 1540s by D. João de Castro) was no more than a stop-gap measure. Eventually, it was Botelho who had his way, and what emerged was the new intra-Asian voyage system of the last third of the century. But before that could happen, a further process had to occur, to facilitate the Crown's withdrawal from the intra-Asian *carreira* trade. This was in the realm of the China-Japan trading nexus.

THE FAR EASTERN SOLUTION

In the period from the mid 1540s to the mid 1550s, Portuguese officialdom – as we have seen – retained its western Indian Ocean focus. This was natural enough, for we are in the period in which the Ottomans built their Red Sea fleet, the command of which was initially given over to Piri Reis, appointed in 1547 to the post of admiral of the Indian Ocean fleet (*Hind Kapudan-i Derya*) (Shaw 1976: 107). Piri Reis in early 1548 took Aden, which had in the interim lapsed into the hands of the local Shaikhs; a Portuguese expeditionary force, under D. João de Castro's son Dom Álvaro, which was sent to pre-empt the Ottomans, failed to attain its objective, in part because of lack of initiative shown by the Portuguese representative already in Aden, D. Paio de Noronha. With Basra coming under direct Ottoman control, it became possible for the Ottomans to launch annual expeditions against the Portuguese in the western Indian Ocean, thus drawing the fire away from trade between India and Southeast Asia and the Red Sea. The period thus witnesses the rise to prominence of the Sumatran Sultanate of Aceh, which allies itself to the Sublime Porte. Ottoman

In 1552, Piri Reis drove the Portuguese out of Maskat; his successor as admiral, Seydi Ali Reis, also enjoyed a few successes before being routed by the Portuguese in 1554 in a naval battle off Hurmuz. Forced to abandon ship and to return to the Ottoman domains overland after an extended sojourn in Gujarat, Sind, Afghanistan and Central Asia (which is set out at some length in his self-congratulatory but highly entertaining *Mirat ul-Memalik*), Seydi Ali Reis died in 1562 (Reis 1899). Thereafter, Ottoman naval activity in the Indian Ocean remained sporadic, such as in a 1568 expedition to aid the Acehnese against Melaka. However, the 1540s and 1550s, in particular the governments of D. João de Castro and

D. Afonso de Noronha (1550–54) are notable for a heightened tension over the Red Sea and Persian Gulf (Ozbaran 1972).

Now while official attention was directed in this direction, private Portuguese – both missionaries and traders – had made much progress in another direction. Immediately after taking Melaka, the Portuguese had made contact with China, at first via the ships of Asian traders and then by means of their own small fleets. These expeditions did not have a happy early history, for while an uneasy standoff between Ming officials and the Portuguese Captains-Major characterised the years from 1513 to 1520, the latter year saw the outbreak of open hostilities, stemming from the activities of Simão de Andrade at Canton; the Portuguese monarch in these years actually toyed with the idea of constructing a fortress in China. In 1521–22, the Portuguese renewed their attempts at trade, but this only brought worse consequences, in the form of an imperial edict banning them from the shores of China. As the Censor Ho Ao wrote a few years later:

> The Franks are most cruel and crafty. ... Some years ago they came suddenly to the city of Canton, and the noise of their cannon shook the earth. Those who remained at the post-station disobeyed the law and had contact with others. Those who came to the Capital were haughty and competed among themselves to become head. Now if we allow them to come freely and to carry on their trade, it will inevitably lead to fighting and bloodshed, and the misfortune of South China may be boundless. (Fok 1987: 147)

Ming writings of these years speak of the Portuguese as kidnappers and slave traders, men who ate children after cooking them as follows:

> [The Portuguese] secretly sought to purchase children of above ten years age to eat. Each child was purchased at 100 cash. This caused the evil youths of Kwangtung to hasten to kidnap children and the number of children eaten was uncountable. The method was to first boil up some soup in a huge iron pan and place the child, who was locked up inside an iron cage, into the pan. After being steamed to sweat, the child was then taken out and his skin peeled with an iron scrubbing-brush. The child, still alive, would now be killed, and having been disembowelled, steamed to eat. (Fok 1987: 145)

However, notwithstanding these images, some of which were possibly designed with the explicit purpose of discouraging Chinese from making contact with the Portuguese, private Portuguese did succeed little by little in making inroads into the private trade of the Fukien and Chekiang coasts. One of these traders was later to write a note entitled 'Information of China', for the Jesuit Francis Xavier in the late 1540s, in which he speaks of trading at the 'old port of Cantão' in the year 1533; we have also seen how in the 1540s, Martim Afonso de Sousa made several grants to individuals of voyages to China (Calado 1960: 114–15). The reason why this clandestine trade was possible in the 1540s and early 1550s was the rise of the *wo-k'ou* (or in Japanese *wako*), pirates who operated in the lower Yangtze region, from bases such as Shuang-hsu on Chusan island. Operating under the shadow of these networks, many Portuguese found a niche in the South China Sea trade, even if a few – like Galeote Pereira in 1549 – were captured and imprisoned by the Chinese.

It is very probably through these *wako* networks that the first Portuguese found their way to Japan, in 1543, from Ningpo; indeed it is possible that they were aided by the celebrated *wako* merchant-mediator Wang Chih (d. 1559), known to the Japanese as Ochoku (Wills 1979). Landing at Tanegashima in the south of Japan, these three Portuguese (in one version, a certain António da Mota and his two companions), were followed within the same decade by others – notably by Jorge Álvares at the head of a fleet of three ships in 1546. Initially, Portuguese trade activity was concentrated at Kyushu, apparently in lands controlled by the Otomo *daimyo* clan. The Otomo, together with the Shimazu and Ouchi, were the major powers of this period in western Japan, in an era in which the Ashikaga dispensation had all but collapsed. On Álvares's return to Melaka in 1547, he met the Jesuit Francis Xavier (who had arrived in Asia on the same fleet as Martim Afonso de Sousa, in 1542); Xavier soon determined that Japan was a likely field of work for him, and collected much information on the islands, some of which appears in the *Livro que trata das Coisas da Índia e do Japão*. This information, given to him very largely by a Japanese Yajiro, whom Álvares brought back with him from Japan, and who was converted to Christianity in Goa in 1548, consisted of details concerning social and political structure, religious practice, ports and trade, agriculture and so on. Xavier concluded that Japan was ruled over by a single king, but that he had below him fourteen other lords 'in the manner of dukes', besides others like counts; the religious in the land were in 'monasteries like friars'; in short, Xavier already had taken it into his head that Japan was practically a European country. Besides, from the point of view of conversion, there was the advantage that the Japanese 'preach that there is only one God, creator of all things; they also preach that there is Paradise, and Purgatory and Inferno' (Calado 1960: 88–99).

Armed with letters of accreditation from the Portuguese Governor at Goa, Garcia de Sá, and the Bishops of Goa and Melaka, Xavier arrived in Japan in August 1549 on a Chinese junk, together with two other Spanish Jesuits. His stay was fruitful in some respects, but disappointing in others; it established the Jesuits in Far Eastern missionary work, but Xavier himself failed to make the sort of political impact that he had hoped in his two-year-long stay. From his initial base at Kagoshima, the Jesuit travelled to Hirado, the Ouchi castle-town of Yamaguchi, Kyoto, and finally to the Otomo town of Bungo. By 1552–53, Portuguese vessels had begun to arrive with some regularity in the harbours of Kyoto, and the *daimyo* Otomo Sorin, who was anxious to attract as much trade as possible to his own port, saw the Jesuit as a means to achieve his end. Thus, from the very earliest years of the Portuguese presence in Japan, missionary work (especially that of the Jesuits) and trade were inextricably interwoven.

The earliest Portuguese traders to Japan probably used the port of Hirado in Kyushu, then under the control of the Matsuura family, more frequently than any other. This was the case in the early 1550s, when Xavier was in Japan; it was still the case in 1555, when two Portuguese ships – those of Duarte da Gama and Diogo Vaz de Aragão – arrived there. Diogo Vaz had already made several visits to Japan by this time, as had Duarte da Gama, and the latter's voyage was a signal success, as we see from a letter of November 1555, written by the Jesuit Padre Mestre Belchior Nunes Barreto:

> Ten or twelve days ago, a *nau* from Japan arrived here [Macau], and she came so richly laden that now all the other Portuguese and ships which are in China intend to go to Japan; and they wish to winter here on the China coast so that they may be able to leave for Japan next May which is the season for the monsoon for voyaging thither. (Boxer 1959: 22)

The China end of the trade at this time was divided between Macau (referred to already in 1554 by Simão Botelho), and the older Portuguese haunts of Lampacau, and the island of Shang-chu'an, all of which were subsidiary to Canton. According to our Jesuit witness of 1555, Barreto, there were imported into these ports over 30,000 *quintais* of pepper (roughly the equivalent of Portuguese trade from Asia to Lisbon in the commodity, but largely originating from Southeast Asia rather than the Indian south-west coast), and – in that particular year at least – over 100,000 *cruzados* worth of silver, brought by the *nau* from Japan. Trade was already so prosperous that Botelho in 1554 noted how '[the goods] that come from China in the hands of Portuguese [to Melaka] pay ten per cent; which was ordered thus, on the grounds that if the duties were raised, so many people would not go there' (Felner 1868, iii: 106).

In this way, almost exactly a half-century after Columbus's projected voyage to 'Cipangu', the islands so termed by Marco Polo did come into contact with an European power – the Portuguese. Not only this: the contact became systematised, and incorporated into the Portuguese intra-Asia trading system, under the institution of the *nau do trato* (or 'Great Ship from Amacon' as it has been termed). The number of vessels on the route usually exceeded one after 1554, there being two each every year between 1555 and 1559, and three in most of the next quinquennium – save in 1561 when there were possibly as many as five vessels used by the Portuguese on the route (Boxer 1959).

These years were unquiet ones, with several violent incidents marring the conduct of trade; in 1561, the Captain-Major of the Portuguese ships, Fernão de Sousa, and over a dozen of his Portuguese companions were killed in an altercation at Hirado, and again in 1565 the Portuguese *nau* of D. João Pereira was attacked by men of the Matsuura *daimyo*. Relative stability came about only after 1570 when the Macau-Japan trade settled on its terminus port, the Kyushu town of Nagasaki. Missionary activity in the port soon assumed substantial proportions as well, with the Jesuits even receiving some form of territorial rights over Nagasaki; in general, we can speak of the next two decades as representing the high point of Portuguese-Japan relations in terms of cordiality, though not in terms of quantities traded. Exports from China to Japan were principally of silk, largely produced in central China, and purchased by the Portuguese at bi-annual fairs in Canton in which the Portuguese were permitted to take part. According to the testimony of the Dutchman Jan Huyghen van Linschoten, resident at Goa in the 1580s, the amount of silk exported by the Portuguese to Japan amounted to some 3,000 *quintais*; an anonymous document in the Seville archives from about 1600 suggests a slightly lower figure, but adds that besides silk the *nau* carried some three to four thousand *taels* of gold, in addition to significant quantities of quicksilver, lead and tin, as also cotton textiles and yarn (Boxer 1959: 179–81).

The principal export from Japan, the very lifeblood of trade in the words of contemporary Spanish writers, was silver. It has been estimated that in the closing years of the sixteenth century, Portuguese exports of silver from Japan amounted to around 20,000 kilograms. This represented a substantial injection of liquidity into the western Indian Ocean, where a good part of it made its way, but it was also a visible symbol of where the profits of Portuguese trade now lay. From the early 1560s, the post of Captain-Major of the Macau-Japan trade became one of the greatly coveted posts, yielding profits to its holder of as much as 70,000 or 80,000 *pardaus*. Some of the more important *fidalgos* in Portuguese Asia in the period made a point of securing the royal grant of this voyage, even if it meant an initial expense from their own pockets. The grant-letter (*alvará*) to João de Mendonça, in 1563, makes the terms quite clear: Mendonça is to make the voyage from India to China via Melaka in his own ship 'fitted out at his own cost and expense'; from China he is to proceed either in person or send an agent to Japan, either in a ship or a junk (Boxer 1959: 173–74). The operative parts of the grant are in the appointment to the posts of Captain-Major over all Portuguese men and ships that he finds in China and Japan, as well as of the purveyor of the estates of the deceased (*provedor dos defuntos*). From these two posts, and their perquisites, and from the freight-duties (as well as his own direct trade) the Captain-Major made his fortune. It is very likely besides that the other ships which accompanied the *nau do trato* had to pay the Captain-Major for the privilege (Mendes da Luz 1954).

It is scarcely possible to exaggerate the importance of the Far Eastern connection for Portuguese trade from the 1560s. By the closing years of the sixteenth century, Macau had some five to six hundred Portuguese, and constituted a significant node of settlement – probably larger than any single settlement in the Bay of Bengal. Copper and silver from the Far East fed the mint of Goa, and helped make the private fortunes of many both in Portuguese Asia's capital city and elsewhere. By the early seventeenth century, the Crown hit upon the expedient of selling the China-Japan voyages, and they thus became an useful source of revenue. But in the sixteenth century, the significance of the Far Eastern connection for the Portuguese official enterprise is not to be seen in terms of its direct contribution to the exchequer via state trade. Rather, by opening up a new avenue of private trade, it diverted the attention of private entrepreneurs to a new field in which they did not compete with the Crown; the other important role it played was in swelling customs-collections in both Goa and Melaka. In the former port, goods going to or returning from China paid 8½ per cent duties, and a slightly lower rate was paid in Melaka; the two combined probably meant that the annual customs-yield of the trade made a substantial contribution to the Portuguese Asian state's revenues.

But we must not forget that the development of this trade, and the great buoyancy it created, were owed to circumstances largely outside the control of the Portuguese. The unsettled conditions in the China Sea at first prevented them from gaining in a substantial way from this trade; it was only after the resolution of the *wako* crisis (in which the Portuguese had no more than a marginal role to play) that returns from the trade could be reaped. The key in the post-1560 period lies once again in the fact that the Chinese state imposed restrictions on the participation of its subjects in the trade to Japan; it was this that left the way open for the Portuguese to gain the lion's share (even if they did not have a total monopoly) in the lucrative China-Japan trade for nearly half a century. In contrast, Japanese overseas trade in the last quarter of the sixteenth century appears to have concentrated on the Philippines and Southeast Asia rather than China, while the Chinese only occasionally traded in Japan (under pretext of sailing to Taiwan). Thus, in a sense the great 'Far Eastern turning' of Portuguese trade that occurred at the end of the crisis of the mid-sixteenth century, and which in reality provided a resolution to the crisis, was not a Portuguese creation at all. The door was opened to them by shifts in the political situation in coastal China and Japan; and the improved exploitation of silver mines in Japan from the mid-century helped make the opportunity lucrative. The Portuguese, even if they did not realise it, appear in this instance to have been the flies on the wheel, who played a role that was convenient to the Ming state and the Japanese *daimyo*.

THE *ESTADO* IN 1570

By 1570, the Portuguese had a presence in almost every region of Asia that they were to penetrate in the course of the sixteenth and seventeenth centuries. In a sense therefore, this period marks a limit to the geographical extension of Portuguese Asian expansion, with what remained being the more intensive exploitation of spaces that had been explored by 1570. Small colonies of Portuguese, missionaries, private traders, renegades or Crown representatives, were to be found by now in Japan, China, mainland Southeast Asia, the Indonesian archipelago, the South Asian landmass, Iran and the Ottoman domains, and East Africa. The historian of almost any part of coastal Asia can by this period be certain that some Portuguese sources and accounts exist of his region, some of them impressionistic and wildly inaccurate, others based on more detailed experience. This is what makes possible the creation in this period of such compendia as the *Códice Casanatense*, a portfolio of seventy-six watercolours, depicting the racial characteristics, customs, and costumes of the peoples of coastal East Africa and Asia. Beginning with the 'Cafres of Good Hope', the anonymous painter takes us through Ethiopia, the Red Sea, Iran, Gujarat and Goa (to both of which he devotes several watercolours), the Kanara and Malabar coasts, Coromandel and Orissa, Bengal, Burma, the Malay world, Sumatra, Java, the Moluccas, eventually ending his visual odyssey in China. We are now far from the fantasies of the ancients, and even Marco Polo; what has been imposed on the area is a vision in which the experiences of the sixteenth century have made their mark (Matos 1985).

Still, the *Códice*, and most other materials generated by the Portuguese up to this period – the chronicles of Barros and Castanheda, for instance – still stick fairly close to the littoral in what they retail. The Portuguese *Estado da Índia* – as the settlements and territories under the control of Goa came to be called from roughly this period – remained therefore essentially a maritime affair. Even the little official expansion and conquest undertaken in the 1560s continues to be in line with this conception of things; in 1568–69, three Kanara ports – Honawar, Basrur and Mangalore – were taken by the Portuguese, for quite traditional reasons, such as the need to control the Kanara pepper trade, and the need to secure Goa's supply lines from these rice-producing areas. The fact that this period was chosen was fortuitous, since the defeat of the Vijayanagara kingdom in south India in 1565 by her northern rivals – the Sultanates of Bijapur, Ahmadnagar and Golconda – created a political vacuum in the area which the Portuguese were quick to exploit. It was this essentially littoral character that was put into question in the decades that followed 1570.

CHAPTER FIVE

Between Land-bound and Sea-borne: Reorientations, 1570–1610

It is often argued that after the mid-century, the Portuguese Asian enterprise lost its vigour, falling into a pattern usually summed up as that of *decadência*. In this view, then, the crisis that we have discussed in the preceding chapter can be seen as a decisive one, which left the Portuguese Asian empire hollow on the inside, and ripe for demolition by the Dutch and English. Such a reading of the record is based in good measure on the great chronicler of the epoch, Diogo do Couto (1543–1616); unlike the first half of the century, when we have the often contradictory voices of *three* chroniclers – João de Barros, Gaspar Correia and Fernão Lopes de Castanheda – to reckon with, the period after 1550 is far poorer in terms of this sort of material, which for long has formed the core around which the history of Portuguese Asia has been written (Boxer 1948b; 1985b). However, recent writings on 'imperial decline' in the early modern period should give those historians who have accepted Couto's vision uncritically some pause, for it emerges that 'decline literature' was in fact itself a sort of genre, which emerged in the development of historiography in the broadly contemporary Ottoman and Mughal cases as a reaction to social realignments that were taking place. As Cornell Fleischer's study of Mustafa Ali (1541–1600), a contemporary historian of Ottoman 'decline' in the late sixteenth century, notes, such writers in their *nasihatname* (reform tracts) often portrayed the passing of a particular order, or the decline in the importance of a particular social group, as manifestations of a general process of decline (Fleischer 1986). As he puts it:

> Modern historians striving for 'objectivity' necessarily have some difficulty in weighing and evaluating the historical evidence provided by pre-modern historians, such as Ali, who present their arguments in explicitly moral and ethical terms, entering judgements that appear to color and distort the nature and degree of social and political change... The ideal of the 'Golden Age' and the notion of decline, which recur throughout that political literature, were

rhetorical devices that served more to express dissatisfaction with the present than to portray an historical reality.   (Fleischer 1986: 268)

Thus, rather than being a phase of generalised decline, the argument of this chapter is that the years from 1570 to 1610 form a phase of reorientation in the history of Portuguese Asia, a period when two tendencies vie for dominance. The residual momentum of the system (or perhaps its inertial tendency) still lay in the direction of controlling maritime trade, in one fashion or the other. But increasingly, a new tendency emerges: in places as far distant from one another as mainland Southeast Asia, Sri Lanka, and East Africa, the Portuguese enterprise shows a far greater predilection for territorial adventurism than in any earlier period. Given that the period was one marked by growing Spanish political control over Portugal (particularly after the union of the Spanish and Portuguese Crowns in 1580), the temptation is naturally to see this process in terms of the growing Hispanification of the Lusitanian conception of empire. The most obvious way of determining the accuracy of such a diagnosis is to examine the building-blocks of the Spanish overseas enterprise of the same period, and it is to this task that we will turn.

TRADE AND CONQUEST: THE SPANISH VIEW

After an initial phase of twenty-five years (1493–1518), when the Spanish largely concentrated on the islands of the New World, their activity moved to the mainland – thus inaugurating what has been termed the 'true colonisation' of the region. Two enterprises are central here: the first, which begins in 1519, is usually associated with the name of Hernán Cortés, and the second – which occupies the years from 1531 – with Francisco Pizarro. Cortés was the head of an army that succeeded in the short space of two years in defeating the Aztec rulers of Mexico, opening up the possibility of enormous riches to be collected at a relatively small cost. Pizarro, whose venture into the Inca kingdom in South America was certainly influenced by the earlier success enjoyed by Cortés, had no less dramatic a career: leaving Panama in January 1531 with an army of no more than two hundred men, he entered the Inca capital Cuzco in 1534 as a conqueror, founded Lima the following year, and lived to enjoy the laurels of a *conquistador* until his assassination in 1541. The phase to the mid-sixteenth century is thus dominated by the figures of the *conquistadores*, who were the stuff of later legend, and for the most part men who had no great social position in Spain before embarking on their overseas adventures. Originating very frequently from the west and south-west of the Spanish kingdom (and comprising in their great majority Andalucians and Extremeños), these men soon transformed themselves into settlers (*pobladores*) and thereafter into holders of grants called *encomiendas* (Lovett 1986: 61–113).

The contrast with Portuguese Asia could scarcely be clearer, and the question naturally arises of why the two kingdoms in their overseas enterprises had such different conceptions. Broadly speaking, two explanations might be thought to exist. The first would focus on the relatively landbound mentality of the Spaniards, especially those who emigrated, and the second on the determining character of local circumstances. Taking the latter tack, the argument could be made that the Portuguese in Asia found a dense and active commercial network, and inland states of some power and resources, capable of resisting their incursions. Activities like those of Pizarro and Cortés were thus out of the question, and the empire had necessarily to be a maritime, trade-oriented one. In contrast, one might say, the Spanish in the New World found little by way of local trade that they could tax, and were hence forced to resort to the control of labour, thus producing seemingly seignorial (or quasi-feudal) institutions. In support of this argument is the fact that the *encomienda* – which gave the holder (or *encomendero*) the right to collect a *tributo* in money, goods or labour services from the Amerindians, in return for 'protecting' them and instructing them in the Catholic religion – had a basis in pre-Spanish institutions such as the Inca *mita* or the Aztec *cuatequil*.

But there is also some reason to be sceptical of this argument. We may note, first of all, that the holders of *encomiendas* stiffly resisted attempts by the Spanish Crown to do away with the system, suggesting that there was more to the institution than mere pragmatism. By the early 1540s, it had become clear that there were no more great inland cities to plunder, or easy tributes to be collected from already mined stocks of gold and silver. Two fruitless expeditions – that of Hernando de Soto into what was later to be Louisiana and Arkansas in 1539–42, and that of Francisco Vázquez Coronado into Arizona, New Mexico, Colorado and the Kansas valley in 1540–41 – made it clear to any would-be *conquistadores* that their best option was to settle for the *encomienda* and its incomes. Seignorial pretensions were much in the air, and as early as 1528, the *conquistadores* had petitioned the Crown for a general partition of New World lands into hereditary holdings; the Crown temporised by making *encomiendas* valid for the lifetime of the grantee and his heir, after which they were to revert to the Crown. This was scarcely to the taste of the *encomenderos* whose philosophy is largely encapsulated in the expression 'God is in Heaven, the King is far, and I give the orders here' ('*Dios está en el cielo, el rey está lejos, y yo mando aquí*'), but worse was to come (Céspedes del Castillo 1972: 360). By the so-called New Laws (*Leyes Nuevas*) promulgated by Charles V in 1542, it was announced that all *encomiendas* would become extinct when the current holder died; what was intended was a more centralised system of government, to be run via a system of two viceroyalties (*virreinatos*). The northern, Mexican, viceroyalty was created in 1535 with the first appointee to the post of viceroy of New Spain (*Nueva España*) being Pedro de Alvarado; the southern viceroyalty, based at Lima, was that of *Tierra Firme*, and the first viceroy was Blasco Núñez Vela.

The viceroys, charged with implementing the New Laws, were faced with a thankless task. Of the two, the southern viceroyalty fared worse: Núñez Vela was deposed and later killed, and a local junta, headed by Francisco Pizarro's half-brother Gonzalo, held power until 1548. The consequences of this rebellion are significant: the threat to the *encomiendas* was withdrawn and the system continued to be of importance until the close of the sixteenth century, after which it crumbled under a more subtle legislative onslaught than that of 1542. But the decline of the *encomienda* did not mean the decline of the territorial and aristocratic pretensions of expatriates, who had taken to styling themselves with such titles as *gentilhombre*, *caballero*, and most commonly with the prefix *don*. Instead, what emerged in the passage from the sixteenth to the seventeenth century in the place of *encomienda* and *encomendero* was the *hacienda* and the *hacendado*, which is to say a system of large rural properties, whose integrity was guaranteed by the juridical practice of *mayorazgo* (which like the Portuguese *morgadio* made the property indivisible). It is not the intention to argue here that the *hacienda* was no more than the *encomienda* in disguise; we are aware that substantial differences existed between the two. But what is significant is that until the end of the seventeenth century, the backbone of the Spanish overseas enterprise remained the control of labour, certainly, and at times labour in conjunction with land. As G. Céspedes del Castillo has put it, the personage of the *hacendado* 'finds its only parallel in the rural nobility of Andalucia' (1972: 455). This is in sharp contrast with the participants in the Portuguese Asian enterprise of the pre-1570 period.

Indeed, even in their foray into Asia, the Spanish worked in much the same fashion as they had in the Americas. Miguel López de Legazpi, sent to the Philippines in the mid-1560s, with the explicit intention of finding a way around the terms of the Treaty of Saragossa (1529) by which the Habsburgs had renounced claims on Asia to the Portuguese, rapidly introduced the *encomienda* system there; by 1591, two hundred and sixty seven *encomiendas* existed, claiming control over some 668,000 inhabitants (while in contrast, in 1570, some four thousand *encomiendas* were to be found in the Americas). Again, this is sometimes explained by pointing to the essentially rural character of the pre-Spanish Philippines, where the major form of settlement was the *barangay*, a unit of some five or six hundred people; thus it is argued that local conditions were what prompted the adoption of this institution, rather than a pre-conceived

110

scheme. But recent research shows that the extent of urbanisation and involvement in trade of the Philippines prior to 1560 was quite significant; Malay traders had pursued their commerce there for some centuries (as recently discovered inscriptions testify), and by the mid-sixteenth century, several Islamised Sultanates, with urban centres (including Manila itself) were in the making (Villiers 1987). Yet, despite this, and despite the importance of trade for the colonial economy of the Philippines, the Spanish nevertheless adopted a part-seignorial system there.

This is not to deny that the Spanish overseas enterprise, even in the Americas, was based in some measure on trade. The Atlantic route, the *Carrera de las Indias*, linked Spanish ports – in particular Seville – with ports in the New World such as Veracruz in Nueva España, and Cartagena and Nombre de Dios in Tierra Firme. Exports from Spain were of wheat, oil, wine and some manufactures, while the returning ships brought a rich cargo of bullion, particularly in the period after 1550. But this trade was conducted in a manner quite different from that which we have observed in respect of the Portuguese *Carreira da Índia* in the years up to 1550. In the Portuguese case, we note that, despite the participation of some private shipping on license (like that of the Italians Sernigi and Marchionni, or of members of noble households, like Catarina Dias d'Aguiar, Duarte Tristão or Dom Nuno Manuel), the Crown still accounted for the great part of both shipping and trade. In the Spanish case, on the other hand, we have an enterprise which has a far more private character; the Crown restricted itself to regulating the trade, taxing it, and from the 1540s organising convoys across the Atlantic to avoid corsair attacks. Apart from the surpluses remitted by the two viceroyalties (which seem to have fluctuated between 25 and 35 per cent of total bullion flows to Castile in the sixteenth century), the financing and organisation of trade remained in the hands of the so-called *cargadores de Indias*, a small group of merchants who were mostly based at Seville, the town which was the principal centre of the trans-Atlantic route in the mid-sixteenth century. The merchants of this centre, which was known to contemporaries by the none-too-flattering term of 'la gran Babilonia de España', held off threats from rival ports – particularly Cadiz, but also San Sebastian, La Coruña and so on – reserving for themselves the virtual monopoly of the trade to the Americas in the sixteenth century. But as for the Crown, it did little for the trade, beyond organising its security and milking it. On fifteen occasions between 1523 and 1596, the Crown confiscated the return private bullion cargoes in part or whole, claiming fiscal needs, the worst run being of four years from 1555 to 1558; in exchange, the merchants received bonds (or *juros*) from the Crown, which were not always redeemed promptly (Lovett 1986: 90).

There is little doubt that in the eyes of the Spanish monarch Charles V, the overseas possessions had a different role than that given to

111

Portuguese Asia by Dom Manuel or Dom João III. As late as 1537, the Portuguese Crown had available to it at least twenty vessels, of over 6,500 *toneladas* combined, which it could choose from for the *Carreira da Índia*, while in contrast, the Spanish Crown had to lease vessels for even the escort function on convoys (Gavetas, v: 179). It was the dimension of territoriality, of the control of land and its product (including bullion, extracted from the mines), that Spanish expatriates in the Americas saw as central to their activity; the Crown too implicitly acquiesced in the vision.

SPAIN, PORTUGAL AND THE ATLANTIC TURNING

During the latter years of the reign of Dom João III (1521–57), and most certainly after his death, Spanish influence is felt in ever increasing measure on the Portuguese court, on the nobility, and eventually on the merchant class. The influence was filtered through men like the Infante Dom Luís, as also through Dom João's wife, Dona Catarina, herself a Habsburg and sister of Charles V. Dona Catarina acted as regent from 1557 to 1562, on behalf of her grandson Dom Sebastião (born posthumously in 1554), a post in which she was succeeded by the Infante-Cardinal Dom Henrique, brother of Dom João III; and in this period, Charles V's son and successor Felipe II came to play a decisive part in Portuguese elite politics. His principal agent in the matter in the 1570s was a certain Cristôvão de Moura, a Portuguese who had long resided in the Spanish court, whose role was to mobilise the support of the Lisbon bourgeoisie, with offers of a possible participation in the network of Habsburg imperial and colonial finance; the Portuguese nobility, for its part, needed no great urging to join ranks with the Spaniards. Even before Dom Felipe made his bid for the Portuguese throne, in the wake of the death of Dom Sebastião in 1578, he had succeeded to a great extent in altering the Portuguese royal house's self-image and comportment. From trader-monarchs, we see the Portuguese kings entering gradually into a different role, one that bears an ever closer resemblance to that of the Habsburgs.

We can see this clearly enough when we examine the manner in which trade on the Cape route – the *Carreira da Índia* – came to be reorganised in the 1560s and 1570s. To recapitulate, in the very early years of trade to Asia (in particular 1499–1504), the Portuguese Crown had formed a company in collaboration with private traders, including some Italians. This was followed by a brief phase, 1504–06, theoretically of free trade, but during which royal authorisation was in fact still needed to send ships to Asia. In these years, not only private Portuguese, but international traders from southern Germany (such as the Welser, Fugger and Hochstetter families), and some Italians, sent ships to Asia, paying a tax to the Crown on their return of 28.5 per cent. However, after 1506, a more complete monopoly was exercised, albeit with some exceptions. A particularly celebrated one was the fleet sent under Diogo Mendes de Vasconcelos in 1510, to open direct trade with Melaka, with numerous vessels owned by the Florentine Sernigi; however, this operation was a failure, since Albuquerque refused to permit such trade and instead commandeered the vessels for his own purposes. Other instances of private vessels can also be found, in 1518 and so on. But far more common as a way around the Crown monopoly was the system of *quintaladas*, or cargo space awarded to individuals to carry particular goods. These could be as large as 300 *quintais* of pepper, and could be held for life or granted for a more limited period. It has been suggested that the use of *quintaladas* and other private trade aboard Crown vessels in fact was quite substantial, even in the middle years of the sixteenth century, although we have no exact means to verify this.

The first changes to this system, which we stress was one of Crown monopoly of trade – and therefore in considerable contrast to the Castilian New World trade – were announced in 1562–63, during the regency. What precisely was adopted as an alternative is not clear; it appears to have been some form of contract, by which private merchants were given the right to trade in the key commodities, pepper and the spices. The new system did not last long, and the old direct trade option was exercised again after 1564. The next major attempt at change occurred in 1570, by which time Dom Sebastião had begun his direct rule. Private persons were now allowed to trade freely in pepper, spices and other hitherto contraband goods; however, they were still obliged to buy these in Asia from Portuguese factories, at a fixed price. Here then are the first clear signs of the Crown's desire to divest itself of responsibility for trade on the Cape route, and even of shipping to the extent possible.

In the same year, 1570, the Italian Luca Giraldi was given a five-year shipping contract, requiring him to send three ships to Asia every year; when his enterprise failed, the contract was taken up by a certain António Calvo, who agreed to send five ships a year to Asia. But a further modification was to follow. In 1576, the pepper trade was farmed out on a five-year contract to a combine, headed by Konrad Rott (but also including Welser and Italian investments); Rott later pulled out of the operation, but his partners the Welsers, and the Milanese Giovanni Battista Rovellasca, continued. By the mid-1580s, several contracts existed: that on pepper trade from Asia, that on distribution of pepper within Europe, that of organising the fleet, and finally the farm of the revenues of the *Casa da Índia*. Initially monopolised by foreigners, these contracts came by the 1590s to be controlled by several *cristão novo* families, such as the Gomes d'Élvas, the Mendes de Brito and so on. Institutionally, then, by

New christians

113

the late 1580s, the trade of the Cape route and the trade of the trans-Atlantic route from Seville had come to resemble each other far more than before. But the modification was not brought about simply as a consequence of Spanish rule in Portugal after 1580. The process, completed after 1580, was in fact begun already in the 1560s and 1570s (Godinho 1981–83, iii: 57–69).

If first indirect and then direct Spanish influence was one reason for the shift, there were others too. We have seen in the previous chapter how the 1540s saw a debate in Dom João's council on the relative merits of the Asian empire versus North Africa. By the 1560s, a new rival had arisen to the *Estado da Índia*: namely Brazil. In the late 1540s, almost half a century after the accidental discovery of Brazil by Cabral while *en route* to Asia, Brazil was still thinly populated by settlers, who numbered perhaps two thousand, less than one-twentieth of the settler population in Spanish America. From the mid-century, however, the settlement of Brazil advanced apace, and was accompanied by two other processes: the import into Brazil of slaves from Luanda and other west African ports, and the cultivation and export of sugar based on this slave labour. By 1583, Brazil had some 25,000 white settlers and a slave population of 33,000; by 1600, the white settlers had increased to 30,000 and the slaves to 120,000. In the same period, sugar production expanded dramatically too: 180,000 *arrobas* in 1570, 350,000 in 1583, and 600,000 by the end of the century. The rise of Brazil, documented in some detail by Frédéric Mauro, had significant consequences. First, unlike the India trade, the trade to Brazil was not organised as a Crown monopoly, and allowed a far greater scope for the participation of private traders – both Portuguese and foreigners. Second, not being organised as a Crown monopoly, the trade was not centralised from Lisbon either. Other ports such as Oporto, Aveiro and Viana do Castelo to the north, and Setubal, Portimão and Faro to the south, come to play a major role in this trade, thus leading to a limited decentralisation of the commercial economy (Mauro 1970: 15–35).

The 'Atlantic turning', as the shift of emphasis from India to Brazil is sometimes termed, was a part of the global conjuncture within which Dom Felipe's takeover of Portugal was accomplished in 1580. We are still somewhat unclear as to how precisely this political act was orchestrated, even as we are unclear about the precise politics of the 'Restoration' – the expulsion of the Habsburgs from Portugal sixty years later, in 1640. But the force of the conjuncture is visible in various ways: in particular, we may note that many of Dom Felipe's policies after 1580 exhibit a great deal of continuity with policies followed in the late 1560s and 1570s by his nephew Dom Sebastião. One of these we have already noted, namely the contract system in respect of trade on the Cape route. A second aspect, which we shall examine in greater detail in a later section, is the attitude of the Crown towards intra-Asian trade, and the growth of the so-called 'concession-system' of voyages within Asia. A third aspect concerns territorial adventurism in Asia, already encouraged by Dom Sebastião in the 1570s, and taken a step further under Dom Felipe and his son.

But there was also *one* major difference. For some reason that remains obscure to us, Dom Sebastião was determined to re-activate the North African front, largely abandoned in the 1540s by his grandfather. One explanation for this has been that the 1560s and 1570s had seen the birth of a new conception, linking the fate of North Africa to the Atlantic islands and Brazil; the purpose of intervening in North Africa could hence be seen as creating a new network, once again excluding Asia. In immediate terms, what provoked the intervention was a dispute within the Sa'di dynasty, following on the death of al-Ghalib (r. 1557–74); his successor Muhammad al-Mutawakkil was defeated and displaced by his own uncle, Abd al-Malik, who was aided in this by the Ottomans and Habsburgs (Mantran 1970). Al-Mutawakkil fled to Portugal, and asked for assistance, which Dom Sebastião determined to give him – against the advice of many in his court, as well as against the fairly clear signals sent to him by the Habsburgs, whom he asked to cooperate in the venture.

A small and ill-equipped Portuguese expeditionary force, led by the king himself, set out in July 1578 for Arzila, and on 4 August 1578, a battle took place at al-Qasr al-Kabir. It was a disaster from the Portuguese viewpoint, and the first battle for over a century when the king himself had taken the field. Al-Mutawakkil was drowned, many of the Portuguese nobles including the Duque de Barcelos captured, and Dom Sebastião himself killed, although rumours rapidly spread that he was in fact alive. The battle was described thus by a participant:

> The dead were on top of the living and the living on top of the dead, all cut to pieces, Christians and Moors locked in each other's arms, crying and dying, some on top of artillery, others dragging limbs and entrails, caught under horses or mangled on top of them, and everything was much worse than I can describe to you now because the memory of what I went through grieves me so. (Spence 1984: 38)

Still, the consequences for the Sa'dis were happy ones, even though Abd al-Malik himself died on the battlefield (probably from natural causes). His brother Ahmad al-Mansur now came to the throne, and remained in power for a quarter century, in the course of which he reorganised administration, rebuilt the capital of Marrakesh, and managed to extend his power as far as Timbuktu in the 1590s. Portugal, on the other hand, found itself in the throes of a political crisis with close parallels to that of 1383–85. The immediate successor to Dom Sebastião, the Infante-Cardinal, was clearly too old and infirm to be much more than a stop-gap measure. Three logical alternatives existed: Dom Felipe, who was related to the Portuguese royal houses by many routes, on account of the close intermarriage of the two houses (the marriage of first cousins being a common feature, and permitted by Papal dispensation in these instances); the house of the Dukes of Bragança, also lineal descendants of Dom João I of the House of Avis; and a candidate whose position was remarkably similar to that of Dom João I in 1383, Dom António, prior of Crato, and illegitimate son of the Infante Dom Luís.

The Cardinal Dom Henrique died in January 1580. Of all the candidates, Dom Felipe was the best-prepared; the support of Lisbon *and* the nobility, as well as the high clergy, had been negotiated for him by his representatives. The Braganças were poorly placed, for the Duke was too old, and his son had had to be ransomed from the Sa'dis by the Habsburgs, who ensured thereafter that his movements were kept restricted. Only Dom António was prepared to resist, and did so, declaring himself ruler at Santarém in 1580. But he was scarcely equipped to resist the Habsburg army of the Duke of Alba (Parker 1979: 145–46). This is particularly because he failed to gain political support, and the fact that Dom António's mother (who bore the suggestive nickname 'the Pelican') came from a New Christian family may have had something to do with the nobility's reluctance to deal with him. Although the resistance of his partisans continued until the mid-1580s, eventually extending into the Açores, by early 1581 Felipe could justifiably say of Portugal (as legend suggests he did): 'I inherited it, I bought it, I conquered it (*Yo lo heredé, yo lo compré, yo lo conquisté*)'.

GIRDLING THE GLOBE

Felipe II of Spain was officially acknowledged ruler of Portugal in April 1581, when the Portuguese *cortes* met at Tomar, and he was presented to the representatives of the three estates. The idea was that when the normal succession from father to son (by *jure sanguinis*) was interrupted, power notionally returned to the people (*povo*) whose representatives the *cortes gerais* then transferred power to the new ruler, by entering into the *pactum subjectionis* (Thomaz 1985). There were clearly negotiations that preceded the *cortes*, and Felipe agreed to observe the customs, laws and statutes of Portugal, to allow Portugal some autonomy in government, and so on. Historians of the Habsburgs have been anxious to establish that the Portuguese received a good bargain at Tomar, and have gone so far as to claim that it was Castile that lost from its link with Portugal, which is supposed to have been a 'drain' on Habsburg resources. Such judgements are suspect, for the balance of gain and loss is a more complex affair than a mere retailing of the expenditures set aside in Castilian budgets for Portuguese affairs. But it is certain that some Portuguese groups gained in the aftermath of Tomar. Most conspicuous among these were the *cristãos novos* – the New Christians, descended from the converts from Judaism of the late 1490s.

The New Christian network of trade and state finance that arose in the half-century 1580–1630 literally girdled the globe. Its major European centres included Lisbon, Oporto, Medina del Campo, Madrid, Seville, Valladolid and Antwerp; in the New World, we find them at Pernambuco, Lima, Olinda, Mexico and Cartagena; in Asia in Melaka, Macau, Nagasaki, Manila, Goa and Cochin. Essentially, the New Christian network worked by the principle of integrating several circuits of trade and finance, which had hitherto remained poorly connected. One was the old one between the Iberian cities, the Low Countries and Germany, which had been strengthened by the fact that Lisbon and Seville had become the twin nodes of trade to Asia and America. The letters of two great trading families, the Gomes d'Elvas and the Rodrigues d'Évora, directed at correspondents in Medina del Campo, set out this section of the network clearly enough; other letters of traders in Antwerp, from the years 1561–1609, enable us to list other families – such as the Caldeira, the Henriques, and the Nunes – who can in turn be traced to contiguous circuits of trade (Silva 1956; 1959–61; Vasquez de Prada 1960). As for the New Christians of Lisbon itself, we have the following rather uncharitable description of them from the pen of the Florentine Filippo Sassetti, writing to his friend Baccio Valori from the Portuguese capital in 1578:

> The inhabitants of Lisbona would be some two hundred and twenty thousand: these are Old Christians, New Christians, and slaves. The Old Christians are divided into *fidalgos* and the other lower classes (*popolo minuto*); and the New Christians are the former Jews who decided to remain here and be baptised: they are little better than infamous, wicked (*cattivi*), perfidious, and without faith or honour or anything that might be good, save their most subtle understanding, which taken together with the above qualities, makes up a mixture such that anyone who can trade with them and not be duped is a man whom one can entrust with everything, and to whom one can give, as the saying goes, completely free rein (*la briglia sul collo*).
>
> (Bramanti 1970: 216–19)

The second of these major circuits was the Atlantic one, embracing the smaller Portuguese ports, Olinda, Salvador de Bahia, Luanda in West Africa, and some of the eastward-looking ports of Spanish America, like Cartagena or Veracruz. This is a network then which involves sugar, and slaves, and feeds back into the trade of Europe already sketched out. A third circuit was that which stretched across from Spanish America to the Philippines and Macau. The creation of this commercial nexus was owed to the opening up of trans-Pacific trade from the 1560s, and had a good deal to do with the changed Portuguese-Spanish relationship of the 1560s and 1570s. It would be recalled that earlier treaties of the fifteenth century, notably Alcaçovas-Toledo and Tordesillas, had envisaged a division of the world outside Europe between Spanish and Portuguese. The understanding was naturally flawed, since the true map of the globe was as yet unavailable to the contending parties, and this was partly what led to the wrangle in the 1520s, following the circumnavigation of the globe by a Spanish expedition, captained by a Portuguese, Fernão de Magalhães (or Ferdinand Magellan). The tangle was again resolved, this time in the treaty of Saragossa, with the major Portuguese concern at the negotiating table being the rights over the Moluccas and their spices (Thomaz 1975). But in the 1560s, the question was reopened by the Spanish, who used the Philippines as a lever with which to prise open the earlier system. Clashes followed between Portuguese and Spanish squadrons in the Moluccas, since the latter clearly intended to divert a part of Southeast Asian trade to Manila, and thence to the New World. But the door, once opened, could not be shut with ease. The Manila galleon, the trading vessels bringing New World silver from Acapulco to the Philippines, needed goods to take back, and the products of the Philippine economy clearly would not suffice.

It is nearly impossible to quantify the extent of this trade, since a great proportion of it was on private account, rather than that of the state. The figures of John J. TePaske, which are no more than rough guesses, suggest the picture shown in Table 5.1 (TePaske 1983).

Table 5.1 Silver remittances from Mexico to Manila (kilos)

Period	Public Account	Private Account	Total
1581–1590	32,198	?	32,198
1591–1600	11,912	14,779	26,691
1601–1610	30,030	89,886	119,916
1611–1620	64,967	129,035	194,002
1621–1630	92,545	138,638	231,183
1631–1640	93,882	89,716	183,598
1641–1650	56,408	44,980	101,388
1651–1660	38,556	51,523	90,079

(*Source*: TePaske 1983: 444–45)

In addition, there was also private trade from the ports of Peru (such as Callao) to Manila, which until 1582 was legal; in 1582, a ban on this trade was promulgated in response to complaints from Seville merchants, and later extended in 1591 to trade from all parts of Tierra Firme to the Philippines. Despite further restrictive legislation, it has often been suspected that illegal trade occupied more than a fair share of total trans-Pacific commerce, and that it particularly involved Callao. The official legislation, in effect from 1594 to 1702, limited trade to two galleons of 300 tons each, and further stipulated that the silver exports should not exceed 15,300 kilogrammes, with return cargoes to Acapulco also not to exceed 300,000 *pesos* worth of goods. But at least one contemporary observer in 1597 claimed the smuggled flow of silver was over 300,000 kilogrammes, which even if it is an exaggeration is an evocative one (TePaske 1983).

In this trade, from Acapulco and Peru to the Philippines, the Portuguese New Christians came to play a role of great importance. Their trading world has been difficult to penetrate, possibly because they remained relatively insecure, and hence secretive; the fact that their trade was, in this instance, only semi-legal further complicates the issue. Indeed, our best sources on them are a result of their persecution, particularly by the Inquisition, whose tribunals thus collected considerable data on their trade and influence. Portuguese traders in and around Lima, called *peruleiros*, were particularly important after 1560, and were involved not merely in trade, but in mining and transportation. Important figures among the community by the early seventeenth century include Sebastião Duarte, Álvaro Mendes, António da Cunha and Jorge da Silva, but also one celebrated entrepreneur called Manuel Baptista Peres, concerning whom we have quite detailed knowledge.

Born in 1583, Peres was a great-grandson of Henrique Rodrigues d'Évora, and nephew of Diogo Rodrigues de Lisboa; he thus belonged to a branch of a celebrated New Christian family. Before arriving in Lima in 1618, he appears to have been in Coimbra, and then Seville. Together with his brothers-in-law Sebastião Duarte and Luís da Veiga, Peres ran an enormous and diverse business, estimated by the Inquisition at some 650,000 ducats in the mid-1630s. His interests included the slave trade via Cartagena and Rio de la Plata into the Atlantic, silver mining in the Andes, and a *hacienda* at Bocanegra – near the present site of Lima's airport.

But Inquisition records concerning Peres are interesting not merely for these details. They speak of an art-gallery and a map-room in his estate, and contain a listing of books in his possession, which included religious texts, belles-lettres, and a good deal on Asian and European history, including the *Décadas da Ásia* of João de Barros, the *Rimas* of Luís Vaz de Camões, the *Crónica de Dom João III* of Luís de Sousa, the *Jornada del Rey Don Sebastián*, and the *Ystoria de las Molucas* of Bartolomé Leonardo de Argensola (Reparaz 1976: 105–09). In this sense, Peres was clearly a man of his era: his collection effectively embraces Europe, Africa and Asia, while he himself resided in South America.

The 1630s and 1640s saw the fortunes of the Portuguese New Christians in Mexico and Peru plummet, on account of persecutions by the Inquisition, with Peres himself being burnt at stake in 1639. A hundred or more arrests were made in Lima alone in 1635, with those arrested being accused, quite absurdly, of a great conspiracy to overthrow

119

the viceroyalty (Cross 1978). But for a half century or more, they held sway, as this description by a Lima-based rival in 1636 states:

> Over the past six or eight years, a great quantity of Portuguese have entered this kingdom of Peru (where there were already many), by way of Buenos Ayres, Brasil, Nueva España, Nuevo Reino [Granada], and Puerto Velo. This city was thick with them. Many are married but more are single. They have made themselves masters of commerce; the street (*calle*) which is called that of the merchants is almost theirs; the passageway is all theirs as are the dry-goods stores. They swarm through the streets selling from trunks as do the linen-drapers at this court. All of the best spots where the people congregate are theirs. Such luck has been theirs that they are in absolute control of the traffic in merchandise ranging from brocade to sackcloth and from diamonds to cumin seeds. (Liebman 1971)

The fourth of the circuits, which completes the picture, was that in the Indian Ocean itself. It is the most difficult of all to uncover, partly because the records of the Goa Inquisition have survived only in fragmentary form. But using these and other materials from related branches of the Inquisition, James Boyajian has shown the presence in late sixteenth-century and early seventeenth-century Portuguese Asia of a substantial network of New Christian trade, embracing Nagasaki, Manila, Macau, Melaka, Cochin and Goa, but also with tentacles extending beyond the limits of the *Estado*, into Agra, Bijapur and inland south India. Of particular importance is one family and its connections: these are the Fernandes d'Aires, who were in turn related to other New Christian families like the Tinoco, Dias de Santiago, Paz d'Azevedo and Brandão. We know from Inquisition records that one of their important agents, Manuel Serrão, born at Elvas in 1521, arrived in Goa in 1554, but left shortly thereafter from fear of the Inquisition (Boyajian 1986). Over the second half of the sixteenth century, Serrão's activities centred in such places as Vijayanagara and Agra, while his son-in-law João Monteiro continued to act for him in Goa. Serrão kept close contact with the Fernandes d'Aires, who for their part acted as agents for New Christian families in Mexico, Seville and elsewhere.

We may note another example, this one from the 1590s and early 1600s: this is the business alliance of António Dias de Casseres at Macau with Diogo Fernandes Vitória at Manila, Henrique Dias at Lisbon, and Diogo Dias Neto and Bernardo de Luna at Mexico. Here we see two features of the system as it had emerged. First, this particular network straddled the eastern part of the *Estado da Índia* and Spanish America, as did that of the Montóia brothers somewhat later: Jorge Dias de Montóia at Macau, Francisco Dias de Montóia at Manila, and Duarte de Montóia at Mexico. Second, the Casseres-Vitória-Dias-Neto link shows that kinship was not always the binding force of such relations. One way of getting around this was the use of fictive kinship ties, such as god-parentship (*compadrío*). Thus, Garcia de Melo (1563–1630), a

120

celebrated official (*vedor da fazenda*) and private trader in early seventeenth-century Portuguese Asia, was linked through such ties to the Augsburg-born Ferdinand Cron; both lived in Goa in the first two decades of the century, and Cron was also linked by way of business to several viceroys and to *other* New Christian entrepreneurs such as Fernão Jorge da Silveira (1575–1640), and Valentim Garcia (1580–1645) (Leiden University Library, BPL Nr. 876).

The geographical spread and timing of New Christian activity was determined by several factors. One of these was the level of efficiency of the Inquisition, which was always on the look out for 'Judaizers'. In the decades from 1561 to 1580, the Inquisition was particularly active in Goa, where it moved for example against Isabel d'Aires, daughter of the Lisbon-based New Christian Henrique Fernandes d'Aires. In these two decades therefore, prudent New Christians exercised two options: they either stayed within the *Estado da Índia* but moved as far as possible from Goa (say to Macau), or they moved out of the *Estado* altogether. By the last decade of the sixteenth century, however, the extent of persecution had fallen off, and earlier legislation, including an order passed in 1585 expelling all of them from Portuguese Asia, was winked at. The post-1600 years thus mark a high point for their activity, and the extant lists of private goods shipped to Lisbon from Goa and Cochin by the *Carreira da Índia* show an extensive participation by such men as Valentim Garcia and Fernão Jorge. In these years, a new strategy was discovered and implemented by New Christian entrepreneurs wishing to protect themselves in Asia, namely the alliance with important *fidalgos*, and even with the governors and viceroys of Portuguese Asia itself. A clear case of such a strategy emerges from examining the life of Duarte Gomes Solis (1562–1630), who was born in Lisbon, brought up in the great financial centre of Medina del Campo, and who made several trips to India, the first in 1585. By the time of his final return to Iberia in 1602, Solis was a rich man, a circumstance that permitted him to buy himself the title of *cavaleiro fidalgo* of the Royal Household. This was managed by seeking the protection of the governor Manuel de Sousa Coutinho (1588–91), and later of the viceroy Dom Francisco da Gama. Similarly, in later years, men like Valentim Garcia and Francisco Tinoco de Carvalho were to be protected by the viceroy, Dom Miguel de Noronha, Conde de Linhares (1629–35), in exchange for the official and unofficial aid and advice they gave him (Boyajian 1983; 1986; Calvet de Magalhães 1966).

Eventually a second wave of persecutions, related to those in Mexico and Peru, and occupying the 1630s and 1640s, put paid to some of the centres of the New Christian network like Goa. Prominent victims of the second wave included Baltasar da Viega, a relative of the Lima-based Manuel Baptista Peres, and an ally of Linhares during his administration. By the 1640s, therefore, the conspicuous New Christian activity in the

Estado da Índia had dissipated, with the half-century or so following the *cortes* of Tomar being a sort of golden age for the community in this respect. Persecution was only one reason for the decline; the decline of the trans-Pacific trade, the attacks by the Dutch on Portuguese-owned shipping, and the tendency for prosperous New Christians to buy into titles and move out of business also are likely to have played a part in the change that occurred.

THE 'LAND' QUESTION

The early years of the direct reign of Dom Sebastião are remarkable for a series of administrative reforms, which have seldom been adequately studied, because they ostensibly did not have time to take root. As we have seen, however, in respect of the organisation of trade on the Cape route, many of the reforms and changes attributed to the Habsburgs in fact had roots in the decade before 1580, at times even as early as 1560. This is also clear in respect of the most important feature of early Habsburg control over the *Estado da Índia*, namely the growing preoccupation with terrestrial affairs – whether in East Africa, Sri Lanka, or Southeast Asia. One of Diogo do Couto's implict complaints in his *Diálogo do Soldado Prático* ('Dialogue of the Veteran Soldier'), concerns precisely this growing neglect of the maritime vocation – so much so indeed that the Portuguese were (he claims) called 'chickens of the sea' by Asian competitors (Couto 1988).

No more startling administrative reform can be found in these years than the decision to divide the *Estado da Índia* into three separate governments: one running along East Africa, the second from Hurmuz to the Bay of Bengal, and the third extending from the eastern Bay of Bengal littoral to Macau. Separate governors were appointed in 1571 to the three sub-*Estado*s, the first to be based in East Africa, the second at Goa, the third in Melaka. The plan was sabotaged though, by the then viceroy at Goa, Dom Antão de Noronha, who refused to permit the captain of Melaka, António Monis Barreto, to become governor of the eastern province. Annoyed at this interference, Dom Sebastião took the harsh step of removing Noronha in the middle of his term, and appointed Barreto to govern in Goa, giving Melaka over to Dom Leonis Pereira (Couto 1973–74, ix: *passim*). But once more, no devolution of powers took effect, and the scheme came to be abandoned on the death of Dom Sebastião.

Was this scheme no more than an eccentric and arbitrary shift in direction? On the contrary, there appears to be some method behind the apparent madness. We may recall that it was early in Dom Sebastião's reign that Paulo Dias de Novais was given a *capitania-donatária* or charter to commence the territorial conquest of Angola, in the face of deteriorating relations with the Ngola ruler there. Similarly, in the case of East Africa, the years leading up to the tripartite divison of the *Estado* saw the grant to Francisco Barreto, a former governor at Goa, of the Captain-Majorship of the 'Conquest of Monomotapa'. This grant, made at Almeirim in March 1569, followed on a consultation with theologians, who argued that for a variety of reasons the Portuguese ruler had a right to conquer the inland kingdom; a significant factor that influenced their arguments was the killing of the Jesuit Fr. Gonçalo de Sequeira, in March 1561, while at the court of the Mutapa ruler Negomo Mupunzagutu (r.1550–86) (Mudenge 1988: 201–03). The three specific arguments that were made to justify the right of *conquista* all are familiar ones: the killing of an 'ambassador' (even if the Jesuit had not had precisely this status); the denial of the free right to trade whereas 'hospitality and commerce ... are the common rights of peoples'; finally, an argument typical of the Counter-Reformation, namely the Muslim presence in the kingdom of the Mutapa.

Barreto was subsequently made governor of the East Africa sub-*Estado* by a grant of February 1571, with jurisdiction over Sofala, Moçambique and other parts of the 'conquest', which presumably included the little trading settlements that private Portuguese had established up the Zambezi, in such places as Sena and Tete. But even before this, he had set sail from Lisbon in April 1569 with an invasion fleet, which expected great returns from the conquest; as the Portuguese chronicler Manuel de Faria e Sousa later put it, 'The great inducement to this conquest was the information and experience of the vast quantity of gold found particularly at Manica in the kingdom of Macaranga' (Mudenge 1988: 203). But Barreto does not seem to have been entirely possessed of the same spirit as Pizarro and Cortés; instead of proceeding inland, he dawdled on the coast at Moçambique Island and Pate, toyed with the idea of making for the Indian west coast, and only in 1571 – after receiving news of his governorship – went ahead with his expedition. His force, of some seven hundred musketeers, left Moçambique for Sena in November 1571, and after six weeks' travel arrived at Sena. The cost in terms of lives on the journey was considerable, and the returns in gold began to seem unlikely; despite the religious zeal shown by the Jesuit Fr. Francisco de Monclaro, who was desirous of recovering the bones of the deceased Sequeira, negotiations were begun from afar with the Mutapa. Nothing emerged from them, and a military campaign was resumed, which lasted intermittently until October 1572; thereafter, Barreto returned to Moçambique Island, only to return with fresh supplies to Sena, where he died in May 1573.

The Barreto expedition, even in the optimistic vision of Monclaro, cannot be seen as a great success. The Portuguese never encountered the

Mutapa's forces, instead spending their energy fighting the forces of the relatively petty Samungazi ruler; it was climate, disease and a lack of a sense of purpose that undermined the expedition, so that by 1573 a mere one hundred and eighty men from the original Portuguese force were left. But the Portuguese Crown had not given up its dream of an African *El Dorado*; Barreto's place was taken by Vasco Fernandes Homem, who led an expedition inland by an alternative, and less taxing route, from Sofala. This attempt, which began in late 1574, was less aimed at chastising the Mutapa than at gaining hold of the Manyika gold-source, and Homem did in fact find his way to that kingdom by the latter half of 1575. What they found there was nevertheless disappointing: the process of washing gold from the rivers was laborious, and the Portuguese of Homem's expedition did not have the wherewithal to do so. Matters dragged on to 1577, with desultory expeditions being sent out to explore rumours of other gold and silver sources; once again, the climate, and local resistance (which accounted for a force under António Cardoso Almeida) won the war of attrition (Mudenge 1988).

The parallel between these expeditions and the less successful Spanish expeditions, like those of Coronado, and especially de Soto, of the 1530s and early 1540s is obvious. Taken together with the developments in Angola, however, an argument can be made that the tendency to move inland might have had a more complex evolution than imitation of the Spanish 'model': the donatory captaincy system in Brazil, and the *prazo*-estates created in the *província do norte*, north of Goa, also provide models of land-based expansion. Certainly, in the Sri Lankan case there is something to be said for such an explanation. But the East African adventure of the 1570s, which continued into the 1580s – during the captaincy at Moçambique of Nuno Velho Pereira – has little in common with the Angolan-Brazilian model, which was more concerned with the control of people and, through them, of labour power and agrarian produce, than with quick returns from the plunder of inland polities.

Still, had these expeditions been unique, it might have been possible to argue that they lived and died – like the Moroccan revival – with Dom Sebastião, being purely the product of local circumstances and the expedient politics of the moment. There had after all been earlier expeditions inland into Africa: in the 1530s, the Christian ruler of Ethiopia, Lebna Dengel (r. 1508–40), had been routed by forces of the Adal-based Ahmad ibn-Ibrahim al-Ghazi (better known as Ahmad 'Gran', the left-handed), and the Portuguese had mounted a counter-expedition under Dom Cristôvão da Gama in 1541. This expedition, despite the death of Gama, helped restore to the Ethiopian throne the emperor Galawdewos (r. 1540–59), but – significantly – did not attempt to seize the revenues of the kingdom for itself (Pankhurst 1961).

The spirit of the years from 1570 to 1610 was quite different. The

Bishop of Melaka from 1581 to 1601, Dom João Ribeiro Gaio, had a number of schemes that speak of substantial territorial conquest, which he put up for the Crown's consideration. Many of his schemes, which were conceived in the Habsburg period, required Spanish-Portuguese cooperation, with Manila to provide one of the bases from which operations would be conducted, together with Melaka. One of these concerned the possibility of conquering the Thai kingdom of Ayuthia, as well as its ports such as Patani; the Bishop argued that Thailand would provide agricultural supplies and cattle, besides being a rich centre of trade that could be taxed, and among the products he mentions are indigo, benzoin, sappan-wood, and timber for ship-building. This notion, far from being regarded as an eccentric pipe-dream, was seconded by Luís Pérez Dasmariñas, interim Governor of the Philippines in 1593–96. Besides the fact that the conquest of Ayuthia, Patani and territories around would make Felipe II the 'richest and most powerful ruler in the world', legal-ethical considerations were brought into play, in a manner parallel to what had occurred in respect of East Africa in 1569 (Boxer 1969b). The anti-Christian conduct of the Ayuthia ruler Phra Nareth – evocatively described as the 'Black King' – was dilated on at some length by Dasmariñas; it was also argued that the Thais themselves wished, almost to a man, to be rid of their ruler, and enjoy peace and security, 'something which everyone desires, and which now they lack completely'.

The archives of the period are littered with papers containing proposals of this kind, which tend to become formulaic in their construction by the 1590s. Acts of cruelty against missionaries by Asian rulers are alleged, as well as the mistreatment of ambassadors or Portuguese representatives; once this has been pointed out, the tyranny of the ruler in question while dealing with his own subjects is used as a device to show his illegitimacy; at times, genealogical tables are produced to demonstrate the illegitimacy of the ruler in terms of descent from earlier kings; finally, an appendix is usually to be found, which speaks of the agricultural and mineral wealth of the kingdom, the aspect of *realpolitik* thus not being neglected either. It is such a construction one encounters for Thailand, and similar papers exist in the cases of Cambodia and Burma; more sketchy proposals may be found dealing with China, and southern India. In none of these cases could the argument of Holy War be invoked, since the rulers in all of these cases were not Muslim, nor indeed were the majority of their subjects.

Two of these proposals did bear fruit of some kind in the 1590s, these being projects in respect of Burma and Cambodia. In the latter case, the proposal originated not from Melaka or Manila, but from Cambodia itself – with the prime mover being a Portuguese mercenary called Diogo Veloso, who was employed by the Cambodian ruler Satha II in his campaigns against Ayuthia. Veloso in the 1580s appealed for aid first to Melaka, and then to Manila, himself travelling to the former port as

Satha's ambassador on two occasions. In 1596, the Spanish decided to intervene, sending back Veloso and his associate Blas Ruiz de Hernán González with a small expeditionary force of three ships and one hundred and twenty men, to help Satha II's son against a usurper, Phra Ream. The precise circumstances of what followed are not entirely clear; it is apparent that the expedition could not by itself have had great effect, but the letters and papers of Veloso and his associates do not tell us who their 'native' allies were. At any rate, Phra Ream was displaced from Srei Santhor, the capital-city, and Veloso and Blas Ruiz were given extensive favours, including permission to build a fort, by the new king Barom Rechea (Groslier 1958).

But neither Veloso nor his allies, who included several Augustinians like Frei António de Piedade, were satisfied with this. In letters to Melaka, they proposed no less than the conquest of Cambodia, and thereafter of Champa, in its entirety. Already in 1595, a junta of theologians at Manila had decided that the King of Champa was a tyrant, deserving of a campaign against him 'of fire and blood' (*una guerra a fuego y sangre*) (Boxer 1969b: 130). In the Cambodia case, such a legal or theological justification was never sought; however, we do have a pragmatic document, entitled 'Things that are to be found in the Kingdom of Camboya', written in 1599, which states the following.

> First of all, Camboya can sustain all of India in all its necessities.
> One can make galleys in Camboya, as well as all other sorts of vessels at a very low cost, and from the best wood there is in India.
> The island that the King has given [to Veloso] in order to make the fortress is the key to the whole Kingdom, and it is upriver from this island that the port which receives all the ships is located. And across from it, at the distance of a cannon-shot from the island, is a city, the principal one in Camboya.
> The land has in itself yellow silk, gold-bearing streams, cardamom, sappan-wood, much wax, much ivory, much cloth of every sort, much saltpetre – the best in all of India, ebony-wood, aloes, eaglewood – only a little.
> And [from there] the port of Lao is open, whence come many goods and precious stones, and whence comes all the benzoin. The greatest trade there is in Camboya is of salt, all of it passes by this island, and they cannot live without it. We can, from Camboya, take Chanpaa with no additional cost to the King, and after it is taken make a fortress there that can be sustained by twenty men.
> The voyage to Japan, at present made by the Camboyas, will if made by us amount to thirty thousand cruzados.
> Pegu, which used to provide Melaka with rice, no longer does so.
> There is in Camboya much oil, pitch, and tow.
>
> (Subrahmanyam 1990b: 158)

By the early seventeenth century, however, we hear little further concerning this project, possibly because its principal proponent Veloso had been killed by Malay traders in a fracas in 1599. But other similar projects were floated in the period, and even brought to some form of conclusion. In the eastern Bengal region, where once Martim de Lucena and Cristôvão Jusarte strode the stage, there had agglomerated by the 1590s a substantial number of Portuguese, who acted as private traders, pirates and mercenaries. Some of them are likely by this period to have been of mixed blood, but others – like a certain Filipe de Brito e Nicote – were men who had arrived from Portugal, and who after a brief period in Goa or Cochin, had left the Indian west coast settlements of the *Estado* for the Bay of Bengal. Burmese ports such as Martaban, Pegu and Dagon had a substantial number of Portuguese resident in them already from the 1530s, as did the western Irrawaddy delta port of Cosmin (Bassein), the great centre where trade to Bengal and Coromandel was concerned. Trade was however not the only activity with which these elements concerned themselves; in about 1540, a mercenary captain called João Caeiro is reported to have been active in the area, and in the 1540s one Diogo Soares de Albergaria had a role of some importance in local politics. The Burmese Great Chronicle (*Maha-ya-zawin-gyi*) of U Kala, while making no specific mention of Albergaria's role, does speak of Portuguese influence over the ruler Tabin-shwei-hti (r. 1531–50), who is reported by the chronicler to have become an alcoholic as a result of associating with these 'unseemly heretics' (Lieberman 1980).

It is sometimes argued that the principal role of these Portuguese was as experts in the use of firearms, by means of which the first two rulers of the so-called Taung-ngu dynasty, Tabin-shwei-hti and his brother-in-law and successor, Bayin-naung (r. 1551–81), are supposed to have consolidated rule over what was the largest single state in mainland Southeast Asia in the epoch. The role of firearms in this process may be disputed, but there is certainly no gainsaying the success of these two rulers. In particular, under Bayin-naung, the Burmese state came to control not merely the coast but the uplands, as well as a large area of Tai-speaking principalities from Kalei in the north-west to Chiengmai in the south-west. The process of conquest, set out at some length in the contemporary Mon-language account *Nidana Ramadhipati-katha*, made Bayin-naung a ruler of some dimensions, as the Venetian Cesare Federici (who visited Burma in the 1560s) points out:

> To conclude, there is not a King on the Earth that hath more power or strength then this King of Pegu, because hee hath twenty and six crowned Kings at his command ... This King of Pegu hath not any army or power by Sea, but in the Land, for People, Dominions, Gold and Silver, he farre exceedeth the power of the great Turke in treasure and strength. This King hath divers Magasons full of treasure, as Gold and Silver, and every day he encreaseth it more and more, and it is never diminished.
>
> (Lieberman 1980: 217)

Despite the extent of his power, however, Bayin-naung was never able to gain control over the coastal region to the north of the Irrawaddy delta, which hence became the core region of another flourishing state – the state of Arakan, based at the river-port of Mrauk-u. Several attacks were made on Mrauk-u by the south Burmese, but with little success, and on the death of Bayin-naung in the early 1580s, the tide began to turn in Arakan's favour. During the reign at Pegu of Nanda-bayin (r. 1581–99), a phase of political disintegration was inaugurated, which seems to have had two principal causes. The first was the conflict between the southern Mon-speakers of the Pegu region, and the northern Burmese, who were favoured by Nanda-bayin; this eventually led Buddhist monks from the southern province to lead a revolt against the Taung-ngu rulers. Second, the Burmese state of Bayin-naung had overstretched itself, and come to encompass a territory far larger than that which it could control effectively. This led to a resurgence of the power of Ayuthia in the 1580s and early 1590s, while at the same time the Arakan ruler, Minyazagyi, attacked the lower Irrawaddy delta (Reid 1990).

Like Bayin-naung, the Arakan ruler too had several Portuguese mercenaries in his entourage, and it was to one of these – Filipe de Brito e Nicote, who had reputedly been in his service from the 1570s – that he gave control over a small wooden fort at Syriam, in the Irrawaddy delta. But De Brito had his own ideas; he seems to have been anxious to rehabilitate himself in the mainstream of Portuguese Asian society, and therefore sought a link with Goa and thence with Lisbon and Madrid. His offer was simple: the Portuguese *Estado* did not have a single fortress, customs-house or possession on the eastern Bay of Bengal littoral, with the exception of Melaka. This was particularly ironical, for the Bay of Bengal trade had been growing with great rapidity in the 1570s and 1580s; new ports like Masulipatnam had arisen, whose trading networks were wholly outside the *Estado*'s control. Syriam was thus ideally placed to be the counterpart of Melaka further to the north: a fleet based at Syriam, and a customs-house there, would control trade from Arakan to Tenasserim, and encompass all the ports of Burma and the northern limits of the Malay world.

Goa was eager, but nervous. On De Brito's arrival there in the early seventeenth century, he was well received by the viceroy Aires de Saldanha, but legal issues remained to be sorted out. First, Minyazagyi had to be persuaded to desist from his claim over Syriam, even though he later did change his mind on the question; next, the question of residual sovereignty rights over the Pegu-Syriam region had to be sorted out. The Goa High Court (*Relação*) resolved that these were vested, by virtue of a marital link with the late Nanda-bayin, in the ruler of Chiengmai ('Jangoma'), and an embassy was hence sent to him. The Dominican priest who served as ambassador has left us a long memoir, expounding on the legal and moral aspects of the question: he concludes, not surprisingly perhaps, that the strongest claim over the entire region is that of Felipe of

Spain and Portugal. Appended to his learned report is – almost inevitably – a shorter, more pragmatic, statement: 'Notes on the things that the Kingdom of Pegu produces'. It is remarkably similar to the report on Cambodia that we have examined above, speaks of the agricultural richness of the region, the precious stones, gold, and other products, and even points out that

> with the forces that can be got together here, one can conquer Bengala, so that His Majesty would no longer have to send the annual aid (*socorro*) to the south from India, but rather from here and from Bengalla, on account of the great facility there is in this, for the voyage is easy and along the coast, and besides there are very abundant lands here that can be divided amongst the poor of India who have scarcely anything. (Subrahmanyam 1990b: 159–60)

The Pegu enterprise thus has an obvious resemblance to that of Cambodia; however, unlike Veloso, De Brito did succeed in creating something of substance. He was granted the captaincy of Syriam by the Portuguese Crown for his lifetime and for that of his first heir; the viceroy gave him his neice, Dona Luísa de Saldanha, in marriage; and he returned to Burma with a small *armada*, and the regulations (*regimento*) for his customs-house. In the first decade of the seventeenth century, when the Dutch first arrived in the Bay of Bengal, the fortress *Santiago* of De Brito at Syriam preoccupied them a great deal, suggesting that it did have a certain importance in re-directing traffic in the eastern Bay of Bengal. In their reports on the trade of the Bay of Bengal and Coromandel, Dutch factors like Stalpaert van der Wiele and Pieter Willemszoon stress the 'great trade and profits' that the trade of the Bay of Bengal held, save for the fact that the Portuguese had closed it to them by means of their fort (*stercte*) (De Jonge 1865: 150–52, 289–90).

The East African and Southeast Asian projects – with the exception of Syriam – were, we have seen, not particularly successful in the years up to 1610, although they represent a tendency that is significant. The creation of the *prazos da Coroa* in the Zambezi region by a gradual process in the first half of the seventeenth century flows out of these earlier attempts, and is the result of a more propitious political climate in the Zambezi region in that period – so that Portuguese, Goan and *mestiço prazeros* are able to gain control over small Malawian, Sena and Tonga chieftaincies on the margins of the river. The last of the major cases of territorial expansion by the Portuguese in the period is similar to the East African one in logic, in the sense that only shifts in local alliance-structures and political formations make it possible. Unlike East Africa or Southeast Asia, however, it already takes place in the late sixteenth century: here we speak of the Sri Lankan case.

When the Portuguese first arrived in Sri Lanka in the first decade of the sixteenth century, they found the island loosely divided into three competing sovereignties: to the north the Tamil kingdom of the Arya

Chakravartis of Jaffna, ruled over by Pararajasekeram (r. 1478–1519); in the interior, the upland (Uda-rata) kingdom of the Kandy region was ruled over by Vikramabahu (r. 1475–1511); to the south-west was the most powerful kingdom of the three, Kotte, at the time ruled over by Dharma Parakramabahu, and then by Vijayabahu (d. 1521) (Bouchon 1971). This structure was itself the product of a gradual shift that had taken place on the island after the twelfth century, for until then power had centred largely in the east-north-east, with the major courtly centre of the 'Golden Age' of Parakramabahu I (r. 1153–86) being Polonnaruva (halfway between Kandy and Trincomalee). The resources of the Polonnaruva state had largely been drawn from an elaborate irrigation-based rice-cultivating economy, but – for reasons that are unclear – this was abandoned from the thirteenth century in favour of rain-fed subsistence agriculture. A concomitant shift of population from interior to coast seems to have occurred, and the resources of two of the three states of the early sixteenth century – Jaffna and Kotte – were drawn largely from trade. The Kotte rulers controlled the cinnamon-producing forests of the south-western wet-zone, and the trade in this spice – together with that in the forest's other resource, elephants – was what drew the Portuguese there in the first place (Abeyasinghe 1966; De Silva 1972).

In the first phase, the principal interest of the Portuguese state, operating for the most part from the fortress-centre of Colombo, in the Kotte kingdom, was cinnamon. By 1526, they had succeeded in having their principal commercial rivals – the Mappilas of Malabar – largely excluded from this trade, and in 1533 a contract between them and the ruler of Kotte, Bhuvanekabahu, confirmed a system of *páreas* (tribute) in cinnamon to be offered yearly by the Kotte ruler, which amounted to three hundred *bahars* (or nine hundred *quintais*) a year; the Portuguese state was also to have a monopoly on the rest of the cinnamon that was traded, at a fixed price (De Silva 1989: 31–32). But this monopoly was not really effective, since the cinnamon lands now fell partly outside of Kotte's control, on account of a division of the kingdom that had taken place in 1521, at the death of Vijayabahu: of his three sons, Rayigama Bandara controlled one section, Mayadunne of Sitavaka another, and Bhuvanekabahu remained with Kotte and its environs. The Sitavaka ruler soon emerged as the principal source of resistance to Portuguese control of external trade, and also the principal threat to Kotte itself. As he pressed on Kotte, Bhuvanekabahu was forced into the Portuguese camp; in 1540, he sent an embassy to Lisbon, as a result of which Dom João III swore in 1543 to protect the succession at Kotte of the former's grandson, Dharmapala. The Portuguese state had thus emerged by the early 1540s as the guarantor of Kotte's sovereignty in opposition to Sitavaka.

This was a position that they were to exploit mercilessly. In the early 1550s, Bhuvanekabahu was murdered, possibly at Goa's instigation, and the viceroy Dom Afonso de Noronha mounted an expedition to the Sri Lankan west coast, plundering the palaces at both Kotte and Sitavaka with impunity. The new king, Dharmapala, was persuaded in 1557 to convert to Catholicism; in 1565, after renewed attacks by Sitavaka forces, he abandoned Kotte to them and fled to the safety of Colombo; and in the late 1570s, as Dom João Dharmapala, made a curious will, naming the Portuguese King as his heir, a will that was confirmed when the House of Avis gave way to the Habsburgs. At the time, the will probably was seen as of little significance, for it is not even mentioned by the anonymous author of the *Livro das Cidades e Fortalezas* (1582), who was attempting to inform Felipe II of his possessions in Asia (Mendes da Luz 1954). The reason for this was simple: the period from the 1560s to the early 1590s are the apogee of Sitavaka power, with Mayadunne's successor Rajasinha reducing not only Kotte but also the upland kingdom at Kandy to insignificance.

But in the 1590s, a reversal occurred. On the death of Rajasinha of Sitavaka in 1593, the Portuguese began to expand along the south-west, while the power of Kandy was re-established by Vimala Dharma Surya (r. 1591–1604) and his son Senarath (r. 1604–35). From the Portuguese viewpoint, the turning point may be seen as the appointment to the post of Captain-General of Ceilão of Dom Jerónimo de Azevedo in 1594. Here, unlike in either East Africa or Southeast Asia, no tortuous process of religio-legal sanction for conquest had to be invoked: Dharmapala's will provided it. Only the north of the island remained to be accounted for: from the middle years of the sixteenth century, the Portuguese had gradually come to play a crucial role in Jaffna politics, and in the 1560s had actually toyed with the idea – under the viceroy Dom Constantino de Bragança – of promoting agrarian settlement in that part of the island by Portuguese from the Coromandel settlements. Now, the collapse of Sitavaka provided the ideal opportunity, and rapid expansion followed, as we can see from the *Tombo* (or land-register) compiled in 1599 by Jorge Frolim de Almeida, and the subsequent one put together in around 1614 by Antão Vaz Freire, *vedor da fazenda* of the *ilha de Ceilão*; by the latter date the Portuguese held rights over some 4,640 villages (Abeyasinghe 1966: 125). The principal idea now became to promote the settlement of a type of rural-based intermediary, who would collect revenue, and maintain a force (usually set out in terms of a number of muskets – *espingardas*), thus constituting a form of volunteer militia.

These settlers, termed *casados fronteiros*, possibly to distinguish them from the common *casados* who were urban-based, bear an obvious resemblance to Portuguese settlers in certain nuclei in North Africa (such as Azemmour), but are also clearly akin to the settlers in the New World – be it in Brazil or Spanish America. The focus of their activity is not so much trade – though trade too played a role in the lives of early

131

seventeenth-century *casados* of the island, like Lançarote de Seixas Cabreira – as the control of labour and its produce. Characteristic of this is the relationship that is built up with specific social groups like *salagama* (or *chaleas*, as the Portuguese term them), who were denominated traditional state-slaves by the Portuguese (and later the Dutch), although no evidence of such a tradition seems to exist prior to the sixteenth century. In particular, the *sulubadda* sub-group among the *salagama*, resident in the villages of the valley of the Kelani river, and the coast to the north of it, were pressed into service as cinnamon peelers; in the early seventeenth century, their obligation to peel cinnamon was determined by the amount of land they held, but by the middle of the same century, every male *salagama* was required to supply a fixed amount of cinnamon, whether or not he held land (De Silva 1989).

The *fronteiro* system as adopted in Sri Lanka from the 1590s thus provides further evidence of a growing tendency to territoriality in the *Estado da Índia*. It is, of course, not wholly unprecedented as an institution, bearing a resemblance to the *prazos* of the *província do Norte*, where too the *prazo*-holders were endowed in a process termed *aforamento* (as obtained in Sri Lanka). However, in the latter case, the rights of the *prazeros* approximate the *iqta* – or revenue-assignment – previously in effect under the Sultans of Gujarat, stressing land-revenue collection rather than labour control, whereas in Sri Lanka, the case is somewhat different. After 1619, when the Portuguese *Estado* took over Jaffna as well, its returns from village-revenues come greatly to exceed customs-revenue. Table 5.2 illustrates the picture as late as 1634.

Table 5.2 Portuguese revenues in Sri Lanka, 1630s (in *pardaus*)

Source	Jaffna	Colombo	Galle	Total
Customs-duties	319	8,250	1,348	9,917
Village *foros*/land taxes	21,210	17,982	1,829	41,021
Deçus	–	2,296	–	2,296
Sale of areca	170	9,324	–	9,494
Foros on Portuguese	729	–	–	729
Elephants	–	3,999	–	3,999
Other revenues	464	959	1,059	2,482
TOTAL	22,892	42,810	4,236	69,938

(*Source*: Godinho 1982: 108)

To sum up therefore, we can argue with some conviction that in the late sixteenth century, there was a growing tendency towards territoriality, even if the drive to territorial expansion did not bear fruit in many instances. What occurred, the extent of success, the institutions that evolved in each case, were of course the product of local circumstance as much as anything else. The assumption that the Portuguese (or indeed the Spanish) had an institutional tool-kit which they applied in the course of expansion, irrespective of local circumstances, is one that few historians would make today. But we should not err in the other direction either: of seeing each case as a wholly unique thing-in-itself, bearing no relationship to the other contemporary instances, which involved a parallel set of actors.

THE MARITIME CHALLENGE

Towards the end of Diogo do Couto's *Soldado Prático*, which purports to deal with the 1570s (even though it was revised later), the chief protagonist and authorial voice, the Old Soldier (*soldado velho da Índia*) puts the following question to his interlocutors: which is it more important to conquer – Ceylon or Aceh? The Soldier has his own answer, of course, which is neither; he prefers the conquest of Munhumutapa, 'and from there it would be possible to penetrate that heart of Kaffirdom, unto the other part of Angola, and make the Atlantic sea accessible from the Indian [Ocean]; for I myself believe that it is no more that two hundred leagues across' (Couto 1988: 132). But the question is an important one, showing us that even in the late sixteenth century, the land was not everyone's preoccupation: instead the sea, and maritime rivals like Aceh, were also a substantial worry.

The Acehnese Sultanate had been founded in the early sixteenth century in the extreme north of Sumatra in the area known in the sixteenth century as Lamri. Rich in the production of pepper, the northern tip of Sumatra also sheltered two other ports of importance in the period, Pedir and Pasai, the latter the first centre in Indonesia to have been converted to Islam. In the early years of the sixteenth century, and immediately after taking Melaka in 1511, the Portuguese kept a vigilant eye on the politics and trade of Pasai, maintaining a factor there, and – for a brief period around 1520 – even having a fortress in the port. Pasai had been overshadowed in the fifteenth century by Melaka, but still maintained an important role in trade to Bengal and to a lesser extent Coromandel. The first major step in Acehnese expansion was therefore the capture of this port, accomplished by the founder-Sultan of Aceh, Ali Mughayat Syah. The second step came with the reign at Aceh of Sultan Alauddin Riayat Syah al-Kahhar (r. 1539–71); now the pepper trade from Sunda and the Malay peninsula to the western Indian Ocean came to be increasingly routed through the ports under Acehnese control, and Portuguese frustration at this 'contraband' commerce mounted (Boxer 1969b).

But it is only in the 1560s and 1570s that Aceh actually came to be the focus of an entire maritime system, rival to that of the Portuguese *Estado*. Three factors accounted for this transformation: first, the development by Aceh of a diplomatic and military link with the Ottomans; second, the articulation within the Bay of Bengal of a maritime network, encompassing Masulipatnam, Bengal, Aceh, Pegu and the Malay peninsula ports; and third, the growth of Acehnese influence over the Javanese north coast, and the Moluccas.

To begin with the Ottoman link, we have already seen how in the 1540s and 1550s, the Ottomans had maintained a naval presence in the western Indian Ocean, causing considerable concern to the Portuguese. Being aware of Ottoman interest in keeping alive trade to the Red Sea from South and Southeast Asia, and also desirous of the legitimacy provided by a link with the Caliphate, Sultan Alauddin sent an embassy to the Ottomans in 1564. The Portuguese got wind of the embassy through two spies at Venice, Gaspar and João Ribeiro, whose report mentions a substantial present of 'a casket containing a large necklace of valuable pearls and many diamonds and rubies', for the Ottoman ruler Suleyman; in return, the Acehnese requested military aid for a planned attack on Melaka (which eventually took place in 1568) (Boxer 1969b: 420; Manguin 1988). The Ottomans did provide Aceh with expert gun-founders and artillerymen, but the major consequence of this embassy was to cement economic ties between the ports of the Red Sea (like Jiddah) which were under Ottoman control, and the Acehnese. Also, the moral and material support of the Ottomans gave Aceh pre-eminence in the Islamic context, allowing the state to become a major patron of *ulama* from India and further west; thus, the Sultans of Aceh were able to overshadow the Sultans of Johor, even though the latter were descended from the rulers of Melaka (Lombard 1967).

After 1569, the Portuguese largely abandoned any idea of controlling this trade by patrolling the mouth of the Red Sea, and thought in terms of attacking Aceh itself. Ottoman control over the Horn of Africa and the Red Sea went from strength to strength, eventually forcing the Portuguese in the early 1590s to set up a fort on the Swahili coast (Fort Jesus at Mombasa) to limit its spread. The proximate cause for the new outpost was the expeditions in 1585 and 1588 of Mir Ali Bey, who persuaded most of the cities of the Swahili coast between Mogadishu and Kilwa to recognise Ottoman supremacy, and whose success was eventually checked only in 1589, by a substantial Portuguese expeditionary fleet (of twenty ships and nine hundred men) under Tomé de Sousa Coutinho. Following this, in 1593, Mombasa was fortified, and a customs-house set up the next year, the revenues of which were divided between the Portuguese *Estado* and the Sultan of Malindi (Azevedo and Boxer 1960). However, the fort at Mombasa and the fleet maintained by its captain could not choke off traffic through the Red Sea. Early Dutch and English observers at Jiddah thus found numerous ships there from Aceh, of which a fair number seem to have been Gujarati-owned.

But trade from Aceh was not limited to the western Indian Ocean alone. From the late 1560s, we are aware of links between the north Sumatran ports and such centres as Masulipatnam in the Bay of Bengal, from where Aceh received munitions and textiles, the former for use against the Portuguese, and the latter for redistribution within the Indonesian archipelago. Prominent merchants of Masulipatnam, and even the Sultan of Golconda himself (under whose control Masulipatnam fell) were active in this trade. Equally, Aceh received rice and provisions from the ports of Bengal, Orissa, and southern Coromandel, and even private Portuguese traders from such ports as Nagapattinam engaged in this commerce. English traders in early seventeenth century Aceh, like John Davis, note the presence in the harbour of Kutaraja (the capital-city) of several such vessels, besides those from Dabhol and Surat in Gujarat, which were engaged in carrying pepper and spices to the Red Sea (Subrahmanyam 1990a: 151–53, 203–04). The Portuguese Diogo Gil, with whose help the Bishop of Melaka produced the *Roteiro das Cousas do Achém* in 1588, claimed that the relative balance of westward trade from Aceh was as follows: one or two ships each year from Gujarat, one or two from Dabhol, two or three from Coromandel, five to six from Pegu, and three or four from Jiddah (Alves 1990: 106).

The third factor in Acehnese success was the link eastward, into the Indonesian archipelago itself. When the Portuguese sent their first exploratory missions to the Moluccas, they found that an elaborate network of trade linked these islands to the great entrepot of Melaka. At the eastern end, the islands of Ternate, Tidore, Makian, Motir and Bacan – all lying along the west coast of the larger island of Halmahera – produced cloves, while the Banda Islands (also five in number) produced nutmeg and mace. The population resident in these islands were as yet only partly Islamised; the economy was largely one of subsistence, and the principal product against which spices could be procured were Indian textiles, with the means of exchange being barter. Linking these islands to Melaka was a chain of intermediate ports, Sumbawa, Gresik and Panarukan being the most important, with the trade being dominated by a Keling merchant of Melaka, Suryadevasena, and the Gresik-based Pati Yusuf (Thomaz 1975).

The Portuguese moved quickly to control this trade, setting up a fort at Ternate in 1521, and later attempting (in 1532) to take control of the Banda Islands, Gresik and Panarukan as well. Their regime, initially one of Crown trade, gradually became privatised, as we have seen was the case with much of their intra-Asian and Euro-Asian commerce in the sixteenth century. After 1539, trade was notionally freed, with private traders being obliged to sell a third of their cargo to the Crown at Melaka for a fixed price, as well as pay a freight-charge (*choquel*) if they used Crown shipping. This regime was quite successful; in 1547, the Portuguese were able to send over a thousand *quintais* of cloves to Europe, and in 1553, over 1,300 *quintais*. Besides, the intra-Asian clove trade of private parties also yielded a tidy profit, with India in particular being a substantial consumer of the commodity; over two-thirds of total Portuguese procurement thus was re-sold within Asia (Thomaz 1975; Villiers 1981).

But from about 1570, two problems arose. Clove production began to spread southward, into the islands of Halmahera, Ceram and Ambon, forcing the Portuguese to attempt to extend their control over these new sources as well. In 1564, they constructed a small fort at Ative on Ambon, and in 1568, Gonçalo Pereira Marramaque built a far more substantial one at Hitu. This was done in part to forestall Castilian ambitions in the area; but a far more significant threat had arisen in the form of a rival network linking Aceh, via Banten and Japara, to the Banda and Molucca Islands. The second problem was of the Portuguese' own making, resulting from the assassination in 1570 of Sultan Hairun of Ternate, at the instigation of the Portuguese captain there, Diogo Lopes de Mesquita. A revolt ensued against the Portuguese garrison, and Ternate was eventually lost in 1575. The Portuguese now shifted their focus very largely to Ambon, returning in 1578 to Tidore and mounting several expeditions against Ternate (Jacobs 1985).

Nevertheless, from about 1570, the relative weight of trading networks in eastern Indonesia had begun to shift. The success of the Aceh-Banten-Japara nexus was at two levels: first, the spice trade was diverted into the hands of merchants operating out of these ports, with the spices that were procured being sent on not only to the Red Sea (as is usually implied), but to consuming centres in the Bay of Bengal and western India; second, eastern Indonesia now came definitively under the influence of the Malay-Islamic culture of Aceh and its partners, with the conversion of the Sultan of Makassar in the early seventeenth century being the culmination of this process.

The rivalry between Aceh and Melaka did not mean, however, that the two were in a continuous state of war. Intermittently, diplomatic relations between the two were maintained, and also Portuguese private traders and mercenaries at Aceh kept open a corridor of communication. In the late 1590s, the Portuguese state came very close to obtaining a fortress at Aceh, and only the arrival of the Dutch and English diverted the negotiations under way between Melaka and its 'mirror-image'.

The same can be said of another maritime challenge to the Portuguese *Estado* that came to a head in much the same period: that of the Mappila Muslims of the Malabar coast. Here too, one notices alternating phases of negotiation and conflict, with an additional complicating dimension – namely the imperfect integration between the Mappila community and the two rulers on the Malabar coast whose territories they used as bases: the Kolathiri of Cannanore and the Samudri raja of Calicut. Like Aceh, the Mappila ports were centres that rivalled Cochin and other official Portuguese ports, and the small, lightly-armed, and highly mobile vessels of the Mappilas became a threat to Portuguese shipping all along the Indian west coast. The authorities at Goa were obliged by the 1560s annually to bring convoys of merchant vessels from Cape Comorin to their own ports, as well as to organise regular cruising along the Kanara and Malabar coasts to deal with the Mappila challenge. Eventually, in the late 1590s, a solution of sorts was found. The head of one of the Mappila communities, Muhammad Kunjali Marakkar of Ponnani, was defeated and killed by an alliance between the *Estado* and the Calicut ruler, who had grown nervous about the royal pretensions of the Mappila magnate; the other leading Mappila family, the Ali Rajas of Cannanore, were granted permission to send ships even to the Red Sea, as a way of ensuring their cooperation (Pearson 1981). Thus, Zain al-Din Ma'bari's vision of an unremitting *jihad* between Muslims and infidel Portuguese remained more an ideal than a reality.

CONCESSIONS AND CAPTAINS-MAJOR

If the four decades after 1570 are characterised on the one hand by a growing interest in the land and territorial adventurism, and on the other by the rise of a set of maritime networks to rival those of the Portuguese *Estado*, one must not neglect the changes that took place in official Portuguese intra-Asian maritime trade either. When Felipe II of Spain became ruler of Portugal, these changes were already under way, and they accelerated further in the next three decades.

Being a pragmatic ruler – as well something of a workaholic with a mania for paperwork – Felipe appears to have commissioned, in the very first year of his reign over the Portuguese empire, a compendium on the extent and nature of his Asian possessions. This text, the *Livro das Cidades e Fortalezas* ('Book of Cities and Fortresses') is somewhat misnamed, for at least a quarter of it deals with neither cities nor fortresses, but instead with maritime trade within Asia (Mendes da Luz 1954). We do not know who its author was, but it is very likely to have been a former *vedor da fazenda* in Portuguese Asia, for the *Livro* is most precise on financial matters, and also quite pragmatic (rather than legal-minded) in its construction; internal evidence also suggests that the author in all likelihood spent some time in Melaka during his career.

The reader of the *Livro das Cidades e Fortalezas* finds himself in a quite different maritime trading world than what we have seen to be the case in the mid-sixteenth century, when Simão Botelho wrote his penetrating, and at times even caustic, letters on the affairs of India. Whereas the early 1550s was still a period when the *carreira*-route, dominated by Crown shipping, was the rule, this had largely changed by 1580, when only three intra-Asian routes were still plied by the *naus del-Rei*: these were the routes from Goa to Mozambique, Sri Lanka (Colombo), and the Moluccas. In the rest of the routes earlier plied by Crown shipping, the period from the late 1550s had seen a gradual transition, to the system that came to be called that of the *viagens de lugares* (or concession-voyages). We have already examined one of these at some length: this is the Goa-Melaka-Macau-Japan voyage, perhaps the most lucrative of the *viagens* under consideration. In the words of the *Livro*'s anonymous author:

> [These] Voyages of which we are treating, I say that they are the best and most profitable of any that are made in the parts of India, and hence they are always given to very honoured *fidalgos*, of service and very special merit.
>
> (Mendes da Luz 1954: 130)

Even if this was not strictly true, it was certainly the case that those who were granted the Macau-Japan voyage were most often men of wealth and power, if not of birth and 'merits'. They did not always make the journey in a single ship, for the concession was that of the post of Captain-Major, and in fact in seven out of ten years in the 1580s, two ships made the voyage rather than one. But the ship that left an impression was the Captain-Major's own vessel, termed the *Kurofune* ('Black Ship') by contemporary Japanese, and ranging between 1,200 and 1,600 tons by the end of the sixteenth century. Trade on these ships, based on the export of pepper and spices from Melaka to Macau, of silk and gold from Macau to Japan, of silver from Japan to Macau, and of silk, copper and precious metals from Macau back to Goa, made the fortunes of many an entrepreneur, ranging from the picturesque Bartolomeu Vaz Landeiro (nicknamed the 'King of the Portuguese' in Japan), to the vigilant Padres of the Society of Jesus, who from the late 1570s made frequent and profitable investments in the silk export from China to Japan. So high was the return to the Captain-Major, that despite the risk of encountering typhoons in the Far East, or – after 1603 – of having to deal with ill-disposed Dutch men-of-war off Macau, a brisk re-sale market came to exist in the concessions.

The Macau-Japan concession represented one pattern, that of the post of Captain-Major. In fact, until 1623, Macau had no permanent resident Captain, so that the Captain-Major of the concession-voyage also served as the town's Captain-Major during the trading season. This pattern seems to have obtained in certain other cases, such as Pipli in Orissa, where grants of the post of Captain-Major can be traced back to the late 1550s or early 1560s. The Orissa concession, like the Macau-Japan one, was one invented in the middle decades of the century, by way of exploiting what was for the Portuguese a new maritime route. But there was also another type of concession, which obtained over routes which had earlier been intra-Asian *carreiras*; these *viagens* were on routes such as Coromandel-Melaka, Coromandel-Cosmin, and so on, replacing the earlier *Carreira de Choromandel* or *Carreira de Pegu*. The author of the *Livro das Cidades e Fortalezas* hastens to explain why the transition took place from *carreira* to *viagem*:

> [The] manner in which at the beginning the Royal Treasury benefitted from the commerce of India, while necessary at that time, and considered as profitable, for reasons that we shall see is not appropriate at this time, nor is it useful but instead most prejudicial: For if in this way the money and capital of the State, that is necessary for the sustenance and augumentation of the same is consumed therein, one neither can nor should engage in trade and commerce.
>
> (Mendes da Luz 1954: 112)

A second reason is added: in the early phases, the Crown was forced to act as merchant because there were no private Portuguese merchants, but now since the Portuguese 'make trade and commerce in all the Orient, with almost all of them mixing trade with arms', the Crown can afford to desist.

What we are witnessing then is the *dénouement* of the Cabral-Fernandes debate, initiated in the period of Dom João de Castro, and continued by Simão Botelho in his letters. As our author of the early 1580s makes clear, the initial shift from *carreira* to *viagem* did not come so much from Lisbon but from Goa:

> Finally for all these and many other reasons, the Viceroys and Governors of India came to desist generally from such commerce and trade, in the manner that seemed necessary to them, so that profits would result for the Royal Treasury, either by freeing them to the people, or by contracting them out. And leaving aside the rest, for it is not a matter to be dealt with here, and dealing with the voyages that used to be made in *naos del Rey* and with his [the King's] goods (as has been mentioned above), in the same way they ceased to make them in the accustomed manner, and ordered the persons who had received a grant (*mercê*) of any of them from the King to make them in their own *naos* or ships, fitted out at their own cost.
>
> (Mendes da Luz 1954: 113)

The transition in the Coromandel-Melaka case took place in about the mid-1560s, later grants thus bearing the tell-tale phrase 'fitted out at their own cost' (*armado a sua própria custa*). But during an intermediate phase, since it was also necessary to deal with those who had received a *mercê* under the old regime, and who felt 'greatly defrauded' by the new dispensation, a sum of three thosand *cruzados* was set aside to help each of them fit out or freight a vessel.

This change is truly a significant one, the intra-Asian counterpart – in broad terms – of the shift in regime that took place in the 1560s and 1570s in respect of the Cape route (Thomaz 1979). For a concomitant change took place in Portuguese claims over intra-Asian trade, especially in the case of the routes that had earlier been plied by the *naus del-Rei*, and were hence given out as specific voyages rather than grants of the post of Captain-Major. As the *Livro das Cidades* makes clear: 'It is to be known that all the places from where, and to which such voyages are made are reserved (*coutados*), so that it is forbidden to other ships save those of the regular route [viz. royal grant]'. This meant that whereas in the 1540s and 1550s, several ships had annually taken textiles from Coromandel to Melaka, by the late 1560s only the concessionary's carrack did so. Being a monopolist, the concessionary could thus gain that much more from trading, or indeed even by freighting goods. But such a monopolistic regime meant in turn that private Portuguese and Asian shipowning merchants turned more and more to routes and ports that fell outside the concession system. Ships from Coromandel took to using ports on the Malay peninsula, such as Perak and Trang, as a way of avoiding Melaka; Aceh too is likely to have gained from the displacement that took place (Subrahmanyam 1990b: 39–46).

But for the concessionaries, the returns were considerable. Table 5.3 lists some of the more lucrative concessions in about 1580, in addition to which there were numerous other petty ones – with the Captains of Melaka alone being entitled to hold eighteen concessions for the duration of their captaincy (which usually was three years) (Thomaz 1979; Matos 1982).

Table 5.3 Major intra-Asian concession voyages (*c.* 1580)

Route	Net average profit (in cruzados)	Auction price (in cruzados)
Goa-Macau/Nagasaki	35,000	20,000
Goa-Moluccas		
: captain	9,500	
: scrivener	3,000	
Melaka-Macau	10,000	5,500
Coromandel-Melaka	6,000	
Coromandel-Cosmin	6,000	
Melaka-Pipli	9,000	
Melaka-Sunda	10,000	5,500
Melaka-Borneo	5,500	
Macau-Sunda	6,500	

(*Source*: Mendes da Luz 1954: 116–44)

In the three decades after 1580, these concessions tended to fluctuate in value, although the Macau-Japan did retain its pre-eminence despite several years – 1592, 1594, 1599, 1601, 1603, 1607, and 1608 – when the voyage could not be made (Boxer 1959). The Coromandel-Melaka voyage too still remained lucrative, and was usually made from the central Coromandel port of São Tomé (or Mylapur), less often from Nagapattinam. The trade to Burma, on the other hand, suffered from severe dislocations, beginning in the late 1570s when Bayin-naung expelled all Portuguese from his dominions, and forbade formal trade, to avenge himself for the capture of one of his vessels by Dom João da Gama, captain of Melaka. Several years of hostile relations followed, with the Portuguese sending out expeditions from Goa to attack trade between Masulipatnam and Pegu on at least two occasions, in the early 1580s and mid-1590s. An exchange of embassies between Nanda-bayin and Goa in the late 1590s promised to restore normalcy, but this was not to be; thus, the concession-voyages only resumed after 1600, with Syriam as their eastern terminus. Several of the other voyages, such as those to the Moluccas, suffered even more, since the Dutch capture of Ambon and Tidore (1605) meant that their *raison d'être* – the clove and nutmeg trade – was put under question. From about 1610, therefore, the Portuguese had to resort increasingly to the south Sulawesi port of Makassar, to which cloves and other spices were brought in the face of Dutch opposition; but no regular concession-route developed with Makassar as its terminus.

The changed profile of voyages is visible through the papers of the 'General Auction' held in 1614–15 by the viceroy Dom Jerónimo de Azevedo, to meet the urgent shortage of liquidity that he faced. He could only sell concessions pertaining to six routes, the Macau-Japan voyage remaining the most lucrative, followed closely by the Goa-Moçambique route (for which no details are available for the early 1580s).

Table 5.4 Sales of concessions, *c.* 1614

Voyage	Number	Purchaser	Amount (xerafins)
São Tomé-Melaka	3	Simão Teixeira	12,010
Goa-Moçambique	3	Bastião Fernandes	27,800
São Tomé-Pegu	3	Henrique de Sousa	1,100
Coromandel-Trang	3	Martim Cota	1,720
Goa-Macau-Japan	1	Vicente Rodrigues	16,016
Goa-Macau-Japan	1	Jerónimo de Macedo de Carvalho	16,000
Goa-Macau-Japan	1	Ferdinand Cron	16,000
Coromandel-Mergui	3	António Gonçalves	1,205

(*Source*: ANTT, Documentos Remetidos da Índia, Livro 38, fls. 334–45)

Thus, by the second decade of the seventeenth century, we can already speak of the concession system as having entered its twilight years, after a brief fluorescence in the closing decades of the sixteenth century. But from the point of view of the Portuguese private trader, the decline of the concession system may not have been without its positive side, for the reasons that we have discussed above.

THE BEGINNINGS OF DECLINE?

Can we draw up a balance sheet then of 'gains and losses' from the twists and turns that we have described in this chapter, and conclude that the Portuguese empire in Asia either declined, or even remained stable, in the years from 1570 to 1610? It would seem clear that the hypothesis of 'decline' can be contested with the greatest of ease, since there was a clear expansion in opportunities, albeit accompanied by a shift in priorities, in this period; the only thing that declines unambiguously is the Crown's role as a trader, whether within Asia or on the Cape route, as a result of a predilection towards 'privatisation' of a kind so eloquently articulated by the author of the *Livro das Cidades e Fortalezas* already in the early 1580s.

The other decline that we see in this period is in the number of ships that returned from Asia to Lisbon each year. T. Bentley Duncan's statistics once again sum up the picture, as illustrated in Table 5.5.

Table 5.5 Portuguese shipping tonnage on the Cape route, 1570–1610

| Period | Europe-Asia | | Asia-Europe | |
	Departures	Arrivals	Departures	Arrivals
1571–1580	42,900 (50)	40,800 (48)	38,250 (42)	35,150 (39)
1581–1590	55,420 (59)	42,870 (45)	48,450 (51)	39,290 (42)
1591–1600	49,200 (43)	42,540 (39)	45,350 (40)	25,000 (22)
1601–1610	77,190 (71)	49,540 (45)	43,390 (36)	32,290 (28)

(Figures in brackets are numbers of ships)
(*Source*: Duncan 1986: 22)

Table 5.5 makes two facts clear. First, the proportion of losses en route increases significantly in the period (for instance, twenty-six out of seventy-one outward-bound ships are lost in the decade 1601–10). But, with the exception of the last decade of the sixteenth century, shipping tonnage returning to Lisbon from Asia is quite respectable, indeed above the levels of the 1540s and 1550s. Thus, any absolute decline in Portuguese trade from Asia on the Cape route that observers have inferred from statistics on the *number* of ships is purely illusory.

Once we call the post-1570 decline in return tonnage and hence cargoes from Asia into question, the hypothesis of a substantial revival in Euro-Asian trade via the overland route of Asia Minor in the last quarter of the sixteenth century (put forward by Lane, Godinho, Braudel and

Steensgaard) begins to look poorly founded on evidence. C.H.H. Wake has argued in this context that the increase in Acehnese and Malabar-based trade to the Red Sea after about 1560 is largely explicable in terms of two factors: first, the growth in Middle Eastern demand for South and Southeast Asian spices, and second, the fact that in some particular years, when the number of Portuguese ships reaching Lisbon was low, Venice may have picked up the slack and filled residual European demand. Still, in a fair number of years, the returning ships of the *Carreira da Índia* came quite close to meeting total European demand for pepper (estimated by the south German banking houses in the late sixteenth century at around 28,000 *quintais* or 1,500 tonnes), with the situation in respect of the other spices being somewhat more ambiguous (Kellenbenz 1956).

This trade was, however, now increasingly financed and managed not by the Crown, but by international merchant-capitalists, first men like the Welsers, the Fuggers, Konrad Rott or Rovellasca, and later more and more New Christian entrepreneurs such as the Rodrigues d'Évora and the Mendes de Brito. Meanwhile, the Crown, propelled by the experience of Spanish America, and with its appetite whetted by sub-imperialist adventurers from east Africa and Sri Lanka to Pegu and Cambodia, sank its military resources in a set of territorial adventures, some of which bore fruit. In particular, the setting up of an outpost at Syriam was – potentially at least – a fecund idea, since it enabled the Portuguese state for the very first time to gain a foothold in the very heart of the Bay of Bengal, and caused considerable heartburning to the Dutch when they first arrived there. It is difficult to evaluate with certainty the extent to which the expansionism of the late sixteenth century reflects central rather than peripheral initiatives at work. Many of the projects of expansion clearly were initiated at the periphery – by men like Veloso, Filipe de Brito or Dom João Ribeiro Gaio – but had they not struck the fancy of men in power in Goa, Lisbon and Madrid, they would have not made headway.

This is easily demonstrated by a letter of Felipe III of 1610, in which he dreams of a land-based empire in peninsular India, based on the ruins of the declining Vijayanagara empire, then ruled over from the twin fortresses of Chandragiri and Velur by Aravidu Venkatapatiraya (r. 1586–1614). Using the Portuguese settlement of São Tomé de Meliapor as a base, the major Vaishnava temple of Tirupati could be plundered of its wealth in the process, and all this 'can well be done with a few more people than there are now [in São Tomé]; because those who inhabit those lands are weak and unused to war' (DRI, i: 359). With the comfortable distance of almost four centuries between us and the letter's writer, we can savour its ironical flavour; for a mere five years later, in 1615, São Tomé was fighting for its very survival against the aggression of the Dutch East India Company, now based at Pulicat.

CHAPTER SIX
Empire in Retreat, 1610–1665

In around 1665, the end of the period that we consider in this chapter, the Portuguese Jesuit Manuel Godinho, who was writing an account of his voyage overland from Goa to Lisbon via the Persian Gulf and the Levant, summed up the history of Portuguese Asia to his day. The early years under D. Manuel were, he wrote, the infancy of the Asian empire, while the reign of D. João III represented the equivalent of adolescence. Then the reigns of D. Sebastião and the first two Filipes saw the *Estado da Índia* attain maturity, but it was struck down in the prime of life (so to speak) by an outside force – the Dutch (Correia-Afonso 1990: 21–26). The anthropomorphic image presented by Padre Godinho does not exactly correspond to our analysis in the earlier chapters, but does highlight one important fact: the Portuguese Asian empire was not so much undermined from within as from without. However, although Dutch military might, and especially naval power, was an important factor in forcing the *Estado da Índia* into retreat in the half century under consideration here, it was by no means the only external factor.

It has often been remarked that Portugal was one of the less 'advanced' countries in Europe at the time that it began its expansion, and indeed historically much less prosperous than northern and central Italy, France or Spain. In all of Iberia, Portugal was the last area to resist the Romans, the last to be incorporated into the empire of the Visigoths, the last to adopt the Christian calendar, and the last to adopt titles for its nobility in accordance with what obtained elsewhere. Again, as early as the sixteenth century, travellers to Portugal from elsewhere in Europe, like Frei Claudio de Bronseval, remarked on the remoteness and poverty of the country, in apparent contrast to Venice, or Florence, or the Spain of Charles V (Thomaz 1989c: 374–75). But in making such comparisons with France or Italy, historians lose sight of the fact that the principal challenge to the Portuguese came not from these nations, but from the Netherlands, an area as marginal, and as peripheral to the medieval European mind, as

Portugal if not more so. In the mid-sixteenth century, the population of the Low Countries was perhaps three million, and only slightly more in around 1600. Up until the late sixteenth century, much of the Netherlands was still under marsh, and it was only the massive canal-building and lake-drainage operations of the years 1590–1640 (when some 80,000 hectares of land was reclaimed) that turned the balance. As late as 1652, the English traveller Owen Feltham's rude description of the Netherlands sums up the upstart character of this economy: the Low Countries, he wrote, were 'the great Bog of Europe ... and the buttock of the World, full of veines and bloud, but no bones in't' (Parker 1980: 145).

However, to see the decline of the Portuguese empire in Asia in the seventeenth century purely in terms of the rivalry with the Dutch would not be just. For even the Luso-Dutch conflict in Asia was not a two-dimensional but rather a multi-dimensional affair: it involved not only the Portuguese and the Dutch but also the Safavid Shah, the Nayaka rulers of Tanjavur and Madurai, the Susuhunan of Mataram and the Sultan of Makassar, to choose five examples from the many that exist. These third parties often crucially mediated the outcome of even the Luso-Dutch conflict, and while at a global level the Dutch triumph may have had an air of inevitability about it in view of their superior resources and mode of functioning, it was by no means so in a number of specific instances. And had all these instances gone one way rather than the other, this might well have had a decisive influence on the global outcome as well.

There is also the important fact that some of the major losses that the Portuguese suffered in the half-century after 1610 had nothing at all to do with the Dutch: this is the case with first Syriam (1612), then Hurmuz (1622), followed by Hughli (1632), then the Japan trade (1638), and finally the Kanara ports (1654). We must begin our examination of this phase of decline in Portuguese official fortunes in Asia therefore with an analysis of the situation they faced with their major adversaries and allies in Asia, and the nature of the Asian political dynamic in about 1610.

POLITICAL RECONSOLIDATION IN ASIA, 1570–1610

The first phase of the Portuguese presence in Asia was, coincidentally, one of rapid political realignments in the western half of the continent. In the first thirty years of their presence in the Indian Ocean, the Portuguese were witness to Ottoman expansion into Egypt and the Red Sea (arguably one of the most important phases in Ottoman history), to Safavid consolidation in Iran under the founder of the dynasty Shah Ismail, to the setting up of Mughal rule in northern India by the Timurid Babur in the 1520s, and to the apogee of the power of Vijayanagara in southern India under Krishnadevaraya (r. 1509–29). As the Portuguese themselves saw it in around 1530, the major political powers in Asia were the Ottomans, Vijayanagara and the Ming Chinese: they actively feared and combated the first, dealt by diplomatic means with the second, and kept a wary distance from the third.

The next four decades were relatively less momentous ones, with the only truly significant political shift in the western Indian Ocean from the Portuguese viewpoint being the realignment in power in the Deccan (or south-central India), with the decisive defeat in 1565 of Vijayanagara forces by the rulers of Bijapur, Ahmadnagar and Golconda. Goa, whose trade was linked to the demand of Vijayanagara city, felt the aftershock of this shift, but soon the trade to Bijapur grew in order to compensate partially for this decline. Furthermore, by the 1560s, trade in the Bay of Bengal was of growing interest to the Portuguese private merchant, who brought back news of the great new state machine built by Tabin-shwei-hti and Bayin-naung in Burma; the Burmese ruler ('*o rey Brama*') is a prepossessing presence in Portuguese accounts of these decades.

But from the 1570s, a new political order came into being in the arc stretching from Bengal, through northern India and Iran, to the Red Sea, which endured – with some relatively small realignments – into the early eighteenth century. The single most important factor that influenced this new order was the expansion of the Mughal state from a landlocked kingdom astride the Gangetic valley in northern India to an empire with maritime access not only into the western Indian Ocean but into the Bay of Bengal.

The shift took place during the reign of Akbar (r. 1556–1605), the first of his lineage to be called the Great Mughal ('*Grão Mogol*') by the Portuguese, and was the culmination of earlier attempts by his father Humayun in the 1530s to gain control of Gujarat and Bengal. In 1572, Akbar's forces easily conquered Gujarat, and the Mughals signed a treaty with the Portuguese in March of the following year; then, in 1575–76, the Mughal general Munim Khan conducted a successful campaign in Bengal, bringing the ports of Pipli and Satgaon under Mughal control, and permitting the creation of the Mughal *suba* (province) of Bengal. Finally, in 1591–92, the Mughal *Khan-i khanan*, Abd ur-Rahim, took lower Sind from its ruler Mirza Jani Beg, who was allowed into Mughal service as a noble of high rank; this gave the Mughals control over Thatta and its port Lahori Bandar, at the mouth of the Indus.

In a remarkable period of two decades, therefore, the Mughals had gained control over a complex of land and river routes, and access to maritime trade on a significant scale. Whereas Sher Shah Sur, the ruler who forced Humayun into exile in the 1540s, had had to foster trade along the Gangetic valley as his only means of access to treasure and war-animals, Akbar and his successors controlled a vast network of routes: the ports of Bengal and Orissa were linked to the heartland of north India by riverine navigation, while a major land route linked Agra and Delhi to Lahore, Multan and the great caravan routes to Kabul and Kandahar, as well as to Balkh and Samarqand. Lahore, the great mart and trade centre of the north-west, was equally linked via Multan to the Indus valley, and exported goods through Thatta and Lahori Bandar (literally 'the port of Lahore') to the markets of the western Indian Ocean. Another important route under Mughal control stretched from Agra to Gujarat, where, after the decline of Khambayat (Cambay) in the latter half of the sixteenth century, Surat came to be the great port.

Now unlike the Ottomans, whose control of first the Red Sea and then Basra tempted them to launch a series of anti-Portuguese expeditions in the middle years of the sixteenth century, the Mughals did not in these years attempt a direct maritime challenge to Portuguese power. Historians have sought to explain this phenomenon in terms of the ethos of the Mughals, and seen their alleged indifference to the sea as a consequence of their Central Asian heritage, and preference for the land as a field of activity (Pearson 1976; 1987). The explanation is probably too facile: Akbar did at various points in his correspondence with other rulers (such as the Uzbek monarch, Abdullah Khan), speak of the need for a *jihad* against the infidels to secure control of the maritime route to the Holy Cities of Mecca and Medina. But the problem was a diplomatic one; since Akbar was, from the 1570s, actively striving to rival – if not overshadow – the Ottomans, there was equally the tempting possibility of using the Portuguese against his co-religionists (Farooqi 1989: 37–38).

Thus, until about 1610, the Mughals were largely content to use the threat they posed to Portuguese settlements on land as a way of keeping the *Estado da Índia* from pursuing policies that were indiscreet; and it is significant that in a phase dominated by El Dorado-style projects, no one thought to venture the conquest of Mughal territories as a possibility. The most the Portuguese hoped for was that the Jesuit presence in Akbar's court might tempt him to convert to Christianity and thus make him more malleable; but in the event, this conversion project too was shown to be chimeral. As New World silver, and especially the *reales de a ocho* coined from the produce of the mines of Potosi, began to flow into Goa via the ships of the *Carreira da Índia*, Gujarat and Goa acquired a comfortable trading link. Equally, in the late sixteenth century, ships from Gujarat continued to trade to the Red Sea, and bring back precious metals from there in exchange for Indian textile exports; this silver, like that from Goa, served to feed the mints of the Mughal empire, which turned out *rupias* in increasing quantities from Akbar's reign.

147

The relatively comfortable symbiosis of interests that existed with the Mughals was overhung by only one dark cloud: the *Estado*'s administrators feared that Mughal expansion down the Indian peninsula would eventually bring the Timurid rulers control over the hinterland of Goa itself, and hence lead to their expulsion from their headquarters. They therefore repeatedly sought alliances with Bijapur and Golconda, with the Queen of Ahmadnagar Chand Bibi, and later with Malik Ambar, the Ethiopian-born potentate who controlled the hinterland of Chaul in the early seventeenth century (DRI, ii: 159–60).

A far greater worry than the Mughals were their western neighbours and sometime rivals, the Safavid rulers of Iran. Portuguese official relations with the first rulers of this dynasty, Ismail (1501–24), the long-reigning Tahmasp (1524–76), and Muhammad Khudabanda (1578–87), seem to have been relatively trouble-free. But all this was to change in the reign of Shah Abbas I (1587–1629), who established trade links with Moscow, sent ambassadors and trade representatives to Europe, and began to resent Portuguese control over Hurmuz, which effectively dominated the entrance to the Persian Gulf. Safavid military power, earlier put into question by successes enjoyed against them by the Ottomans on the frontier, was given a new lease of life, as an army of *ghulaman* (Georgian, Circassian and other mercenaries) was created to supplement Turkoman levies; the icing on the cake was the corps of 12,000 arquebusiers (*tufangchiyan*) and 12,000 artillerymen (*tupchiyan*) built up by Shah Abbas from a far smaller force that had been maintained by Tahmasp (Jackson and Lockhart 1986: 264–72). From his new capital at Isfahan, Shah Abbas and his advisers set out an elaborate strategy, to combat the Ottoman threat and to deal with the Portuguese. Access to the land-routes to Europe continued to be limited and difficult even after military successes against the Ottomans in the north-west, and even the intermediation of the Shah's favoured trading community, the Armenians (whom he had settled in large numbers in the New Julfa suburb of Isfahan), had not enabled the northern option to be exercised.

In July 1599, Shah Abbas had sent out an embassy, comprising the Englishman Sir Anthony Sherley and the *qizilbash* Hoseyn Ali Beg Bayat, with letters to the Czar Boris Godunov (1598–1605) in Moscow, to Sigismond III of Poland, and to the rulers of Hungary, France, Scotland, Queen Elizabeth I of England, the Doge of Venice and the Grand Duke of Tuscany, and Felipe III of Spain. He suggested an anti-Ottoman alliance in these letters, a theme taken up again in a later grand diplomatic tour of Europe on behalf of the Shah, by Anthony Sherley's brother Robert, in 1608 (Szuppe 1986). The proposals met with a lukewarm response, particularly from the Habsburgs, forcing Shah Abbas to consider moving against Hurmuz, the only other means he had of conducting external trade freely. The matter was neatly summed up about this time by the English diplomat Sir Thomas Roe, who wrote that Shah Abbas must 'constantly resolve to go through with the Spaniard, or to make peace with the Turk; one of them he must do' (Boxer 1985a, i: 57–8). The exchange of embassies between Madrid and Goa, and Isfahan, continued through the 1610s, but it soon emerged that this was merely a way for Shah Abbas to bide his time while waiting for English support to come through; the setting up of an English factory at Jask in 1616 signalled the beginnings of the Anglo-Iranian alliance against the Portuguese.

To understand why Shah Abbas went through with this alliance, and why he had already turned against the Portuguese from the early seventeenth century (when he attacked several of their Persian Gulf establishments), it is essential to remember that the period witnesses the transformation of the Iranian state into an increasingly mercantile enterprise, rather than a purely agrarian, territorial state. The cash resources needed to recruit mercenaries and pay for armaments in order to combat the external threat was certainly one reason for this growing state mercantilism, but not the only one. Over the course of the sixteenth century, the alliance between the Safavid dynasty and their Turkoman tribal supporters – the so-called *qizilbash* – had begun to show signs of severe strain, with rulers like Tahmasp struggling in vain to shake off the dominance of the *qizilbash* notables (or *amirs*) (Haneda 1987). Thus, the use of trade as a resource to be taxed and from which funds could be raised enabled Shah Abbas to free himself and his court from dependence on the original supporters of his dynasty; one of his first steps therefore was to declare the lucrative trade in silk a state monopoly, and to attempt to control its sale price. But so long as the two silk routes – one heading north-west over land, and the other south-east via the Persian Gulf – were blocked, this strategy had strict limitations. This then is what eventually led to the conflict between Safavids and Portuguese.

We have so far concentrated on developments in south and west Asia in the decades leading up to 1610, from which it has emerged that the new political configuration in these areas boded ill for the Portuguese. The same was true in these years for the far corner of the Portuguese Asian enterprise – Japan. As has been noted in Chapter 4, the entry of the Portuguese as intermediaries between China and Japan in the 1540s and 1550s was largely the result of local circumstances. Again, the purely coincidental expansion of silver mining and production in Japan in these years facilitated the growth in Portuguese trade, so that the 'Great Ship from Amacon' became one of the major intra-Asian lines of the concession system. The expansion in silver production seems to have resulted from the import of a new ash-blowing mining technology into Japan from China, via Korea, which was first adopted in the western Japanese Iwami mine, and later used in other mines such as Ikuno.

Between 1560 and 1600, it has been estimated that the Portuguese carried between 22,500 and 37,500 kilogrammes of silver from Japan every year, while Chinese and Japanese vessels over the same period carried off another 11,000 kilogrammes. Over the next thirty years, exports went up further – to between 150,000 and 187,500 kilogrammes per annum, with all exporters being taken into consideration (Yamamura and Kamiki 1983: 351–52).

But the Portuguese were sitting on a powder-keg. The early years of their presence had seen local lords (*daimyo*) vie with each other for Portuguese trade, in a situation of internecine conflict. But in the last quarter of the sixteenth century, matters began to stabilise, under first Oda Nobunaga, then Toyotomi Hideyoshi, and finally Tokugawa Ieyasu – the so-called 'Great Unifiers'. By the 1580s, Hideyoshi had begun taking silver levies from the Iwami mines, and thereafter took to trading himself with the Portuguese in silver, raw silk and gold. Troubles between him and the Portuguese arose on two counts, one religious and one to do with reasons of state. The years since Xavier's arrival in Japan had seen the Jesuit mission grow from strength to strength, with the conversion of many thousands of Japanese, ranging from peasants to members of Hideyoshi's own entourage, to Christianity. Important Christian *daimyo* took to destroying shrines of the native tradition, and some went so far as to forcibly convert peasants in territories under their control. It is evident that Christianity had to be tolerated up to a point by men like Nobunaga and Hideyoshi, given the fact that its 'carriers' – the Portuguese – had their uses. It was, after all, under Portuguese influence that firearms had been introduced into Japan, and become an important part of military strategy under the Great Unifiers. But the Jesuits began, by the 1580s, to threaten to be too assertive, with their vice-provincial of the period at Nagasaki, Padre Gaspar Coelho, comporting himself almost in the style of a *daimyo*, to the extent of travelling about in a light galley armed with artillery.

Hideyoshi took harsh action against Coelho in 1587, after a meeting with the latter on board his vessel, and issued an edict declaring that since Christianity was a pernicious doctrine, it could not be permitted in Japan, 'the land of the Gods'. He therefore ordered all missionaries out of Japan in twenty days. It would appear that this order was not really meant to be executed, but merely to give the Jesuits and their Japanese clients a warning. Thus, in reality, the missionaries were not expelled, but instead forced to tone down their activities; a few churches were razed to the ground; Nagasaki itself, which the Jesuits had earlier been granted as their domain, was confiscated and put under an administrator appointed by Hideyoshi; some Christian *daimyo* were punished, while others returned to their original religion.

Over the next few years, Hideyoshi was too busy with matters overseas to bother with the Portuguese overmuch. In 1592, he launched a major naval attack on Korea, as a prelude to an attack on the Ming Chinese empire (Hall et al. 1981: 199). This was a measure of a shift in Japanese official thinking, the beginnings of the creation of a Japan-centred world-order, at least in East Asia. The Korean war was not a success, for while the Japanese made great inroads into the peninsula and considerable carnage resulted, the intervention of the Chinese meant that the Japanese army was forced to retreat. This costly war dragged on intermittently into the late 1590s, with Hideyoshi's death in 1598 eventually forcing it to a close. By this time, however, he had had one more bout of serious conflict with the Portuguese, after the wreck of a Spanish galleon *San Felipe* off Japan in 1596. Suspecting a larger Spanish-Portuguese plan to create rebellions in his territories, and at the same time possibly frustrated with the lack of success of his Korean campaign, Hideyoshi ordered the public execution of twenty-six Christians (seventeen Japanese, three Jesuits and six Spanish Franciscans), which was accomplished on 5th February 1597.

Thus, by 1610, the Portuguese had had a taste of the changed circumstances that obtained in post-*sengoku* Japan, and what the new, relatively centralised order, as distinct from the old *daimyo*-dominated dispensation, meant. But it is likely, nevertheless, that they underestimated the seriousness of intention of the *bakufu* (or 'curtain government') put in place by Hideyoshi and his successor, Tokugawa Ieyasu. The relative absence of persecutions in the first decade of the seventeenth century was however illusory, as the Portuguese learnt in 1614, when the definitive order for the expulsion of all missionaries was promulgated. Thereafter, the Portuguese conducted their trade on borrowed time.

SYRIAM AND HURMUZ: THE BEGINNINGS OF RETREAT

The first real blows came however neither in the Mughal territories, nor in those of the Safavids, nor indeed in Japan. Rather, they came from the Dutch, who, in 1605, took Ambon, and also occupied a Spanish fort at Tidore; but the Spaniards recovered soon, making inroads into Ternate, while the Portuguese continued to procure cloves and spices via Makassar, which emerged by 1610 as a major entrepot in eastern Indonesia. Far more telling and significant a blow came from quite a different quarter, namely Burma. We have seen how after the collapse of Nanda-bayin's kingdom in the late 1590s, Filipe de Brito had managed to carve out for the *Estado da Índia* (and for himself) a position in the Irrawaddy delta port of Syriam, from where he collected customs on shipping from Coromandel, and sought to restrict navigation in the coastal waters between Arakan and the upper Malay peninsula by means of a small flotilla. It appears that De Brito in the decade and more that he ran this customs-house never remitted any money to Goa, but the significance of Syriam is still undoubted. Early Dutch expeditions to Masulipatnam (which they visited first in 1605), were greatly concerned with Syriam, and the Dutch factor Pieter Willemszoon, who visited Arakan in these years, is quite explicit in suggesting that Dutch trade in the Bay of Bengal could never make inroads until the Syriam menace was combated (Terpstra 1911). His report, entitled 'Information of the Bay of Bengala and Arracan', was delivered to Pieter Ysaacx Eyloff at the Masulipatnam factory in May 1608, and states:

> After I had arrived safely in Arracan, I found the King there, who had come back some five months before from Pegu, where he had besieged the castle of St. Jago (where one Phillipe de Britto maintains himself with around three to four hundred Portuguese, Mestiços and Topasses, and some five to six hundred Peguers), with around one hundred thousand men (*sic*) and around 150 foists and three thousand galeasses or praus, but he could not take the above mentioned castle ...
>
> A great trade and profits are derived from this Bay, and but for the fact that these lands (*dese peys*) have been closed off before our arrival, we too could have taken part in it, [though] the Portuguese will do their best to close it off so that it might cause great losses (*achterdeel*) to the Company and the East India trade, but on the contrary if the Portuguese are driven out of Pegu then they will be excluded from Porto Pequeno to Martabaen, yea in truth from St Thome to Malacca, and besides the Moors of Maslipatam and Choromandel will also sing more sweetly ... . (De Jonge 1865: 288–89)

However, despite his success in staving off the threat from Arakan, things were not running all that smoothly for Filipe de Brito, who, unfortunately for himself and the *Estado* was unable to make common cause with the greater part of the Portuguese and *mestiços* of the Arakan and Chittagong area, who might otherwise have provided him with the necessary manpower to sustain his enterprise. His relations with Sebastião Gonçalves Tibau, a Portuguese who in the 1590s ingratiated himself (like De Brito) with the Arakan ruler, and proceeded to gain control of the island of Sandwip off the Bengal coast, were poor; Tibau therefore conducted his own negotiations with the Arakan court on a number of issues, undermining De Brito's position. Furthermore, his pretensions to collecting customs on the Masulipatnam-Burma trade (and the attacks by his flotilla on more than one Masulipatnam vessel in 1603–04) irked the powerful and well-connected Persian traders of that port, who in turn commanded a good deal of influence in Arakan and Pegu. The turning point came however with a shift in the political situation in lower Burma itself. After Nanda-bayin's death, the focus of political power for the lineage of Bayin-naung shifted upland to Ava, and one of the latter's sons – Nyaung-yan Min – began the process of reconsolidation of the Shan states, as well as Prome and Taung-ngu. But it was a grandson of Bayin-naung, Anauk-hpet-lun (r. 1606–28), who completed the process of unification, so that by 1612, Syriam was an enclave in a unified political zone dominated by the Restored Taung-ngu Dynasty (Lieberman 1980).

Madrid and Lisbon were aware of this; a royal letter dated 15th March 1613, and addressed to the viceroy D. Jerónimo de Azevedo, speaks of how the 'rey do Ava' had defeated the ruler of Taung-ngu 'and taken all his treasures', and how he intended next to attack the Ayuthia kingdom. It was suggested that Goa send a fleet of ten galliots immediately to aid Filipe de Brito, but by the time Goa acted it was much too late (DRI, ii: 391–92). Anauk-hpet-lun, allegedly aided by 'cap-wearing Moors' (possibly from Masulipatnam), attacked Syriam by land and water in 1612; the fort surrendered, and De Brito was impaled on an iron stake, while many of his companions were carried off as prisoners to Ava and tied to the Crown on a hereditary basis as military specialists.

The fall of Syriam opened the way for the free expansion of trade between Masulipatnam and Burma, which reached substantial dimensions by the 1620s. It did not aid the Dutch immediately to any great extent, for it was only in the 1630s that the Dutch made their first serious attempts to trade in the eastern Bay of Bengal littoral ports. But one significant gainer was surely the Restored Taung-ngu Dynasty, which – even if it did not favour as direct a role in maritime affairs as had the ship-owning Bayin-naung in the 1570s and early 1580s – was concerned about the control of customs, trade and the access to firearms. Also the significance of Syriam for the Portuguese *Estado* was not marginal either, and this is why at least one major armada was sent from Goa to Burma to see what could be salvaged of the affair, even after the fortress had fallen. To the *Estado*, Syriam meant a true foothold in the Bay of Bengal, a window into the dreamed-of conquest of mainland Southeast Asia, but equally a centre that would act as a significant aid to Melaka in controlling the Asian trade that was passing into ports outside of the *Estado*'s direct control: Perak, Kedah, Trang, Ujangselang and Mergui (APO, vi: 923–24). But this was not to be.

With the fall of Syriam, a sense of urgency set into the correspondence between Madrid and Lisbon, and Goa. The Dutch presence on the Coromandel coast, in the ports of Masulipatnam, Nizamapatnam, Pulicat and Tirupapuliyur, hitherto largely the concern of locally resident Portuguese traders and missionaries, became a major concern of Goa too, with the decision to appoint Rui Dias de Sampaio to the post of 'Captain-General of São Tomé de Meliapor and the Pulicat Enterprise' in 1614–15. Again, in these years, investigations were made into why revenues from the customs-houses of Cochin and Melaka were not as high as they might be, and the first moves to improve the fortifications of several Portuguese settlements – from Cochin to São Tomé – were made.

The financial crunch of the mid-sixteenth century was being repeated with one significant difference: now the causes were not cyclical, and circumstances did not permit a thorough-going debate.

Instead, a facile solution was adopted, in keeping with the new style favoured during the monarchy of Felipe III (r. 1598–1621). The quarter-century of this monarch's reign has attracted relatively little attention from historians, who have preferred to focus on the reigns immediately preceding and succeeding, which seem to be characterised respectively by dramatic success and dramatic failure. Felipe III's reign, lacking the drama of these others, was nevertheless one in which several important structural changes took place, both within Spain, and in the relationship between Spain and Portugal. It was now that the institution of the *valido* (or royal favourite) came to assume true significance, in the person of Francisco Sandoval y Rojas, Duke of Lerma, who was Felipe III's close counsellor; in turn, it was Lerma's influence that brought about changes in the relationship between Portugal and Spain. In 1601, Lerma sought to introduce, over and above the *Conselho da Fazenda* (Revenue-Council) created by Felipe II in 1591 to oversee Portuguese internal and overseas fiscal affairs, a *Junta da Fazenda*, manned by three Spaniards. The Portuguese opposed the move, and it was soon abolished in 1605, but in its place came the *Conselho da Índia*, also abolished by 1614 in the face of Portuguese opposition. The policy under Felipe III, simply put, was to bring the highest echelons of administration in Portugal gradually under the control of Spaniards; his most explicit move came in 1617, when in the teeth of opposition, he appointed the Spanish Count of Salinas (disingenuously given the Portuguese title of Marquês de Alenquer) his viceroy in Portugal (Lynch 1981; Disney 1978).

The logic of Spanish statecraft in this period was blandly expressed some years later by one Pedro Fernández Navarrete, who observed:

> It is only fair that the burdens should be properly apportioned; that Castile should continue to provide for the royal household and for the defence of its own coasts and the route to the Indies; that Portugal should pay for its own military defences and for the East Indies fleets, as it did before incorporation with Castile. (Lynch 1981: 40)

A rather more caustic Dutchman put the matter with greater bluntness; the king of Spain, he stated, saw Portuguese Asia 'as his concubine, who can shift for herself if need be, but he does not count the cost of maintaining America, which he regards as his lawful wife, of whom he is exceedingly jealous and firmly resolved to maintain inviolate' (Lynch 1981: 65). In the 1610s, despite the truce between Spain and the Netherlands (1609–21), the question arose of how Portuguese Asia would then 'shift for herself' in a situation of financial need. It comes as no surprise to note that resort was taken to a characteristic device already in use in Spanish America, the sale of public offices by auction.

Table 6.1 The sale of offices in Portuguese Asia, 1614

Place	Purchaser	Amount (xerafins)
A. Captaincies		
Goa	D. Diogo Lobo	10,500
Honawar	João Fernandes Leitão	6,000
Basrur	D. Diogo de Sousa	10,500
Mangalore	Salvador Ribeiro Marinho	6,400
Cannanore	André Salema	5,030
Kollam	Jorge Caiado de Negreiros	1,000
Mannar	D. Francisco Roxo	11,000
Nagapattinam	António Ferreira da Camara	6,050
Galle	Domingos Cerveira	4,450
Chilaw	Vicente do Amaral	400
Caliture	André Gonçalves	500
Hughli	Domingos de Albuquerque	340
Pipli	Pero Coelho	150
Melaka	João Caiado de Gamboa	30,030
Chaul	D. Manuel de Azevedo	32,200
Bassein	Gaspar Pereira	22,050
Manora	Gaspar Pereira	5,000
Daman	Manuel de Melo Pereira	37,000
Diu	D. Pedro de Almeida	53,000
Hurmuz	D. Luís da Gama	145,000
Maskat	André do Rego	30,000
Mombasa	Simão de Melo Pereira	23,000
	TOTAL	439,600
B. Other significant sales		
1. Customs-house inspectors (*juizes da alfândega*)		
Goa	António Galvão	23,700
Cochin	António de Araújo	2,000
Melaka	António de Brito Fogaça	500
Diu	António Homem de Azevedo	10,000
	TOTAL	36,200
2. Factors (*feitores*)		
Goa	Manuel Rodrigues	2,820
Dabhol	Jerónimo da Costa Ourives	4,200
Basrur	António Carvalho	410
Cochin	António de Almeida Brandão	2,020
Melaka	Luís Alvares de Lemos	2,500
Chaul	Gabriel Gomes do Quintal	2,010
Bassein	Sebastião Álvares de Fonseca	7,300
Daman	Manuel da Costa	3,060
Diu	António Travassos	9,200
Hurmuz	Manuel da Costa Cortes	11,550
Maskat	Pero Mendes Girão	400
Moçambique	António Monis da Silva	9,010
Mombasa	Domingos Rebelo	2,800
	TOTAL	57,280
GRAND TOTAL (with other posts)		627,030

(*Source*: BNL, Fundo Geral, Codice 1540, fls. 89–91v, 'Relação dos Cargos do Estado da Índia que estão vendidos por ordem de Sua Magestade para as despesas do Estado.')

Table 6.1 summarises the proceeds of the sale, listing the buyers and the amounts paid for each office; the concession voyages that were sold in the same auction have been dealt with in an earlier chapter.

Some of the most lucrative posts that were sold in the course of the auction were those at Hurmuz, with the captaincy being bought by the celebrated D. Luís da Gama (brother of a twice viceroy at Goa, the Count of Vidigueira) for as much as 145,000 *xerafins*. What made Hurmuz so coveted? The answer lies in Hurmuz's substantial trade, as the port that supplied the routes via Basra and Baghdad, Isfahan and the Iranian plateau, with the goods that came in from the east. Of course an alternative existed, in the form of the caravan trade from northern India, Lahore and Sind, via Kabul and Kandahar into Iran, but in normal times this probably accounted for a rather smaller proportion of trade than the maritime route into Hurmuz. But, as Felipe III wrote to his viceroy Rui Lourenço de Távora in 1611, if Hurmuz were under threat (as it had been intermittently since the 1590s), the balance between the two routes would change. He foresaw an attack by Shah Abbas, and wrote:

> And ... if the war continues, my treasury will lose all that the customs-house of Ormuz yields and moreover it will be necessary to send money for expenses and supplies from India, and the routes will be sealed and the residents of Ormuz will no longer send out their goods, nor risk those that they have, and will [instead] open up the route from Sinde to Persia ... .   (DRI, ii: 103)

Still, in normal years, in the early seventeenth century, Hurmuz had a considerable eastward trade, as a retrospective estimate by a Dutch factor in the region in the 1620s, set out in Table 6.2, shows.

Table 6.2 The eastward maritime trade of Hurmuz, *c.* 1620

Partner ports	Number of ships	Partner ports	Number of ships
Sind	8	Dabhol	4
Nagana	3	Goa	12
Diu	5	Cochin	2
Daman	3	Melaka	2
Bassein	3	Bengal	2
Chaul	8	Malindi	2
		TOTAL	54

(*Source*: Steensgaard 1973: 197)

In terms of customs-collections, the yield was substantial, and what is more had been growing from the 1570s on. In terms of *pardaus* (each of 300 *reis*), the total yield in the half-century leading up to 1620 (including some minor taxes besides customs) is shown in Table 6.3:

Table 6.3 Portuguese revenues ar Hurmuz, 1574–1620

Year	Amount (in pardaus)
1574	170,000
1588	180,000
1605	192,000
1610	229,500
1618	105,500 (January–July)
1620	200,684

(*Sources*: Godinho 1982: 49; BPADE, cv/2–7)

It was this trade and its revenue that the aggression of Shah Abbas threatened, and which Goa sought to preserve by the most curious of means, such as the attempted assassination of the Persian envoy to England, Robert Sherley, while he was on his way back to Isfahan via Sind, in 1613–14. But the stark facts were there for all to see; all that prevented Shah Abbas from taking Hurmuz was the lack of a naval force, and if he were to manage that, it was unlikely that the Portuguese garrison would hold out, especially since, as Lisbon wrote to Goa already in January 1612, 'the fortress of Ormuz lacks artillery, and that which it has is so old and lacking in metal that if the occasion were to arise, there is no piece there that could fire for two days at a stretch' (DRI, ii: 144). Still, the motions were gone through; a fleet was sent to Hurmuz under the command of Rui Freire de Andrade from Lisbon, arriving in the Persian Gulf in June 1620. Rui Freire gave the English pause for more than a year, but was finally outmanoeuvred and forced to surrender at Qishm in February 1622. Hurmuz itself surrendered, after a siege, in May 1622 to the forces of Shah Abbas and the English Company (Steensgaard 1973; Boxer 1985a, i).

Now, the significance of the fall of Hurmuz has been dramatised in the literature out of all proportion to its real importance. Let us note, first of all, that it did not mean the end of Portuguese trade in the Persian Gulf – for they still held Maskat on the Arabian coast, and by the early 1630s also had rights over Bandar Kung, granted to them by Shah Safi (r. 1629–42). Maskat, in the 1630s, in turn became an important staging post for Portuguese trade to Basra (and thence to Baghdad, Mosul and other inland urban centres), and remained so until it was lost to Omani forces later in the century. The real significance of the expulsion of the Portuguese from Hurmuz was that it permitted the rise of Bandar Abbas (or Gombroon), the port favoured and protected by Shah Abbas I (and even named after him); even after his death in 1629, it continued to be the port of Isfahan, through which diplomatic missions to Mughal India, Ayuthia and other centres arrived and departed.

At the same time, the loss of Hurmuz did mean a significant fall in

Portuguese revenues, for while their *own* trade in the Gulf may have continued, they no longer had the control of the chief customs-house of the area. Later in the 1620s, Rui Freire de Andrade did continue to captain a fleet in the area, with the intention of discouraging ships from putting in to ports other than Maskat, Qatif or later Kung, but the trade of Bandar Abbas grew in leaps and bounds, as evidence from ports such as Surat shows (Van Santen 1982). However, far worse from the Portuguese viewpoint was to follow in the 1630s, a fact which excessive attention to the case of Hurmuz has sometimes obscured.

REFORM AND ITS CONSEQUENCES

The arrival of the first English and Dutch fleets in Asian waters via the Cape route (James Lancaster in 1592 and Cornelis de Houtman in 1596, respectively) does not seem to have occasioned great alarm in the *Estado da Índia*, as the reader of official papers from the governments of Matias de Albuquerque (1591–97) and D. Francisco da Gama (1597–1600) discovers. To be sure, these fleets stayed clear of all major Portuguese settlements, and Lancaster's capture of a Portuguese concession-carrack near the Nicobar islands was put down to 'English piracy' rather than seen as a prelude to a systematic challenge. Even in 1598, when as many as twenty-two ships of diverse organisations left the Netherlands for Asia, they were mostly instructed to concentrate on Indonesia, and – implicitly – to tap the anti-Portuguese network that linked Aceh with Banten and a part of the Moluccas. The first Dutch attempts to make contact with Gujarat, on the other hand, were disastrous: the Dutch envoys, sent from Aceh, were intercepted by the Portuguese and executed. Thus, the pattern of the early years was to avoid the areas of Portuguese strength and concentrate on Southeast Asia and the Far East.

The first major deviation from this rule came from the English Company, founded in 1600 on a charter from Elizabeth I (Chaudhuri 1965). The English decided to tap the trade in Gujarat even at the risk of provoking conflict with the Portuguese, and in a series of naval engagements managed to stave off the repeated challenges from Goa quite successfully by 1615. Meanwhile the Dutch, now formed into a single company, the United East India Company (founded 1602) had taken a rather different route: from an initial concentration on Indonesia, they spread their operations to the Coromandel coast (1605), but had yet to make serious inroads into the trade of the western Indian Ocean even as late as 1621. Attempts had been made of course, but the circumstances of the Truce of Antwerp made open conflict with the Portuguese difficult after 1609 (save under great provocation), and besides the Dutch had enough on their hands in Southeast Asia with the English, with whom they fought a series of naval battles in the 1610s. In the early 1620s then, the situation was as follows: the English were a relatively strong presence in Gujarat and the Persian Gulf, and far less so on Coromandel and in Southeast Asia; with the Dutch, the exact opposite obtained (Chaudhuri 1965; Glamann 1981).

It had not escaped the notice of the Portuguese that in the decades after 1600, their European rivals had gained ground on various fronts. Several possible solutions were suggested, some of which were military and strategic or diplomatic in nature, others requiring institutional change and reform. The writers of tracts suggesting solutions drew upon a tradition that had existed from at least the late sixteenth century, and are often described under the general Spanish term *arbitristas*. An example is André Coelho, a soldier and ship's captain of some experience in Asia, who wrote a detailed *Relação* in 1621, describing the Dutch possessions and trade in Asia, and the means to 'extinguish' them (as he put it). One of the means he suggests to put paid to Dutch trade on Coromandel is – to state it mildly – somewhat far-fetched, involving the monopoly of a dye-wood (*xáia*) produced in Mannar. His other, more direct, proposal involved the creation of a fleet of eight galliots. Four of these would wait at the bar of Tenasserim, while another four would attack shipping off lower Burma until 10th October, by which time most shipping from Bengal and Coromandel arrived there. The two sub-fleets would then go together to Melaka to get supplies, only to return in December and January to attack ships along the whole coast from Tenasserim to Arakan; then in early February, they would make a lightning raid on Masulipatnam harbour, 'and will burn in that bay (*sic*) all the vessels, carracks, sampans, of the Moors and Dutch, which may be in that port'. The same would be achieved thereafter, the optimistic Coelho stated, at the Dutch factory of Pulicat, after which the fleet would go on to Galle in Sri Lanka (BNL, Fundo Geral, Códice 638).

The means by which this naval force was to be raised is left vague by Coelho, although in another part of his *Relação* he speaks highly of the idea of a privateer fleet to be fitted out by *homens casados* from Goa, warning only that the soldiers on board should be men with a 'house, wife and family and Goa', apparently as a means of discouraging desertion. In the mid-1620s, we are aware that such a fleet (the so-called *armada dos aventureiros*) was indeed created, and that it did have some limited success in the Bay of Bengal, besides engaging in some acts of outright piracy in the western Indian Ocean against ships from Bhatkal and other ports. But getting rid of the Dutch was by no means as simple a task as Coelho imagined. From an average of 5.9 ships a year in the decade 1601–10, the Dutch had begun sending as many as 11.7 ships to Asia per year in the next decade, while Lisbon sent out a mere 66 ships in the decade

1611–20, of which only 47 reached Asia. Even if the Portuguese vessels were larger, the fact was that the Dutch were not adversaries to be dealt with using fleets of eight galliots and the advantage of surprise. This naturally prompted a thought – imitation. Thus, another line taken by reform tracts was of institutional change, and the key was seen to be that marvellous innovation – the national chartered trading company.

By 1620, there were three national chartered companies in Europe for trade to Asia – the Dutch, the English and the Danish. Since the last of these, founded in 1616, was undercapitalised and dependent to a very large extent on the support of King Kristian IV of Denmark, it should have served as a warning to those in Portugal and Portuguese Asia who assumed that the creation of a company for trade on the Cape route was in and of itself a solution to their problems. However, it was not to the Danes but the Dutch that the Portuguese looked, and what they saw was the following. The charter of the Dutch Verenigde Oost-Indische Compagnie (VOC) was granted to it by the States-General of the Netherlands in March 1602 on the payment of a small fee of Dfl. 25,000; it was to be renewed after twenty-one years, as indeed it was in 1623 (and thereafter in 1647, 1672, 1696 and so on). The central management in the Netherlands rested with the so-called Seventeen Gentlemen (*Heren XVII*), consisting of delegates from the principal chambers that comprised the Company, and corresponding to major trading towns: eight from Amsterdam, four from Middelburgh (Zeeland), and one each from Hoorn, Enkhuizen, Delft and Rotterdam, with a floating seventeenth member. The directors of the chambers (the so-called *bewindhebbers*) were brought in on some of the decisions, but final power vested with the Seventeen Gentlemen (Glamann 1981).

There was only a limited extent to which the Portuguese could follow the Dutch model. For one, they already had an elaborate local apparatus in place in the form of the *Estado da Índia*, which included designated cities with municipal chambers, and all sorts of sovereign claims, which could not simply be handed over to a Company. The state in Portuguese Asia already existed; one could not create a Company that would also be a quasi-state, as was the case with the VOC. Nevertheless, the idea of forming a Company 'in imitation of that of Holland' surfaced as early as 1618, and in the early 1620s, the New Christian merchant and *arbitrista* Duarte Gomes Solis actually published a proposal for the formation of a company. Solis's ideas, which involved trade in Chinese goods – raw silk and porcelain – rather than spices, were given a most lukewarm reception by the Portuguese community of Macau, which remained hostile to all trading company schemes for much of this period (Disney 1978; Souza 1986).

But in Portugal and Spain they struck a sympathetic chord, not least of all with Don Gaspar de Guzmán, Count (and later Count-Duke) of

Olivares, who was the former tutor of Felipe IV, and became his all-powerful *valido* from about 1622. Another supporter of the idea was the Marquis of Alenquer, although Olivares soon dismissed him from his post as viceroy of Portugal – rendering his support to the idea valueless in political terms. In 1624, the plan found an ardent lobbyist in the court in the form of D. Jorge Mascarenhas (soon to be made Count of Castelo Novo), who was appointed president of the Municipal Chamber (*câmara municipal*) of Lisbon in that year, with the intention of thereby facilitating the financing of the venture. Mascarenhas had his own axe to grind, using the Company project as a means of enhancing his reputation and influence in the court. Olivares for his part saw matters quite differently, conceiving of the Company as a cog in the larger wheel of his 'Great Project' to disrupt Dutch trade and thereby affect the Spain-Netherlands military balance (Elliott 1986; Disney 1978). The key to this scheme seems to have been a Hanseatic-Habsburg company, to operate between the Baltic ports and those of Iberia; other smaller companies were to deal with trade (and implicitly maritime warfare) in Spanish America, northern Europe and the Middle East (Disney 1978: 74–75).

The underlying idea of the companies seems to have been to relieve the treasury of the costs of war, and transfer the burden on to private parties, and particularly the bourgeoisie. Thus the Hanseatic company was to be financed by German and Flemish merchants, rather than the Crown itself. Similarly, D. Jorge Mascarenhas's brief was to persuade the cities (which is to say the *câmaras municipais*) of Portugal to sink money in the venture of East India trade in a systematic fashion; their earlier role had been restricted to periodically bailing out the Crown at moments of crisis. Mascarenhas signally failed in this attempt; none of the Portuguese cities, nor even those of Portuguese Asia (which were also appealed to) was particularly interested in the idea, even though thirty of them did make a contribution of some sort. Nor was he particularly successful in persuading private entrepreneurs to sink money in the venture; in fact, only two private persons are known to have done so. The burden of investment thus fell, as in the Danish case, on the Crown, as the Table 6.4 shows.

Now it may appear something of a misnomer to term an enterprise such as this, where the Crown alone accounted for eighty per cent of the capital, a chartered trading company. We are also forced to ask ourselves why this venture alone, of all those in Olivares's 'Great Project', bore any fruit. At least a part of the answer lay in the relations between the New Christian merchants of Portugal and the Habsburg monarchy in this period. We have already noted how under the Habsburgs the network of New Christian families and their trade had spread across the Atlantic to Brazil, Peru and Mexico, then sought links via Manila and Macau with Portuguese Asia. Equally, the participation of New Christians in the contracts for trade on the Cape route (as well as the customs-farm at

Lisbon) has been established by the research of Boyajian and others (Boyajian 1983; Disney 1978). However, the attitude of the state towards these traders was one of mixing carrot with a rather large dose of stick, particularly after about 1600. In 1609, Felipe III had promulgated the explusion of the *moriscos*, a substantial minority (of some 300,000 people), mostly resident in Valencia, who were the vestiges of the Muslim ocupation of Spain. In much the same period, the Duke of Lerma acted to squeeze the other 'minority' still within his master's territories: the New Christians of Portugal. He first suggested that they be fined and expelled, then proposed that they be sold immunities; but after 1610, the Inquisition resumed operations against them once again (Lynch 1981: 60–62). Again, in 1618, a large number of Lisbon's leading New Christian merchants – including members of the Tinoco and Dias Henriques families – were imprisoned for refusing to buy pepper from the Crown at an absurdly inflated price, and had eventually to pay their way out of trouble (Boyajian 1983: ix).

Table 6.4 Capital invested in the Portuguese Company, 1628–33

Source	Amount (in cruzados)
Crown	1,056,809
Municipalities	
Lisbon	150,000
Évora	16,620
Castelo Branco	16,569
Coimbra	15,000
Others	121,678
Total	318,867
Private Investors	1,500
Chaul *câmara*	3,750
GRAND TOTAL	1,380,926

(*Source*: Disney 1978: 159–60)

Now it is significant that Jorge Mascarenhas sought from the very inception of the Company project to involve New Christians in it. It was suggested that they could buy titles if they invested in the Company: 1,000 *cruzados* would give them the status of *cavaleiro fidalgo*, while 30,000 *cruzados* would make them *fidalgos da casa real*. The leading New Christian families did not rise to the bait, not least of all because the Company's charter declared that subscribed capital was liable to be confiscated if the subscriber were found guilty of heresy (Disney 1978: 82–83). Rather, they preferred to negotiate directly with Olivares, buying themselves a share in Habsburg finances in the late 1620s and 1630s, and thereby displacing the Genoese bankers on whom Madrid had earlier been dependent. But they were nevertheless involved with the direction of the Company, both in Portugal and at Goa; in the latter centre, New Christian merchants like Valentim Garcia and Francisco Tinoco de Carvalho enjoyed official protection during the viceroyalty of the Count of Linhares (1629–35), and were hence willing to serve on the board of the Company at Goa. Later events suggest that in fact they were probably right to be suspicious. The 1630s and 1640s saw a resumption of severe persecutions against them, with several members of the Mendes de Brito family (which had a representative on the Company's Lisbon board) being arrested by the Inquisition in 1630, and one of the Company's other directors, Diogo Rodrigues de Lisboa, being arrested in 1632. Had their capital been sunk in a venture such as the Company, it would almost certainly have been lost. The eventual dissolution of the Company, by an order of 12th April 1633, put an end to the possibilities of such investment soon enough.

The reasons for the failure of the Portuguese East India Company are plain to see. Return cargoes in Asia were plentifully available, since the pepper production in Malabar and Kanara combined by the early seventeenth century was at least ten times what the *Carreira da Índia* required. Rather the issue was of getting capital in time to the pepper-procuring factories (especially Cochin and Honawar), and of ensuring the safety of shipping. In the late 1620s and early 1630s, both of these problems proved insurmountable, the first being partly a result of the second, for no investor would sink money into a trade with over 33 per cent loss rates on shipping. By failing to secure the *Carreira da Índia* against Dutch attacks, the Portuguese attempt to set up a company was always a non-starter. Table 6.5 shows the loss rates in the 1610s and 1620s; in the latter decade, particularly, losses both on the outward and return voyages are outrageously high.

Table 6.5 Portuguese shipping tonnage on the Cape route, 1611–70

| Period | Europe-Asia | | Asia-Europe | |
	Departures	Arrivals	Departures	Arrivals
1611–20	60,990 (66)	44,060 (47)	40,350 (32)	35,550 (28)
1621–30	48,000 (60)	31,410 (39)	24,150 (28)	15,050 (19)
1631–40	20,020 (33)	15,770 (28)	13,710 (21)	9,910 (15)
1641–50	22,840 (42)	14,280 (28)	16,030 (32)	12,030 (24)
1651–60	14,320 (35)	18,990 (35)	7,970 (16)	8,120 (16)
1661–70	8,635 (21)	5,635 (14)	6,070 (14)	4,820 (13)

(*Note:* Figures in brackets are numbers of ships)
(*Source:* Duncan 1986: 22)

THE DECADE OF DISASTERS: PORTUGUESE ASIA IN THE 1630s

The 1630s are in many ways the most crucial years where the seventeenth-century decline of the *Estado da Índia* is concerned. Almost one half of the decade is, curiously enough however, occupied by the government of one of the most celebrated viceroys of Portuguese Asia, D. Miguel de Noronha, Count of Linhares, who left office in December 1635, having concluded in January of the same year a peace treaty with the English in Asia. This Anglo-Portuguese agreement may be counted among the very few positive aspects to the 1630s from the Portuguese viewpoint, relieving them of the burden of having to combat at least one adversary. But otherwise, Linhares left Goa a bitterly disappointed man, for his viceroyalty was counted a failure by many contemporaries, and was rescued only by the assiduous 'public relations' of some of his close associates, like his secretary Pedro Barreto de Resende. His successor in office, Pero da Silva, fared little better, and despite his trenchant – and often *ad hominem* – attacks on Linhares's government, was unable to show anything during his own term in office (1635–39) other than further losses, some of them quite catastrophic. Further, unlike Linhares, whose approach was to take the fight to the rival camp, and who strove to hatch scheme after scheme to alter the balance of political alliances in various Asian regions in favour of the *Estado*, Silva's was a far more passive regime, which attempted little more than a fiscal holding operation. We may begin by considering some of Linhares's pet schemes, and how events – in the form of Asian geo-political shifts – overtook them.

More than any of his predecessors, Linhares was concerned about the control of the stretch of coast extending from Cape Comorin to Pulicat, the so-called Fishery and Coromandel coasts. Pulicat, and the Dutch fortress and factor there, was in particular a great concern of his viceroyalty, during which the idea of expelling the Dutch from this central Coromandel port occupied a good deal of attention. We may note that in 1629, the Portuguese had won a major victory – the last of those decades – against a besieging Acehnese force off Melaka, and this provided a fillip to trade between Coromandel and Melaka in these years. The Acehnese attack was mounted from the port of Deli, and the attacking force comprised – according to the Portuguese – two hundred and thirty-six sail (including thirty-eight galleys), carrying some nineteen thousand persons. It arrived off Melaka in early July 1629, and began after some skirmishes to build elaborate siegeworks; over sixty Portuguese were killed in the next few months, before the arrival in late October of a relieving fleet under Nuno Álvares Botelho. But it was only with the intervention in late November of the Sultan of Johor, Abdul Jalil (r. 1623–77), who arrived with a substantial war-fleet to help the Portuguese, that the tide turned against the Aceh forces. We are thus reminded again of the Malay text with which this book commenced, and its notion of the Malays as *ultimately* holding the fate of Melaka in their hands (Boxer 1985a, iv).

The defeat of the Acehnese coincided roughly with Linhares's arrival in Goa. The new viceroy was thus relieved of a pressure that had been building up since the mid-1620s, when the Bishop of Melaka had warned that

> if the Acehnese enemy sets his sights [on Melaka], filling the sea with his vessels to ensure that our relief canot enter, he will not seem a little nigger (*negrinho*) as I have heard him called here after I came here, but a very ugly negro. (Subrahmanyam 1990b: 179)

Linhares sought to use the breathing-space created thereby to launch a counter-attack against the Dutch in the Bay of Bengal, but one which differed substantially from, say, André Coelho's scheme.

At this time, central and southern Coromandel was controlled by three rulers, from north to south, the last Vijayanagara dynasty at Chandragiri, the Nayaka of Senji and the Nayaka of Tanjavur. By the late 1620s, Dutch activity was concentrated in the first of these areas, particularly around the port of Pulicat (just north of modern-day Madras), since they had abandoned their factories in the Senji Nayaka's lands. Linhares's idea was to persuade the Chandragiri ruler, Venkata, to besiege Pulicat by land, while the Portuguese attacked it by water. To this end, he sent at least two major fleets out to Coromandel during his viceroyalty, one early on, and the other after the treaty with the English had been signed. Similarly, he strove to persuade the Portuguese settlers at Nagapattinam to fortify their settlement against a possible Dutch attack, while simultaneously trying to acquire another nearby coastal fort, at Tranquebar.

In all of these attempts, Linhares proved less than successful; by the end of his viceroyalty, Pulicat still remained in Dutch hands, largely as a consequence of the superior connections of the VOC into local networks of commerce and political entrepreneurship in and around Chandragiri, and Nagapattinam was still an open settlement. It was only somewhat further to the south that the viceroy enjoyed some limited success, extending the *Estado*'s formal control over the town of Tuticorin on the Fishery coast, in an area largely populated by Christian Parava converts. But even here, the Portuguese captain appointed by Goa had to suffer numerous indignities, as the Society of Jesus resented his presence in an area that they regarded as their own domain. Still, using Tuticorin, Linhares was able to secure supplies of saltpetre from the region, thus improving the availability of gunpowder.

This new source of saltpetre was needed for one particular reason: access to the old source – Bengal – was interrupted after 1632, when the Portuguese settlement of Hughli was attacked and overwhelmed by the forces of the Mughal governor of Bengal, Qasim Khan. Portuguese trade from Bengal had been of great importance for some of the west coast settlements, in particular Cochin, and from the 1580s, the textiles brought from Bengal to Goa and Cochin even began to be exported to Europe as part of the private cargoes on the *Carreira da Índia*. The growth in the relative importance of textiles in the Euro-Asian trade has been shown by Niels Steensgaard, and the few examples we have of the 'Books of textiles and silks' (*Livro de roupas e sedas*) carried by the scriveners of Lisbon-bound carracks suggest that Bengal textiles were an important category among these (Steensgaard 1984).

Table 6.6 Composition of imports into Lisbon from Asia (% weight)

Period	Pepper	Ginger	Cinnamon	Spices	Textiles	Indigo	Other
1513–19	80.0	7.3	2.1	9.0	0.2	0.0	1.4
1523–31	84.0	6.1	3.3	6.2	0.0	0.0	0.4
1547–48	89.0	4.2	0.9	4.5	0.0	0.0	1.4
1587–88	68.0	3.7	6.3	1.6	10.5	8.4	1.5
1600–03	65.0	2.5	8.7	5.0	12.2	4.4	2.2

(*Source*: Steensgaard 1984: 22)

Besides supplying textiles for the *Carreira da Índia*, Bengal also exported textiles for consumption in south-western India itself, and these together with rice and saltpetre formed the major exports of the region, against which bullion, pepper and cowrie shells (procured in the Maldives and used as low-value money in Bengal) were imported. It is unlikely that even at the height of their trade, Portuguese merchants dominated the external commerce of Bengal. But their settlements at Chittagong (and its suburb Dianga), Satgaon, and after the late 1570s Hughli, were important from the point of view of Portuguese intra-Asian trade, especially on account of the routes linking Bengal to Cochin and Nagapattinam.

It was in fact a Nagapattinam settler, Domingos de Seixas, who first brought news to the viceroy Linhares at Goa in late 1632 that the Mughals had taken Hughli. Linhares, his mind intent on other affairs, was clearly taken wholly by surprise by this development, which – unlike the case of Syriam or Hurmuz – was not preceded by a series of threats, diplomatic manoeuvres and negotiations. He quickly sought to point out the silver lining in the situation, declaring in a letter to Madrid of February 1633 that since the Portuguese still remained at the Orissa port of Pipli, and since the Arakanese were none too well-disposed to the Mughals, 'I have hopes of being able to return and open those ports, so that Melaka may not lack what used to go there from Bengala' – which is to say rice (ANTT, DRI No. 30, ff. 281v–82).

Portuguese hopes were soon raised further when they received communications from Asaf Khan, a high Mughal noble of Iranian origin, who was the father-in-law of the reigning emperor Shahjahan. Asaf Khan, like many other Iranians in Mughal service (including his son, Shayasta Khan, later governor of Bengal), was not merely a warrior and administrator but also a trader; he therefore suggested that Goa enter into an agreement with him to receive Bengal goods, and actually sent a ship to the *Estado*'s capital in 1636 (ANTT, DRI No. 37, ff. 17–17v).

In the middle decades of the seventeenth century, the Portuguese presence at Hughli and other Bengal ports thus was eventually partially reconsolidated, but two important facts must be borne in mind. First, this rejuvenated trade was of lesser dimensions, and directed to other destinations, than the pre-1632 trade. In particular, trade between the ports of the *Estado* and Bengal never recovered after the early 1630s. Second, the recovery is truly significant only after the mid-1660s, so that during the 1630s and 1640s, the loss of Hughli was a serious blow to Portuguese intra-Asian trade. This is the context in which António Bocarro wrote his *Livro das Plantas*, and the discussion there of Portuguese trade in the area therefore closes in a suitably melancholy tone:

> Here I leave this, and pass from the great bay of Bengala and river Ganges, which by many and large mouths enters into this sea, which was the theatre wherein the Portuguese possessed so much of substance, with some of them of most humble birth coming to possess very substantial lands that might be equated to large kingdoms, there were in them populous cities with sumptuous churches, and everything came to an end on account of the poor manner of government of the Portuguese, which when combined with the vices and related dealings, stirred up the tyranny and greed of the Moorish and Gentile kings, who tried to do away with them as they did. ...
>
> (Subrahmanyam 1990b: 262)

The chronicler thus resorts to the pet explanations of the epoch to understand why the Mughals expelled the Portuguese from Hughli: Portuguese immorality and misdemeanours, and Moorish tyranny and greed. Linhares himself in his letters presents an explanation in the same spirit, while adding some details. Thus:

> The cause of this movement and resolution of the Mogores [he writes], one understands that it is due to us Portuguese, because this Mogor King being the second or third son and rebelling with the kingdom against his father some seven or eight years ago and taking the field, he gave battle in which he was defeated, and taking refuge in the Kingdom of Bengala there sought the aid of the Portuguese of Goly who refused it to him as they were faithful to the said King, his father, and expelled him, and took some of his women who it is said were mistreated. With this sentiment which he carried away concealed in his breast (*recosido em seu peito*), he took revenge, ordering that all those who were living in that port where they had insulted him should be killed or captured.
>
> (ANTT, DRI No. 30, ff. 281v–82)

The reference is to the mid-1620s rebellion of Shahjahan (then Prince Khurram), during which he did indeed come to Bengal, and – during his stay – seek the help of Hughli's captain Miguel Rodrigues, who turned him down. But, needless to add, this was scarcely the true reason for the attack on Hughli, which seems to have been motivated by two other factors: first, Mughal concern at Portuguese involvement in the slave-trade from Bengal, which had increased a good deal from the late sixteenth century; second, the need to contain the power of the Portuguese over the Ganges delta, since they were seen as allies of the Maghs (residents of Arakan). The taking of Hughli thus cleared the way for the Mughal campaign against Chittagong and Arakan, already under consideration in the 1610s according to Portuguese reports, but which eventually was carried out only in Aurangzeb's reign (DRI, ii: 226).

The siege of Hughli, which lasted from 25th June to 29th September 1632 (according to Linhares), led to the death of a number of Portuguese and the carrying away to Agra of a large group of prisoners. Estimates of both the number of Portuguese in Hughli and the extent of their wealth tend to vary a good deal; Linhares's own suggestion that there were 'no more than two hundred Portuguese, and with their Christian slaves would all in all make up eight hundred', seems plausible. In terms of shipping too the losses seem to have been quite considerable – even if we do not accept one clearly exaggerated version, which claims that the Mughals took sixty-four large vessels and many smaller ones – and account for a good proportion of the total shipping losses for the viceroyalty of Linhares. These losses, which his critics carefully collated, are said to have amounted to 155 ships, 1,499 men and goods worth 7,500,000 *xerafins*, all lost between December 1629 and June 1635 (Boxer 1958: 13).

One other major reversal during the Linhares viceroyalty merits mention, and this concerns Sri Lanka. The Kandy ruler, Senarath, who had succeeded Vimala Dharma Suriya, after initially seeking Dutch support against the Portuguese, had later abandoned this idea for an accommodation with the *Estado da Índia*. In around 1620, a budget for Portuguese Asia shows that 'Ceilão and Manar' taken together were more than fiscally self-sufficient; the expenses for Mannar were 10,342 *xerafins* and those for the rest of the island 42,583 *xerafins*, while revenues were almost double this sum. The budget notes:

> The rents (*foros*) of the said island together with the ports and their customs today yield 80,000 *xerafins*, according to the new *foral*, which has just been completed by the *veador da fazenda* Antão Vaz Freire with the accountant Baltasar Marinho, and this is besides what the elephants which are captured amount to, for which there is an outfitting [expense] of between 20 and 30 *xerafins*, and besides the *maralas* which is the third part of the goods of the Gentiles who die, so that the said conquest no longer has need of supplies from this city [Goa]. (BPADE, cv/2–7, f. 56v)

But by the end of the 1620s, the Portuguese over-reached themselves, in an effort to prevent what they saw as possible Dutch inroads into eastern Sri Lanka, an area still not under the *Estado*'s control. Thus, desirous of controlling the eastern ports of Trincomalee and Batticaloa, the Portuguese Captain-General Constantino de Sá de Noronha broke the treaty signed earlier with Senarath, leading to a series of hostilities. The ports were indeed taken and fortified by the *Estado*, but Sá de Noronha also fell into an ambush organised by the Kandy forces in August 1630 (the Battle of Randeniwela), so that his forces were routed and the Captain-General himself killed (Winius 1971). In the aftermath of this battle, Kandyan forces pressed on Colombo and Galle, and relations between Senarath and the Dutch resumed, causing further concern to Goa.

The next series of major reversals in Sri Lanka were however to happen only in the viceroyalty of Pero da Silva, particularly in the year 1638, by which time Senarath had been succeeded at Kandy by his son Raja Sinha. By late 1637, a formal agreement between the Dutch and Kandy was on the cards, and was eventually signed in May 1638; the agreement stipulated that the Dutch would be the only Europeans allowed to trade in Sri Lanka, and in return they agreed to provide naval assistance in attacking Portuguese coastal forts. By this time, the Portuguese had already suffered from still another shock, when another Captain-General, Diogo de Melo de Castro, was defeated and killed by the Kandy forces in early 1638. Later that year, Batticaloa and Trincomalee fell; in 1640, Negombo and Galle were taken, both by joint VOC-Kandy attacks. Portuguese claims to the 'conquest of Ceilão' were beginning to look increasingly hollow.

Hughli and Sri Lanka do not complete the tale of woes for Portuguese Asia in the 1630s. By the second half of the decade, the Dutch regularly began to send fleets to Goa, to blockade the port, and prevent communications or trade with Lisbon. The VOC even set up a factory at the Konkan port of Vengurla (in Bijapur territory) to facilitate this blockade. With its headquarters under threat, the *Estado* could no longer even think of taking the battle to the enemy, and Pero da Silva's viceroyalty is thus characterised by a desperate need to gain some breathing space. It was not given to him to enjoy this though, as troubles in the Far East – and especially Japan – came to a head. The first of the Tokugawa Shoguns, Ieyasu, had been a promoter of foreign trade and contacts between Japan and East and Southeast Asia. This is visible in the vastly increased Japanese shipping activity of these years, as Table 6.7 summarises.

The period also saw Portuguese silver exports from Japan reach their peak, although their share in the total trade was declining in the face of competition. Japanese traders themselves were now settled in Taiwan,

Macau, Makassar, Luzon, Ayuthia and elsewhere; at least one Japanese magnate, Yamada Nagamasa (d. 1633), played a role of great importance in Thai court-politics in the early seventeenth century. In the 1630s, changes came about though, both in the attitude of the *bakufu* to the foreign trade of Japanese, and in their attitude towards Europeans.

Table 6.7 Shipping from Japanese ports, 1604–1635

Destination	1604–16	1617–35
Hoi-an	48	39
Vietnam	11	26
Champa	5	1
Cambodia	24	20
Ayuthia	36	20
Other	71	55
TOTAL	195	161

(*Source*: Whitmore 1983: 380)

In the case of the Portuguese, we have noted how conflicts between Hideyoshi and the Jesuits had already characterised the late 1580s and 1590s, with the order for the expulsion of the Jesuits and other missionaries from Japan in 1614 setting a seal on the process. Missionaries did continue to come into the island-country, illegally and disguised as merchants and mariners, and this was a fact of which the Japanese authorities were aware. The expulsion of the Portuguese, and the denial of their trading rights after 1639, must be seen in the context of both these trends: first, the *general* changes in Japanese state policy in respect of trade, and second, Japanese-Portuguese relations since the 1580s. Where the first of these is concerned, the rule of Tokugawa Iemitsu (1623–51) marks a departure from earlier trends, and certainly from the policy followed by Ieyasu. It is still debated whether we can really see the decisions of this period as the 'closing of Japan'; in any event, it is certain that the foreign trade regime underwent a substantial change as a result of two orders, of 1633 and 1635, which forbade vessels or Japanese subjects to leave Japan save with a licence, and made residence abroad for over five years an offence punishable by death for a Japanese. Then, in 1636, all foreigners in Japan were made to move to the island of Deshima, recently reclaimed from the harbour of Nagasaki, and their activities and movements were strictly limited. All preparations were thus set in motion for a form of hostile trade, conducted in an ambience of great suspicion and distrust. It was a situation that boded ill for the Portuguese, who were already distrusted by many in positions of power.

Portuguese-Japanese relations had been quite variable since 1614, when the expulsion of all missionaries had been officially decreed. Between

1618 and 1620, a large number of priests and lay-persons were executed in Nagasaki and Kyoto, but none of them was Portuguese; however in 1622, some fifty-five others were beheaded or burnt at stake, including nine European priests. By 1625, persecutions had reached their peak, but trade continued apace; with the Spaniards being expelled from Japan in this year, the trade between Macau and Nagasaki seems, if anything, to have gained force. Administrative relations between Goa and Macau had just been reorganised, and Macau had been given its own independent Captain-General, as distinct from the Captain-Major of the Japan voyage, in 1623. At the same time, trade between Macau and Manila flourished as Table 6.8 demonstrates, and despite injunctions against it by the Crown was estimated at one and a half million *pesos* in the early 1630s.

Table 6.8 Macau's trade to Manila and Nagasaki, 1620–40 (Ships)

Year	Manila	Nagasaki	Year	Manila	Nagasaki
1620	5	6	1631	3	5
1621	2	6	1632	4	4
1622	?	0	1633	3	2
1623	?	7	1634	0	5
1624	?	5	1635	4	3
1625	?	5	1636	1	4
1626	?	6	1637	3	6
1627	6	0	1638	3	2
1628	2	5	1639	3	4
1629	2	2	1640	3	1
1630	6	2			

(*Source*: Souza 1986: 55, 75)

By the mid-1630s, the Portuguese gradually became aware that the *bakufu* was seriously considering denying them access to Japan's trade. Letters to the Count of Linhares from Macau in 1635–36 speak of how the Japanese Council of State (*Roju*) had even considered a proposal to attack Macau itself, presented to them by the Dutch. In 1637, a further incident served to drive the wedge between Japanese and Portuguese deeper. A Japanese Augustinian friar, arrested after a manhunt, confessed under torture to having received the help of several Portuguese merchants, one of whom – Duarte Correia – was at the time present in Nagasaki, as captain of one of the ships from Macau. Seized by the Japanese authorities, Correia was eventually burnt at the stake in May 1639, as the Dutch Company's employees report. The rest of the Macau fleet departed in November 1637, with '2,600 chests of silver worth 80 tons of gold', in the words of a Dutch writer (Boxer 1959: 153), and a Portuguese embassy under D. Francisco de Castelbranco stayed on, to make its way to the court.

The tensions inherent in the situation had to find resolution, and this came in the most unexpected way for the Portuguese, as a result of the so-called Shimabara Revolt. This revolt had its roots in the Arima area of Kyushu, ruled over in the early seventeenth century by Christian *daimyo*, who abandoned this faith though after 1614, and hence sought to persuade their subjects also to do so. Those who participated in the rebellion, which was apparently a peasant revolt using the symbols of Christianity as a rallying point, numbered some twenty thousand; they were crushed and slaughtered in large numbers at much the same time that the Portuguese embassy was seeking to make its case at the Shogun's court.

The Portuguese still had the respite of another year's trade: in August 1638, they sent out two galliots from Macau, which managed to bring back some 1,600 chests of silver, but also a set of stern warnings that they conveyed to the increasingly dismayed City Council of Macau. It was in 1639 that the tide turned, with the *bakufu*'s decision to expel them once and for all, lest they seek alliances with disgruntled and footloose *samurai* (the so-called *ronin*) and foment further rebellions. When two galliots, commanded by Vasco Palha de Almeida, reached Nagasaki in late August 1639, they were prevented from unloading their goods or trading, and later informed of the expulsion order by a representative from the court. The clearest narrative of the period's events, by the VOC employee François Caron, informs us that the *bakufu* representative ended his statement with the following – as it happens, quite significant – words:

> For all these reasons, you people are worthy of death, and His Imperial Majesty should justly kill you, but he has condescended to spare your lives, and hereby ordains that you leave Japan and never return. If you should subsequently break this command, you will then infallibly be punished as you now deserve to be. (Boxer 1959: 161)

Despite all the ominous signals, the decision came as a thunderclap for Macau's citizens, who decided – notwithstanding this warning – to send a special embassy in the following year to Nagasaki. Of this embassy of 1640, sixty-one persons were beheaded as a warning, and their ship burnt; the thirteen who remained were sent back to Macau with the news of what had transpired. The Macau-Japan trade was at an end.

RESTORATION, TRUCE AND FAILURE, 1640–52

While Linhares and Pero da Silva conducted their respective administrations in Goa, political affairs in Portugal were gradually coming to a boil. The Count-Duke of Olivares, Felipe IV's powerful minister, had in mind a new political order, one in which territories like Portugal, Aragon and Catalonia would be brought around, as he wrote in a secret memorandum of 1625, to 'the style and laws of Castile, with no difference whatsoever' (Lynch 1981: 105). A version of this idea bore fruit in terms of the plan for the so-called Union of Arms, under which a combined army of reservists would be created, with levies from all parts of Felipe IV's empire. The point was, in a sense, to increase the power and presence of the centralised monarchical system, which did not however necessarily mean a corresponding increase in the monarch's personal power. It is important to remember that this age of 'absolutism' was equally the age of the great and powerful ministers, from Richelieu and Mazarin in France to Olivares in Spain. Felipe IV continued to be regarded as something of a paper tiger by his subjects, one of whom – the satirist Francisco de Quevedo y Villuegas – penned the following trenchant verse on the monarch:

> Filipo, que el mundo aclama
> Rey del infiel tan temido,
> Despierta, que por dormido
> Nadie te teme, ni te ama.

> Philip, acclaimed by the world entire,
> the King most feared by the Moor,
> Awake! For while you snore,
> no one loves you or fears your ire.[1]

That no one feared the King's ire became apparent from the late 1630s, as the spectre of rebellion appeared in various parts of Iberia. In Catalonia in 1637, it was feared that Olivares wished to use the fact that the province was at the border with France to effect a semi-permanent military occupation. Thus, the Catalans refused to send a military force to Italy as they were asked; then, in May 1640, a widespread revolt broke out, and in January 1641 the province's representatives sued to place themselves under the rule of Louis XIII of France. The Catalan problem continued to plague Castile until the 1650s, through which they gradually recovered control of the province, taking Barcelona in 1652, and finally agreeing in 1659 to a Franco-Spanish peace treaty which left the French with some limited parts of the province (Lynch 1981; Elliott 1986).

The Portuguese too seized hold of this opportunity to effect what is known in Portuguese history as the Restoration, by which the Duke of Bragança was made King of Portugal, assuming the title of D. João IV. If the precise circumstances under which the Union of Crowns took place in 1580–81 are obscure, the Restoration is still more difficult to

---

1 The original of this verse is cited in Lynch (1981), p. 69; the rather loose translation is mine. But at least one recent historian argues that Felipe IV has received a 'bad press'; cf. Stradling (1988).

comprehend. Obviously the policy of infiltration of the administration of Portugal by Spaniards begun in the 1610s explains a part of the resentment felt by the Portuguese; the appointment in 1634 of Dona Margarida, Princess of Savoy, to head the government of Portugal worsened already inflamed tempers. Social support for Habsburg rule in the 1580s had come from two quarters: first, the aristocracy, with their inherently pro-Castilian ideology, who believed moreover that the Habsburgs would interfere less with their rights and privileges than the Portuguese monarchs had; second, the mercantile elements, who saw in the Union of the Crowns an opportunity to expand their trading horizons. For a time, the expectations of the latter were met, as Portuguese New Christians expanded their networks into Spanish America and Manila. But in the 1630s, the Inquisition cracked down on them, and both Mexico and Peru saw anti-Portuguese waves of some dimensions. Equally, Olivares's desire to use the Portuguese nobility in his military plans did not meet with the approval of that class, save those few members of the *noblesse de service* who actually managed to integrate themselves into the Castilian court. Besides, the 1630s had made it clear that Spain had neither the resources nor the will to resist Dutch incursions overseas, as events in Brazil – in particular – made clear. As Dutch forces led by Count Johan Maurits of Nassau took Pernambuco in 1637, and then turned their attention on the crucial sugar-producing region of Bahia the following year, Portuguese resentment at what they saw as Castilian neglect of their overseas possessions grew.

The revolt in Catalonia thus presented the Portuguese with a marvellous opening, which the Duke of Bragança seized in December 1640, declaring himself the lawful King of Portugal. Supported by a large proportion of the nobility, aided by the merchant class, aware that Richelieu and the French were willing to lend him support, and helped along by the propaganda of the Jesuits, João IV had to face relatively little initial resistance from Spain, where the Catalan revolt occupied the bulk of the military forces. The transition in Portuguese Asia too passed off relatively smoothly, with the official settlements being required to swear an oath of loyalty to the new monarch, a process that seems to have been accomplished with relatively little resistance.[2]

One of D. João IV's first acts as ruler was to move for a peace with the Netherlands, besides ratifying the one that already existed with England. The ten-year truce with the Dutch States-General was signed by the Portuguese King in November 1641, although it was only ratified and

2 Papers concerning the acclamation of D. João IV in Portuguese Asia are to be found in ANTT, DRI, No. 49. The settlements and cities mentioned include Chaul (f. 168), Bassein (f. 177), Honawar (f. 187), Basrur (ff. 189–89v), Cannanore (ff. 191–91v), Cranganor (f. 195), Cochin (f. 211), Nagapattinam (f. 214), Tuticorin (f. 218) and São Tomé de Meliapor (f. 220). Dates for the acclamation vary between early September and early November 1641.

proclaimed in February 1642. By this time, the Portuguese viceroy at Goa, the Count of Aveiras, had already made at least one attempt to persuade the Dutch to accept a truce local to Asia; the latter refused to do so however, since each passing month enabled them to press forward in their attempt to gain ground in Sri Lanka and elsewhere. We may note, for example, that it was *after* the Restoration (although before news of it arrived in Asia), that the Dutch finally took Melaka from the Portuguese, on 14th January 1641, following over five months of siege and several earlier attempts by the VOC, dating to the early years of the seventeenth century.

The fact was that successive blows in Bengal, Sri Lanka and Japan had left the *Estado da Índia* punch-drunk, with its administration incapable in the late 1630s of organising a coherent overall strategy. The Dutch could now pick targets at will, confident that Goa could not respond – particularly given the fact that the capital city itself was under blockade. Dutch success or failure in this period depended on local circumstances, how well defended any given Portuguese settlement was, and what the residual balance of forces was in the area in question. Thus, in taking Melaka, the VOC had to ensure that they received the support of Johor's Sultan Abdul Jalil, who we have seen helped the Portuguese stave off an Acehnese attack in 1629. Had the forces of Johor decided to support the Portuguese, they could certainly have ensured more or less regular supplies to the city, and thus delayed if not altered the outcome. Instead they threw their weight behind the Dutch, on the understanding that the VOC after the fall of Melaka would enable Johor to build up its trading network at the cost of Aceh, as indeed transpired in the years from 1641 to 1680. The Dutch Council of Batavia acknowledged this, writing to the *Heren XVII* in July 1645, 'We must continue to remember that the Johorese contributed substantially toward the conquest of Malacca. Without their help we could never have become masters of that strong place' (Andaya 1975: 35).

The fall of Melaka is the last major episode in the string of reverses that extend from Syriam, through Hurmuz and Hughli, to Japan and the Sri Lankan east coast ports. In the 1640s, the *Estado* enjoyed a relative respite, not only from the Dutch but – possibly coincidentally – from other Asian adversaries. It is true that hostilities with the Dutch did not wholly cease even during the Ten Years' Truce, with the VOC taking Negombo in early 1644, and retaining it under the Goa Treaty of November 1644. Again, in April 1642, a Dutch fleet was sent out on a plunder-raid to the Portuguese Coromandel settlement of Nagapattinam, and was held off only because of the intervention of the Nayaka of Tanjavur – once again demonstrating that local forces still held the balance in the struggle. Still later, a similar incident occurred in 1649 at the Portuguese settlement of Tuticorin in the territory of the Nayaka of Madurai, and once again the

Dutch forces of Johan Maetsuycker were checked by the Nayaka's intervention (Subrahmanyam 1990b: 93–95; Boxer 1958).

At the time that the negotiations were under way to implement the truce in Asia, some residual optimism still existed among the officials of the *Estado da Índia*. Their hopes were well expressed by José Pinto Pereira, an influential fiscal official and later adviser to D. João IV, who wrote to the King from Goa in March 1644 as follows:

> The state of affairs teaches and tells us that the most healing remedy for now is for Your Majesty to go along with and adjust to this nation [Holland], tolerating their deceits, double-dealing and frauds, for it is thus that I believe one can check the luck they enjoy, and the greatest war one can make is to enter into a peace with them ... for once trade is free, it is a force that will weaken their trade, and also the force which [you] have, which is of no less importance; and our trade will expand, the customs-houses will begin to yield [money], the royal revenues will increase, [your] subjects who are finished and consumed by the robbery and piracy practiced by this enemy, the reason for his greater expansion, will thrive. (Boxer 1958: 18n)

There were two problems with Pereira's logic. First, 'peace' with the Dutch did not mean that 'free trade' would become the rule. Rather, and this is especially the case in the area around Melaka and on the Malay Peninsula, the Dutch in the 1640s sought to impose a highly restrictive system of *cartazes*, intended to impose a structure of control on not only Portuguese but Asian trade and shipping. It was only in the last quarter of the seventeenth century that this attempt was abandoned, and the policy of *mare clausum* gradually moderated by the Dutch. Second, the Portuguese had lost many of the most lucrative trading lines they had with the losses in Bengal, Japan and Melaka. The Melaka-Macau-Nagasaki-Makassar-Manila network that sustained a good part of Portuguese private trade in the 1610s, 1620s and 1630s had been set into disarray, and the hostile relations between Spain and Portugal after the Restoration did not permit an easy reconstitution of even the Macau-Makassar-Manila triangle. Of course the Portuguese were not the only sufferers in this process; the traders based at Manila too had to bear a part of the consequences. This emerges clearly enough from the testimony of the English factors, Edward Pearce and Thomas Breton, who visited Manila in December 1644 to scout out trading possibilities.

> The Trade in this place [they wrote], is very much decayed since the Portugues left it, and the cittizens mightely impoverished, yet will their prowd hearts heardly acknowledge it, every year they send one or two gallioones to Nova Spania a quarter laiden, with wax, china, silk and coast cloathing (when they can gett any from Maccasser which hath beene in very small quantities since the Portugues are bannished Manilla), theis galliones retorne hither the same yeare with nothing but provicions to supply this place and Reals of 8t to defray the extraordinary charge the King is at. (IOLR, Original Correspondence 1902, E/3/19, fl. 112v)

Nor was the situation much better in the western Indian Ocean, peace or no peace with the Dutch. Cochin's traders still had to recover from the loss of Hughli, their main trading route in the pre-1630 period. As for Chaul, Goa and Diu, their trade was also increasingly coming under pressure from a new direction, namely the rising maritime power of Oman. Now the Omanis had always been a minor thorn in the flesh of the *Estado da Índia*, even in the days when Hurmuz was still a Portuguese possession, during which time minor centres subsidiary to Hurmuz were frequently under threat from the forces of the Imams of Oman. It is with the accession of the Ya'rubi line of Imams, founded by Nasir ibn Murshid (r. 1624–49), that the threat began to grow. Imam Nasir succeeded in unifying much of Oman between 1624 and 1632, leaving the Portuguese limited territories at Maskat, Sur and Quryat. These centres, and especially Maskat, emerged in the late 1620s and 1630s as important nodes for Portuguese trade to Basra, Sind and Gujarat, as well as Chaul and Goa. Towards the end of his reign, Imam Nasir moved against Maskat, besieging it from August 1648 but dying before he attained success. The task was completed by his cousin and successor, Sultan ibn Saif al-Ya'rubi (r. 1649–79), to whom the Portuguese Captain-General Francisco de Távora surrendered in January 1650. But this was merely a portent of things to come, as the Omanis built up a formidable navy, and emerged in the latter half of the seventeenth century as a powerful maritime-oriented state, with ambitions ranging from the Indian west coast to the east coast of Africa. Thus, by 1652, and the end of the Luso-Dutch Truce, the Portuguese King's subjects were as ill-prepared for war as they had been in 1644 (Bathurst 1972).

THE RETREAT COMPLETED, 1652–1665

The years between 1641 and about 1680 represent the height of Dutch maritime influence in Asian waters. This is a fact not generally recognised in the historiography, in which the fall of Banten to the Dutch in 1682 is given excessive importance. In the four decades leading up to 1680 (and especially in the 1650s and 1660s), the Dutch made major inroads on the trade of Makassar, thus ensuring that their spice monopoly paid rich dividends. At the same time, these were the years when the Japan trade of the Dutch was at its apogee; the export of silver was prohibited by the *bakufu* in 1668, but thereafter the Dutch continued to export considerable quantities of gold *kobans*. For the 1640s, Dutch bullion exports from Japan were some 15 million florins, 13 million in the next decade, and 14.5 million in the 1660s (with gold and silver taken together). After 1668, and the cessation of silver exports, gold exports alone in the next decade still

177

amounted to some 11.5 million florins, and it is only in the last two decades of the seventeenth century that the VOC exported less than 3 million florins worth of bullion from Nagasaki (Glamann 1981: 58). Cheap Japanese bullion thus powered the Dutch Company into a position where it could easily fund its purchases of Indian textiles, which were used in part to buy spices, and in part as an export to Europe.

Flush with funds by the early 1650s, the Dutch Company was not an easy rival for the Portuguese *Estado da Índia* to combat. There is thus a certain inevitability to what followed in the decade after the Ten Years' Truce ended in Asia. The focus of rivalry now came down to three areas, Sri Lanka, Coromandel and Malabar. The VOC was interested in Sri Lanka because of its cinnamon production and strategic location, since control of Sri Lanka implied an improved ability to check navigation between the western Indian Ocean and the Bay of Bengal. In the case of Malabar again, it was pepper that drew the Dutch there, and they took advantage of the truce of the period 1642–52 to set up a factory at Kayamkulam, which exported an average of 600,000 kilogrammes of pepper per year to Batavia in the years 1646–52 (Subrahmanyam 1990a: 249). Dutch motives in Coromandel are less easy to fathom, and it can be argued that there was no particular need for them to act as they did against Nagapattinam. If any strategic motive can be discerned here at all, it may have been the desire to protect the tin trade of the Malay Peninsula from possible Portuguese competition. But the policies followed by the Governor-General Johan Maetsuycker in the late 1650s and early 1660s are not always characterised by close calculation, in point of fact; rather, they seem to push the VOC into the exercise of sovereign and monopoly powers wherever possible, rather than wherever justifiable on commercial grounds. In retrospect, therefore, the VOC did not necessarily gain in the long run by the series of possessions it acquired in the Luso-Dutch wars of the 1650s and early 1660s, the establishment costs of many of which came to weigh heavily on the Company.

The major possessions lost by the Portuguese to the Dutch in these years included Colombo (1656), Jaffna, Nagapattinam and Tuticorin (1658), and Cochin, Kollam and Cannanore in the early 1660s. The fall of Cochin in 1663 effectively brought hostilities to a close, although a formal seal was set on the cessation of war only in 1669, with the Hague Treaty. The VOC was now left with Nagapattinam, Sri Lanka, the ports of the Fishery Coast of Madurai (and control over the pearl-fishery in the Gulf of Mannar), and the pepper-exporting ports of Malabar. Also, taking advantage of the resumption of hostilities between the Dutch and Portuguese, Sivappa Nayaka, the ruler of the state of Ikkeri to the south of Goa, moved in the mid-1650s to expel the Portuguese from their possessions on the Kanara coast: Honawar, Basrur (and its subsidiary fort Gangolli), and Mangalore. Despite the proximity of these forts to Goa, the

Estado could not relieve them, even though the Dutch had not yet resumed their annual blockade of Goa. One part of the explanation for this fiasco lay in troubles in Goa itself, where a *coup d'état* saw the viceroy, the Count of Óbidos, displaced by a junta of ambitious *fidalgos*, headed by a certain D. Brás de Castro, who were too preoccupied with local consolidation to think of matters farther afield (Winius 1971). Similarly, on the Coromandel coast, the forces of the Sultan of Golconda, acting on rumours that the VOC planned to take the surviving Portuguese settlement of São Tomé (or Mylapur), decided to pre-empt the Dutch, and took São Tomé in May 1662. In the *Estado*'s descending spiral, the Dutch were the major opponents, but others too continued to make their contribution, even in the 1650s and 1660s.

By the mid-1660s then, it is a vastly reduced *Estado da Índia* that confronts the observer. In one sense, it was not reduced in its spread, for at one extreme it still extended to East Africa, while another extreme was defined by Macau and the Portuguese outposts in the Lesser Sunda Islands. But the 'middle' had caved in, with the loss of Kanara, Malabar, and Sri Lanka, on the one hand, Hurmuz, Maskat and Melaka on the other. But one more loss was yet to come, and this from an unexpected source. In the early 1660s, the House of Bragança negotiated what was for it a prestigious marriage alliance, of D. Catarina de Bragança with Charles Stuart, monarch of England and Scotland. As part of the dowry, it was decided to give away a minor outpost of the *Estado* to the north of Goa, the island of Bombaím. The viceroy of the *Estado*, António de Melo de Castro, protested vigorously, claiming that the island had great strategic value and commercial potential, and sent Padre Manuel Godinho of the Society of Jesus to lobby Lisbon on his behalf. Godinho made his way after an arduous overland journey to Lisbon, and managed to get the ear of the all-powerful minister of the time, the Count of Castelo Melhor. But the Count had no patience with Goa's opinions, so that Bombaím was eventually handed over in 1665, further reducing the much shrunken *Estado da Índia* (Correia-Afonso 1990).

ASIANS, EUROPEANS AND THE RETREAT

In his *Fatalidade histórica da ilha de Ceilão* ('Historical Tragedy of the island of Ceylon'), the celebrated Lisbon-born soldier João Ribeiro (1622–93), veteran of eighteen years fighting in Sri Lanka, summed up the years with which the present chapter has been concerned in the following fashion.

> From the Cape of Good Hope onwards [he wrote], we were unwilling to
> leave anything outside of our control; we were anxious to lay hands on
> everything in that huge stretch of 5,000 leagues from Sofala to Japan; and

what was worse was that we set about this without calculating our strength, or thinking that even with the natives themselves this conquest could not last for ever. (Boxer 1985a, xi: 11)

Like every other writer, wise after the event, Ribeiro offered his views on what he thought should have been the *Estado*'s strategy, namely concentration on Goa, Hurmuz, Melaka and Sri Lanka. Such an approach, which we may term 'intensive' rather than 'extensive' in character, was what the *Estado* had perforce to adopt in the years after 1665. But Ribeiro surely missed the point in arguing that this should have been the Portuguese strategy from the very outset. As we have seen, the logic of interests and pressure groups within the Portuguese Asian empire had already led to spatial diversification in the years from 1515 on. It was again spatial diversification, into China and the Japan trade, that had given a fillip to the *Estado* during the crisis of the mid-sixteenth century; once more, in the years between 1570 and 1610, pushing back the frontier had a crucial role in defusing tensions at the margins of the *Estado*.

But Ribeiro's diagnosis was certainly accurate in one respect. The retreat of the *Estado da Índia* in the years from 1610 to 1665 was not merely a question of a rivalry with the 'enemy from Europe', as the Dutch were then termed by the Portuguese. As our analysis has shown, the Dutch were a catalyst in Portuguese retreat in Asia, and also moved in the closing stages (the 1650s and 1660s) to pick up the spoils. But much of the damage was done by 'the natives themselves' (as Ribeiro put it): Syriam, in part Hurmuz, Hughli, Nagasaki, Maskat, the Kanara ports and São Tomé are the clearest examples, but the taking of the coastal forts in Sri Lanka, Melaka or even Cochin could not have been accomplished by the Dutch save in a propitious local political context. It was the change in this context, as much as rivalry with the English and other Europeans, which caused the Dutch in turn to lose their dominant place in Asian trade in the eighteenth century.

CHAPTER SEVEN

Niches and Networks: Staying On, 1665–1700

The period after the mid-1660s, when the dramatic conflicts with the Dutch and English are increasingly a thing of the past, appears almost anti-climactic. It is often with a sense of puzzlement that historians of the *Estado da Índia* note that it still continues to exist in this period, so clearly one in which the Dutch, the English, and later the French dominate Euro-Asian commerce. We can view the years between 1665 and the end of the century from two perspectives. From the viewpoint of the eighteenth century, the last third of the seventeenth century may appear to be a prelude to the expansion of the *Estado* into the New Conquests of Goa and into the territory that eventually became the colony of Mozambique. From this perspective, it is obviously of interest to focus on Luso-Maratha relations, and on the shifting political and economic scene in the Zambezi valley, which define the context for the changes of the eighteenth century.

But there is also another perspective, namely that of the Portuguese private trader who in some form survived the ravages of the 1630s, 1640s and 1650s. Such private traders are to be found most conspicuously in Macau, but they may also be encountered in other – sometimes unexpected – locations, thus comprising a vestigial Lusitanian presence that is not without importance. In particular, an examination of both English and French trade in late seventeenth-century Asia reveals the existence of structures of cooperation between these nations and the Portuguese, who – while they may have been relatively deficient in financial capital – were far more expert than these other Europeans at understanding the structure and functioning of Asian markets and political systems.

Our examination of how the Portuguese empire in Asia and East Africa fared in the last third of the seventeenth century is hampered though by the relative absence of historical studies dealing with the Portuguese in this period. This is all the more ironical given the great richness of

181

source-materials in this period, and can only be explained by the fact that the epoch forms a sort of 'no-man's land'; historians of Asia in the period neglect the Portuguese, seeing them as marginal, while historians of Portuguese expansion prefer for their part to concentrate on Brazil and the Atlantic. How then did the Portuguese fare in their formal and informal settlements, whether Mozambique and the *Rios de Cuama*, Bandar Kung, Diu, the *prazos do Norte* and Goa, or São Tomé, Porto Novo, Hughli, Macau and Timor? Was their Euro-Asian trade as negligible in the period as it is sometimes suggested? These are the questions that we shall address in the present chapter.

THE CAPE ROUTE AND THE BAHIA TRADE

It has sometimes been suggested that one of the reasons why Sri Lanka and the Malabar forts were lost by the *Estado* to the Dutch in the 1650s and 1660s was the fact that the Portuguese Crown preferred to concentrate its attention, and also its military and financial resources, on the preservation of its Atlantic empire. In this endeavour, the Portuguese succeeded to a very large extent, with the Dutch being driven out of Recife and their last Brazilian strongholds in January 1654, and only retaining a foothold in continental South America at Curaçao. Again, in West Africa, Luanda, Benguela and other major possessions remained under Portuguese control at the time of the Treaty of 1669, with the Dutch making only a few gains on the Gold Coast. This idea of trading off losses in Asia against gains in the Atlantic is not merely a fancy of modern-day historians, for we find it articulated already in the Portuguese Council of War in the early 1650s, where it was stated:

> We should give up in Asia as much as we need to, in order to leave us free in Brazil, because whenever we [Portuguese and Dutch] are neighbours, the peace will never be too secure, nor our spices very valuable; besides which Asia, by its distance and its size, is more difficult and costly and less useful to conserve. (Winius 1971: 117)

To this end, it is noticeable that Portuguese shipping concentrated in the 1650s and 1660s on Brazil rather than the Cape route, with the formation of the *Companhia Geral do Estado do Brasil* in 1649 (financed with New Christian capital that was guaranteed immunity, unlike in the case of the Company of 1628–33) furthering the trans-Atlantic trade. Thus, in the 1650s, a mere 14,320 tonnes of shipping were sent out from Portugal to Asia, a figure that dropped still further in the following decade.

However, as Table 7.1 below demonstrates, there was a recovery in Portuguese trade on the Cape route in the last three decades of the seventeenth century, although the tonnage figures remain far below those for the late sixteenth or early seventeenth centuries.

Table 7.1 Portuguese shipping from Lisbon to Asia, 1661–1700

Period	Europe-Asia		Asia-Europe	
	Departures	Arrivals	Departures	Arrivals
1661–1670	8,635 (21)	5,635 (14)	6,070 (14)	4,820 (13)
1671–1680	11,700 (25)	13,900 (29)	10,730 (22)	9,680 (21)
1681–1690	11,650 (19)	11,650 (19)	9,300 (16)	8,600 (15)
1691–1700	14,900 (24)	13,700 (21)	8,950 (14)	7,550 (13)

(*Note*: Figures in brackets are numbers of ships)
(*Source*: Duncan 1986: 22)

Moreover, the logic of the Cape route trade also began to shift in this period. During the sixteenth century, ships on the *Carreira da Índia* had very occasionally called at Atlantic ports, whether in the Açores, on the African west coast or Brazil. The most common circumstance under which this happened was storm or shipwreck, though at times these were used by returning Indiamen as excuses for calling at ports other than Lisbon and indulging in contraband trade there. After its foundation in 1549, Salvador de Bahia became one such port; calls to Salvador were thus expressly forbidden in the orders governing the *Carreira da Índia*, promulgated in 1565. Now the mere fact of legislation did not of course guarantee that such trade was done away with. But economic logic too did not favour a Brazilian stopover; on the way out from Portugal, Brazil had no goods to offer in Asia, while on the way back, Asian goods did not have enough of a market in Brazil. And once the market for Asian goods (and especially textiles, silks and porcelain) began to grow in the late sixteenth century, it was fed via the trans-Pacific route, which – we have seen – was one where numerous New Christian merchants operated and made fortunes.

The disarticulation of Manila's Asian trading network in the aftermath of the Restoration had a negative effect on the trans-Pacific trade in these goods, which the later re-establishment of links between Spanish and Portuguese Asia did not wholly reverse. Further, as Brazil's population grew, and the practice of using coarse Indian textiles (which the Dutch significantly called *guinees lijwaat* or *negroskleden*) for even the slave population took root, the pressure on the ships of the *Carreira da Índia* grew. It is worth remarking here that the bulk of the textiles carried back in Portuguese Indiamen in the seventeenth century were not in the Crown's part of the cargo, but in the liberty-chests (*caixas de liberdade* or *agasalhados*) of the mariners and officers of the vessels themselves. Thus from the 1660s, once the Luso-Dutch truce ensured that the vessels of the

Carreira did not run an undue risk in Brazilian waters, it became the practice for ships returning from Goa to put in at Bahia. Various subterfuges had to be resorted to, however, since the Crown still frowned upon the use of Bahia as a port-of-call, preferring what was called the *viagem em direitura*, that is direct from Goa to Lisbon. Finally, yielding under pressure, a new set of provisions was passed in 1672, permitting homeward-bound Indiamen to call at Bahia, but with the proviso that only the goods from the *caixas de liberdade* could be sold there. Some officials argued that this was short-sighted, for it permitted private parties to profit, while denying the Crown the same opportunity. For instance, António Paes de Sande is known to have written in the late 1670s that ships of the *Carreira* should be allowed to take on sugar at Salvador and other Brazilian ports, 'since today the goods and capitals of India are not sufficient to provide a cargo even for a single ship, limited though it may be' (Boxer 1960). Eventually, this too was permitted, so that the *Carreira da Índia* gradually became integrated with, and perhaps even subsidiary to, the trade to Brazil.

But for this to happen, a further change had to take place. In the 1690s, rich gold-mines were struck in Brazil, in the region of Minas Gerais. The resulting expansion in gold production gave a fillip to Lisbon's trade, inaugurating what historians of an older generation were fond of terming the 'gold cycle' (in succession to the 'spice cycle' and the 'sugar cycle'). Registered exports of gold from Brazil to Lisbon, which were some 725 kgs in 1699, rose to over 10,000 kgs by the early 1710s, with an annual average between 1712 and 1755 of 10,867 kgs. This is likely to have been no more than about a half of total production, and implied a substantial corresponding increase in the demand for import commodities in Brazil (Cross 1983: 417–18). The increase in the gold production of its colony permitted Lisbon to finance a complex triangular trade with England, in which imbalances were financed through gold flows, but it is also likely to have resuscitated the fortunes of the *Carreira da Índia*. Thus, in December 1692, new orders were promulgated, making it not merely permissible but more or less incumbent on returning Portuguese Indiamen to put in at Bahia, and then sail back from Brazil to Lisbon with the Brazil fleet and its convoy. Of 39 ships that left Lisbon for Asia between 1697 and 1712, as many as 22 certainly called at Bahia on their return voyage. What they brought back, in order to purchase gold and tobacco, was a cargo of Indian cottons, Chinese porcelains and silks and – once into the eighteenth century – slaves from Moçambique. In brief, little by little, rather than being a trade between the termini (Lisbon and Goa), the *Carreira da Índia* was gradually transformed into a route dominated by trade at intermediate ports-of-call, whether Bahia or Mozambique. A glimpse of trade on the transformed *Carreira* as seen from the perspective of Bahia is presented in Table 7.2.

Table 7.2 Carreira da Índia ships touching Bahia, 1663–1702

Years	Outward Voyage	Return Voyage	Others	Total
1663–72	3	11	5	19
1673–82	5	10	3	18
1683–92	1	9	4	14
1693–1702	2	8	2	12
TOTAL	11	38	14	63

(*Source*: Hanson 1981: 284)

It is unfortunately not possible in the present state of our knowledge to estimate the precise dimensions of this trade, nor indeed its exact commodity composition. According to J.R. do Amaral Lapa, some proportion of the Asian goods exported into Brazil were re-exported to Spanish America or even West Africa, and he confirms that textiles and manufactures from Asia dominated the cargoes entering Brazil. Of greater significance is his claim that the late seventeenth and eighteenth centuries also saw the development of a direct Asia-Brazil-Asia trade, which was never given proper sanction by the Crown though (Amaral Lapa 1989). The dimensions of this trade, relative to the trade of the *Carreira da Índia*, are difficult to guess, but the point that emerges is that by 1700, Brazil too had goods that found an Asian market. Principal among these were two commodities: powdered tobacco (meant for use as snuff), and sugar, both of which were sold in Goa and Macau. The tobacco monopoly (*estanco*) in Goa earned the *Estado da Índia* 26,666 *xerafins* in 1681, and by 1704, the revenue on this account had gone up as high as 101,500 *xerafins* (Hanson 1981: 320; Nardi 1989). The trade between Brazil and Asia remained intact through the eighteenth century, and in the years from 1796 to 1811 Asian goods accounted for some 11,107,610,258 *reis* in the two major ports of Rio and Bahia, or roughly a half of what goods imported from Portugal amounted to in these ports (Amaral Lapa 1989: 390–91).

We are also aware that, as had been the case in the 1620s and 1630s, some thought was given in the closing decades of the seventeenth century to the issue of the re-organisation of Euro-Asian trade. In particular, the idea that trade be given over to a chartered Company (as in the case of Brazil, and briefly on the Cape route, over the years 1628–33) surfaces time and again. An early incarnation is a proposal tabled to the *Conselho Ultramarino* (Overseas Council) in March 1650 by Gaspar de Faria Severim, and claiming to be from the 'cities or settlers of India'; the proposal points out that the only way of combating the Dutch is to fight fire with fire (or one company with another), and goes on to request twenty-two concessions, some of them quite extensive. First of all, the Company was envisaged as engaged as much in intra-Asian as in

Euro-Asian trade, and even being permitted to trade in the Red Sea. Second, the Company was to have a monopoly of trade to India and Manila from Europe, and also to be allowed to send ships directly between Macau and Portugal. Further, it was suggested that the Company could be financed entirely from capital available in Asia, and it was this aspect that the Overseas Council treated sceptically. Nothing was decided therefore, and the resumption of hostilities with the Dutch led the proposal to die a natural death (AHU, Caixa 20/344–A, Doc. 177).

The proposal was revived again later in the seventeenth century, with one attempt being in the early 1670s, and another particularly serious attempt being in the late 1680s and early 1690s. The first of these proposals, supported by some influential Jesuits, was set out in the aftermath of particularly strong anti-New Christian movements in Portugal, early in the regency of D. Pedro (who took over as regent in 1668). The idea was that New Christian merchants would volunteer their money and expertise towards a new military-cum-commercial venture in the east, if the state would give them a generalised immunity against the Inquisition, which – in July 1672 – had arrested some of Lisbon's most wealthy and influential New Christians, including such men as Francisco Carlos, Diogo de Chaves and numerous others. The new plan, presented by the Jesuit Padre Baltasar da Costa to the royal confessor Manuel Fernandes in 1673, envisaged the creation of a military force of five thousand men to be sent out to Asia in the first year, followed by one thousand two hundred in every following year, towards which the merchants would contribute 20,000 *cruzados*. Further, the New Christian lobby – headed by António Correia Bravo, Pedro Álvares Caldas and Manuel da Gama de Padua – agreed to set aside a sum of money to pay for missionary activity in Asia, and also to fund the proposed Company. But the attempt failed completely, largely because the Lisbon *cortes* of 1674 rejected the idea of immunities or pardons for New Christians outright, in turn a reflection of the fact that popular sentiment against New Christians continued to run high. The decision by the New Christians to lobby Rome, to persuade the Pope that the Portuguese Inquisition was engaged in irregular procedures, further fuelled the flames. After Pope Innocent XI sent an ultimatum to D. Pedro in 1678, demanding an inquiry into earlier trials of New Christians, slanderous street-pamphlets appeared, one of which stated, for example:

> Whoever wants to be a Jew, heretic, sodomite and marry three times, go speak with Padre Manuel Fernandes, confessor to His Majesty, and with Manuel da Gama de Padua and Pedro Álvares Caldas, who have bulls from Padre Quental [the Papal Nuncio] for everything.   (Hanson 1981: 101)

Faced with this situation, the Regent himself performed a *volte-face*, and decided that it was impolitic to associate himself with the schemes of New Christians. Energetic supporters of a more liberal treatment to these merchants, such as Manuel Fernandes and Padre António Vieira, thus found themselves increasingly marginalised, and the death in 1680 of Manuel da Gama de Padua ensured that the scheme was not heard of again.

However, D. Pedro II, on assuming direct control of Portugal in 1683 after the death of D. Afonso VI, for whom he had acted as regent since 1668, revived the idea in another form. As early as 1685, he proposed to the viceroy at Goa that a company be formed along the Dutch and English pattern, and this idea was pursued in the Lisbon-Goa correspondence in succeeding years. A letter of March 1689 from Lisbon to Goa, for instance, speaks of a 'trading Company between the traders of Portugal and all the persons in the Estado da Índia who might be interested in it' (*BFUP*, 44, p. 158). Goa's response was lukewarm, pointing out that not much enthusiasm had been expressed for the idea by the people in Portuguese Asia whose opinions had been sought, but Lisbon continued to press – speaking in successive letters of 1691 and 1692 of the urgency of the need, of modalities and so on. One particular source of resistance to the idea seems to have lain in Macau, whose settlers had been distinctly lacking in enthusiasm even about the earlier Company of the 1620s, and eventually Macau was excluded from the 1690s Company as well. The proposal of the viceroy Count of Vila Verde in 1693 was that the Company 'be formed together with that of Brazil, given the precarious state in which the Estado da Índia finds itself' (BFUP, 44: 240), but the short-lived Companies that were eventually formed appear to have been concerned with Asia alone.

So far as we are aware, two Companies were formed in the 1690s, one funded in good measure by wealthy merchants based at Goa. It received a twelve-year concession, during which period it was granted a monopoly over trade in a number of commodities: at the Portuguese end cloth, coral, emeralds, gold and silver, and at the Asian end pepper, cinnamon, indigo and a few other goods. In 1696–97, one encounters reference to trade on behalf of the Company at Surat, conducted by the Parsi merchant Rustamji Manakji, and other mentions of trade at the factory in Mangalore. Unfortunately for the Company, however, the fall of Mombasa in late 1698 became the occasion for pressures on the viceroy from private traders to suppress its activities, on the grounds that it neglected the security of Portuguese possessions for the single-minded pursuit of profit. Thus, in 1700, it was merged with another Lisbon-based Company, despite the fact that it had showed a profit for the five years of its existence. The joint Company, with mixed Goan, Genoese and Portuguese participation, lasted only a few years.

All in all then, while trade on the Cape route by the Portuguese was not insignificant in the years from 1665 to 1700, it did not recover either to the dimensions of the early seventeenth century. At specific moments, the *Carreira da Índia* did appear to be doing rather well, as for instance in 1672, when Francis Parry, an English diplomat in Portugal, wrote of the arrival of 'richly-laden' ships from Asia at Lisbon, 'wich is soe good a fortune as hath not been knowne here since Portugall hath been a kingdome of itselfe' (Ames 1989: 296). In the final analysis though, such trade – based on pepper cargoes scrounged from Ankola or Mirjan – was not what made the difference. Ironically, Portuguese trade to Asia had to be rescued by its trade to another colony – namely, Brazil.

THE VICISSITUDES OF THE *ESTADO*: THE VIEW FROM GOA

The Mughal chronicler Khafi Khan, writing in the early eighteenth century, knew nothing of the trade between Goa, Bahia and Lisbon, or of the ups and downs of the *Carreira da Índia*. To him the Portuguese *Estado da Índia* appeared quite different, an enterprise of the *firangis* to be sure, but one with a curiously localised flavour, at least in his version:

> The officers of the King of Portugal occupied several neighbouring ports, and had erected forts in strong positions and under the protection of the hills. They built villages and in all matters acted very kindly towards the people, and did not vex them with oppressive taxes. They allotted a separate quarter for the Musalmans who dwelt with them, and appointed a *kazi* over them to settle all matters of taxes and marriage. But the call to prayer and public devotion was not permitted in their settlements .... On the sea, they are not like the English, and do not attack other ships, except those ships which have not received their pass according to rule, or the ships of Arabia and Muskat, with which two countries they have a long-standing enmity, and they attack each other whenever opportunity offers.
>
> (Elliot and Dowson 1867–77, vii: 344–45)

The view from the Mughal court was thus of an Asianised *Estado*, somewhat along the lines of the anonymous Malay Datu Bendahara, who cared little for the existence of Portugal when describing the Portuguese! Shorn of their erstwhile imperial pretensions, the Portuguese seem to have been reduced in their dimensions to Konkani *zamindars*. But Khafi Khan was being somewhat too parochial, neglecting to mention that Goa still exercised authority in the 1670s and 1680s over Daman, Diu, Chaul, Kung in the Persian Gulf, Mombasa and so on. The great shipowning merchants of the Mughal port of Surat, such as Mulla Abdul Ghafur, still took care to obtain *cartazes* from Goa, and the governor of Surat also made it a point to correspond with the viceroys of the *Estado da Índia*.

Perhaps more surprisingly, it turns out that even the revenues of the *Estado da Índia* had not shrunk appreciably between the late sixteenth and late seventeenth centuries. Save for a brief phase in the first two decades of the seventeenth century, when revenues almost touched 400 million *reis*, and surpluses at times exceeded 100 million, revenues of the *Estado da Índia* had tended in the Habsburg period to lie between 250 and 300 million *reis*. In the 1680s, for which similar budget data are available, the revenues are only slightly lower, and this is all the more remarkable when one bears in mind that the revenues of Mozambique were not included by the latter period in the budget statistics.

Table 7.3 Budget figures for the Estado da Índia, 1581–1687 (in *reis*)

Year	Receipts	Expenditures	Surplus
1581	263,036,953	242,784,701	20,252,252
1588	303,051,620	259,949,854	43,101,766
1607	355,530,600	235,677,600	120,153,000
1609	249,780,000	156,627,088	93,152,912
1610	390,595,800	256,978,200	133,617,600
1620	352,071,300	334,248,000	17,823,300
1630	240,597,600	288,051,600	(–) 47,454,000
1634	355,579,200	334,636,500	20,942,700
1680	219,548,400	136,398,900	83,149,500
1684–87 (av.)	239,812,000	260,571,300	(–) 20,759,300

(*Sources*: Matos 1984: 93; Hanson 1981: 212; Ames 1989: 299)

Two features of these budget statistics of the 1680s are notable. First, we observe that the financial viability of the *Estado* was still open to question; if in some years it showed a surplus, in others there was a deficit. Second, as Table 7.4 demonstrates, the dependence on Goa and Bassein for revenues was growing over the period, but at the same time these two centres accounted for the lion's share of expenditures. Indeed, of the ten centres listed below, one half were deficit-producing, and only Bassein, Daman and Kung produced a substantial surplus.

If one compares this budget with earlier budgets, such as for instance that of 1620, some obvious contrasts are visible. In 1620, the contribution of Hurmuz was still considerable (just under 20 per cent of total revenues). The sharpest fall in revenues among the settlements still held in the 1680s is in the case of Diu, where they have fallen from 203,615 *xerafins* in about 1620 to less than a third that amount by the later period. On the other hand, the revenues of Bassein and Daman have increased, with Goa remaining relatively stable. These contrasts are made clear in Table 7.5.

The fall in Diu's revenues is explicable in terms of two factors. First, Portuguese trade in Gujarat tended from the mid-century to gravitate more and more towards Surat, the great westward-looking port of the Mughal empire, with its links to the Persian Gulf and Red Sea. Fleets

Table 7.4 Average revenues and expenditures in the Estado, 1684–87 (in *xerafins*)

Settlement	Revenue	Expenditure	Surplus
Goa	356,300	551,800	(–) 195,500
Bassein	173,000	107,500	66,500
Daman	103,000	41,200	71,800
Diu	62,300	65,500	(–) 3,200
Kung	44,000	6,400	37,600
Mombasa	34,200	24,600	9,600
Chaul	15,400	44,700	(–) 29,300
Manora	4,900	5,900	(–) 1,000
Mangalore	4,600	1,800	3,200
Anjedive	1,900	19,500	(–) 17,600

(*Source*: Hanson 1981: 212)

Table 7.5 Revenue-collection points in the Estado, 1581–1687

Centres	1581	1588	1607	1609	1620	1684–87
Goa	26.3	28.5	34.2	34.3	32.0	44.6
Hurmuz	21.3	18.2	16.6	17.9	17.1	–
Bassein	17.9	14.1	10.4	9.8	10.5	21.6
Diu	15.0	17.5	18.1	19.1	17.4	7.8
Melaka	7.0	8.3	7.4	7.0	5.1	–
Daman	6.5	6.5	5.0	4.3	3.4	12.9
Others	6.0	6.9	8.3	7.7	14.5	13.1

(*Sources*: Matos 1984: 98; Hanson 1981: 212)

from Goa to Surat became an annual feature once the peace with the Dutch was established, and – as we have already seen – the Portuguese used the Parsi merchant Rustamji Manakji as their agent in Surat in the last two decades of the seventeenth century. In December 1690, for instance, Dutch factors at Surat report the arrival there of thirty-three vessels (referred to as the 'annual armada' of the Portuguese) from Goa carrying spelter, areca, eaglewood, quicksilver, tin and other goods, and again in 1691 the same source speaks of the arrival of an armada of twenty-two vessels, with goods worth some 120,000 *rupias*. The Dutch factors on this occasion mention that the Portuguese at Goa were trying to establish trade on a new footing, apparently referring to the proposal for the formation of a Company. In 1694–95, further details of this trading venture become available. According to the Dutch, in the winter of 1694–95, the Portuguese arrived with a fairly large-sized convoy of vessels, with 'a good amount of merchandise', intending to leave a permanent factor at Surat. However, when disagreements arose with the

Mughal officials of the port, this idea could not be implemented (ARA, VOC. 1476, ff. 269–v; VOC. 1529, f. 398; VOC. 1571, ff. 93–94). Nevertheless, through its Parsi agent, the Portuguese Company of 1694–99 managed to buy and sell at Surat without great difficulty.

The second factor which may explain the decline of Diu is the fact that the port felt the brunt of the naval power of the Omanis throughout this period. It has already been noted how in 1650, Sultan bin Saif al-Ya'rubi of Oman had taken Maskat from the Portuguese, thus dealing a considerable blow to Portuguese trade within the Persian Gulf, and between Maskat and Sind, and Maskat and the Indian west coast. Following this, Omani forces attacked Bombay in 1661–62, and then turned their attention to Diu, which was sacked in November 1668, and then again in January 1676. A report of 1669 notes:

> The Arabian enemy entered the city of Dio, which he sacked, and burnt the vessels that he found in the port, imprisoning all the people who were in their houses with all that they possessed, of which they were despoilt and many of them killed, on account of which that land and its settlers were finished and the fortress which the enemy is besieging remained in distress.
>
> (ACE iii: 564–65)

In the 1670s, other attacks followed. Kung was the target in 1670, Bassein in 1674, and throughout this period Portuguese-Omani rivalry continued on the Indian west coast as well as the African east coast. Gradually, on the east coast of Africa, in the stretch extending from Kilwa and Zanzibar to Mombasa, Malindi and Mogadishu (the so-called Swahili coast), Omani influence grew at the cost of the Portuguese. In western India, the situation was not quite so clear, as Mughal governors of the port of Surat, such as Najabat Khan and Itibar Khan, strove to define a middle ground between Omanis and Portuguese, despite occasional outbreaks of hostilities at their very doorstep. In early 1694, and again in March 1699, there were hostilities between Omani vessels and the merchant ships of Surat, while it was commonplace for the Portuguese northern convoy (*armada do norte*) to enter into maritime skirmishes with the fleets of Oman.

It is difficult to comprehend Omani ambitions if one seeks to pose their maritime expansion in the narrow context of sixteenth- and seventeenth-century Red Sea and Persian Gulf politics. Within this ambit, it is evident that no precedent existed for what the Ya'rubis set out to do, which was to build a trade-oriented state, which would focus on the household of the Sultan, but at the same time refine the concept of the *jihad* and seek aggressively to pursue a policy of overseas proselytisation. In so doing, they may have been departing from state-building traditions in their immediate vicinity, but their activities are not so different from, say, those of the Acehnese in Southeast Asia the late sixteenth and early seventeenth centuries. Broadly speaking, the Omani scheme seems to have been to build a thalassocracy extending down to Kilwa, while at the same time reducing the ports of the Indian west coast to a more or less tributary status. In pursuit of this ambition, the Omani ruler Saif bin Sultan (r. 1692–1711) is known to have operated a fleet of twenty-four large ships and twenty-eight smaller ones, and to have had some 1,700 household slaves in an enterprise that is strikingly mercantilist in character (Bathurst 1972; Risso 1986).

Unlike Aceh, which the *Estado da Índia* had actively thought of besieging, the thought of taking the fight to Oman seems never to have crossed the official mind at Goa after the early 1650s. Having lost two opportunities to re-take Maskat in 1652 and 1653, the primary concern became a defensive one, with convoys being sent each year to protect the still lucrative fleet that came from Gujarat to Goa. By the 1680s, this was difficult enough, as a Portuguese fleet discovered in the winter of 1688–89, while encountering eleven Omani vessels (six warships and five merchantmen) off Surat (ACE iii: 575). The correspondence between the viceroys at Goa, Rustamji Manakji, and successive governors of Surat in these years is full of references to the difficulties caused by these engagements, which also led to a periodic souring of relations between Goa and the Mughals (as in late 1694, when the Portuguese armada took two vessels off Surat, which had goods belonging to the port's merchants on board). However, Goa discovered soon enough that the Indian west coast was not where the Omanis really intended to expand their sphere of influence. Rather, these skirmishes were a diversion from the main action, in fact concentrated on the Swahili coast.

The Portuguese stake in the region north of Kilwa had increased from the 1590s, with the construction of Fort Jesus at Mombasa in 1592–93. In the following year, a customs-house of the *Estado* was set up in the port, of which the revenues were shared with the Sultan of Malindi – whose sovereignty over the area was still recognised by the Portuguese. In the early seventeenth century, the revenues of the port for the Portuguese were some 6,120 *xerafins*, but expenditure was far larger – of the order of 11,100 *xerafins*; the fort had a garrison of some one hundred men, and there were also around seventy *casados* resident in the Portuguese settlement in about 1610.

Events in the next two decades almost proved the unmaking of the Portuguese, though, as a consequence of a process strikingly similar to what had happened earlier in Ternate. In 1614, Sultan Hasan of Malindi was murdered at the instigation of Simão de Melo Pereira, captain of Mombasa, and the Portuguese sought to replace him with his son, Yusuf, who had been brought up by the Augustinians with the curious name of D. Jerónimo Chingulia. However, in 1631, the Portuguese at Mombasa discovered to their horror that D. Jerónimo was in fact still a secret Muslim; an armed engagement ensued, and the Portuguese captain of Fort

Jesus was killed. But Sultan Yusuf, as he now styled himself, did not have long to enjoy his triumph. The viceroy Count of Linhares mounted a succession of expeditions from Goa against Mombasa, as a consequence of which the Sultan fled to Arabia, leaving the Portuguese masters of the fort. Thereafter, the *Estado* also moved to create a series of smaller official settlements in the vicinity, including Pate, the great centre of Islamic activity in the area (Azevedo and Boxer 1960).

In the sixteenth century, Pate had emerged as the greatest power of the Swahili region, following the decline of Mombasa in the first half of the century. By 1569, Pate was already a great centre of trade to the Red Sea, and along the coast, a fact that remained true during most of the seventeenth century as well. The town harboured many migrants, those who had fled in the aftermath of the failed *jihad* of Ahmed Gran, as well as others from Benadir, Hadramaut and Yemen. The ruling dynasty at Pate in the sixteenth and seventeenth centuries, the Ba Barayk, themselves came from Shihr, in the Hadramaut. Given this existing 'northern' influence in the area, and the fact that the Swahili coast towns maintained close contact with the heartland of the Arab-speaking world, it was only natural that they should have sought an alliance with the Ya'rubis of Oman (Pouwels 1987). The first real success enjoyed by the Omanis on the coast was thus at Pate itself, where the Portuguese had a small settlement. It is reported in a letter from Goa to Lisbon in January 1689 that the Omanis had done away with this, with contemptuous ease. Thus:

> Patte was lost with the same ease with which it was taken. It is said that we had two galliots in that port and a *charrua* with men-at-arms; and anyway two or three ships of the Arabs entered, without even a musket-shot being fired on our part. (ACE iii: 576)

With the accession of Saif bin Sultan in 1692, far more systematic operations were attempted. In March 1696, a three-thousand-strong force from Maskat arrived off Mombasa, and proceeded to lay siege to Fort Jesus, inaugurating a tussle that lasted for over thirty-two months. While the fort finally surrendered in December 1698, Lisbon had no news of it, and made the futile gesture of sending out a relief expedition in January 1699. They found the Omanis in possession not merely of Mombasa, but of most of the key ports of the coast. The Ya'rubi Sultans took care to maintain small garrisons at Mombasa, Pemba, Zanzibar, and Kilwa in the early decades of the eighteenth century, and it was only for a brief period in 1726–27 that the Portuguese were able to re-capture Mombasa, taking advantage of internal troubles in Oman. However, the Omanis soon recouped their loss, and appointed a strong governor (*liwali*) there, Muhammad bin Uthman Mazrui. He in turn soon broke off from Oman to found his own independent centre and dynasty, which continued to hold power in Mombasa to 1837 (Pouwels 1987: 98–99).

The Omanis, while posing the most systematic threat and challenge to

European seapower in the western Indian Ocean in the latter half of the seventeenth century, were nevertheless not the only Asian polity in the area to do so. In the last third of the seventeenth century, much mention is made in Goa's correspondence of another threat, that posed by the Maratha clan of Shivaji Bhonsle and its allies. By the mid-1660s, the rise of Bhonsle power had already led the Mughals to seek an alliance with the Portuguese in the area, which the *Estado da Índia* however chose to turn down. Despite this, their relations with Shivaji were none too good; in 1667, he invaded Bardes, on the grounds that it housed Maratha clans inimical to the Bhonsles, and despite a peace treaty signed in December that year continued to pose a threat to Goa in 1668–69. The *Estado* had two choices: they could ally themselves with the Mughals, or they could attempt to play them off against the Marathas. It was the latter strategy that they attempted, throughout the last three decades of the seventeenth century. Also the Portuguese tried to instigate the petty chiefs of the Konkan, such as the Sidis of Danda and the ruler of Ramnagar, to create problems periodically for the Bhonsles, often even paying them money to this end. By 1680, Shivaji had some form of control over all lands from Daman to Goa that had borders with Portuguese territory, a situation that considerably limited the *Estado*'s options.

The fact of the matter was that Maratha power was not simply limited to land. For one, they maintained contacts with the Omanis, and even offered them the island of Anjedive as a base. This forced the *Estado* hurriedly to fortify Anjedive in the 1680s (which explains the extraordinarily high expenses under this head in the budgets of 1684–87). Besides, the letters of D. Manuel Lobo da Silveira, Captain-General of the North (that is the *província do norte*) in the late 1670s provide ample testimony of the nervousness that Shivaji's maritime forces inspired in the Portuguese settlers of Daman and Chaul, with at least one letter of 1677 speaking of how 'two leagues from this city [Chaul] there is an armada of the same Sivagy of 23 sail, ten galliots and thirteen ships, that he wishes to place in this river' (ACE iii: 556).

On Shivaji's death in 1680, his successor Sambhaji, with whom the Portuguese had already had a dispute concerning the tribute-payment (*chauth*) of some villages around Daman, appeared even more aggressive to Goa. Again, the Mughals offered an alliance, and once more the viceroy Count of Alvor turned the offer down, declaring rather sanctimoniously that 'the Portuguese did not usually make war on anyone save on highly justified grounds, and that at the moment there were none' (Lobato 1965: 28). He was to regret those words in 1683, when Sambhaji besieged Chaul with six thousand men and two thousand horse, and then sent another force to attack Goa, where he made considerable inroads into Portuguese territory. Chaul was defended by its settlers, organised by the Jesuits resident there into a military force, while Goa appeared more

vulnerable now than at any time since the 1570s. As a minute of the
Council of State at Goa notes in November 1683:

> Sambagi has invaded the lands of this Estado from all parts, entering them in a
> hostile manner with great power of men on foot and horse, both in the lands
> of the North in the Jurisdiction of the fortresses of Chaul, Baçaim and Damão,
> having besieged Chaul with a very close siege, as also in the neighbourhood of
> this island of Goa and its adjacent lands, entering into those of Santo Estêvão,
> and the lands of Bardes and Salcete burning and razing everything, even the
> sacred temples, without our being able to impede him, for all the lands were
> open and there was a great lack of men as the necessary help (*socorro*) had not
> come from Portugal. ....   (ACE iv: 410)

The Portuguese were saved however by the would-be ally whose offer
they had spurned; a Mughal army with 40,000 horse and 60,000 infantry
coincidentally attacked the Marathas at much the same time, forcing
Sambhaji hurriedly to seek an agreement with the *Estado*. The treaty,
signed at Ponda in early February 1684, granted the Bhonsles numerous
concessions that had earlier been withheld, such as specific dues from
Bassein and the *chauth* from Daman, but also sought to limit Portuguese
cooperation with the Mughals. It was within this triangular space then that
the Portuguese continued to defend their Konkan territories in the 1680s:
using the Mughals opportunistically, but not allying themselves to
Aurangzeb against the Marathas.

In 1689, the Mughals enjoyed a major success, defeating, capturing and
executing Sambhaji, and thus making great inroads into the Konkan. Goa
stirred uneasily at this new threat, but the Marathas soon reconsolidated.
Through the 1690s, no major military threat was faced by Goa or the
província do norte, and minor skirmishes with the Marathas were regarded as
part of the normal course of things. The issue of control of the sea still
remained though, and signs of a closer tie-up between Marathas and
Omanis were watched for anxiously. Now the ability of the Bhonsle clan,
and later the Peshwas, to raise naval forces was crucially dependent on
their alliance with the Angria family of semi-autonomous chieftains, who
controlled the area around Kolaba, as well as the ports of Anjanvel,
Ratnagiri and Vijaydurg further south. It was not illogical therefore that
the viceroys of the *Estado* sought to mitigate the Maratha threat by
maintaining good relations with the Angrias, especially Kanhoji, who is
described in one letter of 1703 as *subedar da armada do Sivagi*, the reference
being not to the dead ruler but to the Kolhapur-based prince of the same
name, pretender to the Maratha throne in the period. Similarly, in the late
1690s and early 1700s, viceroys of the *Estado* like Caetano de Melo de
Castro sought to maintain good relations with the Sidis of Janjira, who
acted as naval auxiliaries of the Mughals (*BFUP*, 38–40: 188–90, 199).

Thus, taking one thing with another, diplomacy, finance and the
occasional use of force ensured that the *Estado da Índia* was not quite

teetering on the brink of collapse in these years as is sometimes assumed. The rhetoric of the viceroy, D. Rodrigo da Costa, who in 1689 assured D. Pedro II that 'the *Estado* is so miserable that if Your Majesty does not support it with your Royal Arm, it will be impossible to sustain the revenues', is to be taken with the saline accompaniment it deserves (Hanson 1981: 207). In point of fact, it would appear that the significance of even the loss of Mombasa (with which the century drew to a close) has been somewhat exaggerated, since its contribution to total revenues was not all that large, and its strategic significance dubious at a time when the Ottoman naval threat no longer existed, and the Portuguese no longer cared in the least about controlling shipping to the Red Sea. Nor did losing Mombasa particularly shorten the rather overblown title that the viceroys of the *Estado* still liked to use in their diplomatic correspondence of around 1700, in which they termed themselves 'Viceroy and Captain-General of all the coast of Africa, the Kingdoms of Monomotapa, Persia, the Red Sea, India, Siam, China and of the kingdoms of Manubam, Bataviam, Amarrasse, Lifao, Larentuca, in the islands of Sollor and Timor'. It is to these other far-flung territories to which we shall now turn our attention.

MOZAMBIQUE, MUNHUMUTAPA AND *PRAZO* CREATION

During the late sixteenth and early seventeenth centuries, south-eastern Africa was, as we have noted, a sort of eastern El Dorado for the Portuguese, an area of reputedly uncountable wealth and resources. But even as late as 1660, Portuguese penetration of the interior of this region remained quite limited, with their presence being largely confined to the coastal settlements and the margin of the Zambezi river. The chief institutions through which they participated in the economy of the interior were two: the *feiras*, or local markets where imports and exports were transacted, and the *prazos da Coroa* or 'Crown estates'. Now the *prazo* existed from the mid-sixteenth century in the *província do norte*, along the Konkan coast, as a benefice that could be given to worthy *fidalgos*, or to secure the marriages of 'impoverished gentlewomen' such as the *orfaãs del-Rei* (King's orphans) who came out to Asia in limited numbers in the sixteenth century. The south-east African situation bears certain similarities to that in western India, but is also different in several major respects. If we accept that the mere fact of terminological coincidence ensures that the *prazo* of the Konkan is the same as the Zambezi *prazo*, we run the risk of neglecting local social, economic and historical factors for a purely formal or legalistic analysis. Certainly, when viewed from the Portuguese Crown's perspective, the *prazo* everywhere appeared much the same; they were land-grants, or *aforamentos*, distributed for a certain period of time to the Crown's subjects, after which they could be resumed by the Crown. The only feature that might appear peculiar to the Zambezi case is the rule of inheritance by the female line of the *prazo*. But in Daman and Bassein, the *prazo* was superimposed on a complex system of land rights which obtained in an already commercialised economy, and corresponded fairly closely in practice to the Indo-Islamic idea of the *iqta*. Since in the Zambezi valley pre-existent rights did not correspond to such a pattern, it is logical to suspect that the *prazero* (or *prazo*-holder) too should have been rather different from his Konkani counterpart.

Who then were the early *prazeros*, and what was the extent and nature of their power? Traditional interpretations of the nature of the *prazo* had focused on the use of force, and especially firearms, by the *prazo*-holders, and saw the grants as stemming 'from above', which is to say as creations of the Portuguese Crown, which were then put into effect on the ground. This view has been challenged recently by historians like Allen Isaacman; he argues that *prazo*-formation 'needs to be seen as a continuing process in which Portuguese, mestizo, or Indian colonists acquired recognition as political chiefs over an African population' (Isaacman 1972: 17). Furthermore, it is suggested that the *prazero* had an authority role quite similar to that of earlier 'alien' rulers in the Zambezi region, such as the Karanga and Malawi rulers, and that they also held prerogatives that had earlier pertained to these Zambezi chiefs. In this view then, the Zambezi valley in the early seventeenth century had a fluid political system, in which outsiders could insert themselves without great difficulty, and seek suitable vertical and horizontal links to legitimise their position. The grant by the Portuguese King of a *prazo* was merely one way of legitimising a political alliance and tribute system that already functioned on the ground.

One of the problems that one encounters with defining the *prazo* holdings of the Zambezi valley as a 'system' is this very fluidity. *Prazeros* came and went with great frequency, and even the estates themselves were rarely long-lived. It is hence rather difficult to generalise from the experience of an estate or a few estates to that of the area as a whole. But it is nevertheless instructive to note how some of these estates were set up. In the middle of the seventeenth century, several of the Zambezi *prazeros* are quite conspicuous figures: they include Sisnando Baião, António Lobo da Silva, Manuel Paes de Pinha, and Lourenço de Matos, all of whom operated over extensive regions, conquering many of the Sena-Tonga chieftaincies of the region, and annexing portions of Quiteve and Manyika to their *prazos*. In the case of Baião, we are aware that his chief possession, the *prazo* of Cheringoma, was held not so much on account of sanction from 'above' (here, Portugal or Goa), but rather because of services that he had rendered to the ruler of Quiteve, Berenha (Isaacman 1972: 20). Once they had taken possession of territories, the *prazeros* made sure that their writ ran by means of their *achikunda*, or slave armies, which could in the mid-seventeenth century number as many as five thousand or more. For *prazos* had to be defended against all comers, be they nominally subordinate chieftains of the *prazo*, neighbouring kingdoms or even (perhaps especially) rival *prazeros*.

Thus, rather than being estate owners who ran tightly-knit production units, the *prazeros* emerge as war-band leaders, whose fundamental role was the collection of tribute of various kinds over a loosely defined territory. They rarely if ever succeeded in the seventeenth century in displacing the so-called 'land chiefs' (or *mambos*), and could even seek legitimation through marriage alliances into the families of these chiefs. If successful, they received considerable amounts of goods – ivory, cloth, chicken, dried fish and so on – from the hunters and producers in their territories, by way of tribute (*mutsonko*). But their powers were precarious, and they themselves were walking a political tightrope for much of this period. We would do well therefore to treat with caution the following view of the *prazeros'* power, depicted by a seventeenth-century observer, Manuel Barreto:

> The holders of these lands have the same powers and jurisdiction as the Kaffir fumos (chiefs) from whom they were conquered ... and therefore they are like the potentates of Germany, and can pronounce sentences in all cases, put to death, declare war, and impose tribute, in which great barbarities were committed, but they would not be duly respected by their vassals if they did not hold the same powers as the fumos whom they succeeded.
>
> (Isaacman 1972: 173)

Besides the territorial adventurism that the activities of these *prazeros* represented, the official Portuguese presence in the Mozambique region also had other dimensions. Trade between Goa, Gujarat and Mozambique had been an important and lucrative feature of Portuguese intra-Asian commercial network in the late sixteenth and seventeenth centuries, and the textiles of Gujarat seem always to have found a ready market in the ports and markets of the region. The issue was the regime under which this trade was to be conducted. Normally, in late January and February ships from India arrived on Mozambique island, from where goods were sent by way of coastal craft to Quelimane, and then inland on porters and small river-craft to Sena, Tete and Zumbo, where the imported cloth and other goods were exchanged for gold and ivory. In part the export goods of the region were supplied to the markets by the *prazeros*, from the tribute they had collected, but there were also numerous other participants in the trade.

Now, as we have seen in an earlier chapter, in the late 1560s, 1570s and 1580s, successive rulers of Portugal had thought to control the production centres of gold, but had failed for the most part in the attempt. Their exports of gold from Sofala and Quelimane were nevertheless not negligible: 574 kgs in 1585, 716 kgs in 1591, 850 kgs in 1610 and 1,488 kgs in 1667. The somewhat increased figures in the last period were also the occasion for a proposal, submitted to the viceroy Count of São Vicente, suggesting that inroads be made into the *rios de Cuama* 'vulgarly and truly called the rivers of gold' (BNP, Port. 33, ff. 41–54v).

Now at this time, Goa had some reason to be nervous about the future of the East African trade. The formation in France by Colbert of the *Compagnie des Indes* meant that a French presence had arisen in Madagascar, and the viceroy Luís de Mendonça Furtado feared that the trade of Mozambique would be endangered thereby. He urged the Regent D. Pedro to reverse his decision (put into effect in 1671–72) to free the trade of Mozambique to all comers, and instead succeeded in creating the *Junta do Comércio de Moçambique e Rios*, which was to administer the trade of the region. It was now made mandatory for ships to call at Mozambique island, which became the central point from which imported goods were distributed all along the coast; also goods such as ivory, textiles, gold, firearms and gunpowder were made the exclusive preserve of the *Junta* (Ames 1989). Further, in late 1677, Lisbon despatched a fleet of four ships, carrying some two thousand people, who were sent out with the intention of settling the region – a master-stroke designed to link up gold, trade and the *prazos*. Poorly prepared, and received by their compatriots who were already present in the region with a distinct lack of enthusiasm, these settlers managed to achieve little of consequence. In fact, they were blamed in later years for most of the misfortunes that befell the Portuguese in the region; in the mid-1690s, when the gold trade was disrupted, the viceroy at Goa insisted that 'it was the insolence of our people that caused these wars' (Hanson 1981: 213).

The real reason for the disruption of the gold trade was in fact somewhat different, and lay in the changing relations between the *prazeros*, Dominican priests and the Mutapa rulers of the interior. In the early seventeenth century, the Mutapa Gatsi Rusere (r. 1586/9–1623/4) had carefully maintained the Portuguese at an arm's length, insisting that they pay him a form of tribute (*kuruva*) to be sent annually by the captain of Mozambique through an ambassador. While tolerating Dominican priests in his court, and even permitting them to baptise one of his sons and educate him in Goa, he still possessed sufficient military power to keep the Portuguese private traders and adventurers in the region in check.

The same was not true however of his successors, who came to depend more and more on the Portuguese captain of Mozambique, and the *prazeros*, to shore up their power. Further, the rule of Mavhura Mhande, or Filipe I (1629–31 and 1632–52), inaugurated a phase when the Mutapas accepted Dominican tutelage, and allowed priests of that order a

199

place of importance in court ritual and even politics. As a Dominican priest wrote about that time:

> Doubtless a great day for the sons of St. Dominic! To see in lands so remote, strange and uncultivated, the monarch and lord of them (though a black, a powerful King, and respected as such for the extent and beauty of his empire) burdened with a great stone, not to raise as in heathendom the mount of Mercury, but to erect upon it the temple of the True God, and hear his praises sounded in that unknown tongue like an echo of the apostolic call that invited them thither. (Mudenge 1988: 265)

Facing rivals within the kingdom, in particular those ranged around a certain Nyambo Kapararidze from whom he had wrested power, Mavhura conceded various rights to the Portuguese, and even signed a treaty declaring himself a vassal of the Portuguese Crown. We may interpret this as a sign of his military weakness rather than the *cause* of this weakness; it is in this period that various *prazos* were formed around Tete, and the Portuguese traders of even the interior began to construct forts (or *chuambos*). The phase of *prazo* expansion was thus aided by Portuguese and Dominican influence at the Mutapa court, which secured a favourable balance of forces for the would-be *prazeros*. But a backlash eventually came in the 1680s, in the form of the rise of the Rozvi Changamire ethnic group, and in particular of one war-chief – Changamire Dombo – who in the early 1690s became the power behind the Mutapa throne. Attacking Portuguese traders in the interior, and even relatively organised military forces sent from the coast, the Rozvi thus held off Portuguese territorial expansion, limiting them to the lower Zambezi area.

The trade of the *Junta do Comércio* was thus linked with political and economic developments in the interior, events that the *prazeros* who were located upriver could hope to affect, but which were far beyond the control of those on the coast. The balance between coast and interior shifted only somewhat later, in the eighteenth century, when the demand for slaves by traders on the coast was to have a profound effect not merely on the interior society but on the establishments of the *prazeros*.

THE PORTUGUESE OF THE BAY OF BENGAL

East Africa, and especially the region south of the Swahili coast, represents a hybrid Portuguese presence in the last third of the seventeenth century, one in which the local initiative of private Portuguese, often inserted into the political networks of the region, has a curious dialectic with the designs of Lisbon and Goa. As we have seen, Lisbon was exercised with events in the Zambezi valley and on the coast around Mozambique, and decidedly not content to leave matters in Goa's hands. In the Bay of

Bengal, in contrast, the only manner in which private Portuguese initiative was tempered by an 'official' flavour was via the interest shown by Goa. So far as we are aware, Lisbon suffered from amnesia where this region was concerned, despite its being an area where once the Habsburgs had nursed grand territorial dreams.

The Dutch attack on Nagapattinam in 1658, and the subsequent capture by the Golconda general Neknam Khan of São Tomé de Meliapor in 1662 are often assumed to have put an end to Portuguese trade in the Bay of Bengal. To the extent that the Portuguese continued in the ports of the Bay's littoral – it has been argued – it must have been as fisherfolk, interpreters and go-betweens for the English and Dutch in their dealings with local authorities on the Malay peninsula, in Bengal and on Coromandel. It is certainly true, of course, that Portuguese private and official trade in the Bay of Bengal never quite recovered again to the levels of the late sixteenth century. However, we find that the Portuguese private trader in this region proved far more resilient than has been assumed, with the recovery beginning almost as soon as the ink on the Luso-Dutch truce in Asia was dry. In the 1670s and 1680s, therefore, Dutch and other records on Bengal and Coromandel point clearly to the continued presence of the Portuguese trader and shipowning merchant, resident within a Portuguese trading settlement that forms a part of a larger port-town. An excellent example of this is Hughli, from which, as we have seen in an earlier chapter, the Portuguese were expelled in 1632 by the Mughals.

By the late 1630s, Goa was beginning to think once again of settling Hughli, using its good relations with some of the more powerful nobles of Shahjahan's court. In September 1637, for instance, Pero da Silva wrote to Lisbon of his intention to 'send a man there [Bengal] to deal with matters and get together the Portuguese and Christians who are strewn through that land' (ANTT, DRI No. 40, f. 148). He and his successors wisely chose to eschew the options presented to them by men like a certain Tomé Vás, who at about the same time put forward a proposal to take over Bengal and set up three Portuguese fortresses there – one in Hughli, one in Jessore and the third in Dhaka. This rather circumspect approach paid off in later years, so that Hughli once again emerged as a centre of Portuguese private trade (as well as limited missionary activity) by the 1660s.

In 1665, we learn from a petition of 'the Portuguese settlers, and men of the land and other Christians who live in the Bandel of Ugulym and other parts of Bengala attached thereto', that they numbered some six thousand in all, and that they had a single person who administered them as captain, justice of peace, administrator of the orphans, and so on; they therefore requested and received permission to elect separate officials for each of these posts from the viceroy at Goa António de Melo de Castro

(APO, vi: 1278–80). Occasional letters from these decades inform us of the identities of the captain and other officials of Hughli: in 1667, for example, the captain was one Francisco Cabreira de Seixas, while at much the same time the town had resident in it substantial Portuguese merchants like João Gomes de Soto. Travellers of the period, such as François Bernier and Niccolò Manucci, are quite emphatic in noting that Hughli of the 1660s and 1670s still housed prosperous Portuguese traders, a fact confirmed by other sources as well. The Dutch shipping lists for the port, dating from the early 1680s and late 1690s, make mention of several Portuguese shipowning merchants resident there, who traded principally to the ports of the Coromandel coast, to Goa, and occasionally to Surat. Few of these men were operators on a very large scale, if the Dutch evidence is to be credited, and the same is true of their compatriots in Bengal's other active port of the period – Balasore. In Balasore, Portuguese shipowners, while less numerous than at Hughli, traded to a greater variety of destinations, including Manila and the Maldives (Prakash 1967: 579–82). In contrast, the fate of Portuguese traders in Chittagong remains obscure in the period, even though occasional papers relating to Portuguese presence in that region may still be encountered in the 1680s, in the letters and chronicles of Augustinian priests in the area (ANTT, Livraria 731, f. 528).

The Coromandel case is somewhat better documented, and can be divided into two parts: Porto Novo and São Tomé. Porto Novo had initially been used in the first three decades of the seventeenth century by the Portuguese traders of Nagapattinam, as a subsidiary, textile-producing centre. António Bocarro describes the port in the 1630s, when it was still under the rule of the Nayakas of Senji, as a major supplier of cottons and pepper to Nagapattinam, and it is this image that emerges from Dutch records of the same period as well. In the 1630s and 1640s, the occasional Asian ship is to be found trading from Porto Novo to the ports of Southeast Asia, including vessels belonging to (or protected by) the Senji Nayakas themselves. But it is with the fall of Nagapattinam to the Portuguese that Porto Novo's affairs take on a different complexion. The port gradually became a centre for the trade of local Maraikkayar Muslims, initially concentrated at the more southern centre of Naguru, and at the same time, Portuguese shipping became a conspicuous feature of trade in the port (Subrahmanyam 1988). Thus, by the early 1680s, Porto Novo had transformed itself into the most prominent Coromandel port south of Madras, and a centre in which both the Dutch and the English Companies evinced considerable curiosity and interest. It is thanks to this curiosity that we are able to reconstruct something of the profile of private Portuguese shipping from Porto Novo in the first half of the 1680s. Table 7.6 summarises these findings, based on the Dutch shipping lists.

Table 7.6 Portuguese shipowning at Porto Novo, 1681–86

Destination	1681–82	1682–83	1683–84	1684–85	1685–86
Pegu	2	1	1	1	3
Aceh	3	3	3	2	2
Melaka	1	1	1	1	–
Goa	1	1	1	1	2
Manila	–	–	–	1	–
TOTAL	7	6	6	6	7

(*Source*: Subrahmanyam 1990b: 232–33)

So far as we are aware, the leading shipowner and trader at Porto Novo in this period was a certain Manuel Teixeira Pinto, a man who was wooed by both English and French, and for whom the Dutch Company's factors had a healthy respect. Unfortunately, in the absence of Pinto's own correspondence, or Portuguese documents dealing with his career at length, he remains a frustratingly shadowy figure, although we do know from the Dutch that he was the designated chief (or 'captain-major') of the Portuguese in the port, and therefore presumably the man who dealt with both Goa and local authorities (the Marathas or the Mughals in the 1680s) on behalf of his compatriots.

Pinto also features briefly in Portuguese documents of the period dealing with the other major centre of their trade on Coromandel – São Tomé, or Mylapur. Now Porto Novo, located in southern Coromandel, may be thought to have inherited the mantle of the Portuguese settlement of Nagapattinam, abandoned by them to the Dutch in 1658. While Nagapattinam had certainly been prosperous as a mercantile nucleus, it did not however enjoy the prestige of São Tomé, the town that housed the fabled church and tomb of the Apostle St. Thomas. In 1606, Goa had given São Tomé the status of a city (*cidade*) in its statutes, and also made Mylapur the seat of a bishopric, which remained there even after the town was taken over by Golconda forces in 1662. The association with the Catholic Church is conceivably what prompted the French Company's Admiral De la Haye to attack and take over the city in July 1672, a venture in which he was possibly encouraged by Goa. However, the French were unable to retain the city for long, in the face of hostility not only from Golconda but from the Dutch in nearby Pulicat; in September 1674, they surrendered possession of São Tomé to the VOC, who in turned handed it over to Golconda.

São Tomé's geographical location gave it a strategic importance though, even in its period of decline. Immediately to its north, and across the Kuvam river, lay the English settlement of Madras (or Chennapattinam), where the English had built Fort St. George in the early 1640s, and which was the chief English factory at this time in the

Bay of Bengal as a whole. The English Company was therefore nervous of any other European power taking possession of São Tomé, and attempted through the latter half of the 1670s and the 1680s to persuade Golconda authorities to give them the town on lease, together with Tiruvattur and Egmore; however, the Golconda court was reluctant to do so, apparently on account of a desire to limit the extent of English settlement. Meanwhile, those Portuguese who had remained in São Tomé had been joined in the 1670s and early 1680s by other new residents; these merchants in 1686 sent an independent embassy to the court of Golconda, using as emissary the Augustinian priest Frei Luís de Piedade, and obtained a *farman* (royal grant) in December of that year to create an official Portuguese settlement once again in São Tomé. The prime movers of this project appear to have been three merchants: Lucas Luís de Oliveira, Álvaro Cacela do Vale and António Ferreira; they were supported by the Bishop of Mylapur and other religious in the town. The grant, among other things, stated:

> The duties of the customs-house and of the rest will be paid in conformity with what is paid in the port of Massulapatão by the Dutch, and English, and the said officials will collect the said revenue from the said settlers, and also that in going from the port of Meliapor to Golconda, and on the return, the octroi-collectors (*juncaneiros*) will not place any impediment, and they can travel with all liberty and freedom.   (ACE iv: 573)

Having taken official possession of the town in 1687, and raised 'the flag of the arms of the King of Portugal, our master', the Portuguese settlers of São Tomé did not find matters easy however. There were two reasons for this. First, the fall of Golconda to the Mughals in 1687 meant that the *farman* conceded to them had to be granted afresh, and another embassy sent to Aurangzeb. This was managed in 1688–89, using the services once again of Frei Luís de Piedade, even though the Mughals soon took a rather jaundiced view of the military pretensions of São Tomé's residents, which caused conflicts between the two. The real problem was different. Persuading the Portuguese resident in other ports of Coromandel to return to the fold, and once again become residents of an official settlement of the *Estado* was no easy matter, as was soon discovered. Already in April 1687, the settlers in a letter to the viceroy D. Rodrigo da Costa had asked him to intervene in the matter.

> Firstly [they wrote], it is necesary that Your Lordship sends an order or decree that all the Portuguese settled on this coast should collect in São Thomé and make houses and live under the flag of His Majesty as his loyal vassals, under pain of being de-naturalised (*desnaturalizados*) and being known as foreigners, and with other [penalties] that Your Lordship finds fitting, because otherwise it will not be possible to rebuild this city in such a way that we can defend ourselves in the event of any war that we may have with the lords of the land at a future date when we have the force, in order to settle past scores with them, and so long as this order from Your Lordship does not arrive, we will

not venture to raise the flag, even if we are in possession, on account of the few settlers that we have at present, [but] if all of us get together, no other Foreigners on this coast have a fortress that can compare with the one that we can make.   (BNL, Fundo Geral, Cód. 8358, f. 44)

But this order, which had arrived by October 1687 (thus enabling the flag of Portugal to fly again over São Tomé), did not prove sufficient to persuade the Portuguese resident in Madras, Porto Novo and other spots to shift to São Tomé. This is made evident by the relations between the residents of São Tomé and Manuel Teixeira Pinto.

To Manoel Teixeira Pinto [they write], who came to accompany us from Porto Novo on account of the order of Your Lordship, we have made the blandishments that seemed convenient in order that he should not go back, as he at times has said he will; as soon as he arrived, we went to seek him out, and a few days later we offered him, so long as Your Lordship does not order the contrary, the direction of all matters that might arise, but not of what remained in our charge, both in what has been completed and all that which is being done, offering him our assistance in anything that might be necessary.

The reason for these 'blandishments' (*afagos*) is stated later in the same letter: it was hoped that Pinto's presence would persuade the 'principal persons of Madras' to shift to São Tomé, because 'the so favourable order of Your Lordship was not enough for them to shift their residence, only making a show of coming by pointing out the places where they would make their houses' (BNL, Fundo Geral, Cód. 8358, f. 45).

Despite the gloomy prognosis of this letter, in a sense, the attempt to revive São Tomé was a success. Although in 1697 the Mughals pulled down all fortifications, and insisted that the Portuguese Captain-Major only fly the flag on Sundays and feast-days, the trade of the port grew apace in the early eighteenth century. This was partly the result of the patronage given to the port by the Nawabs of Arcot, a quasi-independent dynasty in the region, who derived legitimacy from the Mughals. The Nawabs clearly used the port as a counterweight to Dutch Pulicat and English Madras. The shipowning merchants of São Tomé in the years from 1700 to 1740 included a large group described in the English records as 'Pathans', who were evidently part of the migratory movement that had resulted from Mughal control of the region. The trade of these and other merchants, including private Portuguese and Armenians, embraced Bengal, Burma, the Persian Gulf, and even Manila. The chief trading partner was Bengal, and imports from there to São Tomé were worth some 200,000 *pagodas* in the 1710s, a period in which the total imports of Madras amounted perhaps to 600,000 *pagodas* (Arasaratnam 1986: 168–71). The re-settlement of São Tomé cannot be counted a success, however, if the Portuguese intention was indeed to 'settle scores' with the rulers of the region for imagined or actual wrongs suffered in the past. The exchange of correspondence between Goa and Mylapur suggests, on the contrary, that by 1704–05, factional conflict had become endemic among the Portuguese settled in São Tomé, and this conflict was so severe that two successive Captains-Major of the town – Mateus Carvalho da Silva in 1704 and Nuno Sodré Frade in 1705 – asked to be relieved of the post (BFUP, 38–40: 231, 260–62).

By the 1730s, the annoyance of the Madras-based English at the continued success of São Tomé was growing. Sanctions were imposed on Asian merchants who chose to trade at the port, who were either forbidden to trade at Madras or fined if they did so; merchants domiciled in Madras were expressly prohibited from trade in the Portuguese enclave. Despite these tactics, however, the 1730s see the continuance of São Tomé's overseas commerce, and numerous vessels were reported there in the years 1732–34 (Arasaratnam 1986: 171). However, the Portuguese connection with the French on Coromandel eventually proved to be their undoing. Taking advantage of hostilities with the French, and the fact that several Portuguese associated with São Tomé (including the celebrated cleric D. António José de Noronha) were closely linked to the French governor Joseph-François Dupleix, the English seized São Tomé in 1749. What could not be achieved by means of competition was thus accomplished by main force (BPADE, cxvi/1–37, ff. 1–34).

The cases of Bengal, Porto Novo and São Tomé in the late seventeenth century demonstrate that it is premature to write off Portuguese trade in the Bay of Bengal with the fall of Nagapattinam and São Tomé in the years 1658–62. Yet, at the same time there is no denying that the Portuguese presence of these years was at a lower level than it had been a century earlier, and equally it is clear that the networks that were in place in the late seventeenth century have the barest veneer of state control over them. The same picture of survival under conditions of extensive autonomy from the control of Lisbon or even Goa is evident in the history of Macau in this period as well, as the next section will be concerned to show. This is hardly astonishing in the case of Macau; indeed, one could argue that what is perhaps more surprising is that the settlements of private Portuguese in the Bay of Bengal and mainland Southeast Asia in the 1680s and 1690s still sought to maintain contacts with Goa.

A brief account of a Portuguese embassy to the court of the Thai ruler Narai in Ayuthia, in 1684, reveals for example that the Portuguese settlement (*kampong*) in the town had a Captain-Major, Francisco Barreto de Pina, a man described by a locally resident Jesuit as a 'noble, loyal vassal' (ANTT, DRI, No. 49, ff. 222–22v). But, as correspondence of the period makes clear in this case as well, the Ayuthia Portuguese sought some degree of autonomy from Goa, accusing emissaries sent from Goa or Macau to Thailand (like the ambassador Pero Vaz de Sequeira) of creating difficulties for the Captain-Major with local authorities. A fine balance thus had to be struck, between association on the one hand and incorporation on the other.

SURVIVAL IN THE FAR EAST: MACAU AND TIMOR

The same struggle to seek an appropriate distance from Goa characterises the trade of Macau's settlers in the second half of the seventeenth century. The continuance of their trade in these years involved the search for new markets and new goods, as well as a willingness to enter into collaborative arrangements with a wide variety of Asian and European trading partners. Macau-based trade in the last third of the seventeenth century extended to the Lesser Sunda islands and eastern Indonesia, Manila, Batavia, Banten, Melaka (even after its fall into Dutch hands) and other destinations in mainland Southeast Asia, and also at times included ships sailing as far west as Goa and Gujarat. The loss of the Japan trade, which occurred in the late 1630s in such dramatic circumstances, was thus not fatal for the Portuguese traders based at Macau and operating in the South China Sea.

In the early 1640s, Macau's total population was estimated at around 40,000, of which some 2,000 were either Portuguese or partly of Portuguese origin. There is no doubt that the number of Portuguese in the port fell in later decades of the seventeenth century; by 1669, the population of *casados* in Macau was down to less than a half what it had been in 1635 (Souza 1986: 32). This fall is partly explained by a rather costly famine in the late 1640s, which resulted in a large number of deaths in the town, but may also have been the consequence of the transition from Ming to Ch'ing rule in China in these decades which made the internal markets of the south-eastern Chinese region uncertain.

The first serious threats posed by the Manchus (or Ch'ings) came in the 1620s, in a period when the Ming state appears already to have been already fiscally unstable. Nevertheless, Ming forces were sent out to deal with the threat, but this left the south-east (where Macau itself was located) somewhat vulnerable to other forces. In particular, the period saw the rise to prominence of local warrior-entrepreneurs like Cheng Chih-lung. During the first phases of his career, Cheng was closely associated with the head of the Chinese community at Hirado in Japan; thereafter, he also entered into cooperative arrangements with the Dutch East India Company, which was in the 1620s trying to make inroads into the Chinese market. In December 1627, after defeating numerous rival pirate forces, as well as a Ming fleet, Cheng was offered a compromise by the Mings, who incorporated him into their regime, and gave him charge of Amoy island. From this time on to the 1660s, the Cheng family played a role of great significance in the politics of the South China Sea. In a sense, it was only after their decline, and the re-establishment of the 'imperial peace' in south-eastern China that Macau's traders could breathe freely again.

The two great figures of the family are Cheng Chih-lung and his son, Cheng Ch'eng-kung (sometimes known as Coxinga), with the father dominating to about 1646, and the son's career reaching its apogee in the 1650s, only to end unceremoniously in 1662. At the height of his power, in 1659, Cheng Ch'eng-kung, claiming to be a Ming loyalist, mustered a force of over a thousand vessels and over fifty thousand men, to sail into the Yangtze delta and attack Ch'ing positions there, including Nanking. Two years later, he besieged and expelled the Dutch from their Fort Zeelandia in Taiwan, in what is possibly the most spectacular naval success enjoyed by an Asian power over any European power in these centuries (Wills 1979: 216–27). This was all to the good for the Portuguese of Macau of course, but nevertheless made for an overall trading ambience that was fraught with uncertainty.

It is clear that in these decades, the Macau settlers' trade was largely concentrated on three destinations: Makassar, Manila, and Tonkin. This was a largely inertial strategy, but required that the Portuguese used a ruse to get around the fact that Spain and Portugal were officially at war: they used the ruler of Makassar (the Sultan of Gowa, to be precise), as a cover for their own trade, and claimed that the ships in which they traded in fact pertained to him. This strategy at one and the same time enabled the Spanish to turn a blind eye, and could be used to keep the Dutch at bay. The fact that several Portuguese private traders, such as Francisco Vieira de Figueiredo and Francisco Mendes, were in these years closely associated with Makassar's rulers, facilitated matters. Figueiredo was also greatly trusted by the *Estado da Índia*'s governors of the period, who went so far as to give him *carte blanche* to deal on their behalf with various rulers in the Indonesian archipelago in the late 1640s, from his base at Makassar (Boxer 1967).

Among the spheres that Figueiredo was supposed to take care of was a small group of islands south of Sulawesi (where he himself was usually located), namely the Lesser Sunda Islands. This was an area over which the rulers of Tallo in Sulawesi at times laid claim, and where the Portuguese had had a presence since the sixteenth century, perhaps from as early as 1520. The four major islands of the group were Solor, Ende, Timor and Flores, of which Timor had a production of sandalwood, which linked it from early days into networks of maritime commerce. However, early Portuguese activity concentrated largely on Solor, where the first Portuguese priests – of the Dominican order – also made their base. By the early 1560s, the area had four Dominicans resident in it, and they claimed some five thousand converts in Solor, Timor and Flores. In these years, the *Estado da Índia* seems to have had relatively little interest in directly controlling the islands, and as a consequence the Dominicans came to exercise a form of temporal power as well – nominating the captain of Solor and Timor up to the mid-1580s. Portuguese traders and concession-ships from Melaka and Macau made their way there in the last quarter of the sixteenth century, largely for the sandalwood that was produced in Timor. And it was the same product that eventually drew the Dutch East India Company to these islands, prompting them to seize Solor in 1613 from the Dominicans, who moved in turn to Larantuka in Flores (Matos 1974; Villiers 1985).

The Portuguese settlement at Flores in the 1620s and 1630s was an integral part of the commercial network centred at Makassar, in which traders from Cochin, Coromandel, Melaka, Macau and Manila all participated. The Dutch watched it grow with some hostility, and eventually moved to crush it by repeatedly attacking its centre – Makassar itself – in the 1640s, 1650s and 1660s. But while doing so, the VOC – which was always eager to seek out commodities that could be monopolised – also sought to secure direct control over the sandalwood trade in the Lesser Sunda islands. Having taken Solor in 1613, they were forced to abandon it for logistic reasons in 1615, but returned a mere three years later, in 1618. In these years, however, the morale in the Dutch fort appears to have been poor; desertions were numerous, and included the chief (or *opperhoofd*) Jan de Hornay, who deserted to the Portuguese in February 1629, forcing the VOC once again to abandon the fort to the Dominicans, who moved quickly to reoccupy it.

The early 1630s thus saw Portuguese trade in the region truly flourish; the Dutch threat was no longer present in the immediate vicinity, and it was estimated that the Portuguese of Macau made 150 to 200 per cent profits in the sale of sandalwood from Timor at this time. This was also the period when the Portuguese presence in the region was described by António Bocarro, who noted the flourishing trade linking Macau to Solor and Timor. But reversals occurred again, and once more the Dutch were the proximate cause – in view of the rather fragile nature of the Portuguese presence in the area. In 1636, faced with a superior Dutch besieging force, the fortress at Solor surrendered once more, even though on this occasion the Dutch chose not to garrison the fort immediately. Instead, it remained untenanted for some ten years, until the Dutch created Fort Henricus there in 1646. With this, the Portuguese presence moved definitively to Timor and Flores (Boxer 1948a: 179–80).

Between the early 1640s and the first years of the eighteenth century, a process of some importance took place in the area. This was the creation of a hybrid Eurasian group, variously called the *Larantuqueiros* or 'Black Portuguese' (Dutch *Zwarte Portugesen*), who were in fact often of mixed Dutch, Portuguese and Timorese ethnicity, and who numbered several hundred by the close of the seventeenth century. This process accompanied Portuguese settlement on Timor, where in the early 1640s the Dominican Friar António de São Jacinto had started building a fort, in the westerly location of Kupang. In 1649, the Portuguese Captain-Major of the islands, Francisco Carneiro de Sequeira, also decided to settle in Kupang, and improved the fortifications, but the Dutch soon saw a threat in the new fort. Therefore, in 1653, the VOC seized Kupang, even as it had earlier taken Solor, dubbed the fort there Fort Concordia, and in the 1650s continued to have skirmishes with the Portuguese in the region. The Portuguese for their part had at first to be content with calling occasionally for trade in Lifau, on the north-west coast, but gradually came to control this port and spread themselves along the coast there. In the early eighteenth century, Larantuka and Lifau remained the two major centres of their trade and settlement, and competed with Kupang for the role of premier port in the region.

The distance from Goa and obscurity of these islands meant that in the latter half of the seventeenth century the *Larantuqeiros* could evolve local structures of power and leadership powerful enough to bend to their will any representative sent by Goa to rule over them. Their society thus evolved in a manner that parallels in certain respects that of the Portuguese in the Bay of Bengal in the late sixteenth century, even if Timor never quite had its version of Filipe de Brito e Nicote. Instead it had two powerful and rival clans, which sought to dominate local coastal society, and to exclude to an extent possible interference from Goa or Macau. One of these clans was of the Hornays, descended from the renegade Dutch *opperhoofd* we have mentioned above, whose principal figure is Jan de Hornay's son, António de Hornay (1613–93). In the mid-1660s, António de Hornay had been closely associated for a time with Francisco Vieira de Figueiredo, then a fugitive from Dutch persecution at Larantuka; subsequently, from 1673 to his death, he effectively controlled the affairs of the Portuguese in the islands, and also sought to bring a large part of the sandalwood trade of the area within his own grasp. During these years, the rival clan, the Da Costas, who were in turn descended from a certain Mateus da Costa who had been Captain-Major in the early 1650s, were somewhat in eclipse. However, they recovered their power in the 1690s, a period when Domingos da Costa of that family took the place of António de Hornay as head of the *Larantuqueiros*. It was Da Costa who led a local rebellion against António Coelho Guerreiro, appointed by Goa to the newly-created post of Governor and Captain-General of the islands of Timor and Solor; from 1702 to 1704, Guerreiro was besieged by Da Costa's forces at Lifau, until he abandoned it and fled to Goa (Boxer 1948a: 184–86).

Thus, even at the end of the period under our consideration, Timor – the last Portuguese possession to be wrested from them by force (in the 1970s) – was still barely under the control of Goa, and indeed continued to be contested by the *Larantuqueiro* leadership until at least the 1760s. It was in this decade that the Governor António José Teles de Menezes abandoned Lifau to the forces of Francisco de Hornay and, in 1769, shifted his capital to eastern Timor, thus founding the town of Dili. Nor was it an area where the traders of Macau could always carry on a particularly profitable trade, if contemporary accounts are to be credited. From the late 1660s on, and especially after the decisive attack on Makassar by a Dutch fleet in 1669, the traders of Macau could only send the odd ship to trade at Timor.

The decline of the Cheng family in the 1660s also meant that the Macau Portuguese had to give up hopes of a Ming revival in China, and concentrate their attention and resources on making a positive impact on the Ch'ing court of the Emperor K'ang-hsi. Two embassies were hence sent to Beijing in these years, those of Manuel de Saldanha (1667–70) and Bento Pereira de Faria (1678). The purpose of these embassies was not only to guard the privileges of Macau, but to ensure that the Dutch Company's access to China was kept limited. Particularly worrisome from the latter point of view was the Dutch embassy of Pieter van Hoorn (1666–68), but in fact the Dutch did not manage to make substantial inroads into the China trade as a consequence of this representation (Wills 1984). In this instance, we find Macau's settlers exercising a fair degree of autonomy from Goa in conducting their 'foreign policy', and we find this to be the case later as well, where Macau's relations with Cambodia, Vietnam and Thailand are concerned. But the 1670s and 1680s were a period when these areas, the traditional stamping-ground of Macau-based traders, were yielding lower and lower dividends to them, and they hence had to shift their attention farther and farther west. First Banten and then Batavia became centres of their trade, while the trade to mainland Southeast Asia continued at a low level. For a brief period in the last quarter of the seventeenth century, the port of Banjarmassin in south-eastern Borneo also attracted Macau's traders, who were hence wary of a proposal in the late 1680s from Goa to establish a factory and fortress there to purchase pepper. Rather, the Macau traders preferred trade without the flag (or at least without the fortress), and in fact they were proved right; the clumsy use of force against rival ships at the port led to the Portuguese being denied access to its trade from 1692 (Souza 1986: 124–27).

It has been estimated that in these years, the shipping operated by the Portuguese out of Macau probably amounted to ten or eleven vessels. Of these, in the late 1680s and early 1690s, two or three ships usually sailed to Dutch Batavia, carrying tea, silk, zinc, and a small quantity of precious metals, and purchasing above all pepper, but also other spices, tin and lead. Earlier, in the 1670s (and prior to their exclusion from there in 1682), roughly the same number of Macau ships had called at Banten, in a trade that seems to have picked up once the Ch'ing peace of which we have spoken had been established in the 1660s. The most prominent shipowning merchant of Macau in the period, Pero Vaz de Sequeira, whom we have already encountered as ambassador to Ayuthia in the 1680s, operated two ships that traded to Banjarmassin, Timor, Batavia and Ayuthia; he seems an operator on a far smaller scale than, say, Manuel Teixeira Pinto further west in the Bay of Bengal (Souza 1986: 44–45). Thus, searching constantly for outlets which the Dutch might permit them, the Macau-based traders of the last third of the seventeenth century are a pale shadow of the prosperous mercantile community of the early years of the same century. Yet survival alone ensured that their day would come once again. As the Dutch began in the early eighteenth century to exercise a less and less dominant presence in intra-Asian trade, the residents of Macau were among those who benefited. In the 1720s and 1730s, their trade shifted to the ports of the Malabar and Coromandel coasts, and at the same time their link with the ports of Vietnam became a major strength. Later, after the 1760s, when the opium trade between Bengal and China became an important growth area, the traders of Macau were once again there to take advantage of the possibilities (Manguin 1984). Our story stops at 1700, but it is then too soon to write off Portuguese private trade in the Indian Ocean.

THE PORTUGUESE, DUTCH AND ENGLISH: A COMPARISON

We have come a fair distance now from Da Gama's misadventures at Malindi and Calicut in the closing years of the fifteenth century. Where pepper and spices had once dominated Euro-Asian trade, by 1700 it was textiles above all that seemed the craze in Europe; tea and coffee were soon to join the lists. In a sense, it was the tyranny of spices that had led Europeans in the sixteenth and seventeenth centuries to develop such an elaborate trading network within Asia; to buy spices, one needed Indian textiles, and to buy Indian textiles one needed goods that would sell in India (or at least bullion). In the seventeenth century, the most successful European mercantile enterprise in Asia, the Dutch East India Company, understood this well, and this is why the Dutch insisted on maintaining such an elaborate network of factories in Asia, that fed on each other, and eventually produced the return cargoes for Europe.

Seen from the perspective of the student of European history, the seventeenth century is marked by the triumph of the chartered trading companies in the trade between Europe and Asia. There is obviously a strong temptation in this context to see the struggle between the

Portuguese and their northern European competitors as one between a medieval, tribute-gathering enterprise, and a rational, profit-maximising one. The very notion of the 'company' suggests immediate parallels with modern capitalism, and the structure of the English and Dutch Companies – with their directors, their systems of auctioning of Asian goods, their use of sophisticated financial and multi-lateral payments mechanisms reinforces this further. There is no doubt, moreover, that between the first and the second halves of the seventeenth century, the Portuguese lost considerable ground on the Cape route to the Dutch and English. How else can we explain this fact, save in terms of the triumph of a capitalistic enterprise over a seignorial one?

It is useful in this context to begin by noting two points. First, the companies borrowed heavily, and often consciously, from the Portuguese example in Asia. The architect of the Dutch Company's early triumphs in Asia, Jan Pieterszoon Coen, was clearly aware of the Portuguese system of concessional voyages within Asia, when he wrote to the Directors of his Company in 1614 of how the profits in intra-Asian trade alone could finance the Company's return cargoes to Europe. Using Coen's 'blueprint', the Dutch systematically built up a network of intra-Asian trade, of which the key centres were the Spice Islands, Japan, the north coast of Java and India (Prakash 1985). Like the Portuguese before them, the Dutch never really succeeded in making inroads into the intense trade between India and the Persian Gulf and Red Sea, and had to remain content with providing freight services to Asian merchants on these routes. It was effectively the triangular relationship between India, the Spice Islands, and Japan then, that accounts of the Dutch Company's great success in the seventeenth century.

However, it soon becomes clear that this success was not one that depended crucially on a more rational organisation, or a better harnessing of market forces. Rather, in the Spice Islands, it depended on naked force, for the Dutch forcibly excluded competitors from procuring cloves, nutmeg and mace to the extent possible. In Japan, the VOC's privileged access to the gold, silver and copper produced under the Tokugawa regime, was once more the result of a specific trading privilege afforded them by the Japanese state, and not the consequence of superiority in economic organisation. And it would be no exaggeration to say that Japanese bullion and copper and Indonesian spices between them accounted either directly or indirectly for the bulk of Dutch profits from Asian trade in the seventeenth century.

Force and diplomacy, rather than the laws of supply and demand, thus play a crucial role in the Dutch success. This should not be surprising for the VOC was not merely a 'company' but a *chartered* trading Company, and one that was closely linked to the Dutch state and its policies. Rather than seeing it as a form of private enterprise pure and simple, we would do better perhaps to see it as a quasi-state organisation, which was after all authorised by the States-General of the Netherlands to wage war, make treaties, engineer conquests, and thus engage in a whole gamut of activities that were not strictly the business of 'merchants', as the Company's employees rather coyly termed themselves.

The case of the English is a somewhat different one. Unlike the Dutch, the English entered Indian Ocean trade in the late sixteenth century in a position of weakness. The principal problems were two in number: the Company's position in England in respect of potential rivals was not as secure as that of the VOC in the Netherlands, and the Company was severely undercapitalised in relation to the VOC. This lack of capital was, moreover, not merely a trading constraint. Given the extent of the maritime power the English Company could command in the Indian Ocean in the first two decades of the seventeenth century, it would never have been able to match the *Estado da Índia* on its own. At best, the English could have hoped for a few stray triumphs, as off the coast of Gujarat and in the Persian Gulf early in the seventeenth century. This weakness in terms of military power was also what accounted for the marginal position the English Company came to hold by 1625 in Southeast Asia and the Far East. When faced by J.P. Coen and his plans, the English Company simply adopted the route of discretion and decided to concentrate its activities in India, and on developing the bilateral trade with Europe. From the middle years of the century, this strategy began to pay off, as the European market for Indian textiles expanded. Gujarat, Coromandel and Bengal became the three great centres of English trade. At the same time, English private traders – who were often either Company servants, or in league with the Company's employees – made gradual inroads into intra-Asian trade. This was done in alliance with Asian mercantile groups like the Muslim Maraikkayars of Coromandel, or the Parsis of the Indian west coast, and helped shore up settlements such as Madras, and later Bombay and Calcutta.

But if we imagine that the English Company was a purely profit-making enterprise, we would be mistaken. The long tradition of corsair activity under licence, which had produced Francis Drake, James Lancaster and others, and which was transformed in the seventeenth-century Caribbean into buccaneering, was not so easily subverted (Andrews 1984; Scammell 1989). From the very first years of its presence in Asia, the English Company used force in trade, and to collect tribute, and was limited largely by its relative feebleness. By the second half of the seventeenth century, the Company's confidence grew in leaps and bounds, culminating in an ill-advised war with the Mughal empire between 1687 and 1689. One of the Company's leading ideologues at the time, Sir Josia Child, wrote in 1686 that it was highly necessary to 'advance the English Interest and make this Company a formidable Martial government in

India'. This was not only to protect the English against the Dutch, who 'despised [us] as a parcel of mere trading merchants or Pedlars as they used to miscall us', but against the 'Natives' (Chaudhuri 1982: 392). He was being too modest, for the Company's objectives were even at the time not merely defensive.

In the eighteenth century, the English gradually took the lead over the Dutch as participants in trade both within Asia and between Europe and Asia. To ask how this occurred is a parallel question to asking how the Dutch triumphed over the Portuguese in the previous century. It appears that one important factor was that the English Company chose to *limit* its trade very largely to that between Europe and Asia, leaving the field of intra-Asian trade open to private entrepreneurs, who then sought loose political and economic links with the Company. As we have noted, centres like Madras and Calcutta became at one and the same time the headquarters of Company operations, and the focal points of networks of 'country trade', conducted by fleets of private British-owned vessels between Asian ports. Fortunes were made in this process already by the 1680s, and continued to be made in the eighteenth century, when these 'East Indian fortunes' helped partly finance English return cargoes to Europe. To the Dutch Company, such an arrangement would have been anathema; to the Portuguese, it might have appeared perfectly reasonable.

The purpose of raising this issue, which will once again be present as a theme in the concluding chapter, is to suggest that the relationship between the Portuguese and later Europeans in Asia is more complex than can be summed up in the notion of a simple replacement of one style of functioning by the other. In 1700, the Portuguese in Asia survived in two forms: as private traders staving off a stifling embrace from Goa (as in Macau and Porto Novo), or as sub-imperialists, carving out territorial dominions (as in south-east Africa or Timor). Contemporary Dutchmen or Englishmen probably saw themselves in neither of these images; but a mere seventy years later the English held considerable territories in India, while in the late eighteenth century private English traders sought desperately to stave off central interference from London and the seats of government in Asia. The moral here is not that history repeats itself – an adage that is a comment on the paucity of historical imagination rather than the reality of historical patterns; rather, it is that the nature of Asian trade and politics guided the actions of pragmatic participants in certain directions in this epoch.

CHAPTER EIGHT

Portuguese Asian Society I: The Official Realm

In earlier chapters, we have been concerned with chronology and a mapping of the different phases in the evolution of the Portuguese presence in Asia and East Africa between 1500 and 1700. In the present chapter and the one that follows, the focus shifts somewhat, as we seek to identify the principal social groups within Portuguese Asia and their dealings with one another. In so doing, the diachronic framework will not be abandoned entirely, for the relative weight of different groups tended to shift over time, as did their influence over the Portuguese presence as a whole. It is useful, in this context, to consider Portuguese Asian society not as a unified whole but as comprising an official part – the *Estado da Índia* and its territories – and an unofficial part, with the boundaries between the latter and the former being fluid, and evolving in the course of time.

The Portuguese presence in Asia in the sixteenth and seventeenth centuries was not based on emigration on a mass scale by the Iberians, and this serves to differentiate it to an extent from Brazil, especially in the latter part of the period under consideration. Furthermore, the official Portuguese presence was for the most part an urban one, with the exception of a few areas – such as the *província do Norte*, Sri Lanka and the Zambezi valley. The institutions that defined the matrix of social interaction with the local context were hence largely urban ones, and frequently had precedents in peninsular Portuguese practice. Some of these institutions, like the *Câmara Municipal* (City Council), or the *Santa Casa de Misericórdia* (Holy House of Mercy), are furthermore to be encountered elsewhere in the Portuguese empire as well, be it in Angola or Brazil. This fact lends a certain artificial uniformity to Portuguese imperial expansion, giving the superficial impression that the same patterns were replicated irrespective of the local context. But a closer examination reveals that such was not in fact the case. Rather, the *Câmara Municipal* when located in Macau could come to play a quite different role than what it played in, say, Goa, simply because the weakness or strength of such 'representative' organs varied with the strength or weakness of the rest of the state apparatus. With this cautionary word then, we may embark on our bird's-eye view of the evolution of 'official' Portuguese Asian society, which is to say the *Estado da Índia* proper.

THE PROBLEM OF NUMBERS

How many Portuguese were there in Asia at various points in the sixteenth and seventeenth centuries, and what activities did they engage in? To answer this question proves difficult, indeed far more difficult than in the case of Spanish America, Brazil, or the Atlantic islands, if only because Asia represented a vast expanse, and it was hence not easy for contemporaries to produce global estimates with any degree of accuracy. But guesses abound. Around 1540, one frequently cited contemporary testimony (that of D. João de Castro) puts the number of Portuguese between Sofala and China at six to seven thousand, and it is also equally often asserted that the number of Portuguese between the Cape of Good Hope and Japan never exceeded ten thousand. More recently, V. M. Godinho has put forward a series of estimates that are of some interest: he notes that in 1513 there were 2,500 Portuguese capable of bearing arms in Asia, 4,000 in 1516, 6,000 to 7,000 in 1540 (here the estimate is again the Castro one), and finally for the 1570s he cites the estimate of Diogo do Couto which puts the total number of Portuguese in Asia at about 16,000 (Godinho 1978). He argues, moreover, that on the Cape route there were at least 2,000 Portuguese going to Asia each year, that this number could be as high as 5,000, but was on average around 3,500. We may consider this number in the context of his estimates for total net emigration from Portugal in these years, summarised in Table 8.1.

Table 8.1 Net Portuguese emigration, 1400–1700

Period	Number	Annual Average
1400–1500	50,000	500
1500–1580	280,000	3,500
1580–1640	330,000	5,500
1640–1700	150,000	2,500

(*Source*: Godinho 1978:9)

Godinho's arguments may be broadly summarised as follows. In the first two thirds of the sixteenth century, the emigrants came from all parts of Portugal, and were destined in their great majority for the Atlantic islands and Asia, with Brazil coming a poor third. However, from the 1560s, two changes occur: first, Brazil begins to dominate as a destination, and second, the emigrants come increasingly from the Portuguese north-west, the area of Entre Douro e Minho, and to a lesser extent Trás-os-Montes.

The former of these two points is fairly clearly established by the evidence on the shifting relative population of different parts of the Portuguese overseas empire. By the end of the sixteenth century, the settler population of Brazil was just under double the 'white' population of Portuguese Asia, whereas in around 1550, it had been about one fourth the latter. From a total Portuguese emigré population about 1600 of over 100,000, Brazil accounted for a third, Asia for a fifth, and West Africa and the Atlantic islands for the rest. The latter point, concerning the origins in Portugal of the migrants, also appears clear from the Brazilian evidence (in particular that from Pernambuco), but would bear closer examination in the Asian case.

Recent researches make it possible to provide a more exact estimate of the movements of persons on the Cape route than those of Godinho. Based on plausible assumptions concerning the relationship at various times between tonnage on the Cape route and numbers of persons on board these vessels, these estimates suggest the picture illustrated in Table 8.2

Table 8.2 Movements of persons between Portugal and Asia, 1497–1700

Period	Arrivals	Departures	Difference	AnnualAverage
1. Seen from Asia				
1497–1540	65,414	36,882	28,532	648
1541–1570	48,408	34,915	13,493	450
1571–1610	93,963	67,326	26,637	667
1611–1660	64,695	40,894	23,801	476
1661–1700	19,747	13,920	5,827	146
TOTAL	292,227	193,937	98,290	482
2. Seen from Portugal				
1497–1540	73,490	33,690	39,800	904
1541–1570	52,111	30,438	21,673	722
1571–1610	105,605	56,049	49,556	1,239
1611–1660	75,108	32,546	42,562	852
1661–1700	24,040	11,289	12,751	319
TOTAL	330,354	164,012	166,342	815

(*Source*: Duncan 1986: 22, 24)

Seen from the viewpoint of Portugal, gross movement to Asia seems to have been somewhat lower than the level estimated by Godinho: just over

1,700 per year leave by the Cape route up to 1570, and just under 2,700 per year in the next four decades. But of far greater interest are the figures presented in the last column of both parts of the table. These represent respectively net 'additions' to the Portuguese population in Asia on account of shipping via the Cape route, and net 'losses' to Portugal by the same means. These figures take account of mortality en route, but are nevertheless limited because of two features. First, they do not deal with those Portuguese who travelled between Asia and Europe via the overland route, passing through the eastern Mediterranean. Second, once into the seventeenth century, it is possible that there were Portuguese who came to Asia not on Portuguese-owned vessels but on those of other nations. However, neither of these qualifications may be thought to have a significant effect on the numbers estimated here.

Even so, it is hard to proceed from Part 1 of Table 8.2 to an estimate of the changing Portuguese population in Asia. This is because we have data neither on Portuguese mortality and expectation of life once in Asia, nor on the rate at which this population reproduced. We must return therefore to the possible manner in which an estimate of population at various points in time can be constructed from contemporary data. Data on population in Portuguese Asia are usually available in terms of a number of categories. They tend, first of all, to be superior for the official part of Portuguese Asia – that is, the *Estado da Índia* – and rather poorer when one turns to unofficial Portuguese activity, be it trade or military adventurism. Even within the *Estado*, it is rarely that one can lay one's hands on a relatively comprehensive listing of the Portuguese scattered across what were, after all, quite distant settlements, ranging from Macau and Solor to Mombasa, Tete and Mozambique.

A possibly unique source of information in this respect is António Bocarro's *Livro do Estado da Índia Oriental*, compiled between 1633 and 1635, with the aid of the secretary of the then viceroy Linhares, Pedro Barreto de Resende. Bocarro's account permits us to arrive at an approximate global estimate (with geographical distribution) of two of the principal categories of Portuguese in Asia: the so-called *casados moradores*, and the ecclesiastics of the four principal religious orders in Asia – the Jesuits, Franciscans (and Capuchins), the Dominicans and the Augustinians.

But before entering into his figures, it is clearly of some importance to consider the categories into which the Portuguese resident in Asia in this period were divided by contemporary writers and chroniclers. Six or seven categories emerge from the documents and chronicles, some common in their usage, others less so. These are (i) *casado* or *casado morador*, which is to say married settler, (ii) *soldado* or soldier, (iii) *religioso* or ecclesiastic, (iv) *ministro* or official, (v) *arrenegado* or renegade, (vi) *alevantado*, or *lançado*, meaning a rebel or someone beyond the pale, and finally (vii) *chatim* or *solteiro*, a semi-derogatory term meaning a free-

219

wheeling merchant of no fixed abode. While the first four categories are relatively clear-cut (with only a few residual confusions or ambiguities in their usage), the last three are used quite loosely, sometimes interchangeably, as we shall see in a later examination of the careers of some Portuguese who were termed as such.

Our primary concern in the present chapter is with those who fell into the first four of these categories, and dwelt moreover in the official realm. Now, of these, the *casados* were numerically the preponderant category, but the term is also of interest for another reason: it is peculiar to Portuguese Asia, rarely or never being used in other parts of the Portuguese empire or in Portugal itself. It is a deceptively simple term, meaning in the literal sense 'married man'. But in reality, it meant something far more specific. First, only those persons resident under the authority of the *Estado da Índia* could be termed *casados*, and they had moreover to be associated with a specific place of residence. In official depositions, petitions and other legal documents, the term always appears as '*casado* resident of such-and-such a settlement'. Being married settlers, these persons were clearly to be distinguished from the ecclesiastics, but they were also differentiated from the soldiers of a settlement's garrison (the *soldados*), and from the short-tenure officials who came from Portugal. No viceroy was ever a *casado*, therefore.

The roots of the term seem to lie in Afonso de Albuquerque's period. Immediately after taking Goa in 1510, the governor wished to settle a Portuguese population there on a permanent basis, and hence gave economic incentives to those who would become married settlers, and would take wives of local origin (who had been converted from Islam or Hinduism). The reason for the latter decision was at least partly pragmatic: since the extent of female migration from Portugal to Asia remained low throughout the sixteenth century, a married settler population could not reasonably be created while insisting on racial exclusivity. We are unfortunately not in a position to provide a clear picture of the social or ethnic origins of those Asian women whom the first Portuguese *casados* of Goa married; only a few of them – those associated with soldiers and administrators from the preceding Adil Shahi administration – are likely to have been 'fair Mooresses', as is sometimes claimed.

Within a generation, this meant that the *casado* community came to comprise both those who were wholly Portuguese, and those of mixed blood (or *mestiços*). Such a distinction was rarely stressed in official or legal documents, but was certainly a commonly used differentiating factor by the *casados* themselves. The *mestiços* were looked down upon by those of 'pure' blood, and the latter tended to be divided too into *castiços* or *indiáticos* (born in Asia of Portuguese, or at least European, parentage), and *reinois* – who were themselves migrants from Portugal. Chronicles of the post-1550 period – and especially the *Décadas* of Diogo do Couto – make a great deal of this distinction, even if it was not an official one. A further distinction is sometimes made between the normal *casados*, who were urban-based, and those of semi-rural parts of the *Estado*, such as sections of Sri Lanka or the *província do norte*. The latter, in a usage that broadly follows the model of the North African garrisons, were termed *fronteiros* ('frontiersmen') and were required by statute to maintain a number of arquebusiers for the service of the Crown in times of war; in return they received alienated land-revenues of one or the other sort.

While the categories and distinctions dealt with above are well-established in the literature, a reading of Bocarro's *Livro* also suggests the existence of an additional category. It would appear from his writings that the Asian Christian converts, who resided as householders in the urban enclaves that formed a part of the *Estado da India* were also termed *casados* by the seventeenth century. Christian slaves are, of course, excluded from purview for this purpose, but in many of the settlements, Bocarro makes mention of *casados pretos* and *casados brancos* ('black' *casados* and 'white' *casados*), at times referring – as in the case of Macau – to the former as *casados* who are 'natives of the land' (*naturais da terra*). The reason for this is not hard to seek: since the written or tacit agreements between the *Estado* and Asian rulers over enclaves that had not been acquired by conquest often gave the Portuguese jurisdiction over all *Christians* resident there, these households too had to be given a place in the official scheme of things.

Table 8.3 summarises the profile of *casados* in Portuguese Asia in the early 1630s.

Whilst the first total of 4,900 is probably fairly accurate, the total for the 'black' *casados* is likely to be an understatement. There are several settlements, such as Mangalore and Daman, where we know that such Christian convert households existed, but we cannot arrive at an estimate for them.

The real problem with our 'white' *casado* figures is slightly different. Since, by 1635, several sizeable Portuguese settlements had already been lost to rivals – as happened with Hurmuz and Hughli – we cannot take the figure of 4,900 to be as true for 1600 as for 1635. Hurmuz in around 1550 had hosted about one hundred and fifty Portuguese and 'black' *casados*; by 1600, the number of Portuguese *casados* alone was around two hundred. Again, the population of several other settlements had fallen sharply between 1600 and 1635; this was certainly true of Goa and Cochin, but also of Chaul and Melaka. While a part of this decline may have been compensated by the rise in *casado* populations elsewhere, it is very likely that on balance the total number of 'white' *casados* in Portuguese Asia in 1600 exceeded 5,500, and may even have been as high as 6,000. This is of course not a very large figure, and one estimate even suggests that there were as many Portuguese in the Spanish viceroyalty of

Table 8.3 White' and 'Black' Casados in Portuguese Asia, 1635

Settlement	'White'	'Black'	Settlement	'White'	'Black'
Macau	850	850	Cranganor	40	60
Goa	800	2,200	Cannanore	40	–
Daman	400	?	Mangalore	35	?
Bassein	400	600	Basrur	35	–
Colombo	350	2,000	Honawar	30	–
Cochin	300	200	Karanja	30	–
Melaka	250	?	Agashe	30	–
Chaul	200	50	Sena	30	–
Nagapattinam	140	360	Caliture	30	?
Jaffna	140	270	Chipangura	25	–
São Tomé	120	200	Manora	20	–
Thana	80	100	Rachol	20	–
Galle	70	130	Trincomalee	20	25
Mannar	70	–	Tete	20	–
Mozambique	70	–	Mombasa	15–20	–
Kollam	60	–	Negombo	6	–
Diu	59	–	Sofala	5	–
Mahim	50	150	Chuambo	4	–
Tarapur	50	200	Gangens	4	40
			TOTAL	4,903	7,435

(*Source*: Bocarro 1937–38, i and ii; Godinho 1968)

Peru in much the same period. In fact, it seems pitiful when compared to the white settler population in Spanish America: 118,000 in 1570, and 655,000 in 1650. But the influence of these Portuguese cannot be gauged in numbers alone; we must also take account of the dimensions of their trade, and qualitative aspects of their presence in Asia.

The other category for which estimates are available from Bocarro is of ecclesiastics belonging to the major religious orders of the period. As we have seen, the first members of religious orders to arrive in Asia were the Franciscans, eight of whom came with Cabral from Lisbon in 1500. Later arrivals were the Jesuits, the Dominicans and the Augustinians, and these orders when taken together with the Carmelites had as many as 1,700 or more religious spread across Asia by the 1630s. The most numerous were the Jesuits, followed closely by the Franciscans (who were divided into regular Franciscans and Capuchin monks). Each of these orders had six hundred or more religious in Asia, including the novices and those in seminaries and colleges. It is no surprise, moreover, to note that these religious were unevenly distributed across Asia, and even the *Estado*. Goa alone had some six hundred members of these orders in it, which is to say over a third of those present in Asia. Another large concentration was in Cochin, and here again all the orders were quite well represented. The *Província do Norte* – including Daman, Chaul, Bassein, Salsette and other

Table 8.4-A Distribution of ecclesiastical orders in Asia, 1635

Region	Franciscans	Capuchins	Augustinians	Dominicans
Goa	149	75	125	102
East Africa	–	8	8	10
West Asia	–	–	33	–
Sind	–	–	3	–
Diu	–	10	–	8
Daman	–	10	6	6
Bassein	38	–	8	12
Chaul	26	15	15	31
Prov. do Norte (other)	27	12	20	7
Kanara	6	–	–	–
Cochin	58	15	20	20
Other Malabar	20	–	–	–
Sri Lanka	96	10	18	18
Coromandel	–	–	8	5
Bengal	–	–	17	–
Melaka	–	12	6	10
China	–	15	15	12
Solor	–	–	–	15
Other	3	–	–	–
TOTAL	423	182	302	256

Table 8.4-B Distribution of Jesuits in Asia, 1635

Location	Number	Location	Number
(i) Goa Province		(ii) Malabar Province	
Goa	148	Total	190–200
Mozambique	14	(iii) China, Cochin-China and Japan	
Ethiopia	21	Total	190
Mughal court	5	GRAND TOTAL	650–660
Tibet	5		
Diu	8		
Daman	8		
Salsette	27		
Bassein	15		
Thana	11		
Chaul	8		
Total	270		

(Source: Bocarro 1937–38 (ii): 55–64)

minor centres – was also an area of relatively intense activity by all the orders; Chaul alone had just under a hundred religious, a rather large number in view of its *casado* population. Table 8.4 summarises the position of these orders in the early 1630s.

A remarkable feature that emerges from Table 8.4 is the fact of geographical specialisation, once one moves away from Goa, the *Província do Norte* and Cochin: the Augustinians are the dominant presence in west Asia (Basra, Iran, the Ottoman domains), as well as in Bengal and Arakan; the Franciscans had a large proportion of their human resources devoted to proselytisation in Sri Lanka; the Dominicans were the exclusive presence in Solor (as we have remarked in the last chapter); and the Jesuits were remarkable for their very large Far Eastern presence, as well as their missions in Ethiopia, the Mughal court and Tibet.

Between the two of them, the categories of *casado branco* and *religioso* account in the 1630s for some 6,700 persons in Asia. Not all of those who belonged to these groups were Portuguese of course, for while the religious orders had several Frenchman, Spaniards and Italians in their lists, some of the *casados* too were not Portuguese properly speaking. This is an issue which we shall address below, of the extent to which contemporaries sought to differentiate 'native' Portuguese from the other Europeans who partook of their Asian enterprise.

THE WORLD OF THE *CASADO*

Before entering into such specificities, it is of interest to set out in broad strokes the social world inhabited by the *casados* in Asia, and see how it came to evolve over time. It may be stated as a broad truth – and excepting always the specific categories that we have discussed above – that the *casado* was the Portuguese Asian equivalent of a burgher, a mercantile-minded townsman. The formal aspect of the social organisation of the *casado* was therefore clearly modelled on the closest equivalent to be found in Iberia: the *homens-bons* or 'good-men', sometimes also known as *cidadãos honrados* ('honoured citizens'). This category ran, at its upper end, into the lower nobility, and so it is with the *casados* in Asia as well; among their number were some *fidalgos* and members of the military orders (especially the Order of Christ). However, unlike the *homens-bons*, the *casados* also included those who might in Portugal have been seen as of the lower classes (*gente miuda*).

In the official settlements of the *Estado da Índia*, which were almost always urban centres, physical space was organised in order to allow the *casados* one or several quarters (*bairros*), side by side with other quarters inhabited by Asian groups. In Melaka, for example, in the early 1580s, there were three quarters, namely Upeh, Hilir, and the Portuguese quarter. In Upeh, one finds the main settlement of the Kelings, the natives of the Coromandel coast who lived in Melaka, while Hilir housed still other groups of Asian merchants. This was a familiar pattern to the

Portuguese, for we have noted in Chapter 2 how the Muslims in Lisbon were all resident in a single quarter (the *mouraria*), which housed their major communal institutions such as mosque, public bath and schools. Equally, in contemporary European towns such as Bruges or Antwerp, it was common to have separate quarters for each of the major foreign communities, a pattern which corresponded fairly well with the Malay idea of the *kampong* in use in Melaka.

It is important to bear in mind that even in their major settlements, the Portuguese were a minority population. In Melaka, the Javanese, Chinese, Kelings and Malays clearly outnumbered them, while in Goa, the Gujaratis and Konkanis were a far larger presence. This was not merely a numerical dominance; many of the key financial instruments even in centres like Goa and even more clearly Macau or Diu remained in the hands of Asian mercantile groups, with their widespread networks of trade. Even in terms of their general culture, relatively few Portuguese settlements developed an overwhelmingly Lusitanian atmosphere. The settlements of the Indian west coast are probably an exception, but contemporary descriptions of São Tomé and Nagapattinam on the Coromandel coast, or Macau, leave us in no doubt of the extremely hybrid character of the settlements. In most of them, such buildings as churches, the house of the captain, and a few other community institutions stood out. In general, the Iberian pattern of whitewashed walls, and red-tiled roofs, arranged around a central arbour, seems to have been followed, if one can credit the drawings of Barreto de Resende in the 1630s of the plans of the principal Portuguese Asian settlements. Within the Portuguese section of these towns, it is clear that the *casados* usually dominated. It was from the set of *casados* that the major representative body of Portuguese cities (*cidades*) in Asia, the *Câmara Municipal* – or Municipal Council – was elected. In the case of Goa, probably the first urban centre in Portuguese Asia to have its own *Câmara*, the Council was closely modelled on what obtained in Lisbon. Ten members were elected for three-year terms, including three nobles (of whom one had to be a *fidalgo*), and besides there were four representatives of the craft-guilds (called *procuradores dos mesteres*), and who obviously included artisans (Boxer 1965: 12–13). This system was followed in Goa to about 1654, even though by this time the Lisbon Council had changed its format considerably. In 1654, the Goa Council decided to follow a rotating roster system for its noble members (or *vereadores nobres*), but otherwise did not greatly alter its structure.

It was the Council that was the central focus of *casado* resistance to the *Estado da Índia* and its policies, but it was equally to such Councils that the *Estado* turned for support in its hours of need. For the *Câmara* typically had its own resources, drawn from fines and a few taxes, but also because it could raise loans from the *casado* citizens of the town; further, adjunct to the *Câmara* was the other great representative institution, the *Santa Casa da Misericórdia* (Holy House of Mercy). The *Misericórdia* was meant in theory to be a charitable institution, a brotherhood founded to run hospitals and hospices, ransom those held by the Moors, bury the corpses of the indigent, and so on: in reality, its governing council (or *Mesa*) became a stage where power-politics within the *casado* community was given full expression, and membership of which conferred a great deal of prestige on a *casado*. The *Misericórdias'* funds came from three sources: bequests, the money of citizens who died intestate, and the legacies of deceased persons which were awaiting transmission to their heirs. The first of these Houses in Asia was founded at Cochin in 1505, followed by another in the next decade in Goa; by the 1540s, Chaul and Melaka also had *Misericórdias*. In the late 1560s, a *Misericórdia* was founded at Macau too, and in the second half of the sixteenth century we are aware that Nagapattinam and São Tomé also possessed these bodies, as did most of the major centres of *casado* activity on the Indian west coast and East Africa.

The power of the *Misericórdias* increased from the late sixteenth century, when they were given a jurisdiction that enabled them to supersede the *provedores dos defuntos* in various parts of Asia, thus permitting them to dispose of the great part of the funds pertaining to Portuguese in Asia who wished in their wills to leave their effects to heirs in Europe. This decision appears in a royal decree (*alvará*) of March 1590 in the following terms:

> I, the King, make it known to those who see this order that ... [I am] informed that the *provedores mores dos defuntos* in the parts of India and the minor *provedores* of the fortresses there are not sending the goods and money of the deceased who die in those parts according to their obligation and statute-book in order that they be handed over to their heirs and in accordance with what the executors wish, but instead are converting them to their own uses and trades both against their consciences and against what they owe to their posts ...   (AHU, Caixa 20, doc. 66)

The *alvará* went on to state that this created 'great scandal'; and so it was ordered that all the goods and money of those who died in Mozambique, Hurmuz, Diu, Daman, Bassein, Chaul and Goa would be handed over immediately on their death to the *Misericórdias* of those forts, and not to the *provedores*. These *Misericórdias* would then hand over the estates to the Goa *Misericórdia*, to be sent to Lisbon. On the other hand, those who died in Kanara, Malabar, Ceylon, Melaka 'and other parts of the south', would have their money go via their local *Misericórdias*, to Cochin, which would send it on to Portugal. The viceroy Matias de Albuquerque's interpretation, dated 18th July 1591, set some further limits on the role of the *Misericórdias*, while still leaving them a substantial place. If, he stated, the heirs were in Portugal, the above *alvará* would hold, but if not, the *provedor-mór* would be left in charge of the estate. If heirs were both in Asia and Portugal, an inventory would be made jointly by the *Misericórdia provedor* and the state *provedor*, and the goods would be divided, each party taking charge of its share. If the whereabouts of the heirs were uncertain, the *Misericórdia* would hold the goods until they were ascertained.

We have already noted that the Municipal Councils at times became the focus of *casado* resistance to official policy in Portuguese Asia. This led some viceroys at Goa, notably the Count of Linhares in 1632, to suggest that their powers be restricted, or that they be done away with altogether. To understand why such conflict should have existed, it is necessary to recall two essential facts: first, that the Crown and the *casados* often had divergent mercantile interests, both during the time when the Crown directly participated in trade, and later when it created monopoly grants and concessions; second, that the interests of the *casados* were not always best served by the officials appointed to serve for three-year terms in locations where they had no long-term stake. The second fact is not peculiar, needless to add, to the history of Portuguese Asia, and obtained elsewhere in the early modern world, where such short-term appointments existed.

The ideal solution to this particular problem from the *casado* viewpoint was to have one of their own community appointed to the captaincy and other posts in their settlement, but the Crown and viceroyalty were understandably reluctant to acquiesce in this. We may note for example the attempt by the settlers of the newly-created Coromandel *cidade* of São Tomé in the 1610s to have one of their own number – a certain Manuel de Frias – made Captain-General of the town; Goa preferred to appoint its own choice, first Rui Dias de Sampaio, and then D. António Manuel (Subrahmanyam 1990b: 203–04). The response of the São Tomé *casados* was characteristic: they made life so difficult for D. António Manuel that he began to fear for his life, and left for Goa halfway through his term.

But the *casado* community did not always get its own way, and one of the reasons for this was that the *casados* themselves were often deeply divided. This phenomenon, common in the late sixteenth and early seventeenth century, is usually to be encountered in contemporary documents and chronicles as the problem of *bandos* (or factions), and is sardonically summed up by the Dutchman Paulus van Soldt in 1606, while passing São Tomé in his ship.

> They lead a wholly unheard-of and barbaric life there, having no authority, laws or police, and are their own lawmen, since when they have any quarrels with one another, they shoot each other dead in the passing out of the windows, and he who has the most friends is the strongest.
>
> (Commelin 1646, xii: 61)

Life even in São Tome, notorious though it was in the period for factional strife, was not quite governed by the law of the jungle, as Van Soldt seems to suggest. Rather, there were clear factions among the *casados*, and the power of different factions and their leaders was partly determined by their connections with the local political structure – which in the early seventeenth century was made up of a set of war-band leaders, headed by the authority of the titular Vijayanagara ruler resident in the inland fortress-towns of Velur and Chandragiri (Rao, Shulman and Subrahmanyam, 1992). One particular difficult and powerful figure in the era in which Van Soldt wrote was a certain António de Sousa Pereira, who features in the correspondence between São Tome and Lisbon. In a letter of 1612, the King D. Felipe wrote to his viceroy at Goa with the following complaints in regard of Pereira:

> I am also informed that in the city of São Thomé de Meliapor there is settled one António de Sousa Pereira, who is unruly and disobedient to my justices, living like a rebel (*levantado*); and that since he uses Gentile and infidel soldiers to kill Christians, and has other boys stolen in order to sell them, the Bishop proceeded against him with censures; and being censured thus he had dead animals placed in the wells from which water is drunk, and has gathered around himself Gentiles and his friends and relatives, planning to kill the Portuguese who live there, or to vex and rob them so much that they would leave the land. ... (DRI, ii: 226)

Pereira's was an extreme case, but others of a less drastic sort can be found from the same period, which also serve to illustrate the often violent nature of factional conflict among *casado* settlers. We are unable to verify whether such conflict always took place along predictable lines: that is whether it pitted *reinol* against *indiático*. There is some suspicion that such was not necessarily the case, for structures of patronage – pitting the clients of one *fidalgo* against those of another – ran across rather than along these distinctions.

Among those who were mobilised if such conflict actually turned violent were the domestic slaves, who existed in considerable numbers in most of the settlements of the *Estado*. In the case of Goa, one early seventeenth-century estimate was that each *casado* household had around ten slaves attached to it; this would suggest a total of some eight thousand slaves in this town alone. A few slaves were also owned by the state itself, and used to man the galleys, and for manual labour. It has been suggested that the import of slaves into Goa was in the sixteenth century largely from Bengal, China and Japan, and later from East Africa (De Souza 1979: 124–25). These three sources – the Far East, Bengal, and East Africa – certainly account for the bulk of the slaves to be found in early seventeenth-century Goa. Consider the household of Garcia de Melo, an important fiscal official, who was arrested for fraud in 1611; when an inventory of his household goods was taken, they were found to include nineteen slaves, six from Bengal (including three eunuchs, or *capados*), six from China, and seven from East Africa (AHU, Cx. 1, doc. 101). All of the slaves had been converted, and possessed only Christian names – not surnames (indicating their social status).

A small proportion of these slaves from Goa and Cochin eventually found their way back to Lisbon, either as merchandise, or when their owners returned to Portugal after their Asian sojourn. It was now that Portuguese peninsular society had its first opportunity to form a first-hand impression of the human geography of Asia, and derive from it a set of stereotypes. Thus, even before he departed for India, the Florentine Filippo Sassetti in the 1580s was, from Lisbon itself, able to provide his friend Baccio Valori in Florence a gallery of pen-portraits of typical Asians: amongst his categories are the Japanese, the Chinese, and two sorts of Indians, 'the Mahommedan Moors, and the blacks who are Gentiles'. Of the Japanese, he wrote: '[They are] olive-coloured people, and who exercise every art with good understanding; small faces and in the rest of their stature reasonable'. The Chinese, on the other hand, are described at greater length:

> The Chinese are men of great intellect and likewise exercise all the arts and above all learn how to cook marvellously; they have pug faces, little eyes as if they had been pierced with a spindle, and all of them (which seems to me their own peculiarity) have their sockets hanging over their eyelids, so that they seem at first sight not to have them, which makes them different and recognisable among all the others. Their colour is between yellow and tan.

Finally, Indians were distinguished into the Moors, who were dark but not black, 'men of such intelligence that no one has more, and from the brightness of their eyes one knows of their cunning; but they have as a result bad tendencies, and are the most wonderful thieves, and if one can find one who is good, he will make a good servant'; the 'black Gentiles', on the other hand, were characterised as good for nothing save physical labour (Bramanti 1970: 220–21).

Besides Goa and the west coast settlements, the Portuguese in places ranging from Nagapattinam to Melaka and Macau all possessed household slaves. These included Chinese, sold in childhood (the so-called *muitsai*), but also African slaves, who formed a part of the military force which beat off a Dutch attack on Macau in 1622. The Dutch Governor-General Jan Pieterszoon Coen was later to write rather unkindly of how the VOC had been beaten off by 'many Portuguese slaves, Kaffirs and the like, [who] having been made drunk, charged so fearlessly against our muskets, that it was a wondrous thing to see' (Boxer 1948a: 85). Coen concluded, in his characteristic way, that keeping slaves for military purposes was therefore desirable for the Dutch as well.

Slaves also had another important function in the life of the *casados*.

The numbers of Portuguese women who emigrated to Asia never exceeded more than a tiny fraction of the total numbers on board the ships of the *Carreira*, and this meant that the gender ratio was strongly skewed in Portuguese Asia. The reasons for this are not wholly clear; it is true that the Crown in certain periods did discourage female migration, but in others actually made an official provision to send out the so-called 'royal orphans' (*orfaãs del-Rei*) to Asia at a rate of around ten a year, providing them a dowry in the form of a *prazo* in the *província do norte*. A recent study has argued that the migration of single men, rather than conjugal migration, was by choice, and because of the relatively secure and stable position enjoyed by women in Portugal; the Portuguese who emigrated thus sought women among other races whom they could subjugate (Silva 1986). If this is indeed true, then the use of female slaves as concubines – which was frequent in the sixteenth and early seventeenth centuries in both Goa and elsewhere – acquires some significance. Filippo Sassetti, for example, the Florentine intellectual and commercial agent who lived in Cochin and Goa in the 1580s, was survived by a daughter whom he had through a female slave, probably from Bengal.

Given the relative preponderance of Portuguese men over women in Asia in the early sixteenth century, the policy adopted by Albuquerque – of promoting mixed-race marriages – was a pragmatic one. Elements of coercion were probably not absent from it, but since we know little or nothing of the women whom these Portuguese settlers married, not much of significance can be said beyond this. It was an implicit part of the arrangement that the wives of the *casados* would convert, and this is likely to have acted as a disincentive to some in a period when economic and social discrimination against non-Christians was still limited. Up until the mid-sixteenth century, two powerful posts were those of *tanadar-mór*, held between 1523 and 1548 with only brief gaps by a Hindu entrepreneur Krishna, and head of the Muslim community (a post offered in the 1540s to Shams-ud-din Gilani).

But with the rise of the Counter-Reformation, and the growing presence in Goa of the religious orders, discrimination against religions other than Christianity grew. Known now, significantly enough, as the 'Rome of the Orient', Goan society saw repressive measures against both Hindus and Muslims, something which appears to have obtained in much lesser degree in other Portuguese settlements east of Cape Comorin. The first step was in the late 1540s, when a special tax was levied on mosques in Bardes and Salsette, and temples were closed down. But a further assault came in the next decade, under the viceroy D. Constantino de Bragança (1558–61). Hindu temples were destroyed on some scale, with perhaps nine hundred in all being demolished in Bardes, Tisvadi and Salsette (De Souza 1979: 91). Both this obvious pressure, and more subtle economic ones, such as the denial to Hindus of access to employment by the state, and preference to converts in various fiscal and legal institutions, eventually led to mass conversion. Between the mid-sixteenth century, when less than a fifth of Goa's population appears to have been Christian, and 1650 – when some two-thirds of it had become so – a sea-change is perceptible. One of its effects was also to solve the problem posed by the skewed gender ratio of Portuguese (whether *reinois* or not) in Goa.

However, the Hindu population of Goa, and particularly the Gujarati *vanias* and the Saraswat Brahmins, continued to play a crucial role both in trade and in fiscal matters. It has been estimated that of the revenue-farms (*rendas*) let out by the *Estado* in Goa between 1600 and 1670, a majority (indeed, eighty per cent of the identifiable cases) were held by Hindu revenue farmers, the great majority by the Saraswats of Goa. Even in terms of value, the case for 'indigenous dominance' of fiscal inter-mediation remains; again Saraswats account for about 45 per cent of total value, other Hindus for some 20 per cent, and Christians for the remaining 35 per cent (Pearson 1981: 98–99). Even where the crucial pepper procurement contracts were concerned, Saraswat merchants such as Govinda, and Pondya, dominate in the early seventeenth century, as do other families with names such as Kini and Nayaka. It is likely that this high profile is more the case after about 1620 than before this date. As *casado* fortunes began to decline, there were fewer and fewer entre-preneurs from within that category who had the wherewithal to make bids for *rendas*, and this is likely to have shifted the balance in favour of the Hindu element. Thus, important though the Counter-Reformation was in redefining Goa's social and religious profile, it was unable in the final analysis to achieve a totally decisive shift in the fiscal and economic sphere.

NETWORKS, FORTUNES AND PATRONAGE

For most of the sixteenth and seventeenth centuries, the *raison d'être* of the *casado* was trade, especially intra-Asian trade. While this is easy to see from a reading of official papers, we are hampered by the fact that the documents rarely if ever permit us a glimpse of the internal functioning of *casado* businesses. Important questions of how they were organised, their size and profitability, and so on, remained unanswered for the most part. If Dutch estimates are to be believed, the extent of *casado* intra-Asian trade must have been rather large in the early seventeenth century: in 1622, total Portuguese intra-Asian trade was estimated by them at some 24 million *xerafins*, and in the 1630s, traders based at Goa alone invested some 850,000 *xerafins* in intra-Asian commerce. Not all of this trade was in *casado* hands, for other free-wheeling *solteiro* merchants had begun to make their appearance by this period, while some part was played in intra-Asian trade by others as well – ranging from high officials in their private capacity, to the religious orders.

The trade of officials (or *ministros*) in Portuguese Asia is a feature that runs through its history from its very inception, though taking different forms in different periods. In the first half of the sixteenth century, when Crown shipping still plied intra-Asian maritime routes on quite a considerable scale, it was partly carried on through the *foros* and *agasalhados* (liberty-chests of various sorts) held by officials as perquisites of office. Melaka, for example, was a major centre of such trade, and the first factor of the town, Rui de Araujo, went even further than this – organising private voyages to the Moluccas and elsewhere on his own account, or in partnership with Asian traders. In the 1520s and 1530s, it was quite common for Portuguese officials based in Melaka to act as sleeping-partners in the enterprises of others, and several of Melaka's captains in the period made quite large fortunes in the process. But some of them also used their office to create short-term monopolies, raising complaints from the Keling traders of the town, who on at least one occasion in the late 1520s actually wrote a letter of complaint to the Crown about the comportment of the captains (Thomaz 1976). As the century wore on, however, the situation tended to deteriorate rather than improve. Simão Botelho, who investigated the situation in Melaka in the early 1550s, declares that 'the greatest merchant is the captain', and accuses them of illegally bringing goods into the town duty-free, thus causing losses to the customs-house (Felner 1868, ii: 29). Some three decades later, the anonymous author of the *Livro das Cidades e Fortalezas* confirms the same picture, adding some further trenchant comments of his own:

> The captains get hold of all [the spices] before they are unloaded, and buy them for a fixed price, and without paying the money immediately, unload them on their own account, and pass them through the customs-house at the low price that has been fixed, and afterwards sell them for double or more of the price that it cost them, and with the money that they make pay back the persons from whom they bought it, and thus, without spending anything from their own purse gain an excessive quantity of money.
>
> (Mendes da Luz 1954: 87)

Besides this monopsonistic practice, the captains of Melaka were also permitted trade of another sort. From the 1570s, at least, when the system of concession-voyages became the rule in the Bay of Bengal and Southeast Asia, the captains of Melaka were given the right *ex officio* to make as many as eighteen of these voyages, to a variety of destinations, ranging from China, to Bengal, Martaban, Kedah, Pahang, Patani, Sunda, Makassar and Borneo.

The implication is thus that the captains of Melaka could, without investing any of their money in trade, still make some 18,000 *cruzados* a

Table 8.5 Concessions held by Melaka's Captains, *c.* 1580

Destination	Value	Auction Price (in cruzados)
Macau	10,000	5–6,000
Bengal	3,000	1,000
Tenasserim	?	200
Martaban	?	200
Ujangselang	?	200
Kedah	?	200
Perak/Bruas	?	700
Pahang	?	500
Patani	?	400
Cambodia	?	500
Blambangan	?	?
Sunda	10,000	5–6,000
Borneo	5–6,000	1,500
Makassar	?	1,000
Timor	?	500
Solor	?	4–500
TOTAL		17,300–19,400

(*Sources*: Mendes da Luz 1954: 137–44; Thomaz 1979)

year from its rents; if we assume that the auction price was roughly one-third of the return if capital was actually invested, the possible profits could be as high as 54,000 *cruzados* a year over the captain's three-year term (Thomaz 1979).

For most of the sixteenth century, the captaincy of Melaka was hence not surprisingly a coveted post, given only to well-connected *fidalgos*, and often seen as a stepping-stone en route to the governorship or viceroyalty of the *Estado da Índia* as a whole. Since by virtue of its distance from Goa, Melaka enjoyed considerable autonomy, the captains of the town often also had experience in running a semi-independent diplomatic policy, in respect not only of Aceh and Johor, but of the trading states of the Malay world – such as Pahang, Patani and Kedah – with which they traded on a regular basis.

The system of concession implied however that both in Melaka, and in other ports where it was applied, such as Nagapattinam on the Coromandel coast, a great potential existed for rivalry between the captain and the *casado* community, which was after all also integrally interested in maritime trade. Captains who were either astute, or had a substantial militarised retinue, could manage this conflict-ridden situation, either by entering into business arrangements with the *casados* (using them as commercial agents, freighting their goods, and so on), or by subjugating them using main force. The captains of Melaka, who had the soldiers of

233

the garrison at their disposal, were relatively better placed in this respect than those of Nagapattinam, of whom Antonio Bocarro wrote in the 1630s, that they were seldom men 'with sufficient resources to be able to force them [the *casados*] to pay him due respect' (Subrahmanyam 1990b: 251). The Nagapattinam captains had two monopoly voyages, respectively to Ujangselang and Bangeri in the Malay peninsula, but it is unlikely that they were always able to make them in the teeth of *casado* opposition. Much depended on their ability to mobilise one or the other group of *casados* in their favour, and often this proved impossible; rather, in the case of Nagapattinam, the *casados* themselves had constituted a sort of unofficial municipal council called the 'Elect of Nagapattinam' (*Os Eleitos de Negapatão*), largely with the intention of negotiating with Goa over the head of the captain. It was thus frequently the case in the 1620s and 1630s that powerful *casado* traders of the port bent the captains to their will, and used them as tools in their trade and factional disputes, rather than the other way around.

It is crucial to bear in mind that the social balance between *casados* and *ministros* tended to be different in towns like Macau, Nagapattinam or Hughli, as opposed to Goa, Hurmuz or Melaka. In these latter settlements, the presence of a relatively large stratum of powerful and well-connected *fidalgos* gave the whole ambience a different flavour, limiting the ability of the *casados* to run the economic life of the town. Settlements such as Cochin represent a halfway-house between the extremes of Goa and Hughli: here a more or less even balance existed between officials and *casados*, so that compromises were the rule. An excellent example of such a compromise emerges from looking at the negotiations of the 1580s over the customs-house reform in Cochin: the Portuguese Crown in this period wished to encroach on the rights of the Cochin rulers, and take over a part of the collection, and also wished to impose taxes that the Cochin *casados* regarded as unreasonably high. A near-rebellion resulted from this, and the *casados* attacked the captain, a fairly important *fidalgo* called D. Jorge de Meneses 'Baroche', in the fort, causing him to appeal to Goa to reconsider. The final arrangement, arrived at nearly three years after the process had been initiated, preserved the privileges of the Cochin *casados* (who it was agreed would pay 3½ per cent import duties and no export duties at the port), but also extended the *Estado*'s fiscal rights at the cost of the Cochin ruler. Significantly, another group whose interests were sacrificed in the process were the so-called *solteiro* traders, who were required to pay higher rates of customs than the *casados* (Subrahmanyam 1990a: 219–20).

A near-rebellion of the sort that occurred in Cochin in 1583–84 seems far less likely in the more state-machinery dominated atmosphere of Goa, but potential for conflict between *casados* and the state still existed. This conflict tended, however, to be channelled into inter-*fidalgo* rivalries, with the *casados* being divided into clients of one or the other *fidalgo* alliances. The picture presented by Diogo do Couto, who suggests an idealised republican solidarity among *casados*, and poses the *fidalgos* as their inveterate rivals and exploiters, is not borne out by an examination of actual conflicts in Goa in the period, including one in 1600, in which Couto himself was marginally involved. Indeed, Couto, who spent the greater part of his life in Asia, was really much too closely involved in events to provide us a coherent and objective critique of social conflicts and their circumstances. One of the great *fidalgo* families of the period, that of the descendants of Vasco da Gama, provided him patronage, and he in turn was peculiarly compromised as a chronicler by his too-close association with D. Vasco's great-grandson, D. Francisco da Gama, who was twice viceroy of the *Estado da Índia*, once in the late 1590s and then again in the mid 1620s.

At the end of Francisco da Gama's first viceroyalty, in 1600, a curious incident occurred that was to prefigure problems faced by other seventeenth-century viceroys, like the Count of Linhares. A statue of Vasco da Gama, which the viceroy had had placed in the Viceroys' Arch at the entrance to the city of Goa, was mutilated and broken up by miscreants one night, and pieces of it strewn in various parts of the city. A lengthy investigation was held into the matter, which was seen as part of a far larger anti-Gama move; at much the same time, the ex-viceroy found an effigy of himself hanging on the yardarm of his ship, and also discovered that all the poultry on board the vessel had been poisoned (Boxer 1985b). Now Couto maintains a discreet silence on many of these issues, but the papers of the investigation referred to above are more explicit. They suggest that the viceroy faced a powerful group of *fidalgos* and *casados* in Goa who were opposed to him, and who included such well-known figures of the day as the superintendent of accounts Francisco Paes, André Furtado de Mendonça (later himself viceroy), and D. Diogo Coutinho, a future captain of Cochin (*Gavetas*, vi: 370–98). A naive interpretation of this incident might see it as one in which the viceroy had fallen foul of a well-entrenched local network of private trade and corruption; but as other records show, Da Gama together with his father-in-law Rui Lourenço de Távora (viceroy of the *Estado* in the 1610s), and his brother D. Luís da Gama, was himself a rather avid private trader, whose second term as viceroy ended in disgrace partly as a result of this fact. While having one set of *fidalgos* and Goa-based settlers ranged against him, Da Gama had links with another group, which included the Augsburg-born Ferdinand Cron, a long-term resident of Goa.

The circumstances of Linhares's viceroyalty, which extended from 1629 to 1635, present a picture that is similar in certain respects. Like the other, Linhares too belonged to a family – the Noronhas – who had a long-standing association with Asia, although the viceroy had never served there himself before 1629. There is little doubt that Linhares, like Da Gama, was a private trader on some scale, and equally all evidence points to the fact that he had close dealings with some of the more important New Christian merchants of Goa in the early 1630s. On the other hand, it is not clear that one can draw the simple conclusion from this that he was an inefficient viceroy, and unlike Da Gama – who returned to Portugal in disgrace, and never quite managed to clear his name – he also made a successful career for almost two decades after his return from Asia to Spain. But nevertheless, while in Goa, Linhares faced a great deal of opposition from a group of *fidalgos*, including the son-in-law of D. Diogo Coutinho (whom we have already encountered), the future viceroy D. Felipe Mascarenhas. The complaints and innuendoes of Linhares's detractors were seized upon by his successor as viceroy Pero da Silva, but had already had ugly consequences before 1635, when charges of favouring certain *fidalgos* – like António Monis Barreto and D. Francisco de Moura – were made by several people against him. The latter half of his viceroyalty also saw a scandal, when an anonymous street placard appeared in Goa, in the form of a judicial charge-sheet against the viceroy, and comprising some twenty-eight rather repetitive accusations, ranging from anti-Christian activities (such as killing the Archbishop of Goa by 'the affronts that he did him'), to trading with the Dutch! The placard ended by stating:

> And having seen all this, it is agreed that the accused (*reo*) Dom Miguel de Noronha is of the Jewish nation, and in all the time of his government was absolute in committing tyrannies, robberies, and using force without any fear of God nor of his laws; we order that he die a natural death ... and that his body be burnt as a Jew. (ANTT, DRI no. 35, f. 346)

It was signed, by way of an ironical gesture, with the names of four of his closest associates in Goa, including D. Francisco de Moura.

Matters came full circle again less than two decades later, this time – again ironically enough – when the viceroy was none other than one of Linhares's great opponents, Felipe Mascarenhas. The symptoms are similar, with one major difference being that D. Felipe had served for many years in Asia before becoming viceroy. But like Da Gama and Linhares, Mascarenhas was a great *fidalgo tratante* – a trading noble – whose fame derived not merely from his valour but his wealth. During two terms as Captain-General of Sri Lanka, he had made a considerable fortune in precious stones, and he counted among his business associates Mir Muhammad Sayyid Ardistani, the Iranian-born minister of the Golconda Sultanate (and later subordinate of the Mughal emperor, Aurangzeb). But Mascarenhas too had powerful opponents in Goa, not only among the nobility and traders, but more ominously within the Society of Jesus (in which too he bears a certain resemblance to Linhares). Within a year of his becoming viceroy, an anonymous letter of accusation was sent to Portugal, in which he was declared guilty of illegal extortions, embezzlement, and numerous other misdemeanours (Winius 1971: 110–12). The next year, 1648, after a dispute between Mascarenhas and a group of *fidalgos* led by D. Brás de Castro, an effigy of the viceroy with a vituperative placard was once again found, this time hanging on the gates of the viceregal residence. D. Felipe acted firmly, arresting two persons, and forcing D. Brás to flee to Bijapur territory. Once again, given the fact of D. Brás's own later comportment, it would be simplistic to see the quarrel as one between viceregal corruption and honest citizenship, or conversely between viceregal efficiency and an entrenched merchant-*fidalgo* conspiracy. Our earlier examples should show that the nature of the problem was structural; struggles of this kind were endemic in the Portuguese Asia of the period.

The cases that we have surveyed so far were usually not resolved; save in the case of Da Gama, all of them petered out, and can thus be interpreted as triumphs of viceregal power. The early 1650s brings us one major exception, which is the closest to a *coup d'état* that one can find in the annals of the seventeenth-century *Estado da Índia*. Again, a key figure is the ubiquitous D. Brás de Castro, now returned from his sojourn in Bijapur, and the incumbent viceroy was D. Vasco Mascarenhas, Count of Óbidos. Óbidos was related to the Dukes of Bragança, and was hence a kinsman of D. João IV himself; this was one of the reasons that influenced the decision to send him out to Asia in 1651–52. One of his first acts after arriving in Goa in September 1652 was to write letters to Portugal bemoaning the incompetence of his predecessor D. Felipe Mascarenhas, and to dissociate his administration from that of the previous three viceroys by the symbolic act of having their portraits taken down from the Hall of Viceroys (Winius 1971: 121–22). But this was not necessarily taken as a positive signal by D. Felipe's erstwhile opponents; the question remained of what Óbidos himself would do. Rumours were spread by persons opposed to him, like the State Councillor António de Sousa Coutinho, that Óbidos was a court-favourite rather than a competent administrator; other State Councillors too seem to have had their reservations about the viceroy. Once again let us stress that it is simplistic to see Óbidos as a reforming viceroy who upset the deep-seated corruption of Goan society; were this the case, we would have to explain why the opposition to him bears such structural similarities to that in the earlier cases we have explored.

The initiative to remove the viceroy came eventually from D. Brás de Castro, now State Councillor. A precedent had already been established in Sri Lanka, where the Captain-General Manuel Mascarenhas Homem had been overthrown by mutiny in November 1652. In the case of Goa, the mutiny came in October 1653, at a time when Óbidos himself was absent from the city. The most detailed account is that of Castro himself, and is automatically suspect for that very reason. He claims that an amorphous mob, tired of Óbidos's 'bad government', forced the City Council and State Councillors to throw out the viceroy; since Castro was the oldest Councillor, he was chosen as successor. It seems clear from other papers, however, that Castro and José de Chaves Sotomaior (the Secretary of the *Conselho do Estado*) had at least some complicity in the matter; and in fact Castro signed the order imprisoning Óbidos (though once again later pleaded that he had been coerced into it). Castro continued to hold power for nearly two years, and it was only in August 1655 that a new viceroy, the Count of Sarzedas, arrived from Lisbon.

To sum up then, Portuguese Asian society in centres such as Goa had its own hierarchy and structures of patronage. Great *fidalgos* maintained entourages of soldiers, taking them along when appointed to some post, and providing for their upkeep in between stints of government employment. Equally, these *fidalgos* were linked to *casado* traders for reasons of business, as well as state finance; after all, the ideal comportment of the *fidalgo* of the period was considered to stem from generosity (here, the 'open house' policy by which indigent *soldados* were fed at the *fidalgo*'s 'table' is crucial), but also from wealth and valour. Being as they often were the second sons of landed nobility, it was understood that the *fidalgo* sent out to Asia had to make his fortune to set up his own patrimony in Portugal. This was understood as much by these nobles as by the viceroys (who after all belonged to roughly the same class), and explains why some twenty or thirty *fidalgos* made their way to Asia each year in the late sixteenth century, a number that exceeded what was needed to man the major military commands there (Cruz 1989). However, once in Asia inter-clan and factional rivalry made itself felt, and was further fuelled by tensions and resentments which existed amongst the *casados* themselves. Any newly arrived viceroy thus had to first plumb, and then navigate, waters that were strewn with the perils of this endemic factionalism; some survived, others barely made it to the end of their terms, and at least one – Óbidos – failed to reach shore safely.

'PORTUGUESE' AND 'FOREIGNER'

From its very inception, the Portuguese enterprise in Asia had witnessed the participation of a number of individuals and groups coming from Europe, but who were not themselves Portuguese. One rather celebrated set was of the Florentines, whose participation was marked from the very first voyages to Asia, and who maintained a particularly high profile in the years of Albuquerque and his immediate successors. The reason for their participation was simple: a Florentine colony already existed in Lisbon from the early fifteenth century, and these merchants were not in the least averse to participating in a trade that undermined the economy of Venice, namely the trade on the Cape route. Besides, the Tuscan economy itself was in the early sixteenth century not in a particularly expansive phase, and it was logical for the impoverished offspring of mercantile families to be sent to Asia – even as the Portuguese themselves did with their own younger sons. Another group with a precocious interest in Portuguese Asian commercial network were the south Germans, from towns such as Augsburg, who also sent out representatives to Cochin and other centres, already in the first decade of the Portuguese presence there.

While some of these Italians and Middle Europeans remained private traders and agents of principals in Europe, others became employees of the *Estado da Índia* even in these early years. An instructive instance is that of a certain Francesco di Parigi Corbinelli, son-in-law of the well-known financier and merchant Bartolomeo Marchionni. Corbinelli was born in Florence in 1466, and moved his operations to Portugal in the late 1490s, apparently motivated by a desire to participate in the sugar trade from the Atlantic islands. He then went on to enlarge his operations, engaged in the trade to West Africa, and then in the early sixteenth century himself travelled to Asia. In 1508–09, he is to be encountered at Cochin as the part-owner of the ship *Santiago*, which later returned to Portugal in 1510. On Corbinelli's return to India, probably at the end of 1510, Albuquerque appointed him the first factor of Goa, a post in which he served till the governor's death. He then returned to Europe, but was back in Goa by 1517, was once again appointed factor of Goa, and continued to hold the post to the end of 1521. Francesco's son Parigi Corbinelli remained in Asia in the 1510 and 1520s, as ship's captain on a number of voyages concerning which we have some information; Francesco Corbinelli himself seems to have died in Asia in 1524–25 (Aubin 1988; Rau 1974). Again Giovanni da Empoli, also a Florentine merchant of the same epoch, served briefly as Portuguese factor at Pasai in north Sumatra, and played a role in early Portuguese trading relations with Bengal (Bouchon and Thomaz 1988). The presence of these Italians is important because it demonstrates that despite the rather early sense of Portugal as a nation, Portuguese expansion in Asia also served as a conduit for other Europeans to operate east of the Cape of Good Hope. Some of these, like Piero di Andrea Strozzi (1483–1522), came out to Asia with the avowed intention of making a quick fortune from trading in spices and precious stones, rather than an overseas career. As the sixteenth century wore on, others came with far more long-term intentions, and even managed at times to put them into practice (Spallanzani 1985).

Such persons were, however, not always from the Italian city-states. In the late sixteenth century, besides the Florentine Filippo Sassetti, who spent much of the 1580s in Goa and then Cochin (where he died in 1588), and Nicolau Pietro Cuccino, a rather shadowy figure who is, like Sassetti, associated with pepper procurement in south-western India, there were several important Flemish and south German traders in Goa and elsewhere in the *Estado*. One of these was the Augsburger Ferdinand Cron (1559–1637), who arrived in Goa in 1587 as agent for the German banking houses of Welser and Fugger, and remained there till 1624. Cron was very well-connected indeed, not only in Germany, but in Antwerp, Lisbon and Madrid. His patrons included the viceroys Manuel de Sousa Coutinho, Rui Lourenço de Távora, and especially D. Francisco da Gama, whose business affairs in Asia Cron handled for nearly two decades (between Da Gama's departure from Goa in 1600, and his return in the 1620s). The Spanish Queen Dona Margarida also appointed Cron her agent in Asia for certain purposes, in particular for raising resources for her favourite project – the construction of the Monastery of Encarnación in Madrid. Cron numbered among his other close associates the New Christian *vedor da fazenda* Garcia de Melo, and appears to have been well-connected with prominent New Christian merchants in Goa in the 1610s and early 1620s. We note too that he owned a rural property (*quinta*) in Goa, was involved in jewel-trading, and was also a speculator in government bonds (*juros*) (Kellenbenz 1963).

Broadly contemporary to Cron were the Flemish brothers Jacques and Joseph van de Coutere, natives of the celebrated merchant-city of Bruges. Arriving in Asia in 1592, ostensibly as *soldados*, the Coutere brothers were initially patronised at Goa by a certain Sebastião Pinto de Frexos. Joseph was married about this time to a Maria Gomes, to whose sister (Catarina do Couto) Jacques was married nearly ten years later, in 1603. In the 1590s, while Joseph remained in Goa, Jacques's commercial interests took him to Southeast Asia, where he traded at Melaka, Pahang, Manila, Johor, Ayuthia and elsewhere. In 1603, he returned to Goa, and became increasingly engaged in the diamond trade in Bijapur, and also traded as far inland as the Mughal court of Agra. In later years, Jacques van de Coutere made at least two trips to Europe via the overland route through the Ottoman Empire and the Mediterranean, and a third brother, Paulus, also came from Europe to settle in Goa in these years. Fluent in Spanish and Portuguese, Jacques van de Coutere has left behind a picaresque (and at times, therefore, quite improbable) memoir of his life and times in Asia, which is the principal source of information about him. His Asia is a world inhabited by villains, tricksters and untrustworthy Asian potentates, and we shall return to his portrayal of the frontier regions of Portuguese Asia in the following chapter (Stols and Verberckmoes 1988).

The position of men like Cron and the Couteres was rendered somewhat insecure in the early seventeenth century on account of a curious xenophobia, wherein a attempt was made in Portuguese Asia to seek out and get rid of 'foreigners' (*estrangeiros*). There is a sense in which the timing of this move is ironical, since the rulers of Portugal in this period were themselves Spaniards; Cron and the Couteres were both natives of the Habsburg dominions if not of Portugal. This xenophobia took the legal form of an order, dated April 1605, which decreed the expulsion of 'all the foreigners who live and may be resident or present in the parts of India, and in Brazil, Guinea, the islands of São Tomé, and Cape Verde, and in the islands of the Açores and Madeira' (APO, vi: 796–98). Ostensibly directed at Dutch spies resident in Portuguese overseas territories, this order was not wholly illogical. After all, the major source of information on Portuguese Asia that the Dutch had in the early seventeenth was the *Itinerario* of Jan Huyghen van Linschoten, whose information had been collected while he was employed in the ecclesiastical establishment at Goa. Besides, the order was not applied indiscriminately; exceptions were made, and men like Cron were granted special permission to stay on.

However, the seeds of trouble had been sown for these 'foreigners', despite their fluency in Portuguese, and marriage to Portuguese women in Asia. Already in 1606, Joseph van de Coutere was under suspicion of being a Dutch spy, and his brother Jacques's activities in Bijapur and Agra only increased this suspicion. By the early 1620s, orders were sent out for their expulsion, and in 1623 they were sent back to Lisbon under a cloud. Ferdinand Cron's political connections did not protect him for much longer, and in fact he fell victim to the anti-viceregal sentiment in Goa in these years (in view of his too-close association with D. Francisco da Gama). By 1625, both he and the van de Coutere brothers were thus back in Iberia, where their fortunes, however, revived. By lobbying the Madrid court, and ingratiating himself with the Count-Duke of Olivares, Cron ended his days in the benign shadow of the Habsburg court as a member of the Order of Christ. Three years after Cron's death in 1637, Jacques van de Coutere – now member of the Order of Santiago – died in Saragossa, after settling scores with a number of his erstwhile commercial rivals in Goa (whom he denounced to the Inquisition), and having written not only his memoirs but also a reform-tract on how to 'remedy' the *Estado da Índia*.

RISE OF THE *SOLTEIRO*

Thus, as attacks by the Dutch increased and the losses in the *Estado* began to mount, the response was – not unexpectedly – to point fingers at 'foreigners', both among the traders and even within the Church hierarchy. Even viceroy Linhares, when hard-pressed to explain why in

241

the early 1630s the area of south-eastern India around Tuticorin saw such frequent troubles, claimed that it was because 'the south is far and the government and monarchy of it is in the hands of foreigners, Italians and French', meaning of course the fathers of the Society of Jesus. At the same time, internal intolerance of New Christians and crypto-Jews increased in the 1630s and 1640s, and this is not only reflected in an increase in the activities of the Inquisition in this period. It was in the 1640s that some of the *casados* of Cochin almost caused a break in the *Estado*'s relations with the Cochin ruler, by assassinating his close associate, the Jewish trader Samuel Castiel (Subrahmanyam 1990a: 337). Castiel had in the late 1610s been instrumental in convincing the chronicler António Bocarro, then a *casado* in Cochin, to return to Judaism, as Bocarro confessed to Inquisitors a few years later (Boxer 1985a, x: 204). At the time, his activities were complained about; two decades later, more stern action was taken, a measure of the intolerance of the times.

It is this growing intolerance in Goa and elsewhere that provides a part of the background to the rise of the *solteiro* merchant in the middle decades of the seventeenth century. The *solteiro*, or bachelor, was someone who was usually counterposed to the *casado*; this was not a question of marital status in the vulgar sense, but rather a question of being a free-wheeling trader instead of having a fixed settlement. It is useful to recall that from 1600, the privileges of *casado* status were gradually being whittled away. The major *casado* institutions like the *Misericórdia* were being milked by the *Estado da Índia*, which took forced loans from them to finance military expeditions, and more often than not did not pay them back. The papers of the 1630s and 1640s are full of complaints from the *casados* of settlements such as Chaul, Goa and Cochin (which were reckoned to be three of the more prosperous *casado* nuclei) complaining of this; in these years, the *casados* also learnt to advertise their poverty in the most extravagant terms, in order to escape the fisc (Subrahmanyam 1990a: 228–31). Still another option, perhaps a sounder one in the medium term, was to opt out of *casado* status altogether. Thus, writing of Macau in the 1630s, the chronicler António Bocarro presents the following picture:

> This city has, besides this, many Portuguese mariners, pilots and ship-masters, many of them *casados* in Portugal, others *solteiros*, who travel in the trading-voyages to Japan, Manila, Solor, Makassar, Cochin-China, of these there are more than one hundred and fifty, and some have large fortunes of over 50,000 *xerafins*, who on no account wish to move to Goa, for fear of falling into the hands of justice for some crime they have committed, or of the viceroys for the service of the King, and there are also many very rich *solteiro* merchants, in whom the same sentiments dwell. (Bocarro, 1937–38, ii: 33)

The quintessential *solteiro* entrepreneur of these years is a certain Francisco Vieira de Figueiredo, whose activities moved from Nagapattinam – where he was in the 1630s – to the Sulawesi port of

Makassar, and eventually to the Lesser Sunda Islands, where he died in either 1667 or early 1668. Born in the early years of the seventeenth century in Azambujal, in the province of Estremadura, Vieira appears to have arrived in Asia in the early 1620s, probably as a *soldado*. His social origins were humble; his father was a stone-mason, and this was later raised as an objection to his being admitted to the Order of Christ. By the early 1630s, Vieira was a *casado* of Nagapattinam, where – it was reported by viceroy Linhares – 'he has more dealings with the Gentiles than with the Christians' (Boxer 1967: 2). From Nagapattinam, he traded to Melaka and Manila, and was sufficiently well thought of in the Philippines to be sent as Manila's envoy to Cambodia in the early 1640s.

It was in these years that Vieira decided to shift his operations to Makassar, which had since the first decade of the seventeenth century emerged as a major centre of intra-Asian trade in eastern Indonesia. The choice is significant, for while Makassar had a large Portuguese settlement, it was really a centre of *Asian* trade, and an important node of political power in the area. Its ruler Ala-ud-din (r. 1593–1637), though a convert to Islam in around 1605, nevertheless tolerated Christianity and spoke Portuguese, as did his successors and their ministers. It was in the shadow of these rulers that Vieira initially operated, using the fact that the Dutch had to observe at least some diplomatic niceties while dealing with someone who claimed to be the envoy of these potentates. Thus, in the early 1640s the VOC had to concede passes for Vieira's ships to trade to Solor and Timor, and later, in 1647, even allowed him to pass through Batavia *en route* to Goa, where he very probably went as envoy of the Sultan Muhammad Said, to the viceroy Felipe Mascarenhas. The most extraordinary aspect of Vieira de Figueiredo's activity in these years is how many hats he was able to wear all at once. In 1647 and again in 1648, he was accredited envoy-at-large of the Sultan of Makassar, but in the latter year, when he put in an appearance at Banten and Batavia, he was *also* envoy from the viceroy at Goa. Some years later, in 1652, he returned to Makassar from Coromandel, claiming to be the envoy of Mir Muhammad Sayyid Ardistani, *mir jumla* and minister of the Sultanate of Golconda. The Dutch, not wholly averse to dealing with him in these roles in the late 1640s and early 1650s, even sold him a ship in 1649–50 which became a part of his fleet of vessels, from which we are aware of the names of at least three in about 1650: *Nazaré*, *Penha de França*, and *São João Baptista*.

It is also curious that Vieira, despite his dubious status as an ex-*casado*, who had left for greener pastures, nevertheless maintained almost uniformly good relations with a succession of governors and viceroys at Goa in the 1640s and 1650s. In this he appears a precursor of men like Manuel Teixeira Pinto, whose activities at Porto Novo and São Tomé in the 1680s have already been discussed in an earlier chapter. In the latter half of the seventeenth century, the *Estado*'s officials had little choice in the matter; any Portuguese who was willing to deal with them had to be dealt with, at his own terms if necessary. Vieira's main problems stemmed therefore not from Portuguese officialdom, which was willing to shower him with honours and compliments, but from the Dutch Company. While in the late 1640s, he received a relatively good reception in Batavia, the relationship was too good to last. The expiry of the Luso-Dutch truce in 1652 meant that the VOC declared open season on Vieira's shipping, despite his association with various Asian potentates. In July 1652, two of his vessels were captured en route from Makassar to Masulipatnam, off Japara on the north coast of Java, and he himself barely escaped falling into Dutch hands. Making his way back to Makassar, he struck back at the Dutch by persuading the Sultan (who for his own reasons was anyway interested in attacking the VOC) to foment a war in Ambon, the chief clove-producing centre for the Dutch Company. Hostilities once begun spread to Makassar itself, which the Dutch blockaded, forcing the new young Sultan Hasanuddin to sue for peace in February 1656.

The Dutch now re-established themselves in Makassar, much to Vieira's discomfort and dismay, as he wrote to Goa in June 1656.

> The Hollanders treat me very courteously and they are very anxious for closer contacts. I am equally polite to them, but very cautious, since I have been warned by well-informed persons in Jacatra not to trust them on any account, and that I should be careful how I drink toasts with them – though I don't drink wine myself. I have also been warned that if the ambassador invites me aboard his ship, I should not go; and this is what I have done, as he asked me and I declined. (Boxer 1967: 19)

He also took measures to continue encouraging anti-Dutch activity in the area, organising, in the words of the junta of governors at Goa in 1658, 'a fleet of galleys which harass the small Dutch ships'. These activities, and the policies of the Makassar rulers themselves, when combined with the monopsonistic claims of the Dutch Company, made for an explosive brew. In June 1660, war was resumed, and the VOC sent a fleet to Makassar, threatening to devastate the town, and forcing a treaty on Hasanuddin by which he was asked to have all the Portuguese leave Makassar. Vieira now played for time, offered the Dutch some trade goods as a sop, and managed to stay on in Makassar in the years 1661–64, on time borrowed from the Dutch Governor-General Joan Maetsuycker. Goa was, naturally enough, anxious for him to stay on, representing as he did a thorn in the flesh of the Dutch, maintained at little or no cost to the *Estado*. To keep him content, the Portuguese Crown in 1664 finally confirmed him in his nomination to the Order of Christ, at the same time asking him to stay on the region. But finally in 1665, the Dutch decided that they had given him enough grace; in early March, he was asked to leave for Larantuka in the Lesser Sunda Islands, where he died two years later.

While there is little doubt that Francisco Vieira de Figueiredo was a man of considerable resources, and political skills, we note that the battle he fought was effectively a losing one. If the *casado*'s trade was declining in this period therefore, it might seem that the *solteiro* did little better. There is a sense in which this is true, but it is equally apparent that Vieira's ability to survive and prosper as long as he did stemmed fundamentally from his ambiguous status; while a devout Catholic, it is not quite so obvious that he was a 'loyal' Portuguese. In his dealings with the Dutch in the years 1662–64, he was after all trading with an enemy of the Portuguese Crown, something that he never could have done while based at an official settlement of the *Estado da Índia*. Vieira's career also pointed the way for future Portuguese traders, whether at Macau or Porto Novo, showing them that a too-close association with the *Estado* was not beneficial in this period. Rather the state had to be used opportunistically by the individual, for benefices, and resources, as also diplomatic privileges – when possible. It was a lesson learnt not only by the Portuguese but by private Englishmen, who in the latter half of the seventeenth century began to make their presence felt in the trade of the Bay of Bengal and Southeast Asia. Attaching themselves when convenient to the English Company, using Company ships and warehouses, entrepreneurs such as William Jearsey, Samuel White and others made a career in the 1670s and 1680s that has a remarkable resemblance to that of Vieira. This was surely no coincidence.

THE IMPACT ON PORTUGAL

Towards the end of his life, we are aware that Francisco Vieira de Figueiredo wished to return to Portugal, together with his second wife Catarina de Noronha, and that he had asked for and received the Crown's permission to do so. In his desire to return, he was surely not unique, for very few of the Portuguese who went out to Asia in the sixteenth and seventeenth centuries seem to have done so with the intention of settling down there. The second generation, the *indiáticos* and *mestiços*, were a somewhat different story, and it is from them that the myth of the Portuguese, who once in Asia had no desire to return to Portugal, was built. In this connection, historians are fond of quoting a statement of the Dutch Governor-General Antonio van Diemen, from 1638. He wrote:

> The greatest number of the Portuguese settlers hold India to be their
> fatherland, thinking no more of Portugal. They trade thither little or nothing,
> living and enriching themselves out of the treasures of India, as though they
> were natives, and knew no other fatherland.   (Boxer 1969c)

The limited insights we have into the mentality and psychological makeup of most Portuguese who arrived in Asia suggest, on the contrary, that relatively few were able to break away from the value-system of the peninsula; even when mercenaries, they hankered after the signs of social advancement that they recognised, such as membership in the military orders, titles in the nobility, and so on. Equally, the figure of the *retornado*, the returnee from Asia, who brought back a fortune, was an important one, as it held out hope in an era when inflation and economic instability (as well as later Habsburg occupation) were sources of discontent in Portugal, to the extent that some contemporaries even felt that the El-Dorado like magnetism of Asia would depopulate Portugal and render her weak. In the sixteenth century, the poet Sá de Miranda was to write:

> Castile I do not fear,
> whence war yet raises not its head,
> but it's Lisbon that I dread;
> her cinnamon smell draws men near,
> and from the kingdom they are led.   (Thomaz 1989c: 390)

Now the returns to the Crown itself from Asia were quite substantial up to the 1620s, if one takes trade on the Cape route alone. Table 8.6 shows figures collated by V.M. Godinho.

Table 8.6   Asia in Portuguese state revenues (*mil reis*)

Sources	1588		1607		1619	
Cape route	191,801	(17.3)	234,360	(16.3)	234,360	(15.0)
Estado da Índia	288,942	(26.0)	355,560	(24.7)	412,500	(26.5)
Atlantic empire	143,920	(13.0)	164,120	(11.4)	173,821	(11.2)
Other	485,482	(43.7)	685,038	(47.6)	735,836	(47.3)
TOTAL	1,110,145		1,439,078		1,556,517	

(Figures in brackets represent percentage shares)

(*Source*: Godinho 1968: 27–63)

Of course, the mere consideration of revenue figures does not tell the whole of the story. The question of the surplus (*saldo*) on each of these accounts should also be taken into consideration, but it could be argued that the total revenue figures are of greater relevance – for the major item of expenditure (salaries and commuted benefices) was equally the major means by which the Crown attached people to itself. A more substantive objection lies elsewhere. Was the return to Portugal of having an Asian empire mainly mediated through returns to the Crown? It would appear that, on the contrary, returns on private account were far more important than returns to the Crown. Not only this: there is some reason to believe

246

that while not monopolised by a single social group, these private returns were nevertheless highly unevenly distributed.

The most conspicuous gainers were the *fidalgos*, many of whom returned to Portugal, as the author of the *Livro das cidades e fortalezas* (1582) informs us, to found 'most noble houses', and 'very large estates (*morgadios*)'. This implies, of course, that they did not already have such houses and estates, which could be the case only if they were younger sons, or illegitimate offspring. The normal career for the oldest son, the sole heir to the parental estate in Portuguese law, was to remain in Portugal, or at best to serve one three-year term in North Africa. If such heirs to great estates went to Asia, it was as viceroys or governors (as we see in the case of Linhares or Vidigueira), rather than as vulnerable military commanders. And even they sought to enlarge their fortunes while in Asia, with Linhares for example bringing back a considerable sum in jewels on his return in the mid-1630s. The careers of the others – the younger sons and illegitimate children – took on a different complexion: typically, it began with a phase of subordinate service, or a captaincy in an armada, then went on (after the 'service papers' of the first phase had been presented and scrutinised) to posts on land (such as the captaincies of forts), and finally culminated in a major position in the Goa administration, perhaps the governorship itself, or the post of Councillor of State (Cruz 1989). In the second phase, concession-voyages were typically lobbied for, and in the third stage trade was conducted through agents among the *casados*, or Asian traders. If the *fidalgo* did not die in mid-career (as happened more often than not), he could hope at the end of it all to return to Portugal in a comfortable financial position, unless, that is, factional rivalry at the court caused his affairs to come under scrutiny.

The *fidalgos* were not the only gainers though. Merchants, whether Old Christian, New Christian or 'foreign', could and did return from Asia with fortunes, often seeking to buy into the lower echelons of the nobility on that basis. We may cite the example of Duarte Gomes Solis (1561–1630), a New Christian who made two voyages to Asia, the first from 1586 to 1591, the second from 1594 to 1601. By the time of his return the second time, Solis had a substantial investment in government bonds (*juros*) alone, and married at the age of forty the daughter of a New Christian magnate, Heitor Mendes de Brito. Here too, Solis is a typical *retornado* in this respect, for such men usually married late, and as a consequence were often survived by their much younger wives. Also typical is the manner in which he managed in the 1620s to ingratiate himself with the Count-Duke of Olivares, proffering advice on the India trade, and being made *fidalgo* of the royal household in the mid 1620s (Calvet de Magalhães 1966).

From the viewpoint of Portuguese society therefore, the Asian empire was a stabilising factor, permitting a certain limited upward mobility to a few, but for the most part shoring up the economic and social power of the *fidalguia*, while at the same time providing a safety valve, to limit conflicts that might otherwise have taken place within that class. To Marxist-influenced writers, this has suggested that expansion into Asia stunted Portuguese development, by reinforcing seigneurial institutions rather than the power of the urban bourgeoisie (Godinho 1968: 266–68). The model that such writers have in mind is, in a sense, similar to that of the so-called 'refeudalisation' of Eastern Europe in this period, with the distinction that here it is not external trade alone but remittances from an external sphere (Asia, and later Brazil) that are seen as shoring up the seigneurial order (Hanson 1981). Yet we are aware that a similar flow of remittances, revenues and private fortunes of 'Nabobs' accompanied the growth in England in the late eighteenth century of manufacturing industry, even if it did not actually fuel it (as was once supposed). Thus, the Asian empire alone (or even overseas expansion in its totality) cannot be seen as a key to Portugal's later 'underdevelopment', the analysis of which requires an understanding of a complex of locational, political, military and resource-base related matters. These are themes to which we shall return in our concluding chapter.

CHAPTER NINE

Portuguese Asian Society II: The Frontier and Beyond

The cities, official settlements and garrisons of the *Estado da Índia* no doubt account for the most visible part of the Portuguese presence in Asia. But there was also another presence, more subtle, all-pervading and difficult to pin down than that of the *casados*, soldiers and officials – whether secular or religious. This other aspect to Portuguese Asian society is made up of footloose and free-wheeling traders and mercenaries, renegades, but also extends into a grey area of Lusitanised communities, which may or may not have had any relationship in terms of descent to the Portuguese in Asia. A facile approach to this underside of the Portuguese presence in Asia would be to dismiss it as little more than a generalisation of the phenomenon later celebrated by Joseph Conrad in *Lord Jim*: of the European 'going native'. It is the contention in this chapter that such an approach is false, because it imposes on the sixteenth and seventeenth centuries the judgements and categories of a later period, judgements that were crucially related to changed attitudes towards miscegenation, and the 'proper' place of the European in Asia. The very fluidity of the frontier between the official and unofficial part of the Portuguese presence in Asia is an important feature, and related to the character of the political systems that they encountered there between 1500 and 1700.

RENEGADES AND REBELS

A particularly important, but also rather neglected, set of figures in this regard are the renegades (*arrenegados*), who are also sometimes rather confusingly referred to by contemporaries simply as 'rebels' (*alevantados*). By and large however, the term renegade, unlike rebel or mercenary, was reserved for Portuguese who converted to Islam and who, furthermore, chose to serve a Muslim ruler. As a phenomenon, this was already familiar to the Portuguese from their fifteenth-century experience in North Africa, where it was not unknown for soldiers to desert their garrisons for the 'other side'. During the sixteenth century, in particular, the renegade was a quite common figure in Portuguese Asia, but despite this we possess biographical details concerning a mere handful. These may be divided into categories on the basis of two principles: the reasons for turning renegade, and the social position of those who did so. These two features were naturally related: very often, those who turned renegade did so because they either had been convicted of some crime, or were in imminent danger of being sentenced or charged. On the other hand, some renegades turned coat (and religion) by choice, to advance themselves in their political and financial ambitions. Chroniclers such as Barros, while speaking of the latter type, are categorical in describing them as 'valiant men, but weak in their faith'.

It is a curious fact that the chronicles of the sixteenth century reveal a certain ambiguity in the Portuguese attitude towards these renegades. Rather than simple condemnation, what is often encountered from the pens of Correia, Couto or even Barros is condemnation tempered with admiration; the fact that the renegades chosen by them were usually men who succeeded in advancing themselves in the alternative system they chose may partly account for this. It is only rarely that one encounters a description that contains pure contempt; one exception is that in the late sixteenth-century *Primor e Honra da vida soldadesca no Estado da Índia* ('The excellence and honour of the soldier's life in the Estado da Índia'):

> In human terms [the renegades] lose their identity as
> Iberians, the envy of the world, and the people most gifted
> with understanding, and become infidels, without good faith,
> reason or justice .... Further they lose the acquaintance of
> their dear fatherland and the companionship of kinsmen,
> friends and compatriots to go off to foreign countries where
> they know no one and are forced to mix with barbarians whose
> customs and speech are quite different from our own. They lose
> their costume and social customs (*pollícia*), which are the
> best in the world, to dress in a hanged man's shroud and to
> wear a hundred lengths (*varas*) of cloth on their heads, and on
> their feet great clogs (*sapatões*) or two bits of leather in
> place of proper boots   (Bury 1975: 247–48).

Perhaps the earliest example we have in Asia of a celebrated Portuguese renegade, and one moreover who managed to rehabilitate himself in the eyes of officialdom in the last years of his career, is João Machado, a native of Braga, who was sent out in Cabral's fleet as a *degredado* (convict-exile), on charges of stealing and sexual misdemeanour with an abbot's niece. In these years, it was common for convicts to be used as emissaries and in advance-parties, to scout out the lay of the land before less expendable members of the expedition were sent out. Machado was hence left on the coast of East Africa with a companion by Cabral, with instructions to gather information about Ethiopia and its fabled ruler, Prester John. Instead, he left his companion and boarded a Gujarati trading vessel, and arrived on the Indian west coast in the early years of the sixteenth century. Machado's activities over the next few years are obscure, but it would appear that he moved from Gujarat to the Deccan soon after his arrival in India, and entered the service of Yusuf Adil Khan at Bijapur. It was an opportune moment for him to do so; the Bijapur court was anxious for information concerning the Portuguese, and Machado was a man who could provide it. The chroniclers are discreet on the details of his conversion to Islam: Barros does not even mention it, but the less staid Correia hints strongly at the possibility.

The renegade's career soon took on some further twists and turns. Machado was a member of the entourage of a certain Rustam Khan, a Bijapuri noble who was sent to besiege Goa in 1511, after it had fallen to the Portuguese in November 1510. From early on in the engagement, Machado, who was head of the *firangiyan* (Franks) on the Adil Shahi side, displayed a strong desire to return to the fold, and even passed strategic information on to Albuquerque in a bid to ingratiate himself. He finally turned coat again though only in late 1511, at a time when Goa was under close siege, and other Portuguese from the garrison (including some *fidalgos*) had begun to desert to him; the choice of moment thus helped restore his credibility. As Albuquerque himself reports the matter, in a letter of April 1512 to D. Manuel:

> After this Pularcam left, he was killed with poison, and Ruztalcam remained here; Joham Machado came here with him and came over to us at a time when he was very necessary to us for our assistance, and he brought nine or ten Christians who had been captured with Fernam Jacome.   (CAA, i: 43)

In view of this, he was also given a dowry, for his marriage with a 'native woman' (*molher da terra*) in December 1512, in a grant where he is termed 'Joham Machado who was a Turk and has now become a Christian' (CAA, v: 303). The dowry was lower than the usual one given to *casados* in the period, suggesting that Albuquerque believed him already to be a man of some resources. We also note that the governor had rapidly come to trust Machado, sending him back to Rustam Khan within a year of his return, as an envoy, to negotiate the latter's withdrawal from Goa, and favoured him in other ways as well. Thus, when Machado returned to Lisbon in 1513 to petition the Manueline court for not only a pardon, but rewards for his services, he was given a liberty-chest on the ship for his goods, which elicited complaints from others. Albuquerque's justification, in a letter to D. Manuel of October 1514, is a masterpiece of diplomacy.

> And, Senhor, as for the cargo of Joham Machado, I gave him that place to load his goods on account of your order, because Your Highness wrote to me that I should give something from your treasury to those who were with the Moors, in order that they should return to the Faith of Our Lord; and Joham Machado returned at the time of greatest danger for Goa, and brought eight or nine with him, lent his money to the factory for the necessities that there were, came forward at a time when he did you service, and for all these respects and since Your Highness ordered me so, I gave him a chance to load up this half-chamber, and to the others I gave nothing.　　(CAA, i: 309)

On his return from Portugal in 1515, Machado was confirmed as *shahbandar* of the port of Goa as well as *tanadar-mór*, a post that he had already held since 1513; he also appears to have served in the same year as part of the embassy to the Safavid Shah Ismail. However, his career was cut short before he could accumulate further triumphs, when he was killed in a cavalry skirmish in 1517–18, ironically enough with the very Adil Shahi forces of which he had once been a member.

In the fact that he was able to rehabilitate himself, Machado represents a very unusual case. Far more severe punishment was handed out to other renegades, despite orders from D. Manuel that they be treated leniently, and be given 'security and pardon' so that they might return. As Albuquerque wrote sarcastically in 1512, if such a policy were made public, more men 'will very shamelessly go and come by this route, the road to the Moors' (CAA, i: 94). Late that year, therefore, when negotiating with Rustam Khan for his withdrawal from Goa, he insisted that the former hand over to him all the renegades who were in his force, so that they could be dealt with. He then wrote:

> I granted the renegades their lives at the request of Ruztalcan, and had them damaged in their members, and maimed, and mutilated, and cut their ears off, as a shock and to remind them of the treason and evil that they had committed.　　(CAA, i: 115–16)

One of those so treated was a *fidalgo*, Fernão Lopes, who returned in 1512 after deserting to the Adil Shah the previous year, and was punished by having a hand and a foot severed, and being exiled to St. Helena in the Atlantic. Of course, most renegades never returned at all, and hence did not have to face such consequences. Two of them are to be found in Bengal in 1521, as part of the locally-resident Portuguese population, and these are Martim de Lucena and João de Borba, who were associated with the pseudo-embassy mounted that year to the Husain Shahi court of Gaur by Cristôvão Jusarte and Rafael Perestrelo. The interpreter of the official, and rival, embassy sent by Goa, that of António de Brito and Diogo Pereira, devotes some attention in his account to Lucena and Borba, particularly the former, whom he regarded with a mixture of fascination and loathing. His first meeting with Lucena has him venturing the following description:

> On that very day, I ran into Martim de Lucena, whom I did not recognise because he came dressed as a Moor; his beard and head shaved, a hood and toque on his head, and his moustaches done up, so that he seemed more Mafamede than the mummy (*çancarrão*) itself. And after I was told he was Portuguese, I went up to him, while he was mounted on a nag, and when I spoke to him he stopped, and made out that he was happy to see me.
>
> (Bouchon and Thomaz 1988: 229–30)

The rather odd reference to the 'mummy' here stemmed from a popular Portuguese belief of the period that the Ka'aba contained Muhammad's mummy, and that this was the reason the Hajj was made by Muslims. Our narrator, the interpreter, seems to suggest with this comparison that the Portuguese renegade he encountered was simply play-acting. Now it is true that with men like Lucena, who were *fidalgos* and associated with the royal household, the decision to Islamise was from choice rather than compulsion. He appears to have been the only one of his family, which was very probably of Andalusian origin, and became a part of the Portuguese service-nobility from the second quarter of the fifteenth century, to come to India in the first half of the sixteenth century; his arrival in 1515 coincided with the shift in policy towards private trade under Lopo Soares de Albergaria. It is of some significance that he is not to be encountered in later chronicles, suggesting that he chose the renegade's career on a long-term basis.

The same is possibly true of João de Borba, who is referred to in 1521 though not as a renegade but as a mercenary, a '*chatim*'. While his earlier Asian career, in Goa, Pasai, and Maskat, can be traced, before his arrival in Bengal, Borba too disappears after 1521. This is not true of Cristóvão Jusarte, who – despite his protestations to the Gaur court that he was in fact a Muslim, unlike the members of the official embassy – did return to the Indian west coast in all probability by 1522.

A slightly later case, and an instructive one also, is that of Gonçalo Vaz Coutinho, a *fidalgo* who in the early 1540s was imprisoned in the prison (*tronco*) of Goa on a murder charge, but who managed to escape and flee the city. Coutinho, who is mentioned several times in Fernão Mendes Pinto's *Peregrinação*, was a powerful and well-connected man, and owned several houses and palm-groves in Goa; he was able therefore to buy and outfit a vessel, with which he set out on a privateering expedition to the Bay of Bengal. There are suggestions, moreover, in Gaspar Correia's *Lendas*, that various Portuguese officials connived with Coutinho; on his way to the Bay of Bengal, for instance, he borrowed artillery from the ostensibly reluctant captain of the pearl-fishery, João Fernandes Correa, against a bond – this despite his status as an escaped criminal. After a brief spell at Nagapattinam, Coutinho made his way with a fleet of six *fustas*, and one hundred and sixty arquebusiers, to lower Burma, where he went on to attack shipping and enrich himself. Thereafter, he returned to Sri Lanka, petitioned Goa from there for a pardon, and on being turned down, went on to attack Muslim-owned ships in the Maldives.

Coutinho's main hope apparently lay with Martim Afonso de Sousa, whom he expected to come to Asia in a position of power, and who Correia claims was 'a great friend of his'. On Sousa's becoming Governor of the *Estado* in 1542, Coutinho returned to Goa, liquidated his belongings there, and taking his wife and children with him, fled to Bijapur territory, where he converted to Islam. In 1543, Sousa suggested that he would be pardoned if he accompanied him on his expedition to the Indian east coast, but Coutinho appears to have decided that he was best off as an Adil Shahi cavalry captain. By 1546, he held charge of the region around Bassein, and – so Correia reports – after conducting himself well against the Portuguese and thereby allaying the suspicions of the Bijapur court was given 'lands with a great revenue, where he remained as a perfect Moor, with his wife and children' (Correia 1975, iv: 149–53, 298, 540). But significantly enough, he did not cut himself off from the official Portuguese even under these circumstances. Two of his nephews, António de Sousa and Cristóvão de Sousa, were in western India at this time, the former as captain of Chaul, while his daughter was married to Domingos de Fonseca, a minor official in Cochin (CSL, iii: 257, 399). In fact, in one of his letters to D. João de Castro of July 1546, António de Sousa goes so far as to ask for a safe-conduct for Coutinho to come to Chaul, adding that 'he is my uncle, and I owe it to him'.

Coutinho, confusingly enough, is referred to not as an *arrenegado* but as an *alevantado*, though he fits the definition of a renegade by all accounts. In a slightly later case, that of Sancho Pires, who again left Portuguese India on account of a murder charge, but fled to the Nizam Shahi kingdom of Ahmadnagar rather than Bijapur, there is no such ambiguity. Couto, our major source for Pires's activities as the Firangi Khan (a title that may imply that he was the designated head of all European mercenaries and renegades who were serving at Ahmadnagar), is all admiration for the man and his valour, regretting only that he gave up his True Faith for Islam. Indeed, Couto goes to some lengths to point out the decisive role played by Pires in the succession struggle at Ahmadnagar in the mid-1550s, in which he supported the winning claimant, Husain Nizam Shah (r. 1554–66). Having arrived in Asia in the 1530s, Pires eventually died in the late 1550s, in the course of a battle at the Deccan fort of Gulbarga, between Adil Shahi and Nizam Shahi forces (Couto 1973–74, vii/1: 342–46; Cruz 1986).

Again, there is little ambiguity concerning the precise status – whether *arrenegado* or merely *alevantado* – of another Portuguese of the closing years of the sixteenth century, Fernão Rodrigues Caldeira, at the Golconda court. Caldeira belonged to an important New Christian family of the period, and his uncle Manuel Caldeira held the contract for fitting out ships on the *Carreira da Índia* in the mid-1580s. In 1585, while *en route* from Lisbon to Goa, he had been shipwrecked off the east coast of Africa, but survived and made his way to Goa; some ten years later, we find him at the Golconda court, advising Sultan Muhammad Quli Qutb Shah on how to negotiate with Goa. In these years, Goa took the unprecedented step of ordering his assassination, together with that of some other renegades at that time in the service of the other Deccan states (Subrahmanyam 1990a: 157).

Whether they met with any success in his case, we do not know, but they certainly did in another one, in the early seventeenth century – the victim being a cannon-founder who had taken service with Bijapur. We find the following laconic description in a letter from the Count of Vidigueira, viceroy at Goa, to the King, in January 1627. The viceroy,

> on being advised that there resided with the Idalcão (Adil Khan) a renegade who was a great founder of artillery, and that he had offered to make every sort of it for him, and in fact made him as a sample a piece of great size, with which the Idalcão became most satisfied and gave him revenues and other advantages that he might remain and continue with the said founding,

resolved to put a stop to the matter. A certain Francisco Henriques de Sousa, native of Santarem, who was in Bijapur (possibly also as a mercenary), offered to kill the artilleryman for a price. Sousa was supplied a barrel of wine and some money, and entertained the renegade with food and drink; 'and after they had eaten and drunk well, killed him and buried him in the same house, and departed forthwith and made his way to Chaul'. The incident caused some trouble, as the Bijapur ambassador at Goa complained, but Sousa was rewarded with the post of magistrate's scribe at Diu for life – an ironically fitting reward for his life of crime (ANTT, DRI No. 24, ff. 83–83v).

This brings us then to the last of the renegade careers we shall consider, a curious case where no Portuguese sources appear to exist on the person in question. In the late 1610s, the Dutchman Pieter van den Broecke, travelling across the Deccan by road for the Dutch Company, makes several references to a powerful Portuguese renegade and cavalry captain, Mansur Khan, then in the service of Malik Ambar of Ahmadnagar. Though not among the Portuguese whom Van den Broecke encountered at the Deccan courts of the period, Mansur Khan was reckoned by him to be a man of means and semi-independent power, as was confirmed in the early 1620s, when he attacked a caravan with English goods near Mandu (Coolhaas 1962–63). This incident nearly provoked a rupture between the English and the Mughals, suggesting that Mansur Khan's actions may have been influenced in this case by Goa – whose interests were clearly served thereby. In 1623–24, we find him

255

mentioned twice in Jahangir's memoirs, the first time as a *mansabdar* with the high rank of 4,000 *zat* and 3,000 *sawar*, and the second time on the occasion of his death in battle, in Malwa. Jahangir wrote on the latter occasion that the Portuguese renegade 'had been drinking on the road, he was coming to the stage drunk with the wine of pride' (Rogers and Beveridge 1909–14, ii: 271). Whether this is true or not, it is certainly of a piece with the generally bibulous reputation of all Portuguese mercenaries at the time.

As we have seen then, renegades did not belong to a single social group within Portuguese Asia; if some were ambitious members of the service-nobility, others were in fear of prison sentences, and still others were poor soldiers who found the remuneration within Portuguese Asia too insubstantial. But conversion to Islam in any of these cases was not something that was done lightly; it was far easier to become a *mercenary*, selling one's services but not giving up one's religion. This latter route was one chosen therefore by a very large number of Portuguese, but this was a choice that was not always available to the individual Portuguese. All the states within easy access of Goa in the years 1500–1660 were Islamic ones, and most of them – Bijapur, Ahmadnagar, the Mughals – had some familiarity with the Portuguese as soldiers and captains. And yet many wavered, as we see in the late 1640s, with D. Brás de Castro. Accused of sedition by the viceroy D. Felipe Mascarenhas and forced to flee Goa for fear of a prison sentence, D. Brás hid in Bijapur (*terra de Mouros*). But he continued to petition the Crown for help, as we note from one of his letters in which he claims that the viceroy has 'pressed false charges against him, on account of which he was obliged, being fearful of his unjust proceedings, to go to the interior, where he is at present, absent from his house, wife, and children, suffering unjustly' (AHU, Cx. 20 344–A, Doc. 179). Now had D. Brás taken up service in Bijapur, and converted to Islam, it is unlikely that he could ever have returned to Goa – as he did a few years later (to the eventual detriment of the Count of Óbidos). The move was thus one fraught with risks, and hence made either by the extremely ambitious or those who had no other recourse.

MERCENARIES, FIREARMS AND FIFTH COLUMNISTS

A much larger group existed, though, of mercenaries and freelance warriors, spread across the Bay of Bengal littoral, mainland Southeast Asia, and Indonesia. It was the claim of João Ribeiro that in the late 1620s, there were some five thousand Portuguese employed by Asian states between Bengal and eastern Indonesia, 'with little hope of remedy for they are accustomed to the free life' (Disney 1978: 21). This is a rather large number when compared either with the number of *casados brancos* in Portuguese Asia in the period, or to the *soldados* in Goa at the same time. In the 1630s, the latter are estimated at about a thousand, and earlier in the seventeenth century at between a thousand five hundred and two thousand.

It was from the ranks of the *soldados* that the common mercenaries were drawn in the great numbers, but the more conspicuous mercenary captains often had a rather more well-to-do social background. Arriving in Goa (or more rarely in Cochin), the average *soldado* had to attach himself to a patron, and have someone pay for his board and lodging before he was assigned to a role in one of the armadas or fortresses. This was a role that *fidalgos* were meant to play, but it was not unknown for wealthy merchants to make loans to arriving soldiers, as we see from Jacques van de Coutere's autobiography. Coutere, who arrived in Goa in September 1592, had lost his clothing and weapons en route from Lisbon; once in Goa, he was therefore forced to take the help of a rich merchant resident there, especially since – as often happened – he fell ill soon after his arrival. His stay in Goa lasted almost a year, before he was able to enter the good graces of D. Diogo Lobo, and leave with him as a *soldado* in Melaka, where Lobo was to be captain (Stols and Verberckmoes 1988: 53–54).

In Coutere's time, as earlier in the sixteenth century, Melaka was an important centre from which Portuguese mercenaries and freelancers spread out through the Bay of Bengal, Southeast Asia and the Far East. More than Goa, and Cochin certainly, and even Hurmuz perhaps, it was a crossroads, a place where the Malay world met that of India, and where – even in the late sixteenth century – a remarkably cosmopolitan population of Tamils (in Malay Kelings), Javanese, south-eastern Chinese, Venetians and Portuguese continued to exist. Coutere, who operated out of Melaka for nearly a decade, until his return to Goa in 1603, speaks of visiting a great deal of the Malay trading world, beginning with Pahang, and then later Johor, Ayuthia, Cambodia, Manila, and Patani (besides most of the ports of the west coast of Sumatra) (De Souza 1989). Coutere claims to have encountered during these travels the celebrated Diogo Veloso (1559–99), a mercenary who from the early 1580s was active in Cambodia and Laos, and whom we have already encountered in Chapter 5, but also numerous other Portuguese, who combined trade with warfare, in a manner characteristic of the period. The earlier account of Fernão Mendes Pinto, who spent twenty-odd years in Asia, from the late 1530s to the late 1550s, and whose travels were very largely in Southeast Asia and the Far East, similarly mentions Portuguese traders, mercenaries and freelancers in the most unlikely places.

A seductive hypothesis that may explain the spread of Portuguese as mercenaries in this period, would link them to the dispersion of firearms in Asia at this time. It has been argued in the past that the sixteenth and seventeenth centuries saw the rise in Asia of 'gunpowder empires', which were presumably predicated on the availability of persons expert in the use of these new-fangled weapons. Broadly speaking, the two groups recognised in early modern Asia as being most expert in the use of cannon and smaller arms were the Portuguese (*firangis*, or in Sanskrit *parasikas*), and the Turks (*rumis*, in Sanskrit *turuskas*). An early seventeenth-century source from south India, the *Sahityaratnakara*, has a description in it for instance of the palace enclosure in the Nayaka state of Tanjavur, where the outermost courtyard is occupied by *parasika* mercenaries; they bear firearms (*agniyantra*), are to be distinguished by 'their eyes rolling from drinking liquor', and are men 'near whom the wind, loudly blowing through their metal *agniyantra* and filling the inner space, seemed to be proclaiming perpetually the imminent mission to destroy the King's enemies' (Subrahmanyam 1987).

However, the causal chain that is needed to make such a hypothesis plausible has several weak links. Let us consider the Asian region where firearms enjoyed their most conspicuous success in the period – namely Japan. Western firearms were introduced here, through the medium of the Portuguese, in the early 1540s; they were already being used quite effectively within a decade or so by some *daimyo*, and by 1575 Oda Nobunaga was able to employ some three thousand musketeers to devastating effect, in the battle of Nagashino (Parker 1988: 140–42). However, evidence of the large-scale employment of Portuguese mercenaries by Japanese warlords is not encountered in this period, suggesting that their presence was not necessary for the military system to adapt to the new technology. At the same time, the mere employment of mercenaries did not imply the transformation of the war-machine. Men like Mansur Khan, or Sancho Pires, whom we have described above, were employed as cavalry leaders and not as artillerymen. Thus, at both levels – the necessary and the sufficient – the link between Portuguese mercenaries and the use of firearms in Asia in the period is open to question.

A far more fruitful line of argument would be to look at the nature of both elite migration and the military labour market in various parts of Asia in this period. We have already noted that the states of early modern Asia were not, for the most part, self-contained, xenophobic, polities; rather one of the characteristics of the period is the openness of state formation, with Iranians and Central Asians to be found in India, Arabs on the west coast of Africa, Chinese on the north coast of Java and so on. Also, at the level of the use of military labour, a large number of groups were recruited on a collective basis, placed under the command of a captain of their own ethnicity, and incorporated into the armies of rulers like the

Mughals, or the Burmese monarchs of the epoch. From the 1540s, in Burma, fairly substantial numbers of Portuguese were to be found both trading and fighting; these were employed both by local rulers, such as the Mon kings who controlled Martaban, and by the Taung-ngu dynasty's Tabin-shwei-hti. Fernão Mendes Pinto claims for example that in 1545, at Martaban, he found a group of seven hundred Portuguese, under the command of a certain João Caeiro, who were first soldiers of the Mon ruler, and after his defeat by Tabin-shwei-hti were forced to switch loyalties. Pinto is not an accurate reporter of numbers, and his estimate is therefore not be taken literally; but it is significant that while calling these men *lançados*, he at the same time asserts that some of them, like Caeiro himself, were well-connected to officials like Pero de Faria, captain of Melaka. Further, not all of them remained mercenaries; one of them, Paulo de Seixas, is reported to have returned to the Coromandel coast some time later, and settled down there with a Burmese woman, whom he married, and by whom he already had two children (Pinto 1983: 440–45).

It was from forces such as these, and similar ones maintained by the ruler of Arakan, that men like Filipe de Brito e Nicote drew their following late in the sixteenth century. Again, while associated with the use of firearms, and the construction and management of naval vessels for Tabib-shwei-hti's sucessor, Bayin-naung, it seems exaggerated to associate these Portuguese simply with changes in warfare technology. As a mercenary force, they were recruited and treated in a manner different from normal levies, and apparently came to be associated with the personal bodyguard of the Burmese rulers, and may have played a similar role in the Ayuthia kingdom (Lieberman 1980). However, the rash of moves by the Portuguese, including Filipe de Brito himself, Manuel de Matos, Sebastião Gonçalves Tibau and others, to seize power for themselves (with the sanction *ex post facto* of Goa and Lisbon), changed this equation. The early seventeenth century witnessed a number of struggles between the rulers of Arakan and lower Burma and the Portuguese mercenaries, at the end of which the relationship with the *firangis* was wholly redefined. In his description of the Bay of Bengal in the 1630s, António Bocarro mentions them as follows:

> Further ahead in the kingdom of Arracão (there are) six hundred Portuguese and two thousand Christians who are employed by that King in his wars against the Mogar, and the said Portuguese and their sons who are fighting men, inclusive of many topaz Christians, comprise the entire force of the King, and he makes them large payments, and gives them extensive farm lands, but all of them take advantage of the enormity of the land so that they more or less know neither law nor King, though they have some Padres and a church. And similarly there are also in Pegu some captive Portuguese, from amongst those who were in His Majesty's fortress of Serião in the said kingdom when it was lost, and who are still captives in name but who live in

the said kingdom with great liberty, with a Padre who administers the
sacrament to them.   (Subrahmanyam 1990b: 262)

Other studies of the Burmese kingdom ruled over by Anauk-hpet-lun, based on indigenous sources, suggest that the men who had served under Filipe de Brito were all deported to the river valleys surrounding Ava, and given lands to maintain themselves, so that they could serve as artillerymen, musketeers and so on. Perhaps four or five hundred in all, these men and their descendants, later joined by imported Indian mercenaries, formed the core of the imperial guard of the Restored Taung-ngu dynasty until the late eighteenth century (Lieberman 1980: 220).

Curiously enough, besides the renegades (that is, converts to Islam), the Mughal state in the seventeenth and eighteenth centuries also institutionalised Portuguese mercenary groups into its forces in a similar fashion. The crucial event here, corresponding to the fall of Syriam, was the fall of Hughli in 1632 to Qasim Khan's forces. A large number of prisoners was carried back to Agra, including – in one estimate – as many as four hundred Portuguese, besides some ten times that number of local Christians. From this community, there grew a larger community of Portuguese and *mestiço* mercenary soldiers, doctors, and courtiers, both men and women. One of them, Agostinho Dias da Costa, originally a *casado* from Cochin, was physician to the Mughal prince Mu'azzam Bahadur Shah between 1659 and 1686, and several others served both Aurangzeb and his brother and rival Dara Shukoh. During the late seventeenth century, when Aurangzeb was ruler, many of their privileges were withdrawn (allegedly as a result of their 'insolent comportment and fondness for drink'). Nevertheless, respecting their autonomy to an extent, the emperor continued to permit them to distill liquor (Desoulières 1986: 163).

Besides the Hughli prisoners and their descendants, other Portuguese continued to take service with the Mughal rulers in the late seventeenth century, in which process a role of importance was played by the intermediation of Dona Juliana Dias da Costa (1655–1734?), daughter of the physician mentioned earlier. From the early eighteenth century, until her death in 1734, Dona Juliana was a figure of some importance in the Mughal court, and had a supervisory and administrative position in the harem. We see this, for example, from the account of the Dutch embassy to the Mughal court in 1711–13, led by Joan Josua Ketelaar. Ketelaar had earlier known Dona Juliana while in Agra, and includes a brief biographical sketch of her in his journal, which appears however to be partly inaccurate (in view of some internal inconsistencies). He attributes Dona Juliana's success to her close association with Bahadur Shah during the period when he was kept imprisoned by his father Aurangzeb (1687–95); when he became king, Bahadur Shah is hence alleged to have given her a *mansab* of 4,000, and appointed her head of all Christians in Agra. At the end of his brief reign, his successor Jahandar Shah continued to extend patronage to her, persuading her not to return to Goa as she wished, and his successors Farrukhsiyar and Muhammad Shah later maintained the same cordiality (Vogel 1937: 178–80). By 1711, Dona Juliana's brother-in-law, João Velho de Castro, was counted among the 'most important courtiers' of Jahandar Shah, holding a *mansab* of 2,500 *zat*/500 *sawar* by virtue of his position as *sardar-i firangiyan* (Vogel 1937: 175).

We can see therefore that the mercenary, or the courtier, had a rather different role to play from the renegade. For the former always had a door that was left half-open, and the possibility of re-entering official Portuguese Asian society. The calculation of many of the mercenaries of the sixteenth century seems to have been precisely this: they intended to use service with foreign rulers as a means of advancing themselves socially and economically, so that they could return to the fold later. To this end, they were never hesitant to use the political and diplomatic leverage that their intermediary positions afforded them; several such mercenary captains were admitted into the Military Orders in the late sixteenth century for services rendered to the Portuguese Crown while employed by another ruler. In this sense, more than the renegades, who – with very rare exceptions like João Machado – usually were men who had turned their backs on Portuguese Asian society, the mercenaries represented a 'fifth column', a potentially seditious element. To understand why Asian states tolerated such elements in their midst, it should be recalled that the loyalties of many courtiers in this period were divided in a similar fashion. While fighting the Safavids around Kandahar, the Mughals always had to keep a nervous eye on the *mansabdars* of Iranian extraction in their midst, and even if these men were in fact loyal to the Mughal state, they remained suspect. This political fluidity, and the composite elite structure that it yielded, obtained not only in South Asia but in Southeast Asia; China and Japan in the period did not, however, accept such outside elements with as great ease into the upper echelons of their elites. In turn, the fluidity and permeability of the elite groupings was what permitted the shift in the political balance that took place in South Asia in the late eighteenth century. The lineal descendants of Filipe de Brito and João Velho de Castro were hence the French and British mercenary captains and warrior-magnates of the later period.

CONVERTS AND CLIENT COMMUNITIES

The frontier between the official realm in Portuguese Asia and the rest of Asian society was not determined by renegades and mercenary soldiers alone. Once conversions to Christianity got under way in the sixteenth century, on account of the activities in particular of the religious orders, a grey area arose on the fringes of Portuguese Asia – inhabited by communities which were not merely Christianised, but also Lusitanised. It has been estimated that as many as a million and a half Christians existed in Asia by the early seventeenth century. Some of these were communities which had existed before the Portuguese arrived, such as the Syrian (or St. Thomas) Christians in Kerala. But the opening of a missionary front of expansion also had certain spectacular results, some of which were longer-lasting than the official, secular, Portuguese presence.

Now, as we have seen in the previous chapter, there were some one thousand eight hundred priests of the major religious orders in Asia by the 1630s, as opposed to fifteen thousand Portuguese and *mestiços* in all of Asia – including priests, *casados*, soldiers, mercenaries, renegades, and *solteiro* and freelance traders. Such a high proportion of ecclesiastics undoubtedly differentiates the Portuguese from later European colonisers in Asia, and gives to their overseas enterprise an exaggeratedly religious flavour. Some seventeenth-century viceroys like the Count of Linhares were strongly of the opinion that the religious establishment was far too large, and made several arguments for reducing its size. The first was that one half of the soldiers who arrived from Europe entered the religious orders as a means of avoiding the rigours of a military life, thus weakening the defences of the *Estado*. He also claimed that the 'lazy religious' were a crippling financial burden, bleeding the treasuries white in order that they be supported (Disney 1978: 21–22).

His complaints were perhaps more valid for Goa and the Indian west coast (which we have seen was massively supplied with ecclesiastics), than for more distant areas, where the religious establishments were supported by the contributions of parishioners, and which were hence economically independent. At times, however, this independence itself caused problems, for the religious orders emerged as a consequence with temporal (and even fiscal) powers, or became semi-commercial enterprises. An excellent example of the latter type is the Jesuit presence in China and Japan, areas in which they had a an extraordinarily large number of priests in the late sixteenth century, to minister to a Christian population that in Japan alone was estimated at some 300,000 by Jesuit writers (Sansom 1961: 377).

The earliest evidence of Jesuit commercial involvement in the region comes from the late 1550s, when a surgeon called Luís de Almeida, who joined the Society of Jesus, donated a sum of money to the order, which was promptly invested in the silk trade from China to Japan. The Jesuits in this instance had a justification, for while the Council of Trent had urged penalties and even excommunication for those who engaged in such ecclesiastical trade, they had no other recourse in their Far Eastern missions. The Portuguese Crown, which had made a grant to them of

1,000 *cruzados* a year, to be paid from the Melaka customs-house, was erratic in its payment, and remittances by the Society itself from its incomes in India were insufficient (Boxer 1959: 39; Spence 1984: 175–77). Thus, Alessandro Valignano, the energetic *visitador* of the Society of Jesus, worked out an arrangement with the Macau City Council, which was legitimised *ex post facto* by the Papacy and by Goa. The arrangement guaranteed the Jesuits a share of the silk trade, and was justified in a royal decree of 1584 on the grounds that 'the Fathers of Japan have no means of sustaining themselves until now, and meeting the great expenses that are made in maintaining nearly five hundred persons, and diverse houses, seminaries and colleges, and nearly two hundred churches that they have in their charge in diverse kingdoms' (Boxer 1959: 197).

The Christian population of Japan, while startling in its extent, is also remarkable for the fact that it did not endure long. By the second decade of the seventeenth century, when the Portuguese had begun to retreat from Japan at least in terms of their missionary presence, the number of Christians is likely to have begun to diminish, and after 1640, only a small underground population probably remained. A more lasting presence was achieved through missionary activity in other areas, most importantly in parts of India where the *Estado*'s hold remained tenuous. Now, one of the most important communities of converts that the Portuguese dealt with in Asia were the Paravas, in the extreme south of the Indian peninsula, in the region of Tirunelveli in Tamilnadu. Their conversion, which took place in the early 1530s, preceded the Counter-Reformation-inspired expansion of missionary activity in Asia, and was achieved through the mediation of the secular clergy of the *Padroado Real* (Crown Patronage of Missions). Preceding the conversion, there had been a decade and more of conflict between the Portuguese – both State forces and semi-autonomous expeditions of the Cochin *casados* – and the Muslim Maraikkayar and Mappila traders, who were active in the region. Seizing hold of the opportunity presented by this conflict, a group of Parava notables approached the Portuguese at Cochin, agreeing to convert in exchange for patronage and protection. Within a few months, some 20,000 baptisms had taken place, and the Portuguese state began to claim rights over economic resources in the area, by virtue of its patronage of the Paravas (Kaufmann 1981).

In essence, the Portuguese intervention in Parava affairs saw the utilisation of pre-existent hierarchies to a new end. As the Portuguese saw it, the entire Parava community of the area could be divided into territorial segments, each headed by a *patangatim* (Tamil *pattankatti*); at the top of the hierarchy was the *patangatim-mór* (or *jati talaivan*), a hereditary post held by João da Cruz and his descendants. This hierarchical structure was at first intended to mobilise labour to prosecute certain imperial projects, such as Portuguese expansion in Sri Lanka. Placed under the control of a Goa-appointed factor of the Fishery Coast (from the pearl fishery carried on twice a year in the straits between India and Sri Lanka), the Paravas were seen as a reserve pool of military labour, as well as a source of tribute through the conduct of the fishery itself. But this equation was not to last very long. In the 1540s, the Society of Jesus, having entered the field of missionary activity in Asia, made the Fishery Coast one of its main areas of interest. Francisco Xavier himself spent time in the area in the early 1540s, and by the early 1550s a three-cornered struggle had begun to develop, between the Jesuits, the *Estado da Índia*, and local political structures – the Nayaka of Madurai and his subordinates. This conflict was to persist in one form of the other until the mid-seventeenth century and stemmed on the one hand from the weak Portuguese state presence in the area, and on the other from the temporal ambitions of the Jesuits.

By the mid-1550s, Simão Botelho speaks of these tensions quite openly. His main concern was financial, for he saw that the tribute derived from the pearl fishery had fallen between the early 1530s and the 1550s, for which he naturally sought the cause. His view was as follows:

> And later, when the fishermen who conduct this fishery began to convert to Christianity, and they came to be favoured, the value of the fishery began to fall, and it yielded much less; the truthful information concerning this cannot be known, because the Padres of the Company of Jesus who now reside there and who work to make and sustain the said Christian folk say that the captains commit great tyrannies for their own interest, and that on this account no one wishes to fish, and they have instead made themselves merchants and traders.
>
> (Felner 1868, ii: 245)

Perhaps on account of reports such as these, the *Estado* began to retreat from the area, leaving matters more and more in Jesuit hands. By the late 1560s, the nearest official outpost was in the island of Mannar, and the Society of Jesus was left to mediate between the Paravas and temporal authority at Goa and Lisbon; in the closing years of the sixteenth century, there were seven Jesuit residences on the coast, with twenty priests and some sixteen churches.

Such an equilibrium could not last for a number of reasons. First, the Parava community's *patangatins* themselves were ambiguous in their feelings about the Jesuits, and at least some of them seem in the early seventeenth century to have wanted other channels of communication with Goa. Jesuit interference in succession disputes to the posts of *patangatim* and *patangatim-mór* appear to have exacerbated the problem. Second, the increasingly erratic revenues of the pearl fishery began to trouble the Goa administration, which started to suspect that the Jesuits were privately siphoning off the returns from the fishery. A long run of years in the late sixteenth century, when no fishery could be held for lack of ripe oysters, increased Goa's suspicions further. Finally, it was rumoured that the Jesuits had struck an arrangement with the Nayakas of Madurai to exclude the secular clergy from Cochin, and that they were planning to construct a fortified centre in an offshore island.

These three factors taken together precipitated a quite exträordinary conflict, by which the Jesuits were expelled from the Fishery Coast in 1605 for a period of sixteen years, and replaced by diocesan priests. In these years, the other religious orders – which had hitherto been excluded from access to the area – also made inroads, so that the Jesuits found on their return in the 1620s that the situation was considerably tangled. The years 1623 and 1625 once again saw quarrels on the coast between rival Parava factions (with the bone of contention being the post of *patangatim-mór*), and the Jesuits were again centrally implicated. Still worse was to come though. In the early 1630s, the viceroy at Goa, the Count of Linhares, decided to stake a claim to direct control of the coast (and especially the settlement of Tuticorin, which had grown in importance since about 1580) on behalf of the *Estado*. His reasons were two-fold: first, since the Madurai region produced saltpetre, a commodity much in demand in times of war, he hoped to buy it through a representative at Tuticorin; second, he suspected the Jesuits of collecting taxes and tolls on Parava economic activity, and wished to put a stop to it. The battle between the *Estado* and the Jesuits was joined once again then, with the appointment in 1630 of Pero Soares de Brito, a *casado* from Cochin, as captain of Tuticorin.

Soares de Brito's brief sojourn on the Fishery Coast was not pleasant. Soon after his arrival, he became embroiled in a quarrel between diocesan priests and Jesuits concerning the control of the church of St. Peter at Tuticorin. The Jesuits being denied control of the church, they appealed to Goa, which restored it to them; the Jesuit provincial at Cochin sent a Padre Fernão Lopes to regain possession. A contemporary report tells us of the fracas that ensued:

> (Fernão Lopes) collecting on his way more than ten thousand men armed, and in a mood for war, with drums and flags, arrived one day at dawn in the aforesaid place of Tuticorin, and breaking down the walls of the settlement entered it, and so much was the perturbation and fear of the people that they collected by the sea, where it is claimed that three or four children were drowned; and when Pero Soares de Brito, captain of the said place came to help with some armed people, and coming to a halt near a crossroads, he was fired on from the Company (of Jesus's) house, and two persons wounded by two musket shots, and a fight followed between the people on the captain's side and those who had come with the said Padre Fernão Lopes.
>
> (HAG, Monções 17, f. 95)

Deciding that Soares de Brito was incompetent, Linhares intervened after this incident, replacing him as captain by António de Meirelles. The new captain fared no better, being harassed by the Madurai Nayaka's local representatives, possibly at the instigation of the Jesuits. Things had reached such a sorry pass by the mid-1630s that Goa even sent out a fleet under the command of D. António Mascarenhas to attack and burn the coastal villages of the Paravas (ostensibly their own clients!), in order to 'castigate' them for the disturbances on the coast.

The struggle between Jesuits and *Estado* for control of the Paravas, the pearl fishery and the Fishery Coast never reached a satisfactory conclusion. Between the early 1640s and 1658, when the *Estado*'s presence in the region ended, matters were further complicated by the Dutch presence in the area, both in Sri Lanka and in the port of Kayalpatnam. In 1649, for instance, the Dutch carried out a rather puzzling raid on Tuticorin and other Parava settlements, occasioning further letters of complaint from the Paravas to Goa, since it appeared to the former that the Portuguese were unable even to afford them minimal protection. Finally, in 1658, the VOC took control of the major ports of the Fishery Coast, itself became administrator of the pearl fishery, and – in a somewhat surprising turn – became effective patron of the Paravas (despite their continued adherence to the Catholic religion). Jesuit activity in the region continued, both on the coast and more particularly in the Madurai mission further inland; at least one celebrated Jesuit, João de Brito, was martyred in the late seventeenth century in this very region.

Unlike Japan, where the disappearance of the official Portuguese presence was a major blow to the client community, the Japanese Christians, some of the Paravas seem to have gone from strength to strength even after 1658. Their major religious centre, the church of *Nossa Senhora das Neves* (Our Lady of the Snows) at Tuticorin had by the mid-eighteenth century become the focus of a major ten-day Chariot Festival, in which the Virgin was taken through the town on a chariot (Tamil *ter*) (Kaufmann 1981: 210–11). When the pearl fishery was held in these years, Parava participation was considerable; Tuticorin was the main centre from which their boats were sent out to the fishery, but other ports like Punnaikkayal also played a role. In the 1708 pearl fishery for example, Tuticorin alone sent out 122 boats from a total of 528, and major boatowners included Pedro Gomes (*pattankatti* of Tuticorin), António Henrique de Moraes, Manuel António da Cruz, Diogo Vaz, and Pedro Francisco Meirinho. But it is apparent from the Dutch records of the period that the Paravas were by now clearly economically differentiated; at one end of the spectrum were the boatowning *champanottis*, at the other the pearl-divers, both of the same caste but with a vast social and economic gulf between them (ARA, VOC. 1756, ff. 1177–88). Conversion thus may have helped some families from amongst the Paravas improve their status and well-being, but its long-term effects on the community as a whole are a complex issue, that cannot be summed up with the traditional formulae of 'improvement' and 'westernisation'.

Significant for our purposes is the preservation by the Paravas, even after the fading away of the *Estado*'s authority in the area, of their collective identity, but this perhaps was also partly the result of the fact that – unlike in Japan, or even Goa – they already possessed a collective identity before conversion. It was thus logical for them to preserve themselves into the eighteenth century as a 'Christian caste in Hindu society' (Kaufmann 1981).

A LUSO-ASIAN DIASPORA?

Located in and associated with a particular region, the Fishery Coast, northern Sri Lanka, and southern Coromandel, the Paravas were never truly 'assimilated' in any real sense into Portuguese Asia – but instead always maintained their separate identity. Further, since they remained largely endogamous, the extent of assimilation through miscegenation with the Portuguese remained limited, and anyway there was never a large enough Portuguese presence at Tuticorin and other centres for this to become a possibility. At the margins, those who were assimilated to a lesser or greater degree were individuals who had been torn from their native context, of which a few conspicuous examples exist in sixteenth- and seventeenth-century Portuguese Asia.

These include members of ruling houses of various Asian kingdoms, whom the Portuguese patronised and indoctrinated as secret weapons, in the hope that at a suitable moment they could be re-inserted into their original contexts as a Portuguese fifth column. In this way, the children or relatives of rulers from Munhumutapa to the Maldives, Bijapur, Jaffna, and Burma were Lusitanised, though rarely to any real political consequence. Such persons remain historical curiosities, interesting from the viewpoint of their mentalities – adrift as they are between their natal world, and that of the Portuguese. We may briefly examine the case of one of them, the curiously-named D. Martinho de Alemão, a Burmese prince from Arakan.

In his numerous letters and petitions, D. Martinho makes it clear that he is the nephew of the Arakan ruler, and son of the governor of Chittagong, who had been brought up by the Augustinians from the age of eight at Hughli and Goa – with his particular patron being a certain Padre Nicolao da Conceição. From the early 1620s, D. Martinho served as a mariner and soldier in various Portuguese fleets, including that of Rui Freire de Andrade in the Persian Gulf. In the early 1640s, already a *fidalgo*, he was given the Habit of Christ, and later also appointed to the captaincy of the pass of São Lourenço in Goa for his services; in the same decade he appears to have made a voyage to Lisbon in connection with a proposal floated by his patron (the Augustinian priest, Padre Nicolao), to reinstate him in Arakan (ANTT, Livraria 731, ff. 295–v). Nothing ever came of this proposal, and the early 1650s see D. Martinho back in Goa, where he continued to maintain a vigorous correspondence with the Provincial of the Augustinians. In these letters, written with a certain erudition and knowledge of legal texts, D. Martinho signs himself 'son of the sacred religion of Saint Augustine', and speaks of his intention to leave a large proportion of his effects to the Augustinians. To his son, D. Francisco de Alemão, he wished to leave his membership of the Order of Christ, and the position of *fidalgo*, if the Crown would only permit it.

Men like D. Martinho may be thought to represent the counterpart (or mirror-image) to the Portuguese who served the rulers of South or Southeast Asia in the seventeenth century, and who passed the permeable frontier between political systems with the hope (or intention) of retracing their steps, but who never quite succeeded in doing do. But even as the Portuguese at the Mughal court always remained *firangis*, Asians like D. Martinho, though assimilated to an extent, and given access to titles, privileges and posts in the *Estado*, never quite crossed the gulf to being Portuguese. This was for several reasons, not only racial; we have noted in an earlier chapter how men like Ferdinand Cron and Jacques van de Coutere, who were perfectly conversant in Portuguese, and married into Portuguese society in Asia, nevertheless were apt to be termed 'foreigners' (*estrangeiros*), and kept at a distance at certain moments. The problem appears to be that while ethnic identification was not strong enough for clear distinctions to be made at all times between 'insiders' and 'outsiders', it was not loose enough either to permit free assimilation merely because some basic criteria – such as religion or language – were met.

A realisation of this aspect of Luso-Asian interaction also leaves one somewhat ambivalent about the utility of the concept of the 'diaspora', for an understanding of the Portuguese and Lusophone peoples spread across Asia in the late seventeenth century. Did these persons and groups see themselves as a community, or is it merely the modern historian who, after setting out the historical processes by which these groups were formed between 1500 and 1700, attributes to them the characteristics of a community? Thomas Bowrey, an English private trader who sailed the waters of the Bay of Bengal in the last third of the seventeenth century, leaves us with this picture of the *firangis* ('Frangues') of Bengal: 'I judge and am well Satisfied in it, that there are noe lesse than 20,000 Frangues of all Sorts in the Kingdom of Bengala, and above half of them inhabit near Hugly river' (Bowrey 1905: 195). Now it is obvious that the term *firangi* had in Bengal already come to have a far more vague connotation than 'Portuguese', or even their descendants, for otherwise such an enormously inflated figure as twenty thousand cannot be accounted for. Indeed, when Bowrey speaks of the Hughli settlers, he is far more specific – calling them 'Portugals', and mentioning the distinction between *reinois* and *indiáticos*, which clearly still persisted even in Bengal in the 1670s! Thus:

> A great Multitude of Portugals inhabit the Kingdome of Bengala, Especially in Hugly and Some other Creeks or Rivolets of the River thereof. Many of them are filias de Lisboa (as they call them selvs), vizt. Europeans borne, but many more of them are filias de Indies. They have a very large towne, about one English mile above the English Factory; it is called the Bandell. I judge it is 2 English miles in circuit, very populous of men, women and children. They are for the most part very poore, but are much to be commended for their Industrie, in acquireinge a livelyhood by honest means, much more commendable and honourable then for Christians to begge in a heathen Country. (Bowrey 1905: 191–92)

It is thus apparent that the Portuguese of Bengal at least still retained their notional adherence to *patria*, and had not merged into the local landscape as is sometimes assumed to be the case. Again, in the 1680s, the Portuguese of Porto Novo or Ayuthia, while not too keen to embrace the *Estado* and its representatives, nevertheless perceived themselves as a community which was at a distance from the hinterland society. The correspondence between a certain Sieur Germain, employee of the French Company, and Manuel Teixeira Pinto at Porto Novo in the 1680s, is instructive in this respect. In a letter dated 9th August 1687, for example, Germain writes of the arrival of a ship from France at Pondicherry, hastening to bring Pinto up to date on political gossip from Europe, beginning with the proposed remarriage of the widow of the Portuguese king D. Afonso VI, and going on to how 'the Emperors have taken Boeda and besieged Belgrade (so that) the Turk has asked for peace' (ARA, VOC. 1438, f. 1253v). Thus even though Pinto lived in a community of Portuguese traders at some distance from the official *Estado da Índia*, he obviously continued to thirst for news from Europe, and still partly retained an orientation in that direction.

In centres such as Goa, Bassein, Diu and Mozambique then, the official apparatus of empire remained in place (albeit often in a weakened form), as late as 1700. Elsewhere in Asia, those of Portuguese descent who remained still clung to their identity, even if not to the improbable dream of re-creating the *Estado* in its most extended form. It is an irony, but not perhaps wholly surprising, that it is the conquerors of the sixteenth century and not these traders, bakers, and others who made 'a livelyhood by honest means' who are remembered, whether for better or worse, when one speaks of the Portuguese in early modern Asia. But then, nationalism, whether in Portugal, Asia or Africa, must have its heroes and villains, the stuff of its myths.

269

CHAPTER TEN

Conclusion: Between Banditry
and Capitalism

See also
pp. 245-8

In the early seventeenth century, a ship from Europe was wrecked on a small Indian Ocean island. Among the many survivors were a group of would-be mutineers, disciples of a religious group that denied the existence of evil – since all that stemmed from God (which is to say all of Creation) was of necessity good. The captain of the vessel fled in the ship's boat, and the mutineers took command of the bulk of the persons who remained, eventually massacring the greater part of them, save the women – who were taken into concubinage. Eventually, an expeditionary force was sent out by higher authorities, under the command of the same ship's captain, to quell the mutiny; most of the mutineers were killed, and some marooned.

To what nation in Europe did these men belong? Confronted with the events in this stark form, devoid of names, places and titles, it would be hard to guess. Was this one of the stray Italian or French expeditions of the period, which so often ended in disaster and chaos? Were these men Portuguese, and is this an excerpt from the 'Tragic History of the Sea' (*História Trágico-Marítima*), collected and published in Lisbon in the early eighteenth century? Or are these Englishmen, and is this a distorted precursor of the later case of the *Bounty*?

In fact they were none of these, but Dutchmen; the ship was the VOC vessel *Batavia*, wrecked off the Abrolhos Islands near the west coast of Australia in 1629. The captain, Francisco Pelsaert, had earlier been Dutch factor in Surat, and written extensively on the history of the Mughals, in an uncharacteristic form for the Dutch of the period – a chronicle. He was to claim later that the *Batavia*'s wreck was the vengeance of God against the mutineers; and when finally able to confront and try the head mutineer Jeronimus Cornelisz, he ordered that his hands be cut off before he was hanged.

Acts and events of this kind, common among seventeenth-century Europeans in Asia, are often described with a certain selectivity by historians. They appear to them be characteristically medieval in their cruelty, and – in the case of the mutiny itself and its ideology – even irrational. Above all, they cannot be easily reconciled with the image of the Dutch – austere, rational, Calvinistic and calculating – that pervades the historiography on the period. The whole episode would surely be better located in a history of Spanish or Portuguese expansion.

It is an uncomfortable fact that the sources on which historical writings are based do not always confirm the historian in his or her prejudices. And prejudices surely abound in writings on the Portuguese in Asia, both in the histories written by nationalistic Portuguese historians and others, whether Asians, Africans or Anglo-Saxons. Some of these views can be summarily dismissed, based as they are on either an uncritical acceptance of the 'universal mission' of the Portuguese in the pursuance of transcendent aims and values, or alternatively of an anachronistic tracing back of modern international tensions to the sixteenth century. But other views are more worthy of consideration, since they are rooted in the comparative study of institutions, and enjoy wide currency among historians today. Now the key interpretation that dominates studies on the Portuguese in early modern Asia is still a Weberian one. Taking its cue from Max Weber's own distinction in his *Protestant Ethic and the Spirit of Capitalism* (Weber 1930), between circumstantial and cultural factors in determining the history of different European nations, this approach seeks to argue that Portugal, like the rest of southern Europe, was in terms of its institutions and mentalities far closer to Asia in the period, than it was to northern (and specifically Protestant) Europe. Though more adept than the Asians at naval warfare, the Portuguese encounter with Asia could not be fertile since it represented the meeting of familiar institutions characteristic of the pre-modern Old World. A more momentous encounter was therefore that of the English and the Dutch with Asia, in the seventeenth century.

The views summarised above were set out in an explicit form not by Weber himself (though one can imagine that he would have been sympathetic to them), but by a Dutch sociologist, J.C. van Leur. His comparative perspective was as follows:

> Portuguese power was typically medieval in character, a fact that helps to explain its limited effectiveness. There was not much unity to the scattered territory of port settlements spread out over thousands of miles, despite the centralized royal shipping from Goa to Europe. There was no hierarchy of officials with a distinction between civil and military administration, but a conglomeration of nobles and *condottieri* each with his own retinue of henchmen bound to him by a vassal's loyalty or a lust for gain; often the officials in authority provided their own equipment and carried out exploitation for their own benefit by means of offices bestowed on them, frequently on a short-term basis. Portuguese power sought its strength then, not in taking over Oriental trade or establishing a territorial authority, but in

acquiring tribute and booty. Non-economic motives – lust for plunder, not lust for profit – played the chief role in overseas expansion.

(Van Leur 1955: 170)

Further, he stated, the Portuguese had a 'weak empire', built on 'war, coercion and violence', which could not affect 'the traditional commercial structure' in Asia seriously, since the commercial and economic forms of the Portuguese Asian regime were the 'same as those of Asian trade and Asian authority'. His final judgement was then the following:

> The Portuguese colonial regime, then, did not introduce a single new economic element into the commerce of southern Asia. The forms of political and economic domination – monopolies, financial exploitation, 'fiscalization' of the government – all of them originated in the caliphates and Byzantium, and were transferred to Portugal, and perhaps carried on there, by Jews and Italians. ... Not Lisbon and Seville, but Amsterdam, Middelburg, Enkhuizen and London were among the heralds of a new era. (Van Leur 1955: 118–19)

This view, disputed in the early 1960s by some scholars like Meilink-Roelofsz (1962), was given a new lease of life by the Danish scholar Niels Steensgaard, whose perspective – like that of Weber and Van Leur – was once more comparative. Seeing the confrontation between the Companies and the Portuguese in the early seventeenth century as symptomatic of a structural crisis in European relations with early modern Asia, Steensgaard bracketed the Portuguese in Asia with the Safavids and Ottomans, as a 'redistributive enterprise'; in contrast were the Companies, whose rational economic organisation and orientation towards profit rather than power made them 'productive enterprises' (Steensgaard 1973).

The method of both Van Leur and Steensgaard is structural in character; that is, a separate and distinct, essential, structure is postulated for the institutional complex of the Dutch, the Safavids, the Ottomans, and the Portuguese, the characteristics of each of which are then identified, and implicitly attributed to some exogenous factor, say cultural differences. Such an approach naturally defines away the possibility that the mentalities, institutions and methods of the Portuguese in 1510 may not have been the same as in 1610, or indeed that different groups of Portuguese may have had different approaches to, as well as a shifting weight in, the enterprise at any point in time.

Recent work on the Dutch Republic in the seventeenth century implicitly casts doubt on one of the building-blocks of this argument, namely the notion of Dutch social organisation in the period as dominated *in practice* (as opposed to in theory) by an ethic that stressed frugality, saving and the making of profit. Simon Schama points out for example that the great Dutch merchant families of the period, like the Trips, had a lifestyle that was anything but frugal, and that – on the other hand – the love of profit, as well as individualistic entrepreneurial capitalism, both had powerful opponents within the Dutch social establishment of the period.

Besides, a serious problem appears to be that the Dutch in their trade of the period were never too keen on the notion of improving efficiency through competition, but preferred instead to use legislation, state power, and force to promote trade. This is one of the major reasons why the timing of expansion and contraction in the Dutch international trading economy coincides so closely with political shifts (Schama 1987: 339–43; Israel 1982, 1989).

Further, as we are aware, in the global struggle for control of long-distance trade between Dutch, English and Portuguese, the winners were not the same everywhere. The Dutch may have gained in Asia, but in Brazil and the south Atlantic more generally, the Portuguese continued their hold into the eighteenth century. Had the struggle been one between the 'medieval' and the 'modern', with one set of institutions destined to supercede the other (as is implied by Van Leur and Steensgaard), this uneven outcome is inexplicable. We must hence concede either that the outcomes were mediated by local circumstances and forces – hence the variation, or that the results depended on how much military power each of the contenders was able to bring to bear in each of the arenas. If the latter argument is admitted, the Dutch 'triumph' in Asia is reduced to something far more mundane than 'institutional innovation', or the peculiar qualities of the chartered trading Company.

We may also recall that the Dutch did not have long to savour their triumph in Asia. By the last two decades of the seventeenth century, the English Company gained rapidly on the VOC where Euro-Asian trade was concerned. As for trade within Asia, the Dutch Company's role remained static after about 1700, and the real gainers thereafter were English private traders, whose mode of organisation had little in common with the chartered trading Company. Seen from this perspective too, there is something artificial about viewing the early seventeenth century as the decisive end of small-scale trading operations, and the beginning of an era of giant (and ostensibly creative) trading monopolies.

This book has partly been concerned therefore with the inherent dangers that lie in hindsight, an approach that leads the historian into that most perilous of traps – anachronism. The divisions and cleavages of the past century and a half between nations and national cultures have an unfortunate way of imposing themselves on historians who are studying an earlier epoch, and this has affected the manner in which the history of the Portuguese in Asia has been written. The image of the Portuguese, the 'Kaffirs of Europe', in the eyes of other Europeans of the first half of this century, was in some senses not very different from the manner in which the colonised countries of Asia and Africa were seen. Just as the 'backwardness' of the latter countries was often explained with reference to their cultural systems (and inability to shed these, despite their purportedly archaic features), so too Portugal was viewed. There was of

273

course one distinction: Portugal in the twentieth century still held colonies. But this was, if anything, seen as further evidence of the archaic nature of her institutions; rather than being modern colonies, these were territories that were held on account of sheer inertia. Now once this division in space had been established – between Portugal, Spain, and certain other parts of the south of Europe, Africa, Latin America and Asia on the one hand, and northern Europe and North America on the other – a corresponding division in time had to be established too. The attempt to divide the European presence in Asia into two phases, before and after about 1620, is an attempt to establish just such a division, which thus permits us to separate the 'modern' from the 'traditional', while at the same time asserting the historical lack of significance of the sixteenth century as a phase of change in Asian or even Iberian history.

One should recall here that such an approach is one in which Portuguese historians themselves have participated. The most major single work on fifteenth- and sixteenth-century Portuguese overseas expansion, that of V.M. Godinho, closes with a vision of Portugal, already doomed by the end of the sixteenth century to backwardness, resulting from the failure of commercial expansion to affect mentalities, attitudes and social structures, and which remained – it would appear – archaic and seignorial, rather than forward-looking, rational and capitalistic. Thus:

> The commercialisation of the fifteenth and sixteenth centuries (in the rigorous sense that we have defined it) generated an economy and a society which blocked itself into rigid lines, in such a way that it could not succeed later either in industrialising itself or in gaining access to the universe of science and citizenship. (Godinho 1981–83, iv: 223)

As an approach and an argument, this is perfectly familiar to historians of Asia, who have made similar pronouncements of 'equilibrium traps', which ensured that no real change was possible in the sixteenth and seventeenth centuries. However, our argument throughout this book has been that it is precisly the *changing* scene within Asia and in Europe that should occupy our attention, and that the political and commercial world of Asia into which the Portuguese entered in about 1500 was significantly different from that of 1700. What were the fundamental transformations that had taken place?

We have noted, to begin with, that in Asia before 1500, states had broadly fallen into two categories. One of these comprised relatively large, agrarian-based, states, which were often landlocked in character, and the other trade-based states, such as Hurmuz, Aden, Calicut or Melaka. This distinction began to break down in the years after 1500, when a mercantilist spirit began to pervade a wide variety of states, causing them to take a more active interest in trade. In part this transformation came about because of the migration of elites across regions, and the spread of accounting and administrative techniques first developed in the commercial sphere into the domain of the state. But equally, the centuries after 1500 offered a rather different set of possibilities to the states than those which had preceded it. The quantitative dimensions of trade increased, as did the range of commodities traded, which now came to include vast quantities of bullion as well as manufactures, and spices. It was in this changing context that the Portuguese operated.

In 1500, at the time of the first Portuguese maritime expeditions to Asia, the Portuguese state played a significant and relatively direct role. The state itself was riven by tensions, between different social classes, within the elite itself, and between different regions. No obvious consensus existed on the issue of maritime expansion, and this explains the shifting nature of the regimes employed to harness the possibilities of trade. In the early sixteenth century, the dominant ideology was a curious combination of mercantilism and messianism, the first of which promoted trading expansion in the Indian Ocean, while the second provided the motive force for an attack on Jerusalem via the Red Sea. Gradually, this gave way to a different spirit, and by the middle decades of the sixteenth century, the state had begun to withdraw from trade – seeing it as beneath its dignity. However, the structures that were already in place could not be transformed overnight. Piecemeal changes had to be made, as priorities shifted more and more from Asia to Brazil, the new frontier of expansion.

These changes were mediated by a fiscal and ideological crisis that the *Estado da Índia* underwent in the middle years of the sixteenth century. On emerging from the crisis in about 1570, several shifts had been made. First, greater priority was now given to the Far East in the trading network of the Portuguese in Asia, as Japanese bullion began to flow into commercial channels. Second, these years witnessed the development of a form of territorial adventurism, which gained further ground after the takeover of Portugal by the Habsburgs in 1580. The territorial imperative stemmed partly from an imitation of Spanish expansion in the New World, and partly from a desire to take advantage of profound political realignments that were taking place in different parts of Asia – most notably Sri Lanka and mainland Southeast Asia – in the period. But a backlash followed, once states in Asia had reconsolidated themselves. This happened at precisely the juncture when the Dutch and English arrived on the Asian scene. Thus in the half-century after 1610, the Portuguese *Estado* had to face not only the challenge posed by the Companies on the Cape route, but the attacks on its territories by Asian states ranging from the Safavids to the rulers of Golconda and Ikkeri, the Burmese king, and the Tokugawas.

Evidently, the *Estado* was not strong enough to withstand such a multi-pronged attack. Already stretched to the limits of its human resources, its finances began to fail, and the Habsburgs did not prove sufficiently forthcoming in terms of resources from Europe. In part, this

275

was because the interests of the *Estado da Índia* were sacrificed at the altar of the empire in the New World, but there was also another dimension to the process. Habsburg attempts to harness private capital in defence of the commercial aspects of the empire were also a signal failure, because of the ambiguous nature of the Habsburg state's relations with the principal trading group – the so-called New Christians, who had converted from Judaism to escape persecution. Despite numerous attempts, from the 1620s to the 1670s, to channel the capital of substantial New Christian entrepreneurs and bankers to shore up the *Estado*'s fortunes, nothing of any substance emerged.

Thus, in the last quarter of the seventeenth century, when the *Estado da Índia* could finally lick its wounds, it had substantially shrunk in relation to its profile of around 1600. It still comprised a set of far-flung territories, from Timor in eastern Indonesia to East Africa, but its settlements in South and Southeast Asia had dwindled. It was now no more than a collection of territorial niches and mercantile networks, the latter peopled by traders who were often anxious to keep the state at arm's length.

To sum up therefore, the two centuries with which we have been concerned witness changes of great magnitude in both economic and political terms. These may be classified as follows.

First, the economy of the Indian Ocean in 1700 was clearly linked to the economies of both Europe, and of the New World, so that one can from the late sixteenth century speak of a commercial nexus that truly girdled the globe. This nexus was to become stronger, and commerce more intense in later centuries, but the fundamental links had been established by 1600.

Secondly, the logic of states in Asia had seen a decisive transformation. It is no longer possible by the late sixteenth and early seventeenth centuries to maintain the distinction between small trading states, and large agrarian-tribute based polities. Far more typical of the period is a sort of intermediate regime, semi-agrarian and semi-commercial, of which examples include the Iran of Shah Abbas I, the Mughal state, Golconda, and even Burma. Later political transformations of the late seventeenth and eighteenth centuries have these already re-designed state structures as their point of departure (Bayly 1989).

Thirdly, in the two centuries after 1500, commercial networks grew more intense, and production for the market in different parts of Asia grew more important. The period of apprenticeship for a new entrant into Asian trade thus declined, making it easier for English private traders, for example, to gain access to the benefits of Asian trade. What had changed was fundamental. Knowledge concerning markets, trading conditions and political etiquette was now far more widely dispersed than before; a *lingua franca* – Portuguese in base, but with lexical items borrowed from Malay, Tamil, Arabic and a host of other languages – also existed. In a very real sense, risks and uncertainties which had stemmed from the relative fragility of the market for commercial information were now much diminished.

We have listed only the major changes here; a host of other changes exist too, from the greater dissemination of firearms, to the spread of precious metals and less valuable money media, accompanying the greater commercialisation of which we have spoken. Once we see the Portuguese presence in Asia from this perspective, the framework of the 'equilibrium trap' – ingenious though it may be – cannot stand. Therein lies the main argumentative thrust of this book, which has been to suggest that the Portuguese commercial and imperial enterprise in Asia evolved a great deal in its character between 1500 and 1700, and that this evolution was the result of the interaction of changes not merely in the metropolis but elsewhere – be it in East Asia, Africa or South America. If at times factors local to Asia were determining in nature, at other times they were merely accommodative; for just as the increase in Japanese bullion production was autonomous of events in Portugal, the reasons for the European Counter-Reformation had little or nothing to do, causally speaking, with Japan. Yet, without the Society of Jesus, and without Japanese silver, the history of the Portuguese in Asia would have been quite different in the sixteenth and seventeenth centuries; and in the final analysis, the Jesuits and Japanese silver came to have a complex historical interaction! In this sense, the issues we have dealt with are neither specific to the history of Portugal and Europe, nor to that of Asia. It might be said with equal truth that they belong to both, even as they belong to neither of the two.

Glossary

Note: Unless otherwise stated, words in the glossary are of Portuguese origin. For other terms – Ar. = Arabic ; Jap. = Japanese ; Mal. = Malay ; Per. = Persian ; Sp. = Spanish.

agasalhado: right to a portion of cargo space on a ship, also termed *gasalhado*.

alevantado: a rebel (see also *levantado*)

almoxarife: administrative post, concerned with civil supplies

al-murabitin: or Almoravid, a Muslim warrior sect of north African origin, active in medieval Iberia

alta burguesia: upper bourgeoisie

amir: Per. noble or man of substance

armada: fleet

arrenegado: renegade

a'yan al-tujjar: Ar. magnates, substantial merchants

bahar: a measure of weight, different in different parts of South and Southeast Asia, varying roughly from 210 kg. to 230 kg. Used at times interchangeably with *candil* (plural *bares*).

bakufu: Jap. shadow government, or rule by shogunate

bendahara: Mal. chief financial minister of a state

bupatis: Mal. Javanese local lords

caixas de liberdade: liberty-chests

câmara municipal: Municipal chamber of a city or town

candy, or *candil*: also *khandi*, a measure of weight, equivalent in Chaul to 235 kg. Also used for the *bahar*.

capitão-mór: Captain-Major

carreiras: trade route, or route taken by ship

Carreira da Índia: Cape route

carta régia: Royal letter

cartaz: a passport or safe-conduct for a ship, given in exchange for a fee or as a diplomatic privilege

Casa da Índia: India House in Lisbon, at which goods arriving from Asia were unloaded and auctioned, and customs-duties collected

Casa da Moeda: the Portuguese mint in Lisbon

Casa de Contratación: Span. the Spanish state agency centralising trade to the New World

casado: literally a married settler, and in fact used as a juridical category to denote a permanent resident of a settlement of the Estado da Índia; at times sub-divided into 'white' (*branco*) and 'black' (*preto*)

castiço: a person of Portuguese descent, born in Asia

cavaleiros: cavalier or knight, at times used together with *fidalgo*

chatim: from the term *chetti*, common to many southern Indian languages, used in a derogatory sense for unscrupulous Portuguese traders

cidadãos or *homens-bons*: a juridical category, denoting middle-class citizens

cidade: city, the Spanish equivalent being *ciudad*

clero: clergy, one of the three orders in society

condados: counties

conde: count

cong than: Vietnamese, warlords in the fifteenth and sixteenth centuries

conselho: council

Conselho do Estado: the State Council in Goa

Conselho da Fazenda: the Revenue-Council

Conselho da Índia: the Council of the Indies in Portugal, 1604–1614

consulta: a written report, which was usually by a state organ

consulta de partes: a private individual's report, usually to the Crown, made with the intention of gaining a promotion or concession

cortes: the notional meeting of the three estates, called periodically in Spain and Portugal

cristãos novos: New Christians, converts from Judaism

cruzado: Portuguese coin, worth 360 *reis* in the sixteenth century, and 400 *reis* in the seventeenth century

daimyo: Jap. warlord

dom: a title of the Portuguese nobility, from the Latin *dominus*, abbreviated as D. The feminine is *Dona*

encomienda: Span. land grant in the New World, entitling the holder (*encomendero*) to collect a tribute in money, goods or labour services

escrivão: scrivener, usually of a ship or factory

escudeiros: squires, members of the lower nobility

Estado da Índia: the Portuguese State of India (ie. the Indies), a term that came into vogue in the second half of the sixteenth century

estanco: state commodity monopoly

Fazenda Real: the Royal Treasury

feitor: factor, Crown or private trading agent

feitoria: factory, Crown trading post

Glossary

fidalgo: literally *filho de algo*, son of a somebody; a member of the upper nobility, corresponds to Span. *hidalgo*

fronteiro: a frontiersman settler in a Portuguese settlement; common usage in North Africa, less so in Asia

fusta: a small ship

gente miuda or *gente baixa*: the common people (literally, little or low people, to be distinguished from the *gente limpa*, the clean people)

ghulam: Per. household slave

grande nobreza: upper strata of the nobility

guerra do corso: war carried on by means of corsairs

hacienda: Span. large rural property in the New World, from which *hacendado*, its proprietor

harac-i arazi: Ottoman, land-tax

has: Ottoman, that which belongs to the Crown ; variants are Persian *khass*, and Mughal *khalisa*

hermandad: Span. literally 'brotherhood', used to denote a corporate body of the cities in the late medieval and early modern period

hulubalang: Mal. local lords rooted in the land

infançoe(s: a category of middle nobility

jagir: Per. used in a Mughal context for a temporary revenue-assignment (or prebend), theoretically of three years' duration

jornaleiros: journeymen

karrani: Ar. ship's scrivener

khidmat: Per. service

khutba: Ar. the Muslim Friday prayer in which the ruler's name was mentioned, and he was prayed for

lavradores: peasants

letrados: clerks

levantado: rebel (alternative spelling for *alevantado*)

malik ut-tujjar: Ar. chief of the merchants

mansab: Per. used in a Mughal context to denote an official position, numerically calibrated on two scales, *zat* and *sawar*

mestiço: of mixed blood

milreis: a monetary unit of 1,000 *reis*

mouros: Moors, used for all Muslims

muqarrariya: Per. a fixed tribute

nau: a large ship, or carrack

naus del-Rei: Crown shipping

naveta: a small ocean-going vessel

navio de remo: an oared ship or galley

negeri di-atas angin: Mal. the lands above the winds

negeri di-bawah angin: Mal. lands below the winds

nobreza: nobility

orang kaya: Mal. the great men or commercially-oriented nobles of a Malay kingdom

ordens militares: the military orders, such as the Orders of Christ, Santiago and Aviz

Padisah: Ottoman, for the ruler ; variant Mughal *padshah*

padroado real: the Portuguese Crown patronage of religious missions

paradesi: root Sanskrit, foreigners, used to denote Middle Esatern Muslims on the Indian west coast

pardau: silver coin worth 360 *reis* (also termed *pataca* and *São Tomé*)

páreas: tribute payment in recognition of the suzerainty of the Portuguese King, made by Asian monarchs

pasisir. Mal. the north coast of Java

patangatim-mór. the head of the Parava community on the Fishery coast of southern India from the Tamil *pattankatti*, headman

povo: the common people

povoação: settlement, as distinct from *cidade*

prazo: land grant on the west coast of India or East Africa, from which *prazero*, its holder

provedor-mór. chief purveyor, or director

qadi: Ar. a judge, or head of a community

qizilbash: Per. literally red-head, used for the Turkoman followers of Shah Ismail and his successors

quintal: a unit of weight ; the light quintal weighed 51.4 kilogrammes and the heavy quintal 58.7 kilogrammes.

real: basic accounting unit, from which the plural *reis*

real de a ocho: Span. rial of eight, worth 400 *reis* in the seventeenth century

reconquista: the reconquest of the Iberian peninsula from Islamic rule

regimento: regulation or statute

reguengos: Crown estate

reino: literally realm or kingdom, used to denote Portugal

reinol: a Portuguese born in Portugal

reis: the basic accounting unit in the Portuguese monetary system ; see under *real*

rendeiros: rentiers, revenue-farmers

ricos-homens: literally rich men, a category of nobility in medieval Portugal

sakoku: Jap. the closed country

Santa Casa de Misericórdia: the Holy House of Mercy, a religious and charitable institution administered by a brotherhood (*irmandade*)

sengoku: Jap. the country at war

soldado: soldier

solteiro: a freewheeling merchant, without a permanent residence in any Portuguese settlement

syahbandars: Mal. from Per. *shahbandar*, literally the lord of the port, in fact an administrative official or representative of a merchant group in a port

Glossary

tanadar-mór: a high official from Goa, the term derives from the Hindustani *thanadar* (with roots in Prakrit)

tanga: silver coin worth 60 *reis*, from the Indo-Muslim *tanka*

temenggong: Mal. a minister of the state

timar: Ottoman, permanent revenue-assignment

tonel: (plural, *toneis*) a unit of displacement for vessels, sometimes called *tonelada*, equivalent to 1,023 kg.

ushur: Ar. port duties

vania: a merchant caste grouping, usually Gujarati

vedor da fazenda: financial superintendent

viagens: voyages, sometimes used for the concession-voyages (*viagens de lugares*)

wo-k'ou: Chinese (also Jap. *wako*), corsairs in the South China Sea

xerafim: silver coin worth 300 *reis*, from the Persian *ashrafi*

zamindar: Per. landholder, used in India to denote the local lords rooted in the land

zeamet: Ar. origin, Ottoman use, for revenue-assignment

A Note on Quantitative Data

The large number of tables included in the present volume is evidence that reliable quantitative data can be obtained for the period under consideration, on different aspects of Portuguese and Asian economic history. This is a view that may be met with some scepticism, and in order to counter this scepticism some explanations are necessary.

Unlike the archives of the great trading Companies, and especially the Dutch East India Company (or VOC), the Portuguese archives are quite fragmented for the period from 1500 to 1700. A part of the reason for this lies in the famous earthquake that shook Lisbon in the mid-eighteenth century, but everything cannot be laid at the door of this Act of God. The nature of the Portuguese enterprise, and the extensive private participation in it, were simply not conducive to the generation of good statistics on a number of key variables. In particular, it is extremely difficult to trace private trade in its quantitative dimensions, especially within Asia. This said, we may briefly survey the main types of quantitative sources available to us from the Portuguese archives.

(1) Budgets or *Orçamentos* of the *Estado da Índia*: These are available intermittently from the 1550s on, with some long gaps. A competent survey of these may be found in Godinho (1982), which is supplemented by Matos (1982). A variant of the *orçamento* is the *tombo*, which is discussed below.

(2) Cape route shipping: Information on this is surprisingly fragmentary. Some general listings exist in the British Museum and elsewhere, but are thought to be suspect. For the early years of the sixteenth century, some detailed documents exist in the Núcleo Antigo collection of the Arquivo Nacional da Torre do Tombo, Lisbon (for which see Bouchon (1976a) and (1977)). For later years in the century, the Archivo General de Simancas in Spain has some detailed records. Fragments of books maintained by the scriveners on board these vessels

283

may be found in the Caixas da Índia of the Arquivo Histórico Ultramarino, Lisbon. An excellent survey of much of the available material is that of Duncan (1986). He has reconstructed shipping numbers, and deduced plausible tonnages on the basis of extrapolating available data. Duncan also provides estimates of gross and net movements of persons on the Cape route, using a simple statistical technique; he takes available data, arranged period-wise, on the relationship between tonnage and passengers, and inflates it using the tonnage data. His estimates have been followed in all tables on shipping and shipping tonnage on the Cape route, and in Table 8.2.

(3) Contemporary compendia: While the major Portuguese chronicles (Barros, Correia, Castanheda and Couto) are by and large lacking in systematic statistical data, we do have occasional compendia which are more detailed. Two of the most important are the anonymous *Livro das Cidades e Fortalezas*, of which a single manuscript exists in the Biblioteca Nacional of Madrid (cf. Mendes da Luz 1954), and António Bocarro's *Livro das Plantas* from the 1630s, of which at least four copies exist (in the Biblioteca Nacional de Madrid, the Biblioteca Nacional de Lisboa, the Évora archives, and the British Museum). An edition by A.B. de Bragança Pereira uses the Évora version (cf. Bocarro 1937–38); it has a certain number of errors of transcription. I have used both these *Livros* extensively. The author of the 1580s text had almost certainly served as a high financial official in Asia, while Bocarro (and his collaborator Pedro Barreto de Resende) had access to detailed state papers.

(4) Account-books: A few account-books relating to early Portuguese voyages in Asia are preserved in the Núcleo Antigo at the Arquivo Nacional da Torre do Tombo. These are mostly concerned with the years 1505 to 1525; an example is discussed at length in Aubin (1988). Private account-books are far more rare. I am in the process of editing one of these, that of a private trader, Francisco da Gama, from the 1610s and early 1620s. Occasionally, account-books dealing with particular factories (Pasai, Chaliyam) may be found. The current reorganisation of the Torre do Tombo may yield more examples of these. Also to be encountered occasionally are detailed accounts of a particular territory, or even a survey of revenue potential. These are termed *Tombos*, and an early example is that of Simão Botelho (Felner 1868). Similar *Tombos* exist for Portuguese territories in early seventeenth-century Sri Lanka.

(5) Foreign sources: For certain aspects of Portuguese trading activities in this period, the records of other nations prove richer than the Portuguese records themselves. This is the case with Italian sources on certain aspects of early trade on the Cape route. For private Portuguese shipping and trade, a particularly important set of papers is in the Algemeen Rijksarchief, The Hague, in the archives of the Dutch Company (or VOC). These are the *Overgekomen Brieven en Papieren*

A note on quantitative data

(Letters and Papers Received) of the VOC, which include detailed statistical enclosures on a number of variables.

Finally, for a number of issues, the statistics that we have cited are no more than informed guess-work. While the population of Portugal can be estimated fairly accurately from a survey of households in the late 1520s, estimating the population of Asia as a whole in 1500 or 1600 is obviously subject to a far wider margin of error.

Bibliography

Abeyasinghe, Tikiri, 1966. *Portuguese Rule in Ceylon, 1594–1612*. Colombo. Lake House.

Albuquerque, Luís de and Inácio Guerreiro, 1985. 'Khoja Shams-ud-din, comerciante de Cananor na primeira metade do seculo XVI'. In *Actas do II Seminário Internacional de História Indo-Portuguesa*. Lisbon.

Alves, Jorge M. dos Santos, 1990. 'Une ville inquiète et un Sultan barricadé. Aceh vers 1588 d'après le *Roteiro das Cousas do Achém* de l'Evêque de Malaka', *Archipel*, 39.

Amaral Lapa, J. R. do, 1989. 'Dimensões do comércio colonial entre o Brasil e o Oriente', *Studia*, 49.

Ames, Glenn J., 1989. 'The Estado da Índia, 1663–1677. Priorities and strategies in Europe and the East', *Studia*, 49.

Amiel, Charles, 1986. 'The archives of the Portuguese Inquisition. A brief survey'. In *The Inquisition in early modern Europe. Studies on sources and methods*, eds. Gustav Henningsen and John Tedeschi. De Kalb (Illinois). Northern Illinois University Press.

Andaya, Leonard Y., 1975. *The Kingdom of Johor, 1641–1728. Economic and political developments*. Kuala Lumpur. Oxford University Press.

Andrews, Kenneth R., 1984. *Trade, plunder and settlement. Maritime enterprise and the genesis of the British empire, 1480–1630*. Cambridge. Cambridge University Press.

Arasaratnam, S., 1986. *Merchants, Companies and Commerce on the Coromandel Coast, 1650–1740*. Delhi. Oxford University Press.

Archivo Portuguez-Oriental, 6 Fascicules in 9 volumes, ed. J.H. da Cunha Rivara. Goa. 1857–76.

Assentos do Conselho do Estado (1618–1750), 5 volumes, ed. P.S.S. Pissurlencar. Goa. Tipografia Rangel. 1953–57.

Athar Ali, M., 1966. *The Mughal nobility under Aurangzeb*. Bombay. Asia Publishing House.

Aubin, Jean, 1971. 'Albuquerque et les négociations de Cambaye', *Mare Luso-Indicum*, 1.

Aubin, Jean, 1973. 'Le Royaume d'Ormuz au début du XVIe siècle', *Mare Luso-Indicum*, 2.

Aubin, Jean, 1976. 'L'Ambassade du Prêtre Jean à D. Manuel', *Mare Luso-Indicum*, 3.

Aubin, Jean, 1980. 'Les Persans au Siam sous le règne de Narai (1656–1688)'. *Mare Luso-Indicum* 4.

Aubin, Jean, 1987. 'L'apprentissage de l'Inde. Cochin, 1503–1504', *Moyen Orient et Océan Indien*, 4.

Aubin, Jean, 1988. 'Un voyage de Goa à Ormuz en 1520', *Modern Asian Studies*, xxii, 3.

Aubin, Jean, 1989. 'La crise Egyptienne de 1510–1512. Venise, Louis XII et le Sultan', *Moyen Orient et Océan Indien*, 6.

Aubin, Jean (ed.), 1990. *La découverte, le Portugal et l'Europe*. Paris. Centre Culturel Portugais.

Azevedo, Carlos de and Charles R. Boxer, 1960. *Fort Jesus and the Portuguese in Mombasa (1593–1729)*. London. Hollis and Carter.

Banister, Judith. 1987. *China's changing population*. Stanford. Stanford University Press.

Barros, João de, 1973. *Da Ásia*. Décadas I–IV. Lisbon. Livraria Sam Carlos. Facsimile of the 1777–78 Régia Oficina Tipográfica edition.

Bathurst, Raymond, 1972. 'Maritime trade and Imamate government. Two principal themes in the history of Oman to 1728'. In *The Arabian Peninsula, society and politics*, ed. D. Hopwood. London. George Allen and Unwin.

Bayly, C.A., 1989. *Imperial Meridian. The British empire and the world, 1780–1830*. London. Longman.

Blussé, Leonard, 1986. *Strange Company: Chinese settlers, mestizo women and the Dutch in VOC Batavia*. Dordrecht. Foris Publications (Verhandelingen KITLV).

Blussé, Leonard, 1988. 'Brief Encounter at Macao', *Modern Asian Studies*, xxii, 3.

Bocarro, António, 1876. *Década XIII da História da Índia*. Edited by R.J. de Lima Felner. 2 volumes. Lisbon. Academia das Ciências.

Bocarro, António, 1937–38. 'Livro das Plantas de todas as fortalezas, cidades e povoações do Estado da Índia Oriental'. in A. B. de Bragança Pereira (ed.), *Arquivo Português Oriental*, (N.S.). Volume IV/1/1–2. Goa. Tipografia Rangel.

Boletim da Filmoteca Ultramarina Portuguesa. Volumes 1 to 45. Centro de Estudos Históricos Ultramarinos. Lisbon, 1954–1971.

Borges, Jorge Luis. 1972. *Selected Poems, 1923–1967*. London. Penguin Press.

Bouchon, Geneviève, 1971. 'Les rois de Kotte au début du XVI siècle', *Mare Luso-Indicum*, 1.

Bouchon, Geneviève, 1973. 'Les Musulmans du Kerala à l'époque de la découverte portugaise', *Mare Luso-Indicum*, 2.

Bouchon, Geneviève, 1976a. 'L'inventaire de la cargaison rapportée en Inde en 1505', *Mare Luso-Indicum*, 3.

Bouchon, Geneviève, 1976b. 'Les femmes dans la société coloniale Ibérique', *Mare Luso-Indicum*, 3.

Bouchon, Geneviève, 1977. *Navires et Cargaisons retour de l'Inde en 1518*. Paris. Société d'Histoire de l'Orient.

Bouchon, Geneviève, 1988. *'Regent of the Sea'. Cannanore's response to Portuguese expansion, 1507–1528*. Delhi. Oxford University Press.

Bouchon, Geneviève and Luís Filipe Thomaz, 1988. *Voyage dans les Deltas du Gange et de l'Irraouaddy. Relation Portugaise Anonyme (1521)*. Paris. Centre Culturel Portugais.

Bowrey, Thomas, 1905. *A geographical account of countries round the Bay of Bengal, 1669 to 1679*, ed. R.C. Temple. London. The Hakluyt Society.

Boxer, Charles R., 1948a. *Fidalgos in the Far East, 1550–1770*. The Hague. Martinus Nijhoff. (Reprint, 1968, Hong Kong)

Boxer, Charles R., 1948b. 'Three historians of Portuguese Asia – Barros, Couto and Bocarro', *Boletim do Instituto Português de Hongkong*, 1.

Boxer, Charles R., 1958. 'Portuguese and Dutch colonial rivalry, 1641–1661', *Studia*, 2.

Boxer, Charles R., 1959. *The Great Ship from Amacon. Annals of Macao and the Old Japan trade, 1555–1640*. Lisbon. CEHU.

Boxer, Charles R., 1960. 'The Carreira da Índia, 1650–1750', *Mariner's Mirror*, 46.

Boxer, Charles R., 1965. *Portuguese Society in the Tropics. The Municipal Councils of Goa, Macao, Bahia and Luanda, 1510–1800*. Madison/ Milwaukee. University of Wisconsin Press.

Boxer, Charles R., 1967. *Francisco Vieira de Figueiredo. A Portuguese merchant-adventurer in South East Asia, 1624–1667*. The Hague. Martinus Nijhoff (Verhandelingen KITLV).

Boxer, Charles R., 1969a. 'A note on Portuguese reactions to the revival of the Red Sea trade and the rise of Atjeh, 1540–1600', *Journal of Southeast Asian Studies*, x, 3.

Boxer, Charles R., 1969b. 'Portuguese and Spanish projects for the conquest of Southeast Asia, 1580–1600', *Journal of Asian History*, 3.

Boxer, Charles R., 1969c. *The Portuguese Seaborne Empire, 1415–1825*. London. Weidenfeld and Nicholson.

Boxer, Charles R., 1975. *Mary and Misogyny. Women in Iberian expansion overseas 1415–1815, some facts, fancies and personalities*. London. Duckworth.

Boxer, Charles R., 1985a. *Portuguese Conquest and Commerce in Southern Asia, 1500–1700*. London. Variorum reprints.

Boxer, Charles R., 1985b. 'Diogo do Couto (1543–1616), controversial chronicler of Portuguese Asia'. In *Iberia – Literary and Historical Issues*.

Studies in Honour of Harold V. Livermore, ed. R.O.W. Goertz. Calgary. University of Calgary Press.

Boyajian, James C., 1983. *Portuguese Bankers at the Court of Spain, 1626–1650*. New Brunswick. Rutgers University Press.

Boyajian, James C., 1986. 'Goa Inquisition – A new light on first 100 years (1561–1660)', *Purabhilekh-Puratatva*, iv, 1.

Bramanti, Vanni (ed.), 1970. *Lettere da Vari Paesi, 1570–1588, di Filippo Sassetti*. Milan. Longanesi.

Bury, Peter John, 1975. 'The Indian contribution to Portuguese rule in the East, 1500–1580'. Ph.D. thesis, University of Cambridge.

Calado, Adelino de Almeida (ed.), 1960. 'Livro que trata das Coisas da Índia e do Japão', *Boletim da Biblioteca da Universidade de Coimbra*, 24

Calvet de Magalhães, José, 1966. 'Duarte Gomes Solis', *Studia*, 19.

Cartas de Afonso de Albuquerque seguidas de documentos que as elucidam, eds. R.A. de Bulhão Pato and H. Lopes de Mendonça, 7 volumes. Lisbon. 1884–1935.

Céspedes del Castillo, Guillermo, 1972. 'La sociedad colonial americana en los siglos XVI y XVII'. In *História de España y America social y economica*, ed. J. Vicens Vives, vol. III. Barcelona. Libros Vicens-Bolsillo.

Chaudhuri, K.N., 1965. *The English East India Company. The study of an early joint-stock company, 1600–1640*. London. Frank Cass.

Chaudhuri, K.N., 1982. 'Foreign Trade. European Trade with India'. In *The Cambridge Economic History of India*, Volume I, eds. Tapan Raychaudhuri and Irfan Habib. Cambridge. Cambridge University Press.

Collis, M.S. and San Shwe Bu, 1925. 'Arakan's place in the civilization of the Bay', *Journal of the Burma Research Society*, xv, 1.

Commelin, Isaac, 1646. *Begin ende Voortgangh van de Vereenighde Nederlantsche Geoctroyeerde Oost-Indische Compagnie*. Amsterdam. 2 volumes.

Coolhaas, W.Ph. (ed.), 1962–63. *Pieter van den Broecke in Azië*, 2 volumes. The Hague. Martinus Nijhoff.

Correia, Gaspar, 1975. *Lendas da Índia*, ed. M. Lopes de Almeida, 4 volumes. Porto.

Correia-Afonso, John (ed.), 1990. *Intrepid Itinerant. Manuel Godinho and his Journey from India to Portugal in 1663*. Bombay. Oxford University Press.

Couto, Diogo do, 1973–74. *Da Ásia*. Décadas IV–XII. Lisbon. Livraria Sam Carlos. Facsimile of the 1777–78 Régia Oficina Tipográfica edition.

Couto, Diogo do, 1988. *O Soldado Prático*. Introduction and notes by Reis Brazil. Lisbon. Publicações Europa-América.

Cross, Harry E., 1978. 'Commerce and orthodoxy. A Spanish response to Portuguese commercial penetration in the viceroyalty of Peru, 1580–1640', *The Americas*, xxxv, 2.

Cross, Harry E., 1983. 'South American bullion production and export, 1550–1750'. In Richards (1983).

Bibliography

Cruz, Maria Augusta Lima, 1986. 'Exiles and Renegades in early sixteenth century Portuguese India', *The Indian Economic and Social History Review*, xxiii, 3.

Cruz, Maria Augusta Lima, 1987. 'Diogo do Couto e a Década 8.a da Ásia', volume 5 (O discurso histórico). Doctoral thesis, Universidade Nova de Lisboa, Lisbon.

Cruz, Maria Augusta Lima, 1989. 'A viagem de Gonçalo Pereira Marramaque do Minho às Molucas — ou os itinerários da fidalguia portuguesa no Oriente', *Studia*, 49.

Das Gupta, Ashin, 1985. 'Indian merchants and the western Indian Ocean. The early seventeenth century', *Modern Asian Studies*, xix, 3.

De Jonge, J.K.J., 1865. *De Opkomst van het Nederlandsch Gezag in Oost-Indië (1595–1610)*. Deel III. The Hague/Amsterdam.

De Silva, C.R., 1972. *The Portuguese in Ceylon, 1617–1638*. Colombo. H.W. Cave and Company.

De Silva, C.R., 1989. 'The Portuguese impact on the production and trade in Sri Lanka cinnamon in Asia in the sixteenth and seventeenth centuries', *Indica*, xxvi, 1/2.

De Souza, Teotonio R., 1979. *Medieval Goa. A Socio-Economic History*. New Delhi. Concept Publishing House.

De Souza, Teotonio R., 1989. 'Embassies and surrogates. Case-study of a Malacca embassy to Siam in 1595', *Indica*, xxvi, 1/2.

Desoulières, Alain, 1986. 'La communauté portugaise d'Agra (1633–1739)', *Arquivos do Centro Cultural Português*, 22.

Dias, José Sebastião da Silva, 1969. *A política cultural da época de D. João III*, 2 vols. Coimbra. Instituto de Estudos Filosóficos.

Dias, José Sebastião da Silva, 1988. *Os Descobrimentos e a problemática cultural do século XVI*. Lisbon. Editorial Presença, 3rd edition.

Disney, Anthony R., 1978. *Twilight of the pepper empire. Portuguese trade in Southwest India in the early seventeenth century*. Cambridge (Mass.). Harvard University Press.

Disney, Anthony R., 1989. 'Famine and famine relief in Portuguese India in the sixteenth and early seventeenth centuries'. *Studia*, 49.

Documentos Remetidos da Índia, ou Livros das Monções, Vols. I–V, ed. R.A. de Bulhão Pato, Lisbon 1880–1935, Vols. VI–X, ed. A. da Silva Rego, Lisbon 1974–82.

Duncan, T. Bentley, 1986. 'Navigation between Portugal and Asia in the Sixteenth and Seventeenth Centuries'. In E.J. van Kley and C.K. Pullapilly (eds.), *Asia and the West. Encounters and Exchanges from the Age of Explorations*. Notre Dame.

Dutra, Francis A. 1970. 'Membership in the Order of Christ in the seventeenth century. Its rights, privileges, and obligations', *The Americas*, xxvii, 1.

Elison, George, 1973. *Deus destroyed. The image of Christianity in early modern Japan*. Cambridge (Mass.). Harvard University Press.

Elliot, H.M. and Dowson, J. (eds.), 1867–77. *The History of India as told by its own historians (The Muhammadan Period)*, 8 Vols. London. Reprint Allahabad. Kitab Mahal.

Elliott, John H., 1986. *The Count-Duke of Olivares. The statesman in an age of decline*. New Haven/London. Yale University Press.

Farooqi, Naimur Rehman, 1989. *Mughal-Ottoman Relations. A study of political and diplomatic relations between Mughal India and the Ottoman Empire, 1556–1748*. Delhi. Idarah-i Adabiyat-i Delhi.

Felner, Rodrigo José de Lima, (ed.), 1868. *Subsídios para a história da Índia Portugueza*. In 3 parts. Lisbon. Academia Real das Sciências.

Fleischer, Cornell H., 1986. *Bureaucrat and Intellectual in the Ottoman Empire. The Historian Mustafa Ali (1541–1600)*. Princeton. Princeton University Press.

Flores, Jorge Manuel, 1990. 'The Straits of Ceylon and the maritime trade in early sixteenth–century India. Commodities, merchants and trading networks', *Moyen Orient et Océan Indien*, 7.

Fok, K.C., 1987. 'Early Ming images of the Portuguese'. In R. Ptak (ed.), *Portuguese Asia. Aspects in History and Economic History*. Stuttgart. Franz Steiner Verlag.

Fontoura, Otília Rodrigues, 1966. 'Portugal em Marrocos na época de D. João III – Abandono ou permanência?'. Universidade de Lisboa, licentiate thesis.

Ford, J.D.M. (ed.), 1931. *Letters of John III, King of Portugal, 1521–1557*. Cambridge (Mass.). Harvard University Press.

Gavetas. *As Gavetas da Torre do Tombo*, 12 volumes. Ed. A. da Silva Rego. Lisbon, 1960–77.

Glamann, Kristof, 1981. *Dutch-Asiatic Trade, 1620–1740*. 2nd edition. The Hague. Martinus Nijhoff.

Godinho, Vitorino Magalhães, 1968. *Ensaios*, Vol. II (sobre história de Portugal). Lisbon. Livraria Sá da Costa.

Godinho, Vitorino Magalhães, 1978. 'L'émigration portugaise (XVeme-XXeme siècles) – une constante structurelle et les réponses au changements du monde', *Revista de História Económica e Social*, 1.

Godinho, Vitorino Magalhães, 1981–83. *Os Descobrimentos e a Economia Mundial*. 4 Volumes. 2nd edition. Lisbon. Editorial Presença.

Godinho, Vitorino Magalhães, 1982. *Les Finances de l'État Portugais des Indes Orientales (1517–1635)*. Paris. Centre Culturel Portugais.

Godinho, Vitorino Magalhães, 1990. *Mito e mercadoria, utópia e prática de navegar, séculos XIII– XVIII*. Lisbon. Difel.

Goertz, R.O.W., 1986. 'The Portuguese in Cochin in the mid-sixteenth century', *Indica*, xxiii, 1/2.

Bibliography

Groslier, Bernard P., 1958. *Angkor et le Cambodge au XVIe siècle, d'après les sources portugaises et espagnoles* (in collaboration with C.R. Boxer). Paris.

Guerreiro, Inácio and Vitor Rodrigues, 1989. 'O 'grupo de Cochin' e a oposição a Afonso de Albuquerque'. Paper presented to the Fifth International Seminar on Indo-Portuguese History, Cochin.

Halbfass, Wilhelm, 1988. *India and Europe. An essay in understanding.* Albany. SUNY Press.

Hall, J.W., Nagahara Keiji, and Kozo Yamamura (eds.), 1981. *Japan before Tokugawa. Political Consolidation and Economic Growth 1500 to 1650.* Princeton. Princeton University Press.

Haneda, Masashi, 1987. *Le Cha#h les Qizilba#š. Le système militaire safavide.* Berlin. Klaus Schwarz Verlag.

Hanson, Carl A., 1981. *Economy and Society in Baroque Portugal, 1668–1703.* London. Macmillan Press.

Heifetz, Hank and Velcheru Narayana Rao (translated), 1987. *For the Lord of the Animals – Poems from the Telugu. The Kalahastisvara Satakamu of Dhurjati.* Delhi. Oxford University Press.

Isaacman, Allen F., 1972. *Mozambique – The Africanization of a European Institution. The Zambezi Prazos, 1750–1902.* Madison/Milwaukee. The University of Wisconsin Press.

Israel, Jonathan I., 1982. *The Dutch Republic and the Hispanic World, 1606–1661.* Oxford. Clarendon Press.

Israel, Jonathan I., 1989. *Dutch primacy in world trade, 1585–1740.* Oxford. Clarendon Press.

Jackson, Peter and Laurence Lockhart (eds.), 1986. *The Cambridge History of Iran*, Vol. VI (The Timurid and Safavid Periods). Cambridge. Cambridge University Press.

Jacobs, Hubert, 1985. 'The Portuguese town of Ambon, 1576–1605'. In Luís de Albuquerque and Inácio Guerreiro (eds.), *Actas do II Seminário Internacional de História Indo-Portuguesa*, Lisbon.

Kamen, Henry. 1985. *Inquisition and Society in Spain in the sixteenth and seventeenth centuries.* London. Weidenfeld and Nicholson.

Kaufmann, S. B., 1981. 'A Christian caste in Hindu society. Religious leadership and social conflict among the Paravas of southern Tamilnadu', *Modern Asian Studies*, xv, 2.

Kellenbenz, Hermann, 1956. 'Les frères Fugger et le marché international du poivre autour de 1600', *Annales E.S.C.*, xi, 1.

Kellenbenz, Hermann, 1963. 'Cron, Ferdinand, 1559–1637'. In *Dicionário de História de Portugal*, ed. Joel Serrão, vol. I. Lisbon.

Knaap, Gerrit J., 1987. *Kruidnagelen en Christenen. De VOC en de bevolking van Ambon, 1656–1696.* Dordrecht. Verhandelingen KITLV.

Kolff, D.H.A., 1990. *Naukar, Rajput and Sepoy. The ethnohistory of the military labour market in Hindustan, 1450–1850.* Cambridge. Cambridge University Press.

Lewis, Bernard, 1970. 'Egypt and Syria'. In P.M. Holt, A.K.S. Lambton and B. Lewis, eds. *The Cambridge History of Islam*, Vol. I, Cambridge. Cambridge University Press

Lieberman, Victor B., 1980. 'Europeans, trade and the Unification of Burma, c. 1540–1620', *Oriens Extremus*, xxvii, 2.

Lieberman, Victor B., 1984. *Burmese Administrative Cycles. Anarchy and Conquest, c. 1580–1760.* Princeton. Princeton University Press.

Liebman, Seymour B., 1971. 'The great conspiracy in Peru', *The Americas*, xxviii, 2.

Livermore, H.V., 1973. *Portugal. A short history.* Edinburgh. Edinburgh University Press.

Lobato, Alexandre, 1965. *Relações Luso-Maratas, 1658–1737.* Lisbon. Centro de Estudos Historicos Ultramarinos.

Lombard, Denys, 1967. *Le Sultanat d'Atjéh au temps d'Iskandar Muda (1607–1636).* Paris. EFEO.

Lopes, David (ed.), 1899. *História dos Portugueses no Malabar por Zinadim.* Lisbon. Imprensa Nacional.

Lovett, A.W., 1986. *Early Habsburg Spain, 1517–1598.* Oxford. Oxford University Press.

Lynch, J.H., 1981. *Spain under the Habsburgs, II. Spain and America 1598–1700.* 2nd edition. Oxford. Basil Blackwell.

Manguin, Pierre-Yves, 1972. *Les Portugais sur les côtes du Viet-nam et du Campa (XVIe, XVIIe et XVIIIe siècles).* Paris. EFEO.

Manguin, Pierre-Yves, 1984. *Les Nguyen, Macau et le Portugal. Aspects politiques et commerciaux d'une rélation privilegiée en Mer de Chine, 1773–1802.* Paris. EFEO.

Manguin, Pierre-Yves, 1988. 'Of Fortresses and Galleys. The 1568 Acehnese Siege of Melaka, after a Contemporary Bird's-eye View', *Modern Asian Studies*, xxii, 3.

Mantran, Robert, 1970. 'North Africa in the sixteenth and seventeenth centuries'. In *The Cambridge History of Islam*, vol. 2, eds. P.M. Holt, A.K.S. Lambton, and B. Lewis. Cambridge. Cambridge University Press.

Marques, A.H. de Oliveira, 1980. *Ensaios da História Medieval Portuguesa.* Lisbon. Editorial Vega, 2nd edition.

Marques, A.H. de Oliveira, 1987. *Portugal na Crise dos Séculos XIV e XV.* Lisbon. Editorial Presença.

Marques, A H de Oliveira, 1988. *Novos Ensaios da História Medieval Portuguesa.* Lisbon. Editorial Presença.

Matos, Artur Teodoro de, 1974. *Timor Português, 1515–1769. Contribuição para a sua história.* Lisbon. Faculdade de Letras.

Matos, Artur Teodoro de, 1982. *O Estado da Índia nos anos de 1581–1588, estrutura administrativa e económica. Alguns elementos para o seu estudo.* Ponta Delgada.

Bibliography

Matos, Artur Teodoro de, 1984. 'The financial situation of the State of India during the Philippine period (1581–1635)'. In *Indo-Portuguese History. Old Issues, New Questions*, ed. T.R. De Souza. New Delhi. Concept Publishing House.

Matos, Luís de (ed.), 1985. *Imagens do Oriente no século XVI. Reprodução do Códice Português da Biblioteca Casanatense.* Lisbon. Imprensa Nacional.

Mattoso, José, 1985. *Ricos-Homens, Infançoe(s e Cavaleiros. A nobreza medieval portuguesa nos séculos XI e XII.* Lisbon. Guimarães editores, 2nd edition.

Mattoso, José, 1988. *Identificação de um país. Ensaio sobre as origens de Portugal, 1096–1325.* 2 volumes. Lisbon. Editorial Estampa.

Mauro, Frédéric, 1970. *Études Économiques sur l'expansion portugaise (1500–1900).* Paris. Calouste Gulbenkian Foundation.

Meilink-Roelofsz, M.A.P., 1962. *Asian trade and European influence in the Indonesian archipelago between 1500 and about 1630.* The Hague. Martinus Nijhoff.

Mendes da Luz, F.P. (ed.), 1954. 'Livro das Cidades e Fortalezas que a Coroa de Portugal tem nas partes da Índia, e das capitanias e mais cargos que nelas há, e da importância deles', *Boletim da Biblioteca da Universidade de Coimbra.* 21.

Miranda, Ambroxio Huici, 1970. 'The Iberian Peninsula and Sicily'. In *The Cambridge History of Islam*, vol. 2, eds. P.M. Holt, A.K.S. Lambton, and B. Lewis. Cambridge. Cambridge University Press.

Mudenge, S.I.G., 1988. *A political history of Munhumutapa, c. 1400–1902.* Harare. Zimbabwe Publishing House.

Nardi, Jean-Baptiste, 1989. 'Le commerce du tabac vers l'Inde Portugaise du XVIIe au XIXe siècle', *Moyen Orient et Océan Indien*, 6.

Nunes Dias, Manuel, 1963–64. *O capitalismo monárquico português (1415–1549). Contribuição para o estudo das origens do capitalismo moderno*, 2 vols. Coimbra.

Ozbaran, Salih, 1972. 'The Ottoman Turks and the Portuguese in the Persian Gulf, 1534–1581', *Journal of Asian History*, vi, 1.

Ozbaran, Salih, 1986. 'Some notes on the Salyane system in the Ottoman empire as organised in Arabia in the sixteenth century'. *Osmanli Arastirmalari, The Journal of Ottoman Studies*, 6.

Pankhurst, Richard, 1961. *An introduction to the economic history of Ethiopia from early times to 1800.* London. Lalibela House.

Parker, Geoffrey, 1979. *Philip II.* London. Hutchinson.

Parker, Geoffrey, 1980. *Europe in Crisis, 1598–1648.* Ithaca. Cornell University Press.

Parker, Geoffrey, 1988. *The military revolution. Military innovation and the rise of the West, 1500–1800.* Cambridge. Cambridge University Press.

Pearson, Michael N., 1976. *Merchants and Rulers in Gujarat. The response to the Portuguese in the sixteenth century.* Berkeley/Los Angeles. University of California Press.

Pearson, Michael N., 1981. *Coastal Western India. Studies from the Portuguese records*. New Delhi. Concept Publishing House.

Pearson, Michael N., 1987. *The Portuguese in India* (The New Cambridge History of India, Volume I.1), Cambridge. Cambridge University Press

Pinto, Fernão Mendes, 1983. *Peregrinação*, ed. Adolfo Casais Monteiro. Lisbon. Imprensa Nacional.

Pinto, Fernão Mendes, 1989. *The Travels of Mendes Pinto*. Edited and translated by Rebecca D. Catz. Chicago. University of Chicago Press.

Pouwels, Randall L., 1987. *Horn and Crescent. Cultural Change and Traditional Islam on the East African Coast, 800–1900*. Cambridge. Cambridge University Press.

Prakash, Om, 1967. 'The Dutch East India Company and the Economy of Bengal, 1650–1717'. Ph.D. thesis, University of Delhi.

Prakash, Om, 1985. *The Dutch East India Company and the Economy of Bengal, 1630–1720*. Princeton. Princeton University Press.

Qureshi, I.H., 1970. 'India under the Mughals'. In *The Cambridge History of Islam*, vol. 2, eds. P.M. Holt, A.K.S. Lambton, and B. Lewis. Cambridge. Cambridge University Press.

Rao, Velcheru Narayana, David Shulman and Sanjay Subrahmanyam, 1992. *Symbols of Substance. Court and State in Nayaka-period Tamilnadu*. Delhi. Oxford University Press.

Rau, Virginia, 1971 'Bartolomeo di Iacopo di Ser Vanni, Mercador-Banqueiro Florentino "Estante" em Lisbon nos meados do século XV.' *Memórias do Centro de Estudos de Marinha, 1*.

Rau, Virginia, 1974. 'Um florentino ao serviço da expansão ultramarina portuguesa: Francisco Corbinelli'. *Memórias do Centro de Estudos de Marinha, 4*.

Reid, Anthony, 1979. 'Trade and state power in sixteenth and seventeenth century Southeast Asia'. *Proceedings of the Seventh IAHA Conference*, Bangkok.

Reid, Anthony, 1988. *Southeast Asia in the Age of Commerce 1450–1680. Volume One: The Lands below the Winds*. New Haven. Yale University Press.

Reid, Anthony, 1990. 'The seventeenth-century crisis in Southeast Asia', *Modern Asian Studies*, xxiv, 4.

Reis, Piri, 1988. *Kitab-i Bahriye* (with an English translation), Ankara.

Reis, Seydi Ali, 1899. *The travels and adventures of the Turkish admiral Sidi Ali Reis in India, Afghanistan, Central Asia and Persia*. Edited and translated by A. Vambery. London. (Reprint, Lahore, Al-Biruni, 1975).

Reparaz, Gonçalo de, 1976. *Os Portugeses no vice-reinado do Peru (séculos XVI e XVII)*. Lisbon. Instituto de Alta Cultura.

Ribeiro, Orlando, Hermann Lautensach, and Suzanne Daveau, 1987. *Geografia de Portugal III. O povo português*. Lisbon. Ediçõe(s João Sá da

Bibliography

Costa.

Richards, John F. (ed.), 1983. *Precious Metals in the Later Medieval and Early Modern Worlds*. Durham. University of Carolina Press.

Risso, Patricia, 1986. *Oman and Muscat. An early modern history*. London. Croom Helm.

Rogers, Alexander and Henry Beveridge (trans. and ed.), 1909–14. *Tuzuk-i-Jahangiri, or Memoirs of Jahangir*. 2 vols. Reprint Delhi 1989.

Sansom, George, 1961. *A History of Japan, 1334–1615*. Chatham. William Dawson.

Savory, Roger, 1980. *Iran under the Safavids*. Cambridge. Cambridge University Press.

Scammell, Geoffrey V., 1989. *The first imperial age. European overseas expansion, c. 1400–1715*. London. Unwin Hyman.

Schama, Simon, 1987. *The embarrassment of riches. An interpretation of Dutch culture in the Golden Age*. New York. Fontana.

Serjeant R.B., 1963. *The Portuguese off the South Arabian Coast. Hadrami Chronicles*. Oxford.

Serjeant, R.B., 1988. 'Yemeni Merchants and Trade in Yemen, 13th-16th Centuries'. In *Marchands et hommes d'affaires asiatiques dans l'Océan Indien et la Mer de Chine, 13e-20e siècles*. eds. Denys Lombard and Jean Aubin. Paris. Editions EHESS.

Serrão, Joaquim Veríssimo, 1980. *História de Portugal (1495–1580)*. Lisbon. Editorial Verbo, 2nd edition.

Shaw, Stanford J., 1976. *History of the Ottoman Empire and Modern Turkey*, Vol. I. *Empire of the Gazis, the Rise and Decline of the Ottoman Empire, 1280–1808*. Cambridge. Cambridge University Press.

Silva, José Gentil da, 1956. *Stratégie des Affaires à Lisbonne entre 1595 et 1607. Lettres marchandes des Rodrigues d'Évora et Veiga*. Paris. SEVPEN.

Silva, José Gentil da, 1959–61. *Marchandises et Finances, lettres de Lisbonne, 1563–1578*. 2 vols. Paris. SEVPEN.

Silva, José Gentil da, 1986. 'As mulheres dos homens. O outro para a vida'. In *Actas. As dimensões de alteridade – O Outro*. Lisbon.

Souza, George B., 1986. *The Survival of Empire. Portuguese Trade and Society in China and the South China Sea 1630–1754*. Cambridge. Cambridge University Press.

Spallanzani, Marco, 1985. 'Fiorentini e portoghesi in Asia all'inizio del cinquecento attraverso le fonti archivistiche fiorentine'. In *Aspetti della vita economica medievale* (Federigo Melis commemoration volume), Florence.

Spence, Jonathan D., 1984. *The memory palace of Matteo Ricci*. New York. Viking Penguin.

Steensgaard, Niels, 1973. *Carracks, Caravans and Companies. The structural crisis in the European-Asian trade in the early seventeenth century*. Copenhagen. Institute of Asian Studies.

Steensgaard, Niels, 1984. 'The return cargoes of the Carreira da Índia in the sixteenth century'. In *Indo-Portuguese History. Old Issues, New Questions*, ed. T.R. De Souza. New Delhi. Concept Publishing House.

Stols, E.A. and Verberckmoes, J. (eds.), 1988. *Aziatische omzwervingen. Het levensverhaal van Jaques de Coutre, een Brugs diamanthandelaar, 1591-1627*. Berchem. Uitgeverij EPO.

Stradling, R.A., 1988. *Philip IV and the government of Spain, 1621-1665*. Cambridge. Cambridge University Press.

Strandes, Justus, 1968. *The Portuguese period in East Africa*, Trans. J.F. Wallwork, ed. J.S. Kirkman. Dar-es-Salaam.

Streusand, Douglas E., 1989. *The Formation of the Mughal Empire*. Delhi. Oxford University Press.

Subrahmanyam, Sanjay, 1987. 'The *Kagemusha* effect. The Portuguese, firearms and the state in early modern south India'. *Moyen Orient et Océan Indien*, 4.

Subrahmanyam, Sanjay, 1988. 'Asian trade and European affluence? – Coromandel, 1650 to 1740'. *Modern Asian Studies*, xxii, 1.

Subrahmanyam, Sanjay, 1990a. *The political economy of commerce. Southern India, 1500-1650*. Cambridge. Cambridge University Press.

Subrahmanyam, Sanjay, 1990b. *Improvising Empire. Portuguese Trade and Settlement in the Bay of Bengal, 1500-1700*. Delhi. Oxford University Press.

Szuppe, Maria, 1986. 'Un marchand du roi de Pologne en Perse, 1601-1602', *Moyen Orient et Océan Indien*, 3.

Tavares, Maria José Pimenta Ferro, 1982. *Os Judeus em Portugal no século XV*. Volume I. Lisbon. Universidade Nova de Lisboa.

TePaske, John J., 1983. 'New World Silver, Castile, and the Philippines, 1590-1800'. In Richards (1983).

Terpstra, H., 1911. *De vestiging van de Nederlanders aan de Kust van Koromandel*. Groningen. M. De Waal.

Thomaz, Luís Filipe F.R., 1975. 'Maluco e Malaca'. In A. Teixeira da Mota (ed.), *A viagem de Fernão de Magalhae(s e a questão das Molucas*. Lisbon.

Thomaz, Luís Filipe F.R., 1976. 'Nina Chatu e o comércio português em Malaca'. *Memórias do Centro de Estudos de Marinha*, 5.

Thomaz, Luís Filipe F.R., 1979. 'Les Portugais dans les mers de l'Archipel au XVIe siècle', *Archipel*, 18.

Thomaz, Luís Filipe F. R., 1985. 'Estrutura política e administrativa do Estado da Índia no século XVI'. In Luís de Albuquerque and Inácio Guerreiro (eds.), *Actas do II Seminário Internacional de História Indo-Portuguesa*, Lisbon.

Thomaz, Luís Filipe F.R., 1986a. 'Malacca's Society on the Eve of Portuguese Conquest. A tenatative interpretation based on the extant Portuguese documents'. Paper presented at the *Persidangan Antarabangsa mengenai Tamadun Melayu*, Kuala Lumpur.

Bibliography

Thomaz, Luís Filipe F.R., 1986b. 'La prise de Malaca par les Portugais vue par les Malais (d'après le manuscrit Raffles 32 de la Royal Asiatic Society)', in *Studies on Cultural Contact and Textual Interpretation*, Leiden. KITLV.

Thomaz, Luís Filipe F.R., 1987. 'Os Frangues na terra de Malaca'. In *A Abertura do Mundo: Estudos de História dos Descobrimentos Europeus* (Em Homenagem a Luís de Albuquerque), eds. Luís Filipe Barreto and Francisco Contente Domingues, 2 volumes. Lisbon. Editorial Presença. Volume II.

Thomaz, Luís Filipe F.R., 1989a. 'O projecto imperial Joanino. Tentativa de interpretação global da política ultramarina de D. João II'. *Congresso Internacional, Bartolomeu Dias e a sua época – Actas*, Volume I, Porto.

Thomaz, Luís Filipe F.R., 1989b. 'Le Portugal et l'Afrique au XVe siècle. Les débuts de l'expansion', *Arquivos do Centro Cultural Português*, 26.

Thomaz, Luís Filipe F.R., 1989c. 'Expansão Portuguesa e Expansão Européia – Reflexões em torno da génese dos Descobrimentos', *Studia*, 47.

Thomaz, Luís Filipe F.R., 1990. 'L'idée impériale manueline'. In Aubin (1990).

Thomaz, Luís Filipe F.R., 1991. 'Factions, Interests and Messianism. The politics of Portuguese expansion in the East, 1500–1521', *The Indian Economic and Social History Review*, xxviii, 1.

Tiele, P.A., and A.C. Burnell (eds.), 1885. *The Voyage of John Huyghen van Linschoten to the East Indies*. 2 volumes. London. The Hakluyt Society.

Toby, Ronald P., 1984. *State and diplomacy in early modern Japan. Asia in the development of the Tokugawa Bakufu*. Princeton. Princeton University Press.

Tracy, James D. (ed.), 1990. *The Rise of Merchant Empires. Long-distance trade in the early modern world 1350–1750*. Cambridge. Cambridge University Press.

Ungar, Esta S., 1983. 'Vietnamese Leadership and Order. Dai Viet under the Le dynasty (1428–1459)'. Ph.D. dissertation, Cornell University.

Van Dijk, L.C.D., 1858. *Zes jaren uit het leven van Wemmer van Berchem*. Amsterdam. Scheltema.

Van Leur J.C., 1955. *Indonesian Trade and Society. Essays in Asian Social and Economic History*. The Hague. W. Van Hoeve.

Van Santen, H.W., 1982. 'De Verenigde Oost-Indische Compagnie in Gujarat en Hindustan, 1620–1660'. Ph.D. dissertation, Leiden University.

Vasquez de Prada, Valentin, 1960. *Lettres marchandes d'Anvers*, Vol. I. Paris. SEVPEN.

Velho, Álvaro, 1987. *Roteiro da Primeira Viagem de Vasco da Gama*. Ed. Neves Aguas. Lisbon.

Villiers, John, 1981. 'Trade and society in the Banda islands during the sixteenth century', *Modern Asian Studies*, xv, 4.

Villiers, John, 1985. 'As derradeiras do mundo. The Dominican missions and the sandalwood in the lesser Sunda islands in the sixteenth and seventeenth centuries'. In Luís de Albuquerque and Inácio Guerreiro (eds.), *Actas do II Seminário Internacional de História Indo-Portuguesa*, Lisbon.

Villiers, John, 1987. 'Portuguese Malacca and Spanish Manila. Two concepts of empire'. In R. Ptak (ed.), *Portuguese Asia*. Stuttgart. Franz Steiner Verlag.

Vogel, J.Ph. (ed.), 1937. *Journaal van J J. Ketelaar's Hofreis naar den Groot Mogol te Lahore, 1711–1713*. The Hague. Martinus Nijhoff.

Wake, C.H.H., 1979. 'The changing pattern of Europe's pepper and spice imports, ca. 1400–1700', *Journal of European Economic History*, viii, 2.

Wake, C.H.H., 1986. 'The volume of European spice imports at the beginning and end of the fifteenth century', *Journal of European Economic History*, xv, 3.

Weber, Max, 1930. *The Protestant Ethic and the Spirit of Capitalism*, tr. Talcott Parsons. London. George Allen and Unwin.

Whitmore, J.K., 1983. 'Vietnam and the Monetary Flow of Eastern Asia, Thirteenth to Eighteenth Centuries'. In Richards (1983).

Wills, John E. (jr.), 1979. 'Maritime China from Wang Chih to Shih Lang. Themes in Peripheral History'. In *From Ming to Ch'ing. Conquest, Region, and Continuity in Seventeenth-Century China*, eds. Jonathan D. Spence and John E. Wills, jr. New Haven. Yale University Press.

Wills, John E. (jr.), 1984. *Embassies and Illusions. Dutch and Portuguese envoys to K'ang-hsi, 1666–1687*. Cambridge (Mass.). Harvard University Press.

Winius, George D., 1971. *The Fatal History of Portuguese Ceylon. Transition to Dutch Rule*. Cambridge (Mass.). Harvard University Press.

Wink, André, 1986. *Land and Sovereignty in India. Agrarian society and politics under the Eighteenth-century Maratha Svarajya*. Cambridge. Cambridge University Press.

Wink, Andre, 1988. '*Al-Hind*. India and Indonesia in the Islamic World-Economy, c. 700–1800 A.D.' *Itinerario*, xii, 1.

Yamamura, Kozo and Tetsuo Kamiki, 1983. 'Silver mines and Sung coins – A monetary history of medieval and modern Japan in international perspective'. In Richards (1983).

Maps

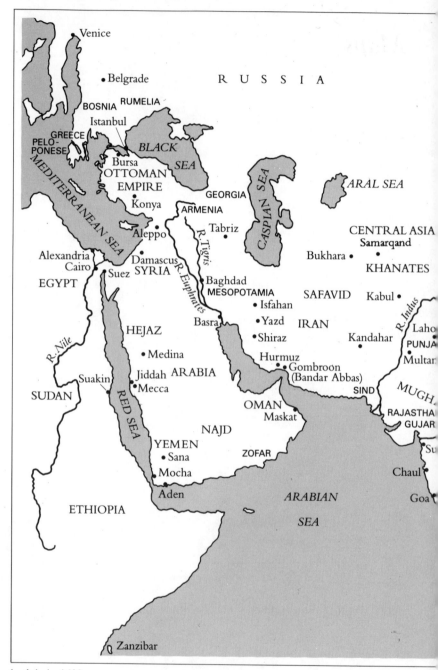

1. Asia in 1600

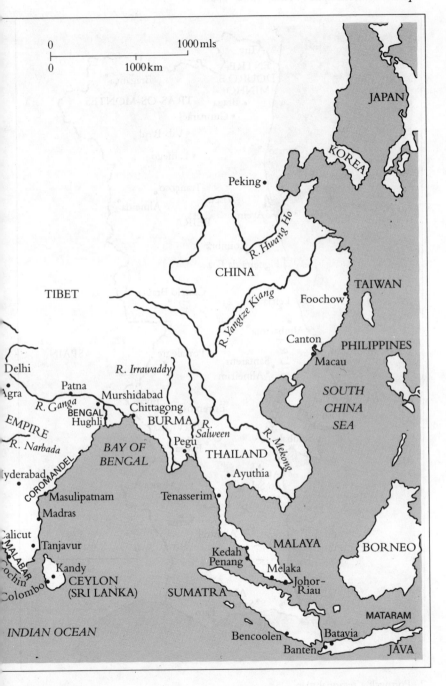

The Portuguese Empire in Asia, 1500–1700

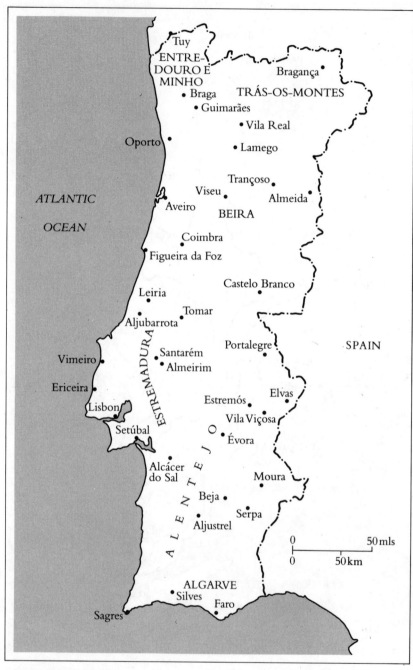

2. Portugal: a regional map

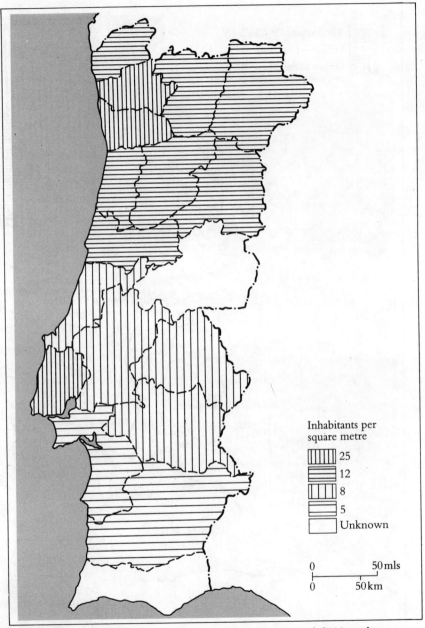

3. Portugal: density of population, 1527–32. [*Note*: the territorial divisions shown here are present-day provinces]

After Ribeiro, Lautensach and Daveau, *Geografia de Portugal III. O povo português* (Lisbon, 1987)

4. Europe in the sixteenth century

Boundary of the Empire   Venetian Dominions
Ottoman Empire   Aragon

1. Swiss Confederation   8. Marquisate of Mantua
2. Franche Comté   9. Duchy of Ferrara
3. Grissons   10. Republic of Lucca
4. Duchy Of Savoy   11. Republic of Florence
5. Duchy of Milan   12. Republic of Siena
6. Republic of Genoa   13. Duchy of Modena
7. Saluzzo   14. Montferrat

SWEDEN
FINLAND

ORDER
• Novgorod
MUSCOVY
• Moscow
• Riga
Konigsberg
TONIC
LITHUANIA
• Smolensk
rsaw
Cracow
Kiev
Lvov
Dnieper
Don
Volga
MOLDAVIA
CRIMEA
WALLACHIA
BLACK SEA
Danube
OTTOMAN
Istanbul
essalonika
EMPIRE
Athens
Crete
Cypus

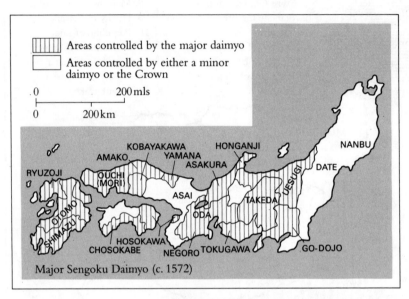

Major Sengoku Daimyo (c. 1572)

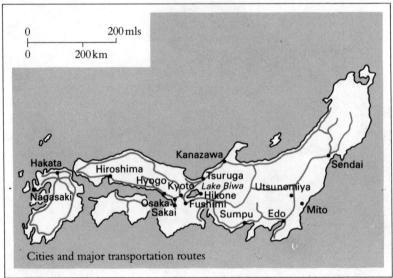

Cities and major transportation routes

5. Japan in 1600

After Hall, Keiji and Yamamura (eds) *Japan before Tokugawa. Political Consolidation and Economic Growth 1500 to 1650* (Princeton, 1981)

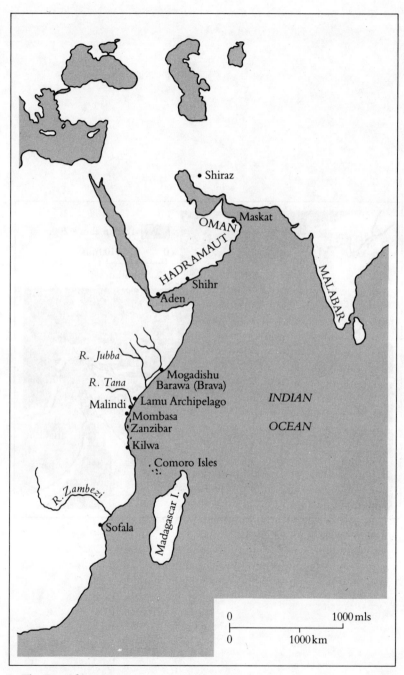

6. The East African coast

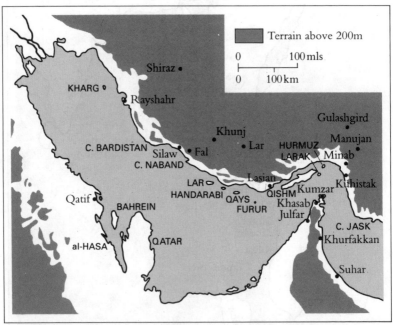

7. Hurmuz and the Persian Gulf

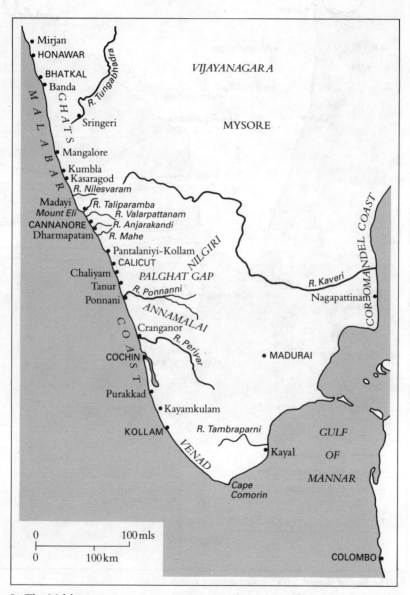

8. The Malabar coast

The Portuguese Empire in Asia, 1500–1700

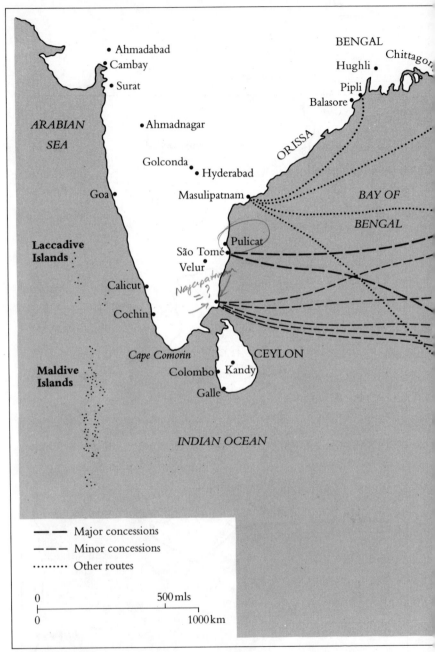

9. The Bay of Bengal, 1600: concessionary routes

After Subrahmanyam, *The Political Economy of Commerce. Southern India 1500–1650* (Cambridge, 1990)

312

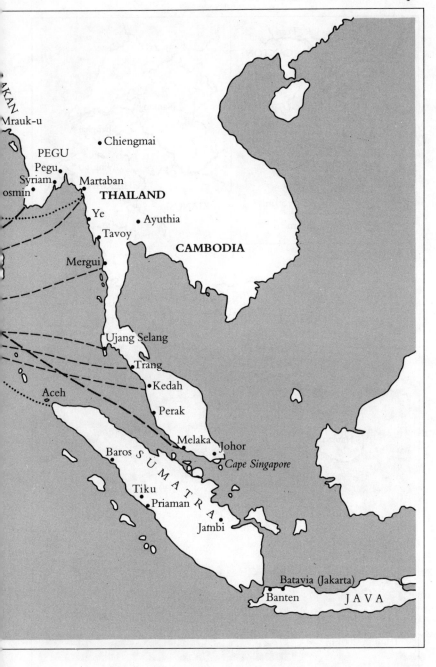

AKAN

Mrauk-u

PEGU

Pegu

Syriam

osmin

Martaban

THAILAND

Chiengmai

Ye

Ayuthia

Tavoy

CAMBODIA

Mergui

Ujang Selang

Trang

Kedah

Aceh

Perak

Melaka

Johor

Baros

Cape Singapore

SUMATRA

Tiku

Priaman

Jambi

Batavia (Jakarta)

Banten

JAVA

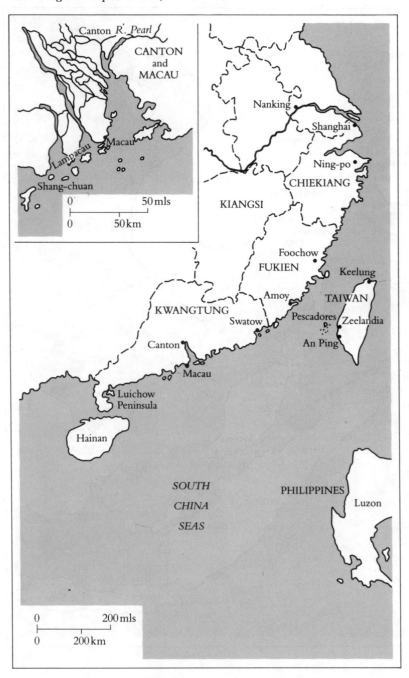

10. Macau and the South China Sea Coast

Index

315